FIGHTER FOR PEACE

For Ada
Ever yours
David Whittaker
14/5/01

Cover photograph: Courtesy of The Hon. Francis Noel-Baker.

Frontispiece: Philip Noel-Baker: Bronze Head by Ian Walters, 1980.
(COURTESY OF IAN WALTERS)

FIGHTER FOR PEACE

Fighter for Peace

Philip Noel-Baker 1889-1982

by

D. J. Whittaker

William Sessions Limited
York, England

ISBN 1 85072 056 8

Printed in 10 on 11 point Plantin Typeface
by William Sessions Limited
The Ebor Press
York, England

Contents

Illustrations

In Memory of John Cross

Scholar, collaborator, friend

d.1988

The author acknowledges a loan from the North Euboean Foundation, towards the publication of this book, in memory of Irene Noel-Baker, Philip's wife, in whose memory the Foundation was established.

Preface

SEVEN AND A HALF DECADES after he entered public life a man who continued to arouse admiration, misunderstanding, elated hopes, and some disdain had charisma meriting biography. Lord Philip Noel-Baker was man and message, a lesson for the present, a portent for the future. Perspectives in time and space make the biographer's task daunting whether he leafs through 1,100 boxes of papers, scans a fair library of books, or assembles notes from written anecdotes and face-to-face interview. I have tried hard to remain analytical, critical, and objective and a statement of my final position can be read as Epilogue in the concluding chapter. My approach is part-thematic, part-chronological. The selection of material is mine and much has had to be left out particularly that dealing with Noel-Baker as M.P. for Coventry and Derby. I am entirely responsible, of course, for any inaccuracies.

Readers are asked to note that Philip changed his surname in 1922 from Baker to Noel-Baker. In the text that follows his name appears as Philip Baker or as Philip Noel-Baker wherever it is thought to be appropriate.

The whole undertaking would have been quite impossible without the unstinted help of many people. I am grateful to the following who have made grants or loans towards the publication of this book – Mrs. Maureen Cross, the Gilbert Murray Foundation, the Joseph Rowntree Charitable Trust, the North Euboean Foundation, which was established in memory of Irene Noel-Baker, Philip Noel-Baker's wife, and the Sessions Book Trust. I owe a further debt of gratitude to all those who gave permission to quote from numerous other texts. They are listed in detail on pp. 378-79. Prof. John Cross who constantly encouraged and advised me throughout almost five years' research sadly did not live to see its outcome. Some of the material used is that which he himself garnered in Cambridge and then shared with me. This biography is dedicated to his memory. I am grateful for the readiness with which others consented to read part of the manuscript and then offer suggestions – Baroness Llewelyn-Davies, Lord Gladwyn, Lord Jenkins of Hillhead, Sir Rex Niven, Prof. K. G. Robbins. Lord Ennals most kindly agreed to write a Foreword. I am inestimably indebted for assistance, friendship, and hospitality to the Hon. Francis Noel-Baker and to his wife Barbara. My gratitude to the following is very real indeed: Horace Alexander, Dr. Don Anthony, Helen Armstrong, Arghyri Balatsos, Sir Roger Bannister, Frank Barnaby, the late Lord (Fenner) Brockway, Grace Crookall-Greening, Dr. Peter van den Dungen, Kenneth East, Cecil Evans, Gordon Evans, Prof. John Ferguson, Michael Foot, Prof. Johan Galtung, John Gray, Brigadier Michael Harbottle, Malcolm Harper, Ron Huzzard, Frances Kelly, Lorna Lloyd, Prof. Isabel de Madariaga and family, Christopher Morris, Prof. Robert Neild, Lady Catherine Peake, Brian Phillips, Dr. R. C. Richardson, William K. Sessions, Nicholas Sims, Henny Spier, Marion Stewart, Christopher Terry, Sir Brian Urquhart, Lady Elisabeth Wilson, Lady Betty Younger.

I owe much to the resource and kindness of library staffs in the Bodleian Library, the British Library of Economic and Political Science, Cambridge University Library, the Archive Centre at Churchill College, Cambridge, Friends House, London, the Royal Commonwealth Society, and Teesside Polytechnic. I am especially grateful to the Master, Fellows and Scholars of Churchill College in the University of Cambridge for permission to use the Noel-Baker Papers housed there in the Archives Centre. My thanks also must acknowledge the cheerful industry of Julie Ibbotson and Helena Whittaker.

January 1989 DAVID J. WHITTAKER

Foreword

by the Rt. Hon. Lord Ennals P.C.

I FIRST MET PHILIP NOEL-BAKER in the summer of 1936 when, as an enthusiastic school boy, I had cycled from my home town of Walsall to Geneva to participate in a League of Nations Union youth summer school. At 15 I was on the first step of my involvement in the peace movement; in his late '40s he was half-way through his.

Even then he was for me a source of inspiration. I was a pacifist – though not for long – and I knew of his stand as a Quaker in joining the Friends Ambulance Unit and landing with the British Expeditionary Force in 1914. It was because there was so much criticism of conscientious objectors that I admired him, for he showed courage in facing the dangers of war which included not only shelling but typhoid and poison gas. Naturally, I was a passionate supporter of the League of Nations and knew that it was involved in a wellnigh hopeless struggle to prevent world war in the face of Hitler's militarism and the totally negative attitude of the Western Powers. I was angry that Britain seemed to be more concerned to isolate the Soviet Union than to stop Hitler, and showed little more commitment to the League than the United States which refused even to join.

Philip Noel-Baker was, to me, a deeply principled, almost heroic figure. Like Sir Norman Angell who, with Philip, was speaking at the summer school, he was a man of vision based on experience. He had been involved in the 1919 Peace Conference, had been a member of the Secretariat of the League in its early years, had been in the British delegation to the League Assembly in 1929 and 1930 and the 1932-33 Disarmament Conference. He had further endeared himself to me because then, as now, very few top-ranking athletes and sportsmen went into politics and fewer still into the Labour Party. He was the newly-elected Labour M.P. for Derby. To an under-aged member of the Labour League of Youth, what more could one ask of a man?

I felt a sense of appreciation of him then; but now, more than 50 years on, surveying a life which was vigorous and deeply principled right to the end, I feel grateful to him for championing the causes which have inspired me. Above all I admire him for his absolute constancy even though I did not totally share his view. Let me give an instance of this. In Geneva that summer he was talking to students from school and universities about the lessons which should be learned from the 1932-33 Disarmament Conference. It was still fresh in his mind and he circulated a memorandum for our use. Nearly 40 years later, on 10th April, 1978, in his introduction to a book on the Disarmament Conference, in a remarkable under-statement – not his normal style – he wrote 'This book has taken me a long time to prepare'. The passage of 45 years had not undermined his phenomenal memory, but, more importantly, it seemed not to have changed his conclusions. Like a swallow the tune he sang had remarkable constancy: for that reason it was clear and sweet to hear.

Let me give another example, because his constancy was his greatest merit. In his last years, in spite of failing health, not surprising for someone in his late eighties and early nineties, Philip Noel-Baker never gave up. Sometimes on his own and in pain, with the aid of a stick, he travelled throughout Britain and the world with the vigour and a sense of urgency of a man half his age. In August 1982 – four months before he died – he was in Japan for the 36th anniversary of the atom bombing of Hiroshima and Nagasaki. On his way back he stopped off in Hong Kong and made a speech, which was highly relevant in the wake of news about the U.S. introduction of the neutron bomb but was vintage Noel-Baker. He called for general and complete disarmament by means of an agreement and eventually a treaty which must include all weapons in all parts of the world. He would never contemplate partial disarmament as a solution; limited agreements affecting certain weapons in pre-determined areas of the world were not on his agenda. He was never deflected by nuclear-free zones, test-ban treaties or agreements which would cover new weapons, or a limited range of weapons. He was dismissive of arms control as a step towards or a substitute for general and complete disarmament. This made him a vehement critic of Western arms control measures proposed in the '70s and '80s.

What merit was there in this seemingly uncompromising approach? His attitude was not easy to live with in an age of compromise. He saw compromise as another word for prevarication or inactivity. Politicians of the post-war arms race era were for the most time trying to think of new ways forward which might build on certain elements of common ground among the major weapon powers. Fair enough: it was like trying to plot a route out of a maze. I was involved in it when I was a Foreign Office Minister in 1974-76 in a post Noel-Baker had held 40 years previously. But Philip was always there to say 'No, that is not the way.' At times this was irritating beyond measure when you were doing your best. He was like a rugby football 'three-quarter'. Not for him the constant passing back and forth which often got nowhere beyond another 'scrum' signalled by the referee's whistle. His eye was on the distant corner flag. His objective was to score.

In another respect he refused to concede accepted wisdom. In his most comprehensive work *The Arms Race*, published shortly before he was awarded the Nobel Peace Prize in 1959 he wrote, 'It is often said that disarmament should follow, but not preclude the settlement of international differences'. Philip argued that you could wait until Kingdom Come for disputes to be settled and that in any case the weight of arms was itself an obstacle to peace making. He accepted that it was desirable to work for both disarmament and the settlement of disputes and that progress with one could improve the prospect of progress with the other. But he vehemently rejected the thesis that disarmament was inevitably dependent upon political relationships. It was, he said, as if the British working classes had said in the 19th century that there could not be a representative parliament, law courts and a police force until the gap between rich and poor had been abolished. He was constantly giving historical examples of the 'fallacy' of the notion that disarmament could only be a consequence, never a cause of an improvement in international relations.

Noel-Baker's absolute commitment to multilateral disarmament by agreement created a gap between him and those who campaigned for unilateral nuclear disarmament. He described as 'desperate' and 'defeatist' any attempt to go for unilateral measures or for limited measures such as the concept of a non-nuclear club. The Left wing in the Labour Party felt offended by his support for N.A.T.O. as a pooling of strength behind international law and the U.N. Charter. I well remember talking with him in the early '60s about the 'Rapacki Plan' for nuclear disarmament on both sides of the divide in Central Europe. I was International Secretary of the Labour Party and felt that there was a basis for a significant East-West agreement. I was working on what became known as the 'Gaitskell Plan'. Courteously, but firmly, Philip told me I was wasting my time. The rift between the multilateral and the unilateral sections of the disarmament movement was painful to him. But he did not despair or flinch. If he had chosen he might have become a leading figure in C.N.D. because of his knowledge, integrity, and commitment: but to him this would have been a betrayal, an easy way out, an over-simplification.

There were two great achievements in his long life – apart from his athletic successes. The first was to keep disarmament high on the agenda of world leaders. Secondly, he threw his tremendous energy into stimulating support for the United Nations and the United Nations Association as he had for the League and the League of Nations Union a generation earlier. He had been in at the beginning of the U.N. in 1945, as Foreign Office Minister of State and as a member of the U.N. Preparatory Commission. Drawing on his League of Nations experience he would argue that the one totally irresistible force was the force of informed public opinion. He had the great power to inspire people and he was a very popular public speaker. After ceasing to be an M.P. in 1970 he decided to throw most of his energy into the disarmament work of U.N.A. and later into the World Disarmament Campaign which he and Fenner Brockway inaugurated. He was convinced that the nations of the world would only make headway with the elimination of all types of weapons if they could bring themselves to act in unison, according to multilateral schedules which were carefully negotiated and systematically supervised. He set out his plans in *The Arms Race*. It was clear to him that the United Nations was the only agency that could cope with the immense amount of work which was necessary to achieve a disarmament treaty. Typically generous, he decided to use the bulk of the Nobel Peace Prize money to support U.N.A. and the World Disarmament Campaign. This enabled him to travel the world in a singleminded campaign for world disarmament. The two organisations gave to Philip and Fenner (both of whom were members of the House of Lords after retiring from the House of Commons) a national and international platform for their disarmament work: a very remarkable pair of octogenarian campaigners they were.

In July 1981 – just over a year before his death – Philip Noel-Baker had flown to Ottawa for the first of the N.G.O. summits at the same time and place as the seven-power Western Summits. He told an audience of 5,000 people that he hoped to live long enough to see the achievement of his life-long objectives. Sadly, neither he nor Fenner Brockway lived to see the ratification of the I.N.F. agreement in Moscow in 1988. Mikail Gorbachev had not assumed office as General Secretary of the Communist Party in the U.S.S.R. in Philip's lifetime, though Fenner lived five years after Philip's death.

Not only did Philip not live to see the historic first step on the road to real disarmament, he missed a new epoch in United Nations peace-keeping – Afghanistan, the Gulf War, Angola, Namibia – which also owed much to Gorbachev's new approach to the world and to the U.N. If he had lived he would almost certainly have accepted my tribute to the Soviet leader, but he would have warned us not to be beguiled by any partial disarmament agreement and not to assume anything unless we had achieved agreement about general and complete disarmament world-wide. He might have been right. Only time will tell. But for me, part of the credit for this first major disarmament agreement and, indeed, for the new prospects for the U.N., goes to Philip Noel-Baker. He, among all men in this century, repeatedly broke the conspiracy of silence about disarmament and pointed the way to world-wide agreement. His speaking and his writing were for ever focussing the attention of world leaders on the urgency of disarmament. His political judgement may have been open to question; otherwise, he would have risen higher in our national political scene. But if he had been a leading party politician he might have reduced his own appeal to people of all parties who rose to their feet to applaud one so dedicated to the cause of peace.

As I have said I have throughout my life felt deeply grateful to Philip Noel-Baker for his inspiration and commitment. Much of that thankfulness must now be shared with David Whittaker who has with love and care, and with skill and dedication brought Philip Noel-Baker to life for those who did not know him but should feel grateful for his life and work

January 1989 — DAVID ENNALS

CHAPTER 1

The Cradle and the Crucible

'I AM MY FATHER'S SON', Philip Noel-Baker announced at the ceremony in Oslo in 1959 when he was awarded a Nobel Peace Prize. The two men, in fact, were remarkably alike in upbringing and in personality. 'Full of the zest of life, of great personal charm, and with a spirit undaunted by difficulties' were words which might well have applied to the son just as it did to the father because of their unrelenting opposition to war preparations, and the manner in which they deplored both the lack of moral authority in their own country's leaders and the reluctance of nations in general to promote arms limitation and reliance upon peaceful arbitration.[1]

The animation of these men owed something to elements on both sides of the Atlantic. A sturdy Quaker, Samuel Baker, Philip's grandfather, emigrated from Ireland to Ontario in 1819, chartering a sailing ship large enough to transport his whole family, their servants, and the furniture to Canada. Woodland was cleared and given over to apple farming. There were good harvests and there were lean times, and his sons, Philip's father among them, had to leave school and apply their hands to making a living. Practical talents among the boys led to their devising a machine which could be worked by hand to sift flour. The idea caught on locally and the Bakers took out a patent in January 1870. Father and one or two sons, in silk hat and frock coat, went from house to house in the larger towns demonstrating to Ontario housewives the excellence of finely sifted flour. Joseph Allen Baker (Philip's father), then a vigorous young man of 24, took the invention over to England in 1876 and the family's menfolk established a workshop in Willesden, North London. Allen, as he was called by the family, spent many hours with blueprint and lathe overseeing the production of ingenious machines which met the needs of English bakers importing their wheat from Canadian prairies. An offshoot of this thriving engineering enterprise was to develop into the firm of Baker, Perkins of Peterborough, who became renowned world-wide for their baking machinery.[2] Philip's father,

(COURTESY: THE HON. FRANCIS NOEL-BAKER)

Pl. 1. The Baker Brothers, 1895. Philip in sailor suit

Joseph Allen, found a Scots wife some two years after his arrival in England and he and Elizabeth Moscrip from Morebattle in Roxburghshire set up in an elegant North London villa and reared three sons and four daughters. Philip was born there in 1889. The biography of Joseph Allen by Philip and a sister says remarkably little about the everyday goings-on of this Quaker family. To observers, the style of life of the Bakers must have seemed prosperous and rather prim, most certainly it was characterised, in the children's view, by unostentatious provision (doubtless a blend of Quaker and Scottish frugality), straightforwardness in relationships, and a thoughtful mix of sociability and reserve.

Elizabeth Baker, the mother of Philip, and daughter of a much-respected Scots 'dominie', appears to have been exceedingly self-reliant in supervising the running of a fair-sized house, attending to the needs of seven children, and receiving quite imperturbably the visits of friends and relations to her 'rural' home (for, in her opinion, the villa at Harlesden was definitely not in Edwardian London itself). The Baker family, in some sense, were 'living on both sides of the Atlantic . . .' There was always 'something breathless happening', records one of Philip's dearest friends who frequently stayed with the Bakers:

'Joseph Allen Baker would have decided that his business needed him at once in Canada, so he had booked a place on the boat from Liverpool the next day, and we all got busy doing what had to be done . . .'[3]

Visitors were so numerous that the Baker home acquired a reputation locally as 'The International Hotel'.

Feelings of social compassion induced Allen Baker to stand as a councillor in East Finsbury in 1895. He joined the radical section of the Liberals, convinced that their views on temperance, housing, wages, and public education wer similar to his own. Everyday experience of London's street life revealed squalor and the excesses of intemperance, both made worse because the unreliability of public transport did little to facilitate escape. Henceforth, for 11 years, Baker was to champion improvement of the tramway system in the Capital, and he worked hard, too, along with his sons, for the betterment of workers' housing, for their schools, and for their further education. A dogged opposition to Britain's Boer War adventure from 1899 doubtless spoiled his prospects of going on to Westminster when the Liberals invited him to stand but six years later he gained a seat in East Finsbury using a platform which resolutely called for welfare rather than warfare and which protested against 'preventable pauperism and social misery'. Philip, then only in his teens, accompanied his father to the hustings, helped him marshall facts and write speeches, and clearly became influenced by concepts and feelings which, in turn, he was to proclaim all his life. The example of the father in turning a cheek to those who used invective showed the son the importance of not being 'frightened by a name from pursuing a policy which seemed on both social and financial grounds to be right'.[4]

As a parliamentarian, Joseph Allen Baker led a Liberal protest against the Navy Estimates in March 1910. Frenzied construction of warships would only lead other nations to do the same. We should give up such an unjustified monopoly of force and other countries would take this to be a civilised and Christian lead.[5] Allen Baker handed on to his son a belief in the force of informed public opinion. An international meeting of minds would educate the public. In 1907 a conference to discuss ways of limiting armaments was called at The Hague. Leading a powerful British delegation was Allen Baker. He and his son Philip had assembled a cogent case for nations resorting to compulsory arbitration. Philip found all this exciting and stimulating though he came to believe that the 'hawks' in many lands would unite to block efforts and stall any attempt to hold a third conference in 1914. This conspiracy theory of history, attributing successes and failures to the activities of single named and unnamed individuals, was to be enunciated with fervour for the rest of Philip's public life.

The two Bakers proposed the use of practical measures to combat 'futile fatalism'; indeed, in 1909 Allen was invited to discuss both with Edward VII and with Kaiser Wilhelm II schemes for international Christian action to prevent the onset of war. Could not a council for inter-church fellowship representing all European lands do something to bridge the gulfs in political and cultural identity which were threatening to wreck civilisation? Baker felt encouraged when Germany's ruler was visibly moved by his suggestion that the Kaiser take the initiative to establish a League of Peace.[6] Conferences on themes of mutual concern were to be held in England and in Germany. Andrew Carnegie gave two million dollars to endow the cause. The movement for Christian reconciliation took root and flourished ultimately as the World Council of Churches although nothing of their earnestness and invention was sufficient to stem the inevitable advance towards battle in 1914.

It seemed clear to the Bakers, father and son, that 'a conflict may be precipitated by the very over-preparedness of the nations concerned'.[7] An arms race, whether it resulted from national fears of a neighbour, or from economic rivalries, whether it was steered by competition in matching Dreadnought hulls (such as the rivalry of Fisher and Turpitz brought about), or was a consequence of geopolitical theory, and of the machinations of arms manufacturers, could have only one result: Armageddon. As far as one can judge, Philip learned from Allen Baker to view the profession of peace with great singleness of mind. To eschew violence in human contest was to live, as George Fox had put it in his Journal, 'in the virtue of that life and power that take away the occasion of all wars'. Correspondingly, to rely on force to settle a dispute was unproductive and inhuman for it could lead only to fear, resentment, and continued hostility. Further, the extension and reinforcement of power via treaties and the balance of forces served only to entangle nations and to mislead their people. Disputes, where they arose, should be settled impartially by arbitration. The new confidence that would grow with peaceful development would find a natural expression in a desire for arms limitation and control.

Despite failures on the international scene Allen and Philip Baker gave themselves wholeheartedly to every cause that captured their imagination. Refusing to grow cynical about politics they never flagged in their resolve to work for what they believed. Eventually, their lives were to end on a similar note for when the father died in 1918 saddened, though not defeated, by vicarious wartime suffering, his son was to declare (as might be said later of himself) that 'he died in the power of faith, rather than in the strength of hope part achieved'.[8]

Philip inevitably went to Quaker schools – to Ackworth, first, then to Bootham, in York, and for one year to Haverford College in Pennsylvania. He impressed his teachers and his peers by a serious-minded approach to studies and by all-round athletic competence as cricketer, footballer, and mile and half-mile runner. 'Muscular Christianity' kept him in singlet and shorts for 10 to 15 hours a week. A letter written from Bootham in the winter of 1905 to his sister, Josie, conveys his enjoyment of school days:

'It's rare sport being a reeve (=prefect) & having a study – and most particularly being able to have cocoa and victuals & things here and being able to ask chaps up. You can imagine it's fun. And it's awfully decent being able to work up in our studies as well'.[9]

Never did Philip forget the school which had educated him. In 1961 he was to give a portion of his Nobel Peace Prize to Bootham and the medal which he received in Oslo. A tree was planted. At the time of Philip's death in 1982 the Head Master, Mr. John Gray, said of the peace medal given to the School that it would help scholars, present and future, understand the foremost tradition of the School, which was that of service to others, and it would enable them all to share something of the ideals for which their celebrated ex-pupil had worked so resolutely.

'My education was guided, not ordered for me', mused Noel-Baker 60 years later. He had had the inestimable advantage of a father, loving towards his wife and children, one imbued with faith and deep understanding of others. Encouragement and open suggestion marked

(COURTESY: DR. DON ANTHONY)

Pl. 2. At 17 – Off to Haverford College, U.S.A. for one year

Allen Baker's paternal role. Would Philip like a year in the United States before going up to Cambridge? Six months in Paris would teach him to speak French fluently. What about a year in Germany to learn the language? Would not History and Economics be the best preparation for playing a part in world affairs? He could hardly do better than King's College, Cambridge. Why not try for a University Scholarship in International Law? If scholarship funds were insufficient, his father would finance the rest. Philip followed the Golden Way never doubting that his father's counsel was right.[10]

The Bootham boy went in 1909 to King's College, Cambridge. The 'Prince of Colleges all' epitomised the *universitas*, a communion of fellowship in learning and in leisure between teacher and taught. Dons such as Arthur Cecil Pigou, Oscar Browning, G. Lowes Dickinson, John Shepherd, were great teachers and somewhat eccentric confidantes concerned rather conspiratorially to disperse illusions and to encourage liberal thinking and refined tastes. Their approach to these tasks ranged over lectures, seminars at the breakfast table, crowded conversaziones, musical evenings, and strawberry teas. In Robert Skidelsky's words, Kings was 'a society of clever, dotty inmates, provided with a continuing supply of charming and clever youths to stir atrophied emotions'.[11] Philip revelled in the society of these golden youths – Maynard Keynes, G. N. Clark, Hugh Dalton, Rupert Brooke, Arthur Waley, Francis Birell, so many of whom were to die in France and Flanders, others to survive into public eminence. A number of them in their first year founded the Carbonari (the Charcoal Burners) an elite society of a dozen or so undergraduates. The name of the group was a tribute to the republican revolutionaries of Italy a century earlier. They dined each week (with a modest libation of claret) and read philosophical papers and poetry in smoke-filled rooms far into the night. 'There was', Noel-Baker recalled many years later, 'a strong tendency for what was revolutionary . . ' He, himself, had been recruited as 'low-brow leaven'.[12] Maynard Keynes, an enthusiastic associate, termed their style of reasoning 'comprehensive irreverence', an attitude towards things formerly held sacred. This frame of mind could lead to self-righteousness and arrogance though it does not appear to have done so in Noel-Baker's case. Pledged to renounce 'Victorian stuffiness' the elite of the Carbonari were regarded with disfavour by the more conventional. One of their first members and a future Chancellor of the Exchequer, the socialist Etonian, Hugh Dalton, paid for his membership by being severely douched in a fountain by less liberal students. He had, after all, been overheard proposing a Loyal Toast: 'The King, God Damn it!' Moreover, as Noel-Baker later said of his fellow-student, Dalton, 'he had a gift for making

(COURTESY: BOOTHAM SCHOOL ARCHIVES)

Pl. 3. Planting a Cherry at Bootham, his old school, 1961

(COURTESY: P. WARN, BOOTHAM SCHOOL)

Pl. 4. The Noel-Baker tree at Bootham School, 1988

people hostile to him. He half-deliberately said very socialist things in order to shock'.[13]

More formally, the academic prowess of the young Baker was soon remarked upon. As he told his mother in his first year, his heart was set on getting a First and for this he would need to do a good deal of vacation reading. Ability was already plain in the papers he presented to the Political Society, chaired by that eminent economic historian Sir John Clapham. Rounding on 'Little Englanderism', hoping the best for a pacific reliance upon a Concert of Europe, his presentations revealed the candour, enthusiasm, and objectivity which were to emerge as hallmarks of personality. He took on the editorship of the King's College journal, *Basileon*.[14]

The pages of *Basileon* show plenty of the light-hearted irreverence customary in student publications and they are not short of real wit and creativity. Rupert Brooke's verses, later to be immortalised as Grantchester, are there. On a rather low level is 'A True Parable of a Kind Don' (modelled on VI Kings X, 1-14) by P. J. Baker. The ending refers to his warm regard for his mentor A. C. Pigou, economist, plant-lover, another of 'King's quasi-mythical characters, trademarked by his sartorial display':

'For the don that was kind to his flowers, was kind also to his pupils, and they flourished together in the sunshine of his loving kindness, and grew both in wisdom and in beauty.'

Pigou, after all, was reputed to indulge both botanical and somewhat aesthetic-erotic interests.

The Carbonari also had their moments of levity. The programme for their Ball in June 1909 was to include 'Mr. Baker, his record prestissimo Jig, for which he has been in training since April' and, as a finale, 'Mr. Rupert Brooke will perform a dream-dance on tiptoe'. A year later, there is a record of a more robust enterprise, 'June 1910 – College Diary – Tuesday April 26. Mr. Baker attempts the N.W. buttress of the Chapel'.[15]

Adulation on all sides was strong in the King's College of those days. For Philip the teaching of A. C. Pigou, Professor of Economics at 30, was breathtaking: 'he literally tore the politicians limb from limb' in the clarity and comprehensiveness of his exposition. Rather a shy man (though ardent on the podium) Pigou, 'the Prof.', enjoyed the companionship of those who revelled in climbing and walking. A 'reading party' for Pigou's students would incorporate strenuous forays from his beloved Buttermere cottage at Lower Gatesgarth or occasional traverses in the Alps for mentor and disciples. 'I followed him', Noel-Baker once put it, 'up the peaks of Switzerland and Norway and up the College walls'.[16] The very lithesomeness in action of his long-distance runner pupil was enough, so it was said, to make the not-so-atrophied Pigou swoon as he watched, for Baker seemed to match all of Pigou's reported criteria for esteem: 'good-looking, good at mountains, good moral tone'.[17] Their friendship was a close one and it lasted until Pigou's death in 1959. Baker easily made friends. There were energetic excursions with Maynard Keynes, with Hugh Dalton, and with Rupert Brooke, with whom he swam in Byron's Pool and talked poetry, breakfasting under the apple blossom in Grantchester. In 1911 Cambridge awarded Baker a Whewell Scholarship in International Law, a much acclaimed honour. Its value in those days was £100 a year. What else in the way of 'glittering prizes' lay before the orator-sportsman?

On a February day the previous year he had told his parents about a forthcoming motion before the Union, namely, 'that this House would view with alarm any advance towards Socialistic principles'. This he felt he had to oppose, indeed, 'I am the only Blue who addresses the learned Assembly, and there is no reason why athletics and intelligence sh'd become divorced in the general mind . . .' In the event, Cambridge approved of a well-reasoned speech from a 'comer-on'.[18] Six terms later, it was being considered that Philip Baker had 'made one of his weighty and convincing speeches: he always impresses the House by his combination of judicial impartiality and evident enthusiasm. He never says anything superficial or extravagant'. His style was thought 'quite Ciceronian'.[19] 'Do you think I should try to become President <of the Cambridge Union>?' Philip had once enquired of a close acquaintance. He went on to do so, in fact, combining as a rare distinction (it was the first time) the presidency of both Cambridge Union and Cambridge University Athletic Club. The same month the undergraduate paper *Granta* once more commended the eloquence, on a particular occasion, of Philip Baker and of Norman Angell, in speaking against Britain's dependence on naval supremacy. This was a theme to which Allen Baker addressed himself forcibly in the House of Commons at this time.

Was it possible, asked *Granta* in May 1912, that anybody could be so enthusiastic as Philip Baker? Underneath a photograph of Baker there appears an account of the holiday the young man contemplated that summer – Olympic track events in Stockholm, visits to German universities, a number of Alpine climbs, and some good fishing in Scotland. Of course, such a good cricketer would be doing three days in the stands at Lords and at the Oval. Undoubtedly, *Granta* remarked (and how far-seeing this epithet was) 'behind variety <there was> unity'. The publication went on to print a verse commemorating the presidential achievements:

'(Mr. Baker, President of the Cambridge Union and Athletic Club, has just gained a First-class in the Economic Tripos)

A two-fold President, you shine
As speech and record-maker
I would your tongue and legs were mine,
O fleet and fluent Baker!
Now, spite of all your bonhomie
Or work no slack forsaker
Through study of Economy
You've proved a first-class Baker![20]

As an individual and as an organiser Philip Baker was distinctly first-class. He had a gift for getting things done effectively and amicably. To arrange for Oxford and Cambridge men to run against Harvard and Yale was an innovation he brought about as an undergraduate. The shining youth who had already won 42 races as a 'Kingsman' was the talk and toast of Junior Commonrooms, praised by Alec Nelson, their athletics coach, some years later as 'an athlete, a fine organiser, a great, deep-thinking scholar'. Baker had come into prominence, 'fleet and fluent', as a consequence of a total mind-and-body approach, with 'a will to win' and a 'beautiful action and <the> balanced mind which quickly absorbed technique and track-sense'.[21] The young man's leadership of 'K.R.A.C.' (King's College Athletic Club) made the year 1910-11 *annus mirabilis*. Oxonians, of course, were scared away, other colleges vanquished, and the fieldside suport of even non-sporting dons showed who was 'responsible for the most remarkable revival of college patriotism ever known'.[22] Even in the vacations the '*bonhomie*' of Philip Baker would ease the arrangement of a winter sports holiday for the Baker family and perhaps 50 friends; there would be skiing at Kandersteg and a meeting for worship on Sunday morning.

In so much that he did he offered ideals, determination, and method. Excellence in athletic performance was the acme of individual effort and the target of group collaboration. One of his famous followers, (Sir) Roger Bannister, was later to see Noel-Baker's precepts illustrated both in Olympics and at lesser events where he had decided 'that his own chance of winning was less than that of a team-mate and so ordered his own race to make the victory of his team-mate more certain'. Sport as part of culture, inseparable from democracy, would bring out the best in the individual and enlist cooperative talents harmoniously. Faith in the sportsman as peacemaker was to sustain him until the end of his long life.[23] Methodical training was his prescription for lifting university athletics out of complacency and with an eye on the Olympics scheduled for Sweden in 1912 he supervised regular 'fitness sessions' and trial events. Promising

(COURTESY: PAUL POPPER LTD.)

Pl. 5. Running in the Stockholm Olympics, 1912. Noel-Baker extreme left

runners now had a chance to exchange with their North American rivals. There was no reason, he complained in 1912, why systematic training should be thought inconsistent with the ideals of fine sportsmanship. The 'noble English press' particularly should recognise the hypocrisy of standing up for 'the divine right of the amateur not to train'. They must have better facilities and a press and public supporting them.[24] Resolute as teamster and as manager, Philip Baker joined a hardened British team which went to the Stockholm Olympics in 1912. Twelve members were from Oxbridge, tested and keen. Philip, who had been holidaying in Sweden, was accepted as an unsponsored competitor for he was not feeling his best mainly due to an injured foot and trouble with an impacted tooth. In the 1,500 metres and before a tremendous crowd Baker showed the ability and the modesty of the fine runner in allowing his Oxford team-mate, Arnold Strode-Jackson, to forge ahead and win. 'Jacker', boxed in by others, was extricated cleverly by his fellow, Philip:

'I made him run with me and I got him to the right place for the last lap and he won the gold medal. I was sixth and very pleased to be sixth because I beat four Americans.'[25]

The *camaraderie*, sportsmanship, and unselfishness of competitors made an indelible impression on Baker, lasting all his life and, through his constant campaigning for sport, influencing countless others:

'I left the sunlit Swedish capital with a deep conviction that international sport and the Olympic movement could become a mighty instrument for making all the nations understand that they belong to one Society with common interests, common hopes and common aims!'[26]

Politics, economics, philosophy and poetry were the staff of intellectual intercourse for those at King's College. Philip, possibly was more spiritually inclined than most of his confrères, attending regularly (but unpunctually) the plain meetings at the Meeting House of the Society of Friends in Jesus Lane. 'The ideal worship', he once remarked, 'would be a Quaker meeting in King's Chapel!' As Chairman he helped to reinvigorate the University's Friends Society. 'Mr. Baker is a sound Liberal', it was thought in 1912, 'a Free Churchman, and one of the most popular undergraduates in Cambridge, where social questions are just now exercising a perfect spell over the serious undergraduate'.[27] The notion of collective responsibility to promote world peace was already taking shape in Philip's mind. He had been with his father to Berlin in October 1912 to an Anglo-German convention representing academics, the churches, and the press. As they surveyed a European scene fast clouding over, they had concluded, so Philip noted, that the fears and jealousies of nations were fanned into disharmony and rivalry by irresponsible elements. Could not the world's journalists contrive a forum to press for common preventive action?[28]

Enthusiasm for politics seems to have been unbridled in Philip. He had spent the Long Vacation of 1911 in the United States. Reappearing in Cambridge he spoke avidly to all his friends about the bluff leadership of Theodore Roosevelt. Hoping to be re-elected President for a further term, Roosevelt sought to harness the progressive and conservative wings of the Republican Party by forming a 'Bull Moose' spearhead. Philip unquestionably admired the candour and enterprise of this rugged, far-seeing 'steward of public welfare'. Here was a man who had secured United States representation at the second Hague Conference of 1907 on which occasion, it will be recalled, Philip's father, Allen Baker, had led the United Kingdom delegation armed with briefs part-drawn up by his Sixth Former son. Here was a world leader accorded a Nobel Peace Prize (and in this a forerunner of Philip himself) who had declared in his acceptance speech in Christiana <Oslo> in 1910 that world peace required 'constructive international activity rather than mere antiwar sentiment'.[29] Fellow-undergraduates were cornered into discussing American liberal ideas with the young Quaker sporting a Bull Moose favour in his buttonhole, captivated by Republican oratory and social evangelism in 1911 as he followed the election train for six weeks. Philip, however, would hardly have followed 'Teddy' seven years later when Roosevelt's position was one of dislike of Woodrow Wilson and of opposition to American adherence to the League of Nations.

A young graduate with a First might be excused for believing he had the world at his feet in 1912. Was his future to be in politics, or in letters, or in academe? Public speaking seemed to be his forte. An appointment to the staff of Ruskin College was in the offing, providing experience on a wide front, yet he felt rather uncertain about the timing of such a move. The only certain thing, he told his sister Josie, with a dash of a young man's arrogance, was that he would remain at King's College for one year, whether or not he secured a Fellowship:

'becos for your private ear I am going to write a joint work with the Prof. which will take a year and will revolutionise public opinion. I shall quite likely get a Fellowship, and shall be blastedly unlucky if I don't because I'm quite good enough.'[30]

As things turned out, he took further soundings at Ruskin and discovered many of the staff to be opposed to the Principal's high-handedness. A frustrated Vice-Principal was even considering premature retirement. Philip Baker was seen as a reinvigorating influence for appointment. The disconsolate Vice-Principal at length was made Principal and Philip became his deputy when the college reopened after a rather

(COURTESY: THE HON. FRANCIS NOEL-BAKER)

Pl. 6. President of the Cambridge Union, 1911

abrupt closing at the country's mobilisation in autumn 1914. 'We hope', wrote his old school (putting it rather loftily), 'he may help Ruskin College to live in harmony with Oxford University and that he may assist Oxford in her search for the social conscience.'[31]

The onset of war was to interrupt his studies as it did for most of his generation. The 'joint work' never emerged in print. A King's Fellowship earned for an essay on the Doctrine of the Legal Equality of States could hardly be enjoyed by a Fellow envisaging residence in the mud of Flanders. Many years later, indeed, Noel-Baker had an amusing story to tell of the progress of that Fellowship. It was in 1924 that the Council of King's College decided, after a hot debate and by a small majority that Philip Baker was not doing academic work consistently enough to justify continuation of the coveted award of 10 years earlier. His former mentor, Pigou, was able to to give him the news confidentially. Leaving 'the Prof.' (the two were meeting at his old College), Baker went into Front Court and could not help walking towards the Vice-Provost of King's, Walter Durnford, who said half-aggressively and half-defensively: 'Well, young man, what's your news?'

'My news, Provost? It's exciting. Yesterday, I was elected to a Chair in the University of London.'
Provost Durnford was dumbfounded.
'Elected to a Chair! The devil you were . . .'

That was all by the way of congratulation. Confirmation arrived by letter the following day.[32]

The international lawyer in Baker impelled him to write to *The Daily News and Leader* on the day World War I broke out. He regarded as 'a wild distortion of the truth' the suggestion that Britain was bound inescapably to the defence of Belgium. In the quarrel between Germany and France, British neutrality would depend upon acceptance by all powers of Belgian independence as had happened in 1839. There must be possibilities of settling the issues by negotiation.[33] This cannot have been a popular point of view quite apart from the validity of the argument though it anticipates some of the strictures about the legality and morality of the 1914-18 War that Noel-Baker was later to make. Generally, Philip's coevals were galvanised, without too much reflection, to respond to a call to arms. Eagerness to join up was more obvious than agitation to seek delay and conciliation in the quarrels that shook Europe's capitals. There was protest and non-violent action and a number of young men, not all members of the Society of Friends, were imprisoned as 'conscientious objectors'.

There is no evidence in the collected papers of Noel-Baker that he ever had to rebut accusations of lack of patriotism in not rallying to the colours.

There may have been those who wondered why Philip's concern for a more peaceful world seemed to stop short of a readiness actively to defend it. A charge such as this would have been readily answered. His life was no more valuable than that of any other enlisted man. He recognised that others, too, yearned desperately for an end to conflict. Nevertheless, membership of the Society of Friends required a response to aggression that was non-violent whenever possible. He had no compunction about supporting an Allied war effort provided his own contribution and that of his associates was a non-combative one. This assurance may not always have dispelled criticism in the anxious days of late 1914.

It was Allen Baker, Philip's father, who was to provide an opportunity for his son to do service overseas. Together with his sons, Arnold Rowntree, and others he formed a Friends Ambulance Unit to accompany the British Expeditionary Force to France.[34] The declaration and agreement which members of this voluntary and non-combative Unit had to sign illustrates the whole-heartedness of those who joined:

'I,N, in undertaking service with the Friends Ambulance Unit, hereby agree to comply with the conditions which entitle me to protection under the Geneva Convention, and to observe the rules, regulations, and orders issued by the Officer commanding or by the Committee <in London> provided that I am not called upon to enlist; and that my conscientious objection to military service is respected.'

More practically, they were obliged to conform to all proper military etiquette when wearing uniform, to obey postal censorship regulations, to serve for the duration of the war (with the right to leave after six months); to do no writing for the press or take photographs; to serve without pay, and to buy their own uniform and kit. Food, lodging, and travel expenses would be paid.[35] Philip Baker, now 25, took over leadership of the first unit despatched to France.

Initially, at the Front, there were some difficulties over protocol with the French and a number of misunderstandings with Britain's Royal Army Medical Corps. On one occasion, for example, in May 1915, the London headquarters of the British Red Cross and the St. John Ambulance Brigade felt they had to pass on a reprimand to the Friends Ambulance Unit because, so it was alleged, members had 'omitted on Tuesday to carry out the dress regulations in all particulars'. This was an unfortunate misunderstanding, they granted, and there was confidence that there would be no further complaints if proper care was taken.[36] Conventional army medical staff resented the intrusion of idealists such as George Trevelyan and Geoffrey Winthrop-Young who were not easily recognisable as 'soldiers'. An academic such as Pigou, eccentric at the best of times, was willing enough to give up a vacation to drive a lurching ambulance along

(COURTESY: CHURCHILL COLLEGE, CAMBRIDGE)

Pl. 7. *With the Friends Ambulance Union, France, 1915. Left to right: Philip Baker, Allan R. Baker, George Trevelyan, G. Winthrop Young*

shell-pocked roads, but disinclined to tolerate the niceties and expectations of regular officers. In another case, to whom was a surgeon major responsible: to his colonel, groomed at Sandhurst and Staff College, or a volunteer Friend? Philip's commonsense and diplomacy usually smoothed things over and earned him the commendation of Sir George Newman at the Unit's London headquarters 'as the commandant of a bully bunch of boys who are doing a fine piece of work of which they and the Committee must be jointly proud'.[37] Appeals by Philip, as Commandant of the forward Unit, for funds and for volunteers brought a good response from readers of *The Friend* and by late 1915 about 80 recruits, chiefly men, had crossed the Channel.

In letters home and in later reminiscence Noel-Baker recounts the anguish and horror of those early wartime days. The Unit sailed into Dunkirk aboard an Admiralty transport past the torpedoed cruiser *Hermes*, her still-crowded decks slipping inexorably beneath the water. On arrival there was confusion on the quays, as walking wounded stumbled across long lines of stretchers on which lay dying soldiers, their gangrenous wounds still undressed. Young men straight from London were bundled into the driving seats of 50 F.A.U. ambulances. They steered disbelievingly past the heaped ruins of villages and the crumbling façade of Ypres Cloth Hall, unable to avoid the terror of Canadians half-blinded and coughing from chlorine gas. A day would end with a hint of excitement and pathos in a rushed farewell at the Menin Gate to Cambridge friends, once Alpine enthusiasts and now pressed into shabby khaki.[38] One hundred thousand casualties or so were to pass through the hands of the F.A.U. in the first 24 months after its embarkation. Philip's tact and patience must have been stretched to the limit for he had to deal with awkward situations behind the Front, amounting almost to callousness when neither R.A.M.C. nor Red Cross could readily countenance a voluntary hospital coping with an outbreak of typhoid, and with delays in Whitehall where funds from the Society of Friends had to await currency clearance.[39]

Qualities of leadership and resourcefulness secured Baker an assignment as adjutant to G. M. Trevelyan's unit destined for Italy. Conditions there were arduous on a front-line that was fast crumbling. At Caporetto, where the salient collapsed, the adjutant spent:

> 'forty hours at the wheel of a Ford Model T, a "Tin Lizzie", with a legless comrade and a nurse sitting in the back, the road blocked all the way with peasants' carts and animals, with abandoned guns and lorries . . .'[40]

There were moments of relief as when Hugh Dalton, his old King's College friend, turned up with his 302 Artillery Battery to play water polo in the River Isonzo and lie afterwards on the banks drying in the autumn sun.

Pathos was evident on other occasions. Many years later, Philip recalled standing in a sun-filled glade, shortly after Dalton's visit, reading aloud from the *Corriere della Sera* a speech of President Woodrow Wilson about the shape of world order after the war's end. His audience was a group of 60 or so battle-weary *Alpini* who chorussed, 'Yes, that's what we want: never any war again'.[41]

It is doubtful whether Philip Baker and Hugh Dalton had much in common apart from their contemporaneity in college. More radically than Baker, Dalton had rejected his class and many of its conventions before 1914, and the edge to his radicalism, as his biographer sees it, was tinged with more aggressiveness and egocentricity than ever his older associate showed. Both had been scarred by war. Dalton nursed anti-Geman resentment allied perhaps to some degree of soured romanticism which regarded the experience of war as a period of youthful fulfilment, while Noel-Baker, in more mature fashion one would think, grounded his growing anti-war feelings upon concrete experience just as much as emotional response. Leaders they were, both in thought and in action, and undoubtedly they were courageous. In the case of Philip Baker the Italian Government awarded him in 1917 the Medal for Military Valour and in the following year the *Croce di Guerra*. Service with the F.A.U. was stressful and dangerous. More than once he was tempted to resign appointment when bouts of depression and lack of confidence assailed him. His sensitiveness had been assailed by the butchery he had witnessed; optimism sorely worn by bureaucracy. Among fellow-Quakers, though, he encountered camaraderie and robust humour and appreciation of all that he was doing for training:

'At the Villa Trento, our H.Q. and Hospital, the F.A.U. training is still in evidence. In the office P.J. mobilizes men and things with his wonted energy. Mrs Baker <Irene Baker, as we shall see presently> does ditto with sheets and household things upstairs and in the hospital, and sees to the comfort, material and social, of *ferati*, *malati*, and *sani* alike . . . And "Professor Pigou's Ford", riddled with shell-holes is started up with great effort each day.'[42]

The adjutant of the Unit was almost run off his feet looking to the paper work concerned with records and procurement for a 60-bed hospital and dealing with the maintenance and deployment of two dozen ambulances. He made a point of giving his men a weekly 'pep-talk'. Somehow he found time to write encouraging letters from the Isonzo front to his sister Josie, now at Newnham and reading Economics, also under Pigou. There were lines of reassurance from his father, 'a first-rate begger for funds', and occasionally, visits from Quakers out from England.

An additional source of comfort was the friendship of Irene Noel who was active in the domestic oversight of the Dunkirk hospital. They became

(COURTESY: THE HON. FRANCIS NOEL-BAKER)

Pl. 8. Irene Noel(-Baker) about 1912

engaged in 1915. She was a fine-looking girl, with deep eyes, a firm, laughing mouth, and an erect bearing, six years older than he, witty, determined, and resourceful. She had inherited an estate at Achmetaga in Euboea, Greece, through the friendship of her forbears with Lady Byron.[43] Both Noel-Baker's sister, Josephine ('Josie'), and A. C. Pigou were upset at the news of the engagement. For Josephine, Philip was 'my dearest lamb' and their relationship an uncommonly affectionate one. He was, however, 'completely and inexorably decided . . .' brother assured sister. For him there could only be one woman with such beauty and 'with such wisdom and power added . . .' and that was Irene Noel.[44] The 'Prof.' felt quite deserted. Was his pupil doing the right thing? He wrote to discount any feelings of jealousy. Of course, he would get accustomed to it in time. In fact, there is every sign during the later years of the scion of King's College (and his Fellowship spanned the years 1902-1959) that he grew into something of a dishevelled recluse, shorn of the stimulating company of youth at weekly breakfast parties and on the fells.

There is a possibility, too, that Virginia and Leonard Woolf did not take the news of the engagement all that calmly. Between Virginia Woolf and Irene Noel there was a strong endearing bond. Virginia and her brothers, Toby and Adrian, had visisted the Noel's Grecian home in 1906. Hearing, in the summer of 1915, of Irene's intended betrothal, Virginia, then married three years to Leonard, found this another blow to her loosening reason and regained her composure only with difficulty.[45]

Apart from those who seem to have fretted over the impending alliance of Philip and Irene there was, by all accounts satisfaction on all sides. A letter to Philip in Dunkirk from his brother Allan, written on 11th April 1915, conveys pleasure and advises that the news be 'broken' as widely as possible to dampen the rather puritanical gossip among F.U.A. members. 'Tell them about your intended engagement', even in advance of Irene's father giving his approval, was his counsel. It wasn't true, was it, that the couple were thinking of living on in Dunkirk after their wedding? The town was much too unpleasant and the fortunes of war too unpredictable.

Philip and Irene were married on 12th June 1915 in the Sussex hamlet of Worth. Professor Pigou was best man. They were to be Mr. and Mrs. Baker until 1922 when they modified their name to Noel-Baker. The marriage was to last until Irene's death in 1956, her husband surviving her by more than a quarter of a century. Plainly, it was a union of two sensitive people whose need of one another's company and understanding underlay phases of detachment, emotional as well as geographical. For Irene, there was the estate on the Aegean island of Euboea to look after. A small band of villagers saw to the maintenance of buildings, the digging of wells, the conservation of some 10,000 forested acres, a small farm, and an olive grove. Irene conscientiously applied herself to principles of husbandry; among the villagers she was *une grande dame féodale*, recognised but not increasingly admired, as Greek radicalism spread to rural areas after 1920.

From the crucible of war Philip Baker emerged physically unscathed and reanimated in spirit. His father was able to arrange, 'somehow', as the son put it, 'a miraculous translation' from the Piave Front to the ordered elegance of Whitehall. There in the League of Nations Section in the Foreign Office he set to work in 1918 with only one thought by way of ambition, namely:

'to carry on what my father so gallantly had sought to do: to work for a League which would establish the rule of law in international affairs and which would ensure that no human being should ever again be killed in war and captured . . .'

As with father, so with son, life's work would deliberately and fully engage 'the whole of my spirit and my mind'.[46] Always in his mind, he was to recall many years later, was the scroll in King's College Chapel commemorating the fallen friends of 1914-18. 'It was', he believed, 'for the things that the Dons taught us that my friends went out to die . . .' He still found it hard to think that they had died in vain.[47]

Allen Baker, Philip's much-loved father, died in the year the war ended. In his last years he had seemed to grow more hopeful that the desperate bleeding of Europe would bring in its train a more peaceful and rational era when international organisations would be set up as a consequence of incessant pleading from the victims of war. Home on furlough, Philip had been an eager participant in family discussions about the proposals of Woodrow Wilson, Colonel House, and Jan Smuts for a world league to prevent war. After release from the F.A.U. in 1918, Philip was now to embark upon an association with the League of Nations as the next chapter more fully relates. He was present at the Peace Conference in Paris in 1918 and the following year went on to Geneva to become a member of the Secretariat of the League of Nations.

When Philip Baker joined the Secretariat four years after their wedding husband and wife must both have foreseen that a measure of disengagement would ensue. The world of Geneva was brilliant, bustling, and demanding. A League Man must devote himself to that world: it was never a nine-to-four job. Preparing drafts, scrutinising reports, attending committees were all tasks making unpredictable inroads into customary method and initiative. Even had Irene felt able to understand the exigencies of this way of working, she would not necessarily have had her husband's company for long intervals. More certainly, she might have complemented Philip's vocational commitment with the poise and social adaptability of the successful hostess. It is a pity that Irene did not fulfill this role more consistently and willingly.

Strangely, Virginia Woolf seems to have had little time for her old friend, Irene, when they met down the years at the Cecils or at other mutual friends. One wonders why there appears to have been such a hard 'edge' to their meeting, for example, in the spring of 1920 three months after Irene's son, Francis, had been born:

'Thursday 18 March 1920. Strange that this should be my last reflection, since without remembering it I told Irene Noel-Baker that I dreaded the thought of meeting her after 6 or 7 years. She said the same thing – but I rather guess this was simulated. Anyhow we met at the Cecil's last Sunday, & I see why she dreads meeting me – because I look at her. Oh you little adventuress, I think to myself, so now you've turned matron, & are pushing your way & Philip's way into political circles – witness the bright comprehending chatter she kept up with Ld R and Ormsby Gore & you've got a son & are proud of nursing him yourself, & you've grown plump, & look less romantic – though the positive search for obvious truth is carried on as pertinaciously as ever!'[48]

Half a year later Virginia's view has not softened:

'Friday 17 October 1920 . . . Phil Baker is standing as a Labour candidate. Irene will have his teeth filed & get him in . . .'[49]

It must have been a matter of great regret, more particularly to the wife, that her husband seldom managed to join her in Euboea for any length of time. There was always the feeling that a telegram might arrive to spirit her Philip off to conference or crisis. Undeniably, Philip's senses were tuned, the tensions eased, by walks through olive groves and participation in Easter celebrations or a local wedding feast.

The reader of correspondence between Philip and Irene Noel-Baker encounters pathos, candour, irritation, humour, querulousness, and much affection. Irene wrote frequently to her husband in Geneva, talking a little about the domestic affairs of the Achmetaga estate but generally giving herself over to admonition tinged with frustration. She confessed inability to rely upon 'an affectionate creature with strong momentary feelings' who lacked consistency and whose judgement appeared too easily swayed by the attentions of others, particularly if they were women. His rather mild protestations roused her to censure. For her gregarious nature there were not many sources of comfort when he was away so frequently. Writing as she left Switzerland in June 1921 Irene promised that, 'When I come back we really will do Christian Science hard combined with a little ordinary religion . . . I want always to say a little prayer with you every day . . .' There were so many things they had in common, she added, that should have made them happy: 'it is ludicrous that just because of my idiotic nerves we should not be. I am determined to overcome them.'[50]

Within a year came an anguishing period in 1922, explicitly revealed in correspondence, when the distant wife suspects the husband of social dilettantism and of philandering. There is, for her, too much of a liaison between her husband and a certain lady, a Dame Rachel Crowdy, who was working as a senior official in the League of Nations Secretariat. Philip, of course, was an acknowledged enthusiast for tennis, ballroom dancing, and swimming, but an emotional involvement in Switzerland was too much for Irene to stomach. Tiresome though insistence must seem, her contention was that Philip must decide between the two of them, Irene, his wife, or that other person in Geneva whose behaviour she castigated as weak and ignoble. If making the choice meant that his work with the League would suffer, then, so be it! There followed the accusation that he had 'failed' her; that he 'didn't care a damn!' His whole attitude she found inexcusable in a letter of March that year:

'Phil there really is something thoroughly wrong with your whole outlook if you believe that you can have a wife and child & never fr one year's end to the other plan *anything* that will give happiness to them or yourself . . . There is a strain of real brutality in you – which you get fr your brutal Puritan ancestors I suppose . . . Your work supplies all the stimulus you need & yr platonic philanderings with people like Dame Rachel supply sentiment enough to keep you going . . .'[51]

The uncertainties of 1922 show in Irene's pathetic letters from a Swiss hotel. She felt she had to be in Geneva to witness Philip's resolution of their marital problems. Which way would he turn after the 'cruelty and the intolerable hardness' of so many weeks? She regarded his tactics as evasive if not deceitful, even irrational. What he seems to have regarded as 'an absolutely free <pure?> friendship with no break' became for her an impossible division of loyalties and a distraction.[52]

How did Philip Baker take Irene's criticisms? Irritated he was, certainly, but such was his tolerant nature that it did not drive him to the point of hostility. After all, they were to stay together for 41 years. It must have been easier for Philip, engaged so actively with issues and with people; for Irene, almost single-handed in Greece, or travelling Europe by herself, the frustrations and regrets became something of a trial. Philip's replies are invariably low-key. They lack remorse; they are seldom decisive. At heart, the husband might have realised that he did not accord his wife the priority she felt she deserved. Had he been more objective and shown greater empathy, he must have sensed that she had grounds for more than one accusation, for instance, that he avoided accompanying her to England or to Greece if an invitation or a conference presented an alternative. Irene's remonstrance comes close to badgering at times. Her counsel is frequently contradictory, also, in that he is rebuked for not paying more attention to wife and son, while on the other hand, he is urged to make up his mind and to deal more promptly with a League situation, with the Prime Minister, and with Lord Cecil.

It took Irene a good many years to overcome her indignation and sadness. The 'Phil' of 1922 she saw as hard and cruel quite unlike his real self. Her brother-in-law, Allan Baker, had suggested she regard this divisive episode as 'a sort of temporary madness'. Yet hardness and cruelty were not natural to her husband. Together, they had somehow become reconciled without bitterness to the loss in infancy of their daughter.[53] Perhaps the whole thing was absent-mindedness on her husband's part? In 1924 her response to his application for a chair in International Relations at the London School of Economics went straight to the point:

'It certainly is heaven sent – a much better fate than you deserve . . . The only drawback to it will be that you will find it more difficult to invent excuses for not coming here <Achmetaga> – so consider that!'

It seems to have been Josie, the 'adoring sister' who had revealed that her brother preferred to spend ten days on the fells in Cumberland, presumably with Pigou. His wife 'might have known' how selfish her husband could be.[54] Irene, needing a great deal of attention and resentful if it were not instantly accorded, may have found it hard to acknowledge that a husband with academic and political ambitions must quite understandably seek the company of others. The terms of the appointment at the L.S.E. were such as to facilitate the building of a career and were not so onerous as to close down horizons or, indeed, abbreviate a man's time. The Cassel Trust had endowed a chair experimentally for a period of five years, the incumbent's duty being seen as 'to work up a school for the study of international relations, both in the historical aspect and in the practical aspect of diplomatic technique'.[55]

Nonetheless, in spite of disagreements, objectivity and fondness begin to show in the observations of Irene mid-decade. She wrote to Philip in the summer of 1926 asking him to take stock of his own shortcomings. On this occasion she admitted that she, too, had deficiencies – 'a formidable list' she believed – impatience, exactingness, a lack of self control, the failure to realise that Philip's important work made 'peace of mind' crucial for him. She had, she owned, been spoiled in her younger days and this had contributed to feelings of self-importance. Now, though, she felt irritated that her husband rarely attempted to 'charm' her away from those failings. She felt too much taken for granted. It had been clear since the sad events of 1922 that Philip showed more concern for women other than herself. Letters from Irene sound in twin tones, the one soothing, the other rather acrimonious. There is some lack of trust and confidence, a disposition to insist and blame, and a willingness, now and then, to make amends. Virginia Woolf, meeting the Noel-Bakers in June 1925 had detected the interior paradoxes and the ambitious thrust behind her friend's talking. There is little that is complimentary in the novelist's observations:

'Monday 8 June 1925 . . . There was Irene and her Phil. I am too sleepy having got up at ¼ to 6 this morning to describe her. She has spread a little, has a double chin, an emphatic nose, & the feet of gulls on sand round the eyes, which are of the old staring sea green blue. And she has her old ways – her straightforwardness, downrightness, ideals; love of adventure, but none of this is so becoming as of old. For in fact she's grown stereotyped, metallic, harsh; her voice brazen & her cheeks crude. She suspected me, & suspected Bloomsbury & adored Leonard, whom she thought so salutary for Phil, but we both suspect <a> scheme for making Phil the foreign sec in the next Labour Government. I liked her best when she talked about the Greek peasants & that side may retain some charm. But she talks, talks, talks; thrusts her way with a hard kind of energy, into whatever may be going forward – would like, I imagine, to wire pull, & be hostess, & know the right people, but instead protests a horror of success, & wants to keep Phil unspoilt. She also wants to be the mistress of men, I imagine, & a little resents that age should have unseated her from that familiar post as it very obviously has. She veered, as usual, towards Desmond, professed her horror of hurting Molly – a very gallant creature & almost drove L distracted by asking him what he thought of the character of every politician.'[56]

Virginia's criticism grows more severe with a note of regret:

'No, she has not worn well, the plating has come off & she's rather steely & common underneath. Needless, to say I had some waves of ancient emotion, chiefly at the sound of her voice & sight of her hands – hands expressing motherhood, perhaps, but mostly very flat, unable to pump up anything, & thus uncomfortable . . . And the taxi never came, & we had a second night of it, hearing good, pure-hearted Philip, with his principles & his ability, & his athleticism, read aloud to Irene till late.'[57]

The comments in Virginia Woolf's diary reflect oscillations in her composure as much as any consistency in attitudes. When things were well with Virginia there was life and laughter at Rodmell and much friendliness and between Philip and Leonard a marked degree of respect and dependence. The diary pages record several instances of this:

'Sunday 9 May 1926 . . . Unthinkingly, I refused just now to lunch with the Phil Bakers, who fetched L in their car. Suddenly 10 minutes ago, I began to regret this profoundly. How I should love the talk, & seeing the house, & battling my wits against theirs.'[58]

And two months previously:

'Wednesday 24 March 1926 <Noel-Baker told Vanessa Bell> . . . he thought L the best living writer, & what a pity it was he spent so much time on *The Nation* & the Press.'[59]

Philip, moreover, had contacts and influence:

'Sunday 27 March 1926. Leonard met Phil Baker, who says he will get £300 as lecturer at the School of Economics easily if he wants it.'[60]

For 'her Phil', here, there and everywhere as he must be, Irene's expressions of endearment and dependence glint in a grey mass of rather oddly phrased correspondence. The wish to be indulged and loved is, though, rather more obvious than any preparedness to be objective in reflection. On occasion there is the wife's disclosure that her 'tiresome *amour propre*' does not make full rapprochement altogether easy with one who has behaved with 'cruelty and idiocy'. At the beginning of 1930 Irene is able to reassure Philip:

'I feel as if I had completely lost that opposition to you which made me feel so hard. I do believe that you love me & Francis & that not being with us is a sacrifice – not just perverseness as I've really felt all these years.'[61]

In the making of Philip Noel-Baker three constituents seem particularly significant. There is the cradle – the generative influence of father and family, the crucible – where the anguish of war turns him into a Fighter for Peace, and the perception of challenge – which he always answered actively and thoughtfully. It is no accident that he became both a vigorous campaigner in a political sense and a notable sportsman. Athletics could not lose their hold of him despite preoccupation with League of Nations affairs. Whenever he could – and this was most days – he kept up methodical training both around the track and more informally in the style of a modern 'jogger'. Eight years after his performance at Stockholm in 1912 the selectors for Britain's Olympic team for the 1920 Antwerp Games were understandably cautious in Noel-Baker's view (many years later):

'And in 1920, after the war, everybody said, "You are 31, you are too old and no good". And I said, "I'll try!" And I went to the mountains to train and ran much better in 1920 than I did in 1912.'[62]

Captain of the British team at Antwerp, he might have won the 1,500 metres had he not unselfishly acted as pacemaker for his team-mate, Albert Hill, a railway guard and a runner even older than himself. A silver medal went to the pacemaker who came in second and less than a second behind Hill. Four years later there might have been another coup from Noel-Baker at the Olympic Games in Paris. A sudden but only temporary illness kept him out of the track events and reduced him to the non-participant role of Deputy Commandant of the British team.

There is an interesting sequel to the fine performance of British athletes in Antwerp. Why not, it was suggested, match the celebrated squad against its United States counterpart at an event to follow Antwerp in 1920? Noel-Baker and a number of Achilles Club officials booked the prestigious

Queens Club in London and guaranteed £1,200 to cover the Americans' expenses. To their chagrin the event appeared to be heading for a 'flop': few tickets had been sold 48 hours before commencement. Midnight oil was burned by an embarrassed committee in composing an appeal to London's Press. Anglo-American collaboration must not go under! The relief of Achilles was great when Lord Northcliffe, sensing the urgency of the occasion, instructed his Press to give maximum publicity to the forthcoming contest. Saturday morning saw every seat sold. The match was a triumph. Profits were substantial. A first charge on the gate-money, Noel-Baker later related, was a sum of several hundred pounds to repair the Queens Club gates, broken down by an excited and impatient crowd.[63]

Cradled in humanism, Philip Noel-Baker regarded the activities of sport as part of culture bringing out the best in individuals and harnessing cooperative talent. He had with anguish seen a young whole generation melted down in the crucible of the first world conflagration. Was it, one of his admirers asks, because of his debt to them that gave him a sense of urgency that never left him and gave to the world nearly a century of good work?[64] His own response to sport had, one might judge, a spiritual content:

'To lots of people running means more than any game or any sport. It is on a plane with the great forms of art . . . it has a dramatic power that nothing else has; it brings in qualities of spirit that are beyond price. And what makes it most important is that it is so simple that its appeal is universal.'[65]

Thoughts such as these were written to dissuade a fellow-Olympist from hanging up his running shoes. Inevitably, though, Noel-Baker would proclaim, comradeship in sport pointed out the way ahead to a more lasting amity born of challenges willingly and peacefully accepted.

CHAPTER 2

A Time for Hope 1919-1939

IN JANUARY 1919 the British Government sent one of its ministers, Lord Robert Cecil, to Paris to prepare for the Peace Conference. A member of the Cecil team was Philip Noel-Baker (Philip Baker as he then was), 'lynch-pin of the whole body' and 'with almost every intellectual gift that a politician can desire coupled with unsparing devotion to the cause of peace'.[1] Through the good offices of his father in 1918, Philip Baker came to the attention of Cecil, who was forming a League of Nations section at the Foreign Office. The young man was asked to join the section and it was in that capacity that he accompanied Cecil to the Paris Peace Conference. There he acted as joint secretary of the Commission, of which President Wilson and Lord Cecil were the dominant members, which was to draw up the Covenant of the League of Nations. This was to be the beginning of a close partnership in work for peace destined to last many years.

Never before had Paris witnessed the gathering of such an enormous crowd of diplomats, jurists, military officers, financiers, parliamentarians, and journalists. The tempo of feverish preparations and encounter was maintained through committees, tea parties, and a never-ceasing flow of messages and messengers. Amid the flurry of consultations and the hurried production of drafts many remained unsure whether the Paris Peace Conference was to be a preliminary meeting to prepare a provisional treaty or whether, in today's parlance, it was to be a think-tank to frame and publish a final treaty. Not all shared the assumption that the objective of the Conference was, as Hankey puts it 'to provide for a peace of justice rather than retribution by devising proposals for a world league to promote peace'.[2]

Nevertheless, the draughtsmen set to work. 'They have', reported James Headlam-Morley of the Foreign Office, 'a separate flat in the <Hotel> Majestic where Cecil, Percy, Curtis and Baker are evolving elaborate schemes; hitherto no one else has been allowed to see what they have produced'. A Whitehall official such as Headlam-Morley found reason to credit these draughtsmen with 'sound workmanship' and carefully thought out scrutiny of the *Realpolitik* of Europe: indeed by mid-February 1919, all reports saw them becoming less visionary for 'Lord Robert Cecil has been warned by the very impracticable nature of the French League of Nations people'.[3]

There was, of course, always the possibility of the draft schemes failing to engage public interest and to win enthusiasm, but the experiment of attempting to furnish security to a battered Europe was worth perseverance. A case in point was Philip Baker's suggestion that aggrieved minorities (and individuals) should approach the League only through their own government. (In the new Europe there were unhappily more than ever of these groups.) There may have been an element of wishful thinking here in his belief that all League members would be as humanitarian as Poland which claimed to 'recognise its obligations towards its citizens to be obligations of international concern, of (sic) which the League of Nations has jurisdiction'. The only exceptions to the rule would be new communities established by a peace settlement and those people who were transferred as aliens to possibly hostile states. Most certainly groups in danger of dispossession should have the right of appeal and in Baker's opinion the best way of effecting a solution was to use a League mechanism rather than the protective inclinations of the Great Powers. There seemed to be a good, strong case here, granted Headlam-Morley, save on one point. Baker was regarding the whole matter from the standpoint of legislative proposals designed to remedy defective legal codes and evident injustice, but Headlam-Morley doubted:

'whether it would be a satisfactory means of dealing with popular persecution on a large scale, extensive riots and pogroms . . . it would be rather absurd to attempt to deal with this simply by means of a complicated system of legal procedure . . .'[4]

At best the procedure would be time-consuming. 'Flagrant facts' had to be dealt with immediately. There is no record of Baker replying to this point, although he was to encounter the problem of how best to achieve prompt and legally binding redress on many occasions in his later years.

Other men were less patient. Maurice Hankey (later Lord Hankey), an ex-Lieutenant Colonel in the Royal Marines, Secretary to the Cabinet and to the Committee of Imperial Defence, and later to be regarded by Noel-Baker as a *bête noir*, had attended the Paris Conference in uniform (seeing it as a meeting of victors), yet he also had recognised the need of reconciliation through international collaboration. Why should he not apply for the post of Secretary General of the League of Nations? Robert Cecil put the matter to him in February 1919. Two months of reflection gave Hankey in the end cause for demurring. 'I have definitely chucked the League of Nations', he resolved, 'My visit to London has convinced me that the British Empire is worth a thousand Leagues of Nations . . .' Britain's capital was for him, 'the sheet anchor of the world. I can do more for the peace of the world there than in Geneva'.[5]

Maurice Hankey and Philip Baker had already had a significant encounter in August 1919. Working late hours in Lord Cecil's League of Nations Section of the British Delegation to Paris, Baker received a sudden summons from Hankey to present himself at the Cabinet Office next morning. The dash to Whitehall necessitated a long and difficult road journey and a swift crossing of the Channel in a warship. All this seemed to have been put in train to enable Hankey to offer an appointment to the personal staff of the Prime Minister, David Lloyd George. Preferring to stay with his admired Cecil, and knowing that the work in Paris was important, he decided against the proposal, according to Noel-Baker's own retrospective account many years later. Both men were quite furious: Hankey, because the offer had been turned down, the other, because he saw the venture as a pretext, a ruse, 'a Hankey plan to break up my partnership with Lord Robert and to divert a young fanatic from his labours for the League'. They parted in mutual contempt. Situations such as these convinced Noel-Baker, and with increasing conviction, that the rather cool advocate of the League was to turn later into a cynic and 'a resolute and most industrious hawk', who had the ear of Britain's Prime Ministers and Foreign Ministers as Cabinet Secretary.[6]

The Peace Conference and the League of Nations were being conceived at a time of war-weariness, fluctuating hopes, and uncertainties. There were those, led by Lloyd George, who were concerned to 'see it through', and among them chauvinists preoccupied with ensuring that any future German revanchism was made impossible. Those of this persuasion had resisted any idea of extensive negotiation with ex-enemies, for they had counted on unity among the Allies undergirded by secret agreements at 'top level' and had fulminated, in the British Premier's words, against:

'pacifist propaganda at home, which, operating on a natural weariness, might develop into a dangerous anti-war sentiment that would undermine the morale of the nation at a time when the event depended on the staying power of the nations . . .'[7]

Ranged against them were those, like the members of the Union of Democratic Control, who aimed at concerting dissent from a government foreign policy which appeared to them powerless to avoid war and ineffectual in ending it and in achieving a lasting post-war settlement. The British public, lured into war, had to be informed through Press and

Parliament. Populist groups elsewhere in Europe must be brought into accord to ensure (in the words of Norman Angell) 'peace terms that neither humiliated the defeated nations nor artificially rearranged frontiers as to provide cause for future wars'.[8] 'Peace without victory', as Woodrow Wilson was to encapsulate it, was something that appealed to the Bakers, father and son, as it did to numerous U.D.C. members, philosophers, writers, journalists, and politicians.

Undeniably, as Noel-Baker has recorded, the Allies in 1918 believed they had 'won' the peace. As Lloyd George saw it, peace would be settled by negotiating safeguards and not by 'public clamour'. On the public stage in Paris Lloyd George was able to see Wilson's 14 Points as entirely acceptable, for, as he put it, 'With the exception of the Freedom of the Seas, there is nothing in these points which is incompatible with the war aims already proclaimed by British and French governments . . .'[9] (Over the next decade that stated reservation was to prove significant.) In his speeches at home and abroad the Premier emphasised the mandate his government had been given. Wavering adherents were ditched and a broad-front pacific policy had been initiated. Was there not also endorsement from those in the Empire who had sacrificed so much for common victory? Hughes, Premier of Australia, though wary of Wilson's 'League of Nations toy', had told the Imperial Cabinet in January 1919 that imperial traditions contributed solidity to a 'league of peace'. Robert Cecil, candidly acknowledging that, 'Foreigners always suspect us of advancing the most altruistic principles for any scheme that promotes British interests', went on to assert that the Empire's enormous power for peace was also 'a position of prodigious responsibility'.[10] And was not J. C. Smuts, co-author of League proposals, an eminent imperial spokesman?

Privately (and most clearly in retrospect) Lloyd George seems to have been more circumspect and less sanguine. It was evident to him, and to observers like Philip Baker, that the peace makers in Paris showed a public mien which might well disguise natural reservations and prejudices. Clemenceau and Sonnino voiced regard for international collaboration while privately much of what they felt and did was actuated by the fears and suspicions of France and Italy respectively. Woodrow Wilson, arriving in Paris with blue-prints for a League, had, in the view of the Welsh pragmatist, 'an ecclesiastical <rather> than a political type of mind'. In all probability, this idealist with no sense of European reality, would discover 'that the chronic troubles of Europe could not be settled by hanging round its neck the phylacteries of abstract justice'.[11] Nor was it likely that the American position would be sustained for long since Wilson lacked political credibility at home and was not able to ensure Republican endorsement for his erratically-drawn and chimerical schemes. Indeed, as United States President, Wilson had to cope with the apprehensions of two flanking American forces. There was the Democratic Party, whose traditional instincts were to 'balance liberty and order . . . <and create> . . . a league strong enough to preserve peace but not powerful enough to destroy freedom'.[12] (This need was echoed by conservatives in Europe.) On the other hand, Republican senators looked to the Monroe Doctrine and an injuction to back away from any form of alliance which might impose external responsibilities and few of them can have felt assured by what the League to Enforce Peace declared in April 1919, that the Covenant of the League of Nations was, 'a thoroughly American instrument – thoroughly American and thoroughly non-partisan'. It was after all known in Washington and elsewhere that American champions of the League of Nations were linked with the League of Nations Union in Britain, with such as Robert Cecil and Philip Baker. If they were honest, both 'Leaguer' and 'anti-Leaguer' should have recognised the truth of the observation that 'Wilson, in opposing reservations, was not opposing alterations to the Covenant exactly, but was opposing the type of mind and the political forces that produced the reservations'.[13]

If Wilson were seen to be a blinkered and uncompromising visionary, the contradictions of Paris in 1919 were plain to others. Ray Stannard Baker (no relation to Philip Baker) detected in the halls and corridors of the French capital:

> 'a conflict between the New, whereof the patent symbol was the Covenant of the League of Nations, and the Old, which was ever identified by its attachment to such items as "territorial guarantees", "economic concessions" or "strategic frontiers". The tactics of the Old were tactics of barter and bluff. The New was disposed to favour the widest possible publicity; the Old thrived upon secrecy and concealment.'[14]

Conflict led to confusions, jealousy, misrepresentation, to wheeling and dealing in public encounter and to agreements hastily negotiated in camera. Harold Nicolson, for one, felt the frustration of 'the inevitable curse of unanimity leading to the no less inevitable curse of compromise', again in public, where recriminations in private led to 'adjustments' which were not recorded in 'hard print'. What was true of the atmosphere in Paris was equally true of Geneva, the seat chosen for the League of Nations, though many had hoped, Philip Baker among them, that removal from an ancient centre of European intrigue to a brighter, neutral locale would bring about a change of heart as well as of scene.

Looking back to the founding days in Paris, Noel-Baker has frequently referred to the enormous influence of Leonard Woolf in promoting the establishment of the League. Woolf's return from the Ceylon Civil Service to the Fabian Society found him working, so he said later 'like a fanatical or dedicated mole . . . By 1916 I had a profound knowledge of my subject: I was an authority'.[15] It was in 1916 that his *International Government* had argued for settlement of disputes between states by codes of international law which should be mandatory. It seems clear that Woolf regarded arbitration not as a panacea for resolving conflict but as a useful means of graduated response which could substitute a deliberative and legislative process for the customary intuitive reliance on *force majeure*. An international authority with a representative council, a secretariat, and a court charged with calling for reports, the setting up of enquiry commissions, and the gazetting of treaties, while it was unlikely to make war impossible, would do much to make it less probable.

In the spring of 1915 one of Philip Baker's dons at Kings College, Goldsworthy Lowes Dickinson, had joined Woolf, J. A. Hobson, and H. N. Brailsford to launch a movement that became known as the League of Nations Society. These innovators worked hard on a number of possibilities. Would it be feasible to require a 'cooling-off' period when disputing nations would be forced to withdraw and consider? Philip Baker's father, Allen, had supported a similar concept at the first Hague Conference of 1899. Might some disputes be distinguished (certainly in the eyes of Fabians) as 'justiciable' and so pre-eminently dealt with through a panel of renowned jurists? If 30 to 40 states were to join the organisation and to be represented in a general assembly and, say, in a smaller supervisory council, then how within such an hierarchical structure could the greater powers retain an authority commensurate with what was judged to be their influence, yet allow the legitimate interests of smaller countries to be represented adequately? Frank Walters, historian of the League of Nations, testifies to the underlying tension these questions raised during the life of the League (and of its successor the United Nations), although, and Noel-Baker has emphasised the point, the smaller nations looked upon the concept of an assembly as enabling them for the first time to make their voices heard, to stand up for their own rights, and to express opinions about the policies of their larger neighbours.

A consensus for international collaboration gathered momentum as the war's final phase brought American entry and frequent stalemate in Flanders. The classicist, Gilbert Murray, and the editor of *The Times*, Wickham Steed, meanwhile had brought into being another group, the League of Free Nations Association. In their view it was imperative that the Allied War Council should develop into a body less concerned with military matters and more with the securing of a peaceful world. It was the human response of men such as these that affirmed the desirability of eventual reconciliation and the admission of Germany to a World League. Coincidental with the 1918 Armistice the League of Nations Society and the League of Free Nations Association combined to form the League of Nations Union and the new group was able to enlist such notable persons at Lord Grey, A. J. Balfour and David Lloyd George as Honorary Presidents. It is significant that these constellations of interest were not only what might be termed today as 'pressure groups'. Their meetings brought earnestness and authority to concentrated discussion. An instance of this was the group of notables chaired by Lord Bryce, and consequently known as the 'Bryce Group'. Further sustained and systematic examination of the thesis of Leonard Woolf was urged through the medium of an Anglo-American committee. Advocates such as J. A. Hobson and H. N. Brailsford stressed the economic usefulness of a world association facilitating the more equitable distribution of resources, investment, and trade and the lessening of world tension. Dickinson was joined by men of letters such as Gilbert Murray and Ernest Barker, by historians and by lawyers, in efforts to sketch a structure for international arbitration. Their tolerance and far-sightedness, later to be elaborated by Noel-Baker in his writings for the Journal *International Law*, had nothing of the rather eccentric exclusiveness of George Bernard Shaw who saw the main difficulty of the League as 'not to get every nation into it, but to keep the incompatible nations out of it!' Amid the core of cognoscenti, broad swathes of public opinion (Noel-Baker's 'great voice') advanced the preferences of liberal internationalists for an end to the limitations and dangers of traditional strategies, reflected caution among moderates who saw a League as a possible complement to the British orthodoxies of naval hegemony, imperial strength, and restrained European commitment, and urged the objections of conservatives who doubted the practicability of instituting an international body with legislative, executive, or judicial functions. Many on the Left were not able to hold with collective force as a notion or with the sustaining of what they regarded as covert imperialism; the Right resented 'interference' and even feared a revolutionary thrust from Geneva.

'It seems to me', wrote Cecil in a Foreign Office minute of 1917, 'increasingly probable that we may have to accept an unsatisfactory peace'.[16] In the aftermath of Versailles, Leonard Woolf was no less candid. 'The Peace is a bad peace, and the League is a bad League . . .' but he went on, 'the League is not quite so bad a League as the peace is a bad peace'. The right policy, and particularly for an America flexing its muscles on the European scene, seemed to be, 'Accept and reject the Treaty'.[17] Might not the League at its very least act as a brake on the force and unpredictability of nationalism? At any rate, as Lord Cecil half-humorously told St. Loe Strachey, one could rely on delay, if not on decisions.[18]

Not only among the wider public but among government officials and diplomats there is evidence that after the war there was difficulty in realising clearly what the role of an international organisation such as the League might be. Would it meet only in times of impending crisis? In what respects would the League differ from the customary alliance of nations who sensed the existence among them of a community of interest? Would there ever be agreement about the 'legitimate interests' of any particular member state? Quite clearly Philip Baker and Cecil discerned among those they met in London or Paris at least an uncertainty, at worst a confusion, about the feasibility of legal codes of control and of imposed moratoria in international disputes. President Wilson's reluctance to be committed to a 'cut and dried' plan only fuelled the inclinations of Maurice Hankey and Philip Kerr to favour the League as a replacement for inter-Allied wartime cooperation and in some respects as an attempt to reconcile emerging idealism with conventional diplomatic procedures and techniques.

The schemes of Woolf and others were not left to float among the clouds. In 1917 Lloyd George's government felt sure enough of its ground to set up a committee to look at the whole question of collaboration among states. The committee, the Phillimore Committee, was composed of a number of lawyers, historians, and civil servants. Woolf's drafts were laid before them. Typically Fabian in their imagination and resourcefulness the proposals were studied and referred to among both official and private groups. In the Foreign Office towards the end of 1918 they were considered very carefully and a summary of their arguments and conclusions was prepared and circulated to members of the Cabinet. This memorandum according to Noel-Baker:

'became a standard work of reference for the League of Nations Section of the British delegation to the Peace Conference and was much used . . . I think it is not too much to say that it thus played a major part in forming the thinking of the authors of the Covenant, and of many men who helped to shape the Secretariat and Council of the League of Nations on questions of international, economic, social and technical cooperation.'[19]

A member of the Imperial War Cabinet, the South African General J. C. Smuts, was able directly to table ideas emanating from Woolf together with his own modifications and those of Lord Robert Cecil and Alfred Zimmern. What had been envisaged was a standing inter-state conference together with a supervising committee of foreign ministers drawn mainly from the Great Powers. Believing that this form of association might be misinterpreted by some as 'a great power conference system, an improved and regularised version of the Concert of Europe extended to include America' Smuts sought to take the proposals further in a carefully written set of suggestions.[20] A league of allies would not be enough. Equitable representation of larger and smaller powers called for a double tier of a council (mainly representative of the great powers) and a general assembly (containing all member countries). Smaller powers would have to be seated in rotation in the council. A direct charge to maintain peace and order would make necessary some system of sanctions, radical proposals for demilitarisation, and a means of monitoring national armaments. An instrument of international government must deal with the causes and consequences of disputes and not function merely as an arbitral device. A League-in-action, direct and relevant was for that shrewd and practical politician, David Lloyd George, 'an ever-visible, inevitable, irresistible part of an international system'.[21] Robert Cecil favoured, too, the suggestions of Woolf, Hobson and Brailsford for mandates to replace colonial suzerainty and for programmes of economic and social development to be coordinated and directed by international agencies.

A permanent secretariat would be responsible for League staff work and a cooling-off period of three months would hopefully delay premature escalation of disputes and make easier the tasks of compiling evidence, conference, and arbitration. Cecil, according to Noel-Baker, 'incorporated virtually the whole of Woolf's ideas into the British Draft Covenant which he gave to Woodrow Wilson'.[22] So straightforward were these proposals in the firm view of Philip Baker, one of their protagonists in 1919, that should any British government default on them, specifically the recommendations (modestly put in the Phillimore Report) that arbitral awards be accepted and that common legal procedures govern the settlement of disputes, then such evasion would profoundly stir a large body of continental opinion then most in favour of a League of Nations. As for the United States, no American should consider the application of these principles of international morality as in any way trespassing upon the rights of Congress.

It was in the Imperial War Cabinet that a phalanx of Tories – Bonar Law, Curzon, Austen Chamberlain, Balfour – expressed themselves as unwilling to make sacrifices of sovereignty in such crucial areas as arms policy and colonial administration. Nor at that time, did they evince much faith in the power of League rulings, finding it difficult, as so many people did, to accommodate both the cooperative and coercive functions of the League's scheme for collective sanctions. Elaborateness may have worried conservatives; it seemed clear also to Robert Cecil (perhaps echoing Foreign Office sentiments) likely to predispose the Prime Minister not to take the League proposals seriously. Thirty years later, one commentator discerns in these attitudes:

'a significant commentary on the state of informed opinion in Great Britain that most of those who saw the need for international organisation insisted, nevertheless, that it must be developed substantially within the framework of a State system that had already demonstrated its inability to insure peace.'[23]

Among Labour leaders Ramsay MacDonald aired the suspicion that the League might turn out to be a new 'Holy Alliance', a league of governments rather than of peoples, organising 'force' rather than 'rationality', and in no way redeeming the harshness of the Versailles settlement. In his view, the League ought to seek to redress those clauses of the Peace Treaty which were commonly regarded as 'punishing' ex-enemy states and which fuelled a sense of grievance.[24]

Was 'the League idea' already beginning to lose ground in late 1918, despite the orchestration of public concern and the beliefs (or blandishments) heard on political platforms? Robert Cecil and his acolyte, Philip Noel-Baker, feared this might be the case. The bureaucracies of Whitehall and the Quai d'Orsay, the protests of French generals, the divided voices chorussed from Washington's Capitol Hill all contributed to inertia. Could the Imperial War Cabinet not now seriously consider Wilson's 14 Point Programme? After all, the Germans had asked explicitly for a peace based on it. There was, moreover, evidence that Wilson was attempting to blackmail his allies into subscribing to the League proposals by threatening to sign a separate peace with the Central Powers. This was perhaps not a very charitable judgement since it is generally recognised that Wilson was anxious to repair what appeared to him to be the flaws of the peace settlement. In any case, to intertwine Treaty and Covenant might help to bring the United States Senate on to his side and placate even the isolationist tendencies of American voters. Cynics were heard to allege that the United States could afford to be idealistic for there were no potentially hostile neighbours on the American Continent. Idealism apart, realistic expectations induced America's President into using the threat of British naval rivalry to cowe his electorate into accepting the League.[25] There is every sign that Allied nations muted their criticism of Wilson's promotion of the League in return for Washington's favourable attitude towards various territorial 'adjustments'.

Generally, though, there was wide agreement on the need for open diplomacy to afford mutual guarantees of political independence and territorial integrity to all states, whatever their size. The problem, as one contemporary observer saw it, was how to put 'bite' into processes of regulation, inspection and requirement, and how to achieve this not via compulsion but by agreement, for 'the bond of common interest is there, the bond of common suffering in the past, and the certainty, if the League fails, of common suffering in the future'.[26] Philip Baker always took for granted that the 'living thing' of the League (to quote Woodrow Wilson) would only flourish if vitality, resilience, and resolve were demonstrated on a common front. In much the same vein, the dynamic vision of J. C. Smuts was often recalled, that the League everyday must be 'an ever-visible living, working organ of the policy of civilisation'.

A delegate from one of the League's smaller states viewing the League after its launching termed the most crucial problem that of 'raising a sufficient head of steam . . . giving power to the turbines'. Cecil, Baker, Sir Eric Drummond, the League's first Secretary-General, were all acutely aware of the need in power-terms to convince both friends and critics of the League's vitality. Together, the power to reduce suffering and the capability to effect decisive influence in situations of conflict appeared to depend a good deal on the twin props of objectivity and international law. Would delegates assembled in common concern overcome competitiveness and chauvinism at least for a month or two? Was it possible that frequency and continuity of contact might lead eventually to realisation of inter-dependence and more specifically and positively to consensus and agreed courses of action? At the base of the structure in what ways might a multinational secretariat displace those all-too-natural feelings of partiality and cultivate (even disseminate) a 'transgovernmentalism' edifying to all who experienced it?

Sir Eric Drummond boldly asserted that as Secretary-General he had recruited an international civil service rather than used national officials temporarily detached from home ministries, as some would have preferred. One of Baker's colleagues, J. A. Salter (later Lord Salter and formerly prominent in Allied Shipping Control), saw in this detachment the weakness of a 'denationalised' staff lacking in status and deprived of informed contact with member countries. A League formed in this manner could prove inefficient and perhaps 'die of dullness'. It is a tribute to the energies of such as Drummond, Cecil, Baker and colleagues that national boundaries were transcended by most Secretariat members united more than ever before in their concern for peaceful inter-action. In actual fact, it seems:

'Diplomats and lawyers still spoke of state sovereignty as if it represented absolute national independence while governments were entering into practical arrangements to facilitate international cooperation and to establish international regulations and institutions where national actions alone would be ineffectual. Most of these agreements were produced by the very diplomats who extolled national sovereignty.'[27]

On the other hand, as the same account sees it, transgovernmentalism developed unevenly within the League, most fully perhaps in connection with matters that governments did not hold salient to their survival, doubtless, in part due to the sheer technicality of certain problems which made their public airing inappropriate, partly because in regard to a number of economic and social issues their conventional solution was held to be within the bounds of national autonomies.

In respect of international law, the danger of being legalistic was something that worried Cecil from the beginning. As a new recruit to Lord Cecil's Section at the Foreign Office, Baker had compiled a series of memoranda on international law which advocated the institution of complicated legal machinery, an approach which Cecil felt only could add to the enormous and crowding difficulties they were encountering: far better, and safer, he thought, 'to have very simple provisions at first which could be elaborated later on'. Colleagues such as Cecil, Eustace Percy, and the lawyer Cecil Hurst may have agreed with their younger compatriot's categorising of disputes, viz.

(i) Purely judicial cases, capable of solution by a legal process in a true court;
(ii) Political cases, which lend themselves to conciliation;
(iii) Purely political causes in which vital political interests are in conflict.

Where they took issue (quite firmly) was with what they regarded as a complicated apparatus to attempt conciliation before a dispute was brought to full conference. Eustace Percy, particularly, doubted the adequacy of a law code as a moral sanction. Should not communities, by means of a long and empirical process, 'grow into a state of law by the slow realization of problems and the creation of rules for their solution'? 'Start simply' was Cecil's notion, 'and allow a thing to grow . . . <that is> the sound way of progress . . .' Baker was less sure, for he had faith in detailed provisions more clearly binding the signatories and thus 'the confidence of each Government will be increased precisely in the proportion as the hands of its neighbours are completely tied . . .'[28]

However the matter was regarded, there was a need for simplicity in the light of two sharp truths which were all too evident: first, that the institution of a League would very likely supplant rather than merely complement traditional British strategies, and, secondly, and a matter of wide regret, the ground under President Wilson's feet was being eroded fast by his political opponents at home. The 26 Articles of the League Covenant had been regarded by those who framed them as essentially simple in the obligation they enumerated, a feature, it was hoped, which would gain wide acceptance.

The main plank of the League's foundation was to be the Covenant. It had to be fashioned quickly. In January 1919 Robert Cecil set up a team to work as a drafting workshop with the Americans led by David Hunter Miller. The Britons were Philip Baker, Frank P. Walters, J. R. M. Butler and Lord Cranborne. Assisting their husbands were Irene Noel and Lady Cecil. From the Foreign Office came Eustace Percy and Cecil Hurst to contribute diplomatic liaison and legal weight respectively. A scheme was drawn up by Baker to take account of three main areas (i) regular conference of all members (ex-enemies to be excluded until admission policies were defined), (ii) the establishment of a Council of Powers such as France, Great Britain, Italy, Japan, and the United States to meet at least yearly and to be served by a secretariat, (iii) detailed procedures for arbitration and sanction. American collaboration was not easily secured, particularly because the far-ranging suggestions of the United States President as to mandates, arbitral measures, and the Council constitution, while they were scrutinised carefully by the drafting workshop, met heavy weather from Wilson's Congressional colleagues, both Republican and Democrat. Indeed, Cecil was in the midst of a welter of personality clashes between Paris, London, and Washington, the concomitant of differences in political attitude. The Covenant must be revised.

Rewriting of Baker's outline of the Covenant was accompanied by constant despatch of notes, growing less conciliatory, between London and Paris. Services chiefs and diplomats stressed the need of 'strength' and 'continuity' in Great Power approach. Canada and Australia asserted the 'solid fact of Empire' in the face of declining British interests. Apart from controversy in Washington, it seemed possible that French fears over the Rhineland, an unsettled German reparations bill, and the conflict between Italy and the Central Powers over Adriatic access, would endanger the drive for international accord.

David Lloyd George, feeling earlier that confrontation was looming over unresolved issues, arranged an intensive and confidential discussion among heads of government at Fontainebleau. The outcome was a set of compromises which pleased nobody. Maurice Hankey's frank opinion in July 1919 was that while, of course, the League of Nations had to be made a success, it was so uncertain an experiment that no-one could afford to base national security upon it. That point was firmly taken in Whitehall and at the Quai d'Orsay; meanwhile, behind a screen of reservations and qualifications, the Americans began to retreat from the Covenant and back away from Europe.

In his book *The League of Nations at Work* (1926) Philip Noel-Baker discusses the foundations upon which the Covenant proposals were based and modestly indicates how the compilers of the draft had somehow to weld the political concepts of European Concert – those of Castlereagh, for instance – which a more modern world would find insufficient, to the movements for organised arbitration and mutuality of guarantee that had their roots in the Hague conferences of 1899 and 1907. Essentially, the Covenant of the League, adopted on 28th April, 1919, may be said, 'to have established the organs of the League, directed their composition, defined their competence, and guided their decisions'.[29]

Noel-Baker had been well satisfied with the League Covenant as it eventually emerged from the inter-Allied discussions in Paris. Writing in 1922, when the League had been in existence for two years, he claimed that, in spite of the absence from membership of the most powerful Allied nation, the United States, experience of the League's actual working had demonstrated that the authors of the Covenant had carried out with great wisdom their task of devising an international contract to promote and guarantee the peace of the world:

'Generally speaking, they created the minimum machinery and laid down the minimum of rules for its working. The obligations they imposed on the Members were the minimum required for placing on a secure foundation the peace of the world. And in practical working as well as theoretically the experience of two years has shown that virtually every sentence of the Covenant is required, . . . corresponds to a real need, and . . . solves a problem in a manner which, so far, has proved satisfactory.'

The Covenant was built upon 'the national sovereignty of its Members. Its purpose was the creation of a system of political institutions in which those members could cooperate freely in the conduct of their common affairs . . . the Covenant, having created the institutions, leaves to the statesmen who have to use them the fullest liberty to work out, untrammelled by detailed constitutional rules, the development of the machinery they use'. Backed by the force of world public opinion, League institutions 'are already rapidly building up a strong and enduring social and political fabric among the nations of the world'.[30]

Even before the League officially came into existence in January 1920, Philip Baker had joined the secretariat which was based in London at first and then in Geneva. He had given his views on its function in a memorandum for Cecil in April 1919, during the Paris discussions of the Commission which drew up the Covenant (and of which he acted as joint secretary). 'The Secretariat of the League, including in that term all the Commissions and other bodies attached to or formed under the League, may well become in a few years the most important part of the whole organisation, the nucleus round which international government can grow'. It was essential for the success of the Secretariat that the member governments should be determined 'to cooperate in every sphere in which there is a real international interest to be promoted, but 'the mere existence of an international organisation like the Secretariat and its ancillary bodies' would do a great deal to promote such cooperation for it would be 'very difficult for any government to defeat the objects of a Commission established at the Seat of the League'. The Secretariat would also need to secure the services of 'the very best class of official'. At the top would be the Secretary-General, prepared to take the intitiative in studying problems and making proposals for action: indeed, he might well be able 'to guide the policy of the League'.[31]

Philip Baker's first specific job was as acting director of the Secretariat's Mandates Section, pending the arrival of the American G. L. Beer and then, when Beer died suddenly, of his successor, the Swiss, W. E. Rappard. It was thought inappropriate for a national of one of the chief mandatory powers to be head of the Mandates Section. On the question of League of Nations mandates there seemed little ground for optimism. The problem from the League point of view was that the colonial possessions of the defeated powers, Germany (in Africa and the Pacific) and Turkey (in the Middle East), had been taken over by the Allied Powers, mainly the British Empire and France, and they were not disposed to permit any effective League involvement until they had decided the nature of the system, despite the inclusion in the Covenant of an unusually detailed Article on the subject (Article 22). Writing in June 1920, when he was in process of handing over the mandates section to its new director, Baker was unable to see any evidence:

'that the prospective Mandatory Powers intend to treat the territories placed under their charge in any way different from that in which they treated their colonial possessions in the past. If the present course of events continues not only will the old evils of "predatory imperialism" be perpetuated but they will bring greater dangers in their train, in so much as practically the whole of the backward areas of the world will be placed under the control of two powers.'

If the mandatory system were to prove a sham it would bring:

'very serious discredit upon the League of Nations . . . it would have been far better never to have invented it.'

However, the supervisory powers of the League under Article 22 were very important ones:

'It might in the future be possible for the League by moral pressure to induce the Mandatories to change their whole policy . . . Moreover if, even in this limted way, the mandate system was successful, there might be great hope of extending it in the future to other territories . . . But to secure even this limited success much public discussion and education is required. The only hope of the Mandate system is that it will bring the force of informed opinion to bear on the relations of advanced and backward peoples . . .'[32]

Stipulations such as these appeared to Maurice Hankey as sophistry. How, for instance, could an ex-soldier such as he entertain a theoretical insistence on an armed force maintained within territory mandated by the League being confined only to basic policing within the frontier limits of that territory? Hankey's grasp of strategy led him to prefer the capability of drafting such forces elsewhere in the style of a fire-fighting force and he had been 'brought to make this proposal by a wild enthusiast from Eric Drummond's staff Philip Baker' who had annoyed him intensely with a proposal for the League Council 'to force on us mandates of a kind we do not want'. 'These cranks will bust the League', he warned, 'if given their head'.[33]

Baker had not been altogether at ease in the Mandates Section. Over a year before finally leaving it he had told Drummond that he had no intention of remaining there since it was inappropriate for a British national and, in any case, the post demanded someone 'who knew something about black men and their problems'. He had set his heart on working for disarmament, but when a new disarmament section was being set up in the Secretariat in May 1921 the Italian Attolico was made director and Baker was passed over as his deputy. He had not intended to serve more than a few years in the Secretariat (among other things, he had parliamentary ambitions) and this seemed the moment to leave, he told Cecil.[34] Irene Baker was quite sure that he should: 'The League while Drummond is S<ecretary> G<eneral> is as dead as a door nail – you can't galvanise it into life unless you are someone of importance in it. You can do *nothing* in a subordinate position but break your heart'.[35] Naturally, she told her husband, he must decide whether or not he should stay in Geneva – she sympathised with his feelings about the League of Nations with all her heart though she could not conceal from him her resentment at being left alone depressed and with taut nerves. 'Please', she urged him in May 1921, 'don't be hypnotised by things that don't really matter into staying on at Geneva *unless* you are given the disarmament job . . .' Cecil's strong advice, however, was for him to remain, and the marriage leave of Frank Walters, Drummond's personal assistant, provided an opportunity for Noel-Baker to deputise for him, and then to share the post with Walters on the latter's return from leave.

In his new capacity Baker was able to roam widely over the issues which came before the Secretariat – and quite a few which did not. Despite his disappointment over the disarmament post, he took a close interest in disarmament issues and such related matters as the private manufacture of armaments; and continued to draft minutes and memoranda on mandates, as he did on various crises which confronted the League in those early days, including Albania, Vilna and the Aaland Islands. While his relations with the Secretary-General were generally good, he undoubtedly shared his wife's views of Drummond's ineffectiveness (views which were based on his own letters to Irene in Greece): certainly Drummond did not seem to be fulfilling the hope that the Secretary-General would 'guide the policy of the League', since he evinced the discretion of a British civil servant rather than the forcefulness of a policy maker. Criticism had to be restrained in public, though, 'as it washes a good deal of the Secretariat's dirty linen'.

Letters home at this time reveal a lighter side to the Genevan toil. He was able to alleviate the boredom of his limited leisure time by indulging a passion for tennis and ballroom dancing (at both of which was a skilled performer). Leaves were spent on his wife's family estate in Greece (although much less frequently and for shorter periods than Irene wanted) or rock-climbing in Cumberland with 'the Prof.', A. C. Pigou. The latter activity provided good training for the Olympic athletic championship in Antwerp in August 1920, where he gained the silver medal in the 1,500 metres. Physical activities served Noel-Baker as an antidote to hours spent in smoky committee rooms. Cultural interests however, were of less consequence, as Irene forthrightly and affectionately reminded him two years later, 'But darling if you are to speak really well you must read *far* more good literature than you do. If you steep yourself in officialese and journalese it must follow as the day the night that you will speak it'. Philip's notes for articles and addresses, in his rather large untidy writing, were to be scrutinised for years by his wife, doubtless with something of candour and proprietorial concern.

Baker's subordinate position did not prevent him, on occasion, from attempting to take a policy initiative, partly no doubt, to stimulate Drummond into taking action. A notable example concerned his work with the Norwegian Fridtjof Nansen. Nansen was to him the League hero, being everything he admired in a world statesman – truly international in his outlook, courageous, impatient of bureaucratic restrictions. Baker was Nansen's main contact in the Secretariat in connection with his humanitarian work as League-appointed High Commissioner, first for the repatriation of prisoners of war in Russia and then for the resettlement of Russian emigré refugees.

It is very probable that the enthusiasm and level-headedness of the young Philip Baker marked him out as an excellent League emissary. In

March 1920 the League Council sent him to Oslo to enquire whether Nansen would accept the post of High Commissioner. Years later Noel-Baker related how surprised he was when the famous man motored down to the British Legation, marched briskly in, and appeared rather impatient at the meagre details offered him. The uncertainty soon paled it seems:

'And then for seven hours without one moment's intermission – right through the Minister's luncheon party, through his tea party, till darkness had fallen outside – Nansen asked me questions about how the repatriation could be done. The Legation Chancery had to find him maps; the encyclopaedia had to be consulted; every possible hypothesis and every plan had to be considered and discussed.'

Three days later Nansen was ready to make detailed plans, knowing this was to turn his back on his beloved fjords, his family, his science and to take on a tremendously wearing enterprise. Noel-Baker is sure that Nansen's compassion for others, his concern to show that international collaboration could work and, not least, his own indomitable self-confidence impelled him to assume the appointment. Nobody else had his restless, vivid, practical imagination, his gift for detailed preparation, his faith and energy. No assistant of his was ever made to feel small for 'the man of iron, who braved the Polar ice and the politicians of Geneva with the same success' was unfailingly considerate towards his colleagues.[36]

At about the same time as Nansen's League role in the resettlement of Russian refugees was being hammered out in August, 1921, Philip Baker was seeing a further role for Nansen and the League in meeting the vast suffering and social dislocation of millions of people caused by the 1921 famine in the drought-ridden Volga region of Soviet Russia. Private relief organisations were playing a part – and the American relief organisation headed by Herbert Hoover – but much more was needed. On 16th August 1921 Baker outlined his ideas in a letter to Nansen, who was about to leave for Moscow. He explained that he had persuaded the Secretary-General to agree to them but only 'with a great deal of difficulty'. Famine relief, if it was to be dealt with effectively by international means, was best done by the League of Nations, as with the repatriation of prisoners of war. But there were objections to this. Three separate groups were already involved: Hoover's relief organisation, which would be chary of cooperating with the League, of which the United States was not a member; the various voluntary bodies which were currently meeting in conference in Geneva and were proposing to set up an international committee to negotiate with the Soviet Government; and the Supreme Council of the Principal Allied Powers, which had also set up a committee. Baker's proposed solution was for Nansen to be nominated as High Commissioner both by the Geneva conference and the Supreme Council committee, while Hoover should be asked to nominate another Commissioner to act with Nansen. The League would then enter the scene under this plan. Hoover was to be asked if American participation would be affected if Nansen were to be appointed League High Commissioner. If the answer were 'No' Nansen should write a public letter to the Supreme Council committee and to the committee appointed by the Geneva conference to say (in Baker's words):

'that you are willing to act as leader in this work, but in view of the great sums of money for which you may have to be responsible and in view of the very grave political questions with which you are certain to be faced, however unpolitically the matter may be dealt with, you would wish in this matter to have the support of the League of Nations and act as League Commissioner, as you did for the repatriation of prisoners of war. This would automatically bring the matter to the attention of the Council of the League . . .'

Baker was 'convinced that in the long run it might prove a most valuable way to bring Russia into touch again with Europe and the League, and might have the most valuable consequences'. The Secretary-General, however, 'has had very grave doubts as to whether League intervention would be useful, and while he is now convinced that it might be, he is not a very ardent supporter of my plans . . . But, of course, if they were adopted, he would do everything in his power to help'.[37]

Drummond was even less enthusiastic about a further elaboration of his assistant's ideas in a minute of 19th August. 'If the organisation of the relief work to be undertaken in connection with the Russian famine were entrusted to the League of Nations', Baker wrote:

'the function of the League would, I believe, be almost exactly those which it fulfilled in connection with the repatriation of prisoners of war . . . it would not create a vast organisation for directly carrying out executive action. The execution of any programme decided on could be entrusted to the numerous agencies – Government and voluntary – concerned in collaboration with the proper Russian organisations and authorities. Indeed, the relation of the League to executive action might be even more remote than this. The area of famine in Russia is so vast that probably the representatives of the Government and voluntary agencies will be able to do no more than supervise the carrying out of relief work by Russian agencies.'

The functions of the League High Commissioner would be to coordinate the efforts of the various executive and supply agencies and to conduct all negotiations with the Soviet authorities: functions which would involve his exercising 'very considerable authority over the voluntary agencies and perhaps over the Government agencies engaged in the work of relief'. This authority would need to be backed by the League Council, especially as the High Commissioner 'will administer large funds and have to take decisions of great political importance'. The League Assembly would provide him with a public platform from which he could bring pressure to bear on governments, while the Secretariat would, as with prisoner repatriation in the previous year, keep the agencies in touch with each other and conduct correspondence both with the voluntary associations and with governments, and be responsible for the banking of, and accounting for, the funds placed at the League's disposal.[38]

Drummond did not like this extension of a subordinate's plans, and doubted its practicability. He clearly interpreted it as involving the League in acting on its own initiative, rather than – as in the earlier plan – leaving it to the Supreme Council committee to appoint Nansen, if it so decided, in which case Nansen would then say that he would like the support and authority of the League to facilitate his work. Drummond would have been even more reluctant to endorse the proposals had he known of the strategic purpose which underlay them. But Baker's friend, Humphrey Sumner, working in the International Labour Organisation, perceived it at once: 'I entirely agree [he wrote] with what I take to be the leading and essential idea behind your plan, viz, the seizing of present opportunity for the starting of practical work in connection with the Russian famine with the ulterior aim of the League eventually being the guiding centre in assisting the economic and general reconstruction of Russia . . .'[39] The Soviet Union did not formally join the League until December 1933, and over 12 years before that date, here was a relatively junior official in the Secretariat already envisaging the League playing a major part in that country's economic development. In any case, the whole operation was frustrated by the unwillingness of governments to make financial contributions, which many saw as strengthening an abhorred Communist regime. Nansen was indeed appointed High Commissioner for Russian famine relief, but by the Geneva conference of voluntary relief agencies, not by the League, with which he had no official connection. Baker's ambitious plan came to naught, but with great energy he nevertheless worked unofficially for Nansen on Russian famine relief, for example, helping to organise Nansen's fund-raising lecture tours to Britain, France and the Netherlands in February 1922, and rebutting charges of Communist sympathies levelled at Nansen for his Russian work.

As assistant to Fridtjof Nansen, Baker's staff work had been enterprising and very thorough. His approaches, whether to Geneva or London or Paris had a three-fold set of priorities for relieving Russia's misery. Immediate needs were for the necessities of life to see people through the winter, namely, flour, meat, blankets, and delivery vans. Secondly, and looking ahead there was a desperate shortage of tractors (and mechanics to service them), ploughs, seeds, and harvesting machines. Thirdly, economic links could be struck through supplying consumer goods to Russian cooperative societies and ensuring adequate marine transport between Italian ports and Odessa. A further line of enquiry was directed at certain philanthropic institutions in the United States. The resuscitation of Russia, it was pointed out, would be impeded, of course, by economic factors and the chaos of famine and also, very significantly, by the denudation of the educated, professional classes, many of whom had fled from the Socialist Republic, vowing never to return. If it were scarcely feasible to intervene in the Russian educational system might it not be possible for dollars to be channelled through Nansen's relief unit in Constantinople to help train and encourage the 200,000 Russian emigrés huddled there? Indeed, he urged his American correspondents to envisage a steady demand among the refugees for assisted passages across the Atlantic to hoped for employment there.

Appeals to the West brought an unpromising response. In London the Treasury were insisting, in tardy replies, on detailed accounting and confirmation of interest before sterling might be disbursed. Paris, particularly, proved exasperating in its prevarication and in its resort to thinly-veiled criticism. These attacks were 'lamentable' Baker told Arthur Henderson. The French, he wrote:

'are willing to play with political quibbles while 20 million people die who might be saved at the cost of half a battleship.'[40]

While the bureaucracy and evasion of governments was not easy to accept, the undeserved criticism heard in several capitals infuriated the Norwegian and his aide. Governments were irresponsible and unjust in their attitude, – they would leave the whole burden to voluntary organisations. Nansen went on:

'I cannot think that right: I cannot think it wise: I cannot think it anything but a disastrous mistake . . .'

Nobody could work efficiently against such a campaign of misrepresentation and rumour. 'My only prayer is that I may avert the crowning tragedy of success that comes too late.'[41] Lord Cecil, in fact, was moved to write many 'appeal' letters staunchly defending the integrity, approach and methods of Nansen and castigating attacks as 'pernicious'.

It is understandable that in the Europe of the 1920's it was not possible to mount the relief operation for Russian refugees on the scale that is met with today. Quite apart from antipathy to Marxism there was not available either a pool of resources or sufficient experience and confidence to provide it. Somehow, though, for the early operation of repatriating half a million prisoners of war from Russia, relief credits had been organised through the League of Nations. Noel-Baker spoke of this tremendous feat in guarded terms some years later:

'There was not the will to co-operate, there was not the machinery of cooperation. There were not the funds to provide the trains and ships and materials that were required. There was the fear of every government across whose territory the prisoners were to move that, in their lamentable condition, they might spread disease among their own population.'[42]

The gigantic task of shipping all their half-forgotten prisoners was an impressive demonstration of how the League of Nations might work. Above all, in Noel-Baker's view:

'it was a work of reconciliation; it brought to half a million families in Central Eastern Europe a knowledge that there is an international organisation for the betterment of human conditions and an international spirit of co-operation that does not always work in vain.'[43]

On another occasion he had said that there was no country on the continent of Europe 'where wives and mothers have not wept in gratitude for the work which Nansen did'.[44]

Yet another fine achievement for the resolute Nansen and his Quaker assistant was the relief of distress among refugees in Thrace and Macedonia. Something like 300,000 refugees, two-thirds of them entirely destitute, were fleeing southwards as a defeated Greek army relinquished border arcas to Turkey. Panic and starvation had these people in their grip. Even one million pounds from the Allied Powers would suffice to stave off typhus, possibly cholera. Eventually, the situation eased when Turkey and Greece agreed to set aside old enmities and organise the relief and exchange of despairing peasants. The field work for the two men was arduous. Noel-Baker spoke of this 14 years later when the plight of refugees in the Spanish Civil War reminded him of the anguish of Greece:

'I saw a picture of an old Ford car, a 'Tin Lizzie' that had seen service in the war and that now stood bunkered by the mud on a little hill in Eastern Thrace. Behind it, pushing, with might and main, to get it up the hill were Dr. Fridtjof Nansen, the great Norwegian statesman and explorer, and the young Englishman who had been sent by the League of Nations to help him in his mission of bringing help to the refugees . . .'

'And all that day and all the next we drove along the primitive track to Adrianople beside an unbending column of refugees that stretched without a break from North to South as far as eye could see. No one who saw it could ever forget that piteous cavalcade . . . But I only grasped the numbers of these refugees when I saw them halted for the night. With their fires gleaming like a myriad of stars, on and on and on through the darkness, it seemed that all the suffering families of humanity must have pitched their camp along the Thracian stream . . .'[45]

Clerical work in the Constantinople office must have seemed heavy-going to Noel-Baker. On one occasion in October 1922 he confided to a friend: 'I have been having a devil of a time with Nansen – 12 hours a day ever since we left Geneva, and no Sundays'.[46] Should he return to London and seek a parliamentary candidacy before polling day? There must have been in his walking thoughts a mix of great compassion and empathy for the sick and homeless, a determination to strain every inch on their behalf, and beyond it an inclination to return and progress to other concerns. He put the matter plainly to his trusted mentor, Robert Cecil in the same month. 'While,' he declared, 'I think all this sort of business extremely important it bores me to distraction and I am most anxious to get back to disarmament.' There is no record of a reply. Cecil doubtless understood the outburst and held his counsel, quietly. The mood evidently passed.

Undoubtedly, Nansen was profoundly grateful for the loyalty and understanding of his colleague, Noel-Baker. 'All I have done in the League or for the League,' he acknowledged later, 'had been done with you, and could not have been done without you, at least in the manner it was achieved. And so it has been from the very beginning and till now.' He went on, 'Oh dear friend, how much you have done for me, and for the League during these many years, and how much time you have given it!'[47]

Elsewhere, Nansen spared no pains in commending the great helpfulness and confidence of his aide. In the work for Russian famine relief, he wrote, Noel-Baker was 'one of those who spurred me on to it . . . [his] sound judgement of international relations was of invaluable importance'. In general terms, Nansen declared:

'I may add that what success the international work under my leadership may have had, is to a very large extent due to Mr. Baker's assistance. His remarkably sound and practical judgement of international relations, his initiative and resourcefulness, combined with his exceptional capacity of working would always find new ways and means to overcome difficulties which often seemed almost impossible . . . And with his inspiring enthusiasm he has also an exceptional ability to make others interested in his subject and to make them work . . .'[48]

Nansen, though, could be severe in his judgements and sharp in criticism. Melancholy and depression at times overtook him as it did, for instance, in the early summer of 1927 when he wrote to Noel-Baker, 'I have a feeling that the League is rottening much quicker than I thought would be possible. Dear me, what a Council! It is decidedly much poorer than it ever was, and with such a gathering of cowards there is nothing doing; and why on earth should one waste one's time coming here . . .'[49] There had been insufficient support for Nansen, as High Commissioner of the League's Refugee Organisation, to achieve his resettlement objectives in southern Russia and in the Armenian frontier lands of Turkey. Stresemann's Germany (now admitted to the League) was prepared to help (although under no obligation). Austen Chamberlain 'gave you the taste of lukewarm water', and the rest said nothing lacking the fight even to save their reputations. 'I miss you sadly,' he assured Noel-Baker, '. . . it is always a consolation to talk things over with you . . . you will always be the unrest which does not allow their conscience to fall asleep entirely . . .' Sorely tempted to leave in disgust the faltering League, Nansen, in fact, did hold on and Sir Charles Trevelyan also advised Noel-Baker to do the same. This 'living symbol of the humanitarian efforts of the League of Nations' was to remain steadfast until his death in 1930.

In the summer of 1922 however, Noel-Baker left the Secretariat for a post which also was closely concerned with the League of Nations, but this time with its public advocacy rather than behind-the-scenes administrative work: Overseas Secretary of the British League of Nations Union, of whose executive council he had been a member of since 1919. It was Lord Robert Cecil, with whom he had maintained close contact since Paris, who suggested he take the L.N.U. appointment and it was Cecil again, in June 1923, who asked Noel-Baker to assist him in his new capacity as Lord Privy Seal in Stanley Baldwin's first Cabinet with special (if ill-defined) responsibilities for League of Nations affairs. When the Baldwin government resigned in late January 1924 Cecil commended Noel-Baker's abilities to Ramsay MacDonald, the incoming Labour Prime Minister. Lord Parmoor, Lord President of the Council, Cecil's Labour successor as minister for League of Nations affairs, was happy to retain Noel-Baker's services as a private secretary. Philip Noel-Baker was less content. If Parmoor had not been 70, with a brain that 'had quite simply ceased to work', he would have been an excellent choice for League of Nations affairs – kind, courteous, singularly patient and sweet-tempered. Enormously dependent upon his Quaker, pacifist second wife, Parmoor seemed unable to deal with the admitted difficulties and was irresolute in not pressing for more debatable aspects of the Covenant to be resolved as at least a stage towards disarmament and acceptance of arbitration.[50]

As always, Irene was quick to press home the point in letters to her husband that work with Parmoor was a stagnant area where little growth in political opportunity might be discerned. Too many people (naturally in her absence), and particularly his adoring sister Josie, had prevailed upon him to labour in a backwater. His 'ideas of standing for parliament have all gone to blazes', she wrote in the spring of 1924 and the plans he made were too often the consequence of selfishness and short-sightedness. The prospect of a chair at the London School of Economics was 'splendid' for that at least would enable Philip and she to see more of each other, afford a measure of less hectic endeavour for half the year and, after all, why not consider combining academic work with politics?[51] Lord Robert, she felt, was sure to agree.

Cecil, for his part, advocated the younger man's relinquishing his private secretaryship, 'for a man of your ability a p.s <Secretaryship> is not a proper career in itself'. His protégé, he believed, meant to go into Parliament. 'And if you do', Cecil affirmed, 'I say again and with renewed emphasis the sooner the better. Politics are a highly skilled calling and require training. Almost everyone makes mistakes at first . . . don't wait another instant. Find a seat as soon as ever you can!'[52]

Throughout his life Philip Noel-Baker made no secret of the debt he owed to Lord Robert Cecil. 'Lord Cecil made the League of Nations', remarked Noel-Baker in a speech many years later as a member of the Attlee Cabinet. 'In the Foreign Office, in the Cabinet, in the United States, in the Chancelleries of Europe, it was Lord Cecil's drive which made the foundation of everything that later on was done . . . He made the League in Paris . . . it was always Lord Cecil who led the debate . . .' And in Geneva (in an observation of Noel-Baker's recorded by Cecil himself), 'It was he who brought the paper institution into life' by this means turning 'a disordered diplomatic gathering into an ordered strong parliamentary institution'.[53]

Robert Cecil (1864-1958), son of the Marquess of Salisbury, was born into one of England's most distinguished families. Schooled at Eton and Oxford, he took silk in 1899 and seven years later entered Parliament as a Conservative with inclinations which soon led him to be an independent. A junior minister during the 1914-18 war, he emerged from that holocaust utterly convinced that all his work henceforth must be to promote the maintenance of peace through international collaboration, and to strive for collective security and disarmament. With J. C. Smuts he had been asked to represent not Britain but South Africa at Geneva. Nonetheless, he was patriot as well as internationalist and when he assumed a Whitehall portfolio of responsibility for League affairs he attended League Council meetings, drafted the statutes of the Permanent Court of International Justice and, to the dismay of some of his London colleagues, had a hand in shaping the League Protocol.[54]

Noel-Baker always considered Baldwin (under pressure from Eyre Crowe and Maurice Hankey) disinclined at first to appoint Cecil to his government. When he heard of this attitude in November 1924 Noel-Baker recalls he telephoned to Drummond in Geneva, who came to London immediately and persuaded the Prime Minister to give Cecil a ministerial responsibility for League Affairs as Chancellor of the Duchy of Lancaster. The final arrangements were perhaps not entirely satisfactory as Noel-Baker recalls:

'We were made to sit in the old Treasury building on the other side of Downing St. . . . I was personally very glad to sit in the Treasury building; it enabled me to be better acquainted with Sir Otto Niemeyer, who had greatly helped to get a League loan for the settlement of Greek refugees in 1923. But since it was essential that either Parmoor or I should see Foreign Office papers which related to the League, I was given a tiny room in the <Foreign> Office – a cubby-hole a little larger than the one I had been given when I first joined the institution. But a desk and a chair and a secretary were all I needed, and my cubby-hole enabled me to keep in touch with Cecil Hurst and other friends.'[55]

Baldwin, and his Foreign Secretary, Austen Chamberlain seem to have been reluctant to recruit Cecil. The new minster has himself stated this and a later commentator has put it in these terms:

'Cecil's inclusion in the Cabinet was due more to Baldwin's perception of the needs of party unity and the wish to symbolise continued theoretical adhesion to the ideals of the League of Nations than to endorsement of his attitude towards disarmament . . . It was made abundantly clear that the Chancellor of the Duchy of Lancaster would not become a kind of alternative Foreign Secretary with special responsiblity to League affairs; he would be requested to toe the line in foreign policy from the outset of the government.'[56]

Few of the peacc campaigners had such ready access to Prime Ministers and elder statesmen as had Robert Cecil. In response to Philip Baker's plea in 1920 that Lloyd George be warned of the undesirability of crude excursions against the newly-established Bolshevik regime in Russia the veteran humorously had replied, 'There is nothing I do better than stir up trouble,' adding, 'if you wish me to do it I will do it with the greatest pleasure!'[57]

Cecil's attitude towards the League and its Covenant was very positive. He was intensely optimistic in believing that international representation serviced by a carefully recruited secretariat and backed by the force of world-wide public opinion would 'remedy grievances' through conciliation and arbitration. Traditional upbringing in the case of Lord Robert did not exclude a kind of paternalism in believing that, as he once put it, 'the real security of the small powers must be the sense of justice of the large ones . . .'[58] He was shrewd in his judgements of Wilson's difficulties, of American reluctance to become involved in Europe, and of the consequent fears of the French that they might be abandoned. He may have been less realistic in giving priority to the technical processes of disarmament rather than to the creation of a strong system of guarantees. In the event, critics of the League, both in France and in Britain, appear to have remained unconvinced that the Covenant would bring about a greater degree of security for their country. Again, to take an example, Cecil's insight may have wavered a little over the Corfu crisis of August 1923. Mussolini, the

Italian dictator, outraged by the murder of an Italian general, a member of a delimitation committee appointed by the Conference of Ambassadors, sent a peremptory note to Greece demanding apology and compensation. A naval force was despatched to bombard and occupy Corfu. Only the League of Nations should judge the Italo-Greek rupture, Cecil and Noel-Baker believed, not the Conference of Ambassadors, a group set up in 1919 to deal with territorial matters requiring adjustment. In this instance, the quarrel constituted a 'threat to peace' and lay within the legitimate ambit of a multi-state league. Apart from that, the Ambassadors would not find it so easy to exercise impartiality since one of their prominent members was, in fact, an injured party. Italy protested vehemently and insisted on the Conference considering the situation rather than the League. Genevan opinion strenuously asserted its right to decide and rule. Cecil's idealism gave way to realism when he very cleverly ensured that Conference and Council worked together in such a way that the apologies and restitution required of Greece went through the Conference. Had Cecil surrendered jurisdiction? Was he skating (dexterously) on thin ice in order to salve League authority now dangerously imperilled? Noel-Baker, himself, was in no doubt:

> 'Cecil had saved Corfu for Greece – Venizelos said later that it was the League's greatest triumph: he had vindicated the competence of the League, rallied the whole Assembly, and obtained most valuable opinions on the meaning of the Covenant from the Permanent Court.'[59]

There is the possibility, however, that Cecil's reliance on probity among nations 'all the way' clouded his discernment somewhat, and that his idealism led to a degree of detachment.[60]

Cecil's discernment may have been on firmer ground when his attitude to divergence from Covenant principles is considered. Was the Treaty of Mutual Assistance which he helped to table in 1923 sufficiently compatible with the main lines of the Covenant? 'Only an organic development of the Covenant', he urged, 'can bring success, not a heterogeneous adjunct thereto'. What was needed was 'not an accumulation of treaties and agreements', but 'an intensification and refinement of the Covenant itself'.[61] This was a point frequently urged, too, by Philip Noel-Baker, who would have associated himself with the distinction, drawn by Gilbert Murray, between what was alliance, vague and partial in extent, and what was drawn up as a result of international agreement and codified by way of Covenant and Protocol. That way – the League way – governments could be assured that 'aggression' would be explicitly defined, together with measures designed to cope with it. In essence, Noel-Baker believed, a Covenant supported by mutual guarantees corresponded, 'almost exactly to the earliest stage of the national police force in every civilised country . . .

the *posse comitatus* – the sheriff calling on all good citizens to join in the pursuit of the criminal'.[62] Any other way was the short-sighted reliance on expediency where countries might find inter-dependent guarantees at first sight attractive but in the last resort not easy to honour or to depend upon. No regional pact could provide real assurance according to Cecil. Was Britain's Foreign Minister Austen Chamberlain so blind, wondered Noel-Baker in a note to Gilbert Murray, that he did not realise 'that his Locarno stuff is *simply* the Treaty of Mutual Assistance – minus, alas, disarmament'?[63] Neither Noel-Baker nor Cecil was ever able to forgive a British government for hastening towards a defensive alliance such as was negotiated at Locarno between Germany, France, Italy and Britain rather than moving forward in the spirit of mutuality aspired to at Geneva.

Subscribing to a treaty of mutual assistance would be 'a great forward step in the political development of international society', wrote Noel-Baker in the summer of 1924. He instanced the case of France to show what might be done to move beyond a discredited system of narrow alliance. No risks would be tolerated by the French, it was said. Herriot's Government would collapse and the fragile Franco-German reconcilliation over reparations and frontier lines would disappear if Paris were less decisive about state impregnability. Yet M. Herriot knew that 'security is a problem which France cannot solve alone'. A radical French Premier such as he, who meant business, and knew what he wanted, would insist on two cardinal points: first, that Germany must be accorded her rightful status as Great Power rather than half-tolerated neighbour, second, that this must involve mutual demilitarisation. What the French (and everybody else) want:

'is not the security of France by the predominance of arms: it is the security of France by the abolition of military force as the controlling factor in international relations.'[64]

In the vigour and clarity of this assertion, Noel-Baker declared, Paris led London. Here was a way to empower the Covenant and work for a common and mutual treaty of assistance under the League's authority. The very vagueness of the former Entente might make it seem easier to revive than to launch into unknown waters. Easier, perhaps, but would its obligations not be more entangling, more likely to recreate the suspicions and uncertainties of the pre-League years? Pacifists who disliked the strength implicit in arrangements for mutual assistance must face the practical alternatives.

The Draft Treaty of Mutual Assistance was replied to by the British Government during the parliamentary recess of 1924. Noel-Baker was quick to comment from his Chair at the London School of Economics. Parliament and public at last were brought face to face with the intertwined problems of arms and security. The flagging discussion of previous years had revealed ignorance as to the possibilities of mutual support and assistance within the context of Europe. Opponents of the draft treaty could only advance platitudes, he thought, about 'the spirit of peace'. Where were the 'practical proposals' apart from tentative suggestions as to neutralised zones and compulsory arbitration? Strangely, it seemed to him, the old militarist tag that disarmament would not remove belligerence was advanced now by the *New Statesman* as well as by the world's Die-Hards. Quite clearly, it was untrue that a reduction, say, of three-quarters of armed forces, or permanent limitation at that figure would have no effect directly or indirectly, in preventing war. If such reduction could be brought about invasion 'out of the blue' was not possible. Military castes and Bismarckian diplomacy would lose their potency. Rival powers competing in 'preparedness' and generating insecurity (which, paradoxically, vitiated their policies, anyway) must lower their sights if the means to domination were denied them. Mutual assistance to promote a heightened sense of security – buttressing the Covenant – could be the result only of an agreed and general limitation of national armaments. There was no other way in the view of Noel-Baker. Our Government's reply was not the end of the matter, in truth, it was only the beginning.[65] Neither the Treaty of Mutual Assistance nor the Protocol, its successors, were to be taken up by governments, the one Labour, the other Conservative, which, in Alfred Zimmern's phrase, adopted 'the policy of the ostrich!'[66] This failure occasioned much dismay in the minds of Cecil and Noel-Baker.

Robert Cecil's honesty and perceptiveness were highly esteemed by the Noel-Bakers. Irene recognised that it would be sad for Philip to leave his friend's service, though that would be necessary if he became an M.P. Her letters between 1921 and 1924 attest a cautious regard for her husband's mentor: they reveal, too a certain mixture of amibition, loneliness, and resentment.

Already in the spring of 1921 Philip had been reminded by his wife of Cecil's suggestion that work for the League of Nations could be a concomitant of preparation for parliament. Those qualities that would make for a good public campaigner and parliamentarian – industry, sincerity, and straightforwardness – were being commented on at this time by many, including Beatrice Webb and Oswald Mosley. 'On the rebound from Armageddon,' Mosley had been captivated by the ardour and optimism of Lord Cecil, and was to emerge for a time as an able front-runner in Labour Party ranks.[67] It seems as though these two observers as well as Ramsay MacDonald esteemed the honesty and knowledge of Noel-Baker more highly, for instance, than that of Hugh Dalton.

Nevertheless, on reflection, Irene was less sure about Parliament, 'as you will always undertake the work of at least three men I prefer on the whole that the two jobs should be more or less compatible – things you really want to do'.[68] A year later she wrote (and telegraphed), 'Do please make up your mind about it soon . . .' Nansen's work would not collapse. In London, and independently, Noel Baker could do more for the League than by staying in Drummond's Secretariat, he would be in touch with 'the people that count', and in this way the L.N.U. would 'bully the Government who will in turn bully the Secretariat'. Through 1923 and 1924 and written from Achmetaga, Paris, or a Lausanne hotel, there are appeals from Irene to that better side and that caring nature of a husband who worked too hard, devoted himself to problems among states, and seemed, in consequence, detached from his family. Her admonitions are couched frequently in terms which range from acrid to affectionate and there seems little doubt that the inevitable long and frequent absences that this entailed all served to render their marriage anything but tranquil. On the other hand, it must be said that each partner appears to have needed the other.

The Baldwin Government's intransigence over naval reduction at the 1927 Coolidge Conference eventually led Robert Cecil to resign office. The resignation should be seen as occurring over a disarmament issue rather than as general disagreement with Whitehall's League policies. Thereafter, his efforts for peace were undiminished and, together with Philip Noel-Baker, he campaigned vigorously for disarmament, as assistant and adviser to Arthur Henderson, the bluff and courageous trade unionist turned M.P. Noel-Baker, as M.P. in 1929, was Parliamentary Private Secretary to 'Uncle Arthur' (as Henderson was called). Whether organising the Peace Ballot in which 11 million Britons favoured the League's efforts for disarmament, or in speaking all over the world for the League, Lord Cecil's 'wide knowledge and complete candour were undeniably persuasive . . '[69]

In 1924, as we have already noted, Noel-Baker accepted the offer of a Chair of International Relations at the London School of Economics. He was to stay there for five years until his election to the House of Commons as M.P. for Coventry in 1929. There was now more time for reflective writing. At a distance from the hurly-burly of the Hotel National in Geneva the international civil servant-turned don attributed much of the League's smooth functioning (in the main) to that 'Genevan atmosphere' ('all air, water, and no more war' according to Salvador de Madariaga), where statesmen of 40 countries did their best to 'act at sittings of the League in a way which differs from that in which they sometimes act in their own Parliaments at home'.[70] Not all would have shared this benevolent impression. A former colleague in the Secretariat and one who was eventually to become Deputy Secretary General of the League, Frank P. Walters, expressed it more phlegmatically. League officials, he later wrote, 'watched with a mixture of hope, anxiety, and jealousy the efforts of the powers to carry out the purposes of the Covenant without accepting its principles or using its institutions'.[71]

Twenty-four hours were never adequate to contain the daily concerns of Philip Noel-Baker. Lecturing on international problems to his students, labouring over a book, assiduous committee work, long journeys by rail and steamer to visit towns in Britain and Europe still somehow left him time for daily physical limbering-up with a swim to finish or a decision about which climbs next to attempt in the Lake District or the Alps. Irene's constant and rather querulous letters reminded him of financial worries over expensive accommodation in London and Geneva and the ever-present uncertainty surrounding the family's Achemtaga estate. Always, of course, there was Cecil, near neighbour in South Eaton Place, to be written to and consulted. Granted, the elder man was insistent, invariably polite and patient, though he did write in November 1925, 'I wish the island of Euboea <the location of Achmetaga> and all that it contains were at the bottom of the sea. Developments in connection with the armaments question are taking place which make one realise how much I should like to talk to you . . . Do please sell your estates to some of the native barbarians, and do not try and live this double life any more!' He added, 'This is not meant too seriously'.[72]

There may have been in Cecil's observation a recognition of the division of loyalties that Philip had to bear in so far as it was provoked by Irene. Cecil can not have been unaware of Irene's petulance and jealousies though he would not have been privy in December 1923 to a mix of upbraiding and advice. Writing from 43 South Eaton Place, London, Irene had scolded her husband in these terms:

'You might have postponed your historical discussions with Lord Robert until the train had started, if you thought it was too much above my intellectual level to make it possible for me to listen to it! It's no good – I simply hate being so taken for granted that I am absolutely ignored. However, I'll quell the demon in me and only determine that at least I won't meet you on your return . . .[73]

Should her husband not now further his parliamentary ambitions and leave Cecil? 'Phil darling', she declared more amenably, 'if you haver abt leaving him now I really shall be more miserable abt you than I have ever been but once. You simply have got to come forward now . . .'

Cecil and Noel-Baker, of course, were quite uncompromising in their support for the League of Nations. His Majesty's Government, as Lord Robert saw it, must stand by, 'the Covenant, the whole Covenant, and nothing but the Covenant'.[74] Yet within three years of the League Covenant being ratified there were anxieties that the incompleteness of European security weakened the effectiveness of provisions for disarmament. Across the Atlantic anxieties about the European scene, and by implication what that might involve for a United States already bloodied in distant continental war, predisposed the Administration and the majority of citizens towards isolationism. President Harding's determination in 1921 is not hard to understand, for, in one view, he 'denounced the Covenant, merely *hoped* for an association of nations, and proposed ratification of the Treaty of Versailles with the Covenant deleted and with proper reservations and modifications that would commit the United States to nothing'.[75]

In what way might a 'gap' in credibility best be dealt with? Robert Cecil, as we have seen earlier, assisted by Noel-Baker and others, sought to plug the fissures by drafting for the Fourth Geneva Assembly in September 1923 the so-called Draft Treaty of Mutual Assistance. Signatories were to inform the League of Nations Council of the arms reductions they felt they could afford in the light of the assurances of the Covenant and, further, they were to make such reductions effective within two years. Not surprisingly, there were League members who interpreted this as stretching Covenant undertakings thinly without building procedures for rapid response to aggression which usefully would include arbitration and sanctions.

It is interesting to note how certain influential Americans attempted in 1924 to exercise influence on a situation of stalemate at Geneva. Was it possible to go *'beyond the League'* (as Zimmern put it) by accepting a Protocol as a pragmatic device morally acceptable to the United States where the Covenant might seem too flaccid and indefinite? Building on the resolve of Senator Borah of Idaho to outlaw war, a group consisting of General Bliss (a Paris Conference delegate), the Covenant draughtsman David Hunter Miller, and Professor James T. Shotwell of Columbia University circulated documents to the Council of the League and to the Assembly. Essentially, as they saw it, 'the outlawry of war' depended upon parties solemnly recognising the underlying proposition, unanimously judging any transgressor, and being prepared, again in common, to apply strict economic sanctions. Edouard Herriot, recently installed as Premier of France, lent them an approving ear. Was there a risk in tabling such proposals in full Council without preliminary study? Philip Noel-Baker, on receipt of the Bliss papers from Washington in June 1924 evidently thought that such action would be premature and – with the British representatives in mind – might even 'provoke an explosion'. Three years were to pass before proposals such as the American ones were seriously considered; eventually, they contributed to the context of the Kellogg Pact, or the Pact for the Renunciation of War, signed in Paris on 28th August 1928. Indeed, the United States had gone further than the Covenant had. However, they remained on the periphery and the direction and extent of any future action on their part was not predictable, and might be thought of as something of 'an addition to the effective power of the League, real but not capable of being calculated'.[76]

In Whitehall, Ramsay MacDonald's minority government, now in office, instructed its delegates at Geneva to seek a more precise and more comprehensive programme which would have as its aim the establishment of extensive machinery for the compulsory settlement of inter-state disputes of every kind and thus work for disarmament. The linkage between security and reduced arms had been made plain but an agglomeration of general guarantees among all states appeared to be a compromise unlikely to afford watertight assurances to those countries ('the weaker') which could rely only on partial alliance. What was contemplated for the Fifth Assembly of the League – it was to be emphasised there by Ramsay MacDonald himself – was the preparation of a Geneva Protocol for the Pacific Settlement of International Disputes, to translate the requirements of the Covenant into active terms and by this means enable a policy of disarmament to be based upon 'a more complete settlement'.

As an independent consultant, now a professor at the London School of Economics, Philip Noel-Baker was closely involved in the preparation of the Protocol – 'the most truly satisfying <weeks> of my life'. Three main planks were to constitute the foundation, namely, arbitration, security, and disarmament. It was granted that the League, 'did not want to create the illusion that by a single step mankind could finally destroy a chaotic but an age-long system <viz war> and forthwith enter a new heaven and earth', nonetheless, the Protocol seems to have been thought of as a kind of self-denying ordinance in that members would acknowledge the criminality of war and while war itself was not abolished, they would refrain from resorting to armed force to resolve a quarrel.[77] Thus, their right to self-defence was placed within the limits of, first, an assurance, collectively subscribed to, of freedom from warlike aggression, and, secondly, a requirement that the victim of any hostile attack demand the mediation of the League. Pacific settlement of disputes was to operate in two ways. What were termed 'justiciable cases' would be taken either to the Permanent Court of International Justice at The Hague or to a special arbitral tribunal. Such matters might have to do with contentious aspects of a treaty or a claim for damages. Verdicts would be binding. 'Non-justiciable cases' would be put to mediation and to the conciliatory scrutiny of the League Council. In the event of the Council failing to achieve a settlement then the matter should be submitted either to The Hague Court or to some form of voluntary arbitration and, in the last resort, following stalemate, arbitration would have to be imposed compulsorily.[78]

It was not entirely clear even to one of the draughtsmen of these novel proposals, Philip Noel-Baker, just what were the legal or quasi-legal rules arbitrators might apply. There appeared to be somewhere in the background the belief that unanimous recommendations of the League Council would be sufficient to bring about solutions. In Noel-Baker's opinion, for instance, 'pacific measures for the enforcement of decisions will, in the vast majority of cases, be enough'. Contentious disputes might even be sent from the Council to the Assembly (as had happened in 1920 over a Serbo-Albanian frontier disagreement) to be subjected, as Arthur Henderson reminded the Fifth Assembly in September 1924, to 'the immense moral pressure of the League as a whole'. Retrospectively, one may judge sentiments such as these as somewhat naive (if not unrealistic) and yet there seems to be something plainly hopeful in the expressed thought that under arbitration, 'the appeal to national honour is a factor, not for war as it has been so often in the past, but for peace'. Moreover, the arbitral process becomes 'an actual source of strength to those elements of moderate opinion who are willing to accept an impartial and reasonable solution'. Hope such as this was to sustain Philip Noel-Baker for another 60 years though later, too, he was to repeat the caveat that in politics not everything that appears logical is wise. (Hankey might have agreed with this, at least.)

In regard to security two consequences of the Protocol gave rise to earnest consultations in European chancelleries. First, the extent to which members' rights of domestic jurisdiction (acknowledged by the Covenant) remained free of external intervention. Clearly, there could be a conflict here between the safeguarding of that autonomy and the duty under the Covenant (and, similarly, later, under the Charter of the United Nations) to act to preserve world peace. A rider to this uttered at the Admiralty in London was the question of within whose orders would a League peace-keeping force operate: that of the League or of the commanders of national naval contingents? 'Disarm the Fleet?', thundered Admiral Sir Rosslyn Wemyss in 1919. Cecil seems to have been quick to understand the conservative nature of this response and Philip Noel-Baker went further to stress that 'the relative weakness of a scattered International Fleet faced by a well-directed national navy illustrates the necessity of having Military and Naval Sections of the Permanent Secretariat <of the League>'. This 'would add enormously to the restraining value of the sanction . . .'[79] National autonomy was generally seen in Foreign Offices as underpinning the status quo. Was there a fundamental contradiction here in the terms of the Protocol? Philip Noel-Baker felt he had to confirm to his fellow-countrymen that Britain was indeed interested in maintaining the status quo:

'Is it probable that we shall submit to foreign decision the rights of domestic jurisdiction over such questions as control of immigration? Or is it likely that any British government would submit even such relatively simple territorial questions as those of Gibraltar, Malta, Cyprus, the Sudan? What we will not accept ourselves we cannot impose on others.'[80]

A further problem was that of defining aggression. It was notoriously difficult to frame an objective definition in relation to any situation, hypothetical or actual. The justifications of 'legitimate interests' and 'right to self-defence' had all too often been resorted to in order to legitimise certain strategic moves. A straightforward suggestion was that of Edouard Herriot, Premier of France, to the Fifth Assembly, namely, that the aggressor would be that state 'which went to war instead of submitting its case to arbitration, or having so submitted its case, went to war rather than comply with the award'.[81] An automatic test such as this was the sort of litmus procedure that a 'protocol' was to include to enforce the provisions of the Covenant. This was not quite adequate a formula in Noel-Baker's eyes for the need to impose sanctions on an unrepentant aggressor he thought should be stated quite explicitly. The members, however, in imposing sanctions, would not lose all freedom of action. It was absolutely plain, Noel-Baker asserted:

'that under Article 11 of the Covenant Great Britain would in no sense be subject to the orders of a council of foreigners; that its liberty would be fettered in no way in which it is not already fettered by the Covenant; and that it would be free to regulate the assistance which it gave in accordance with its own Imperial needs.'[82]

The point was not lost in Whitehall, however, and particularly in October 1924 when MacDonald's government was replaced by a Conservative administration under Stanley Baldwin with Austen Chamberlain as Foreign Secretary. Chamberlain had qualms about the effectiveness of sanctions, indeed in regard to any restriction of British independent action, and his critics were not slow to allege that his sentiments might have been influenced by commercial considerations, whether economic sanctions took the shape of boycott or blockade. More importantly, the attitude of Whitehall was to doubt the generality of the sanctions proposal, asking, in Noel-Baker's words, 'Is the sense of internal solidarity sufficiently developed to induce governments and peoples to make the sacrifices that may be required to maintain the peace in quarrels in which they have no direct concern?'[83] Additional guarantees were needed. The stated conviction of Lord Parmoor, Britain's representative in Geneva, and of Philip Noel-Baker that, 'the extension of the obligation to take part in sanctions is outweighed by the diminution of the chance that the obligation will, in fact, arise', did not perhaps go far enough.[84]

Chamberlain was soon to tell the League of Nations Secretary-General, Sir Eric Drummond, and to announce it to the League Council in March 1925 that his government were unwilling to accept the Protocol. They believed that security and disarmament would be achieved more permanently by making 'special arrangements in order to meet special needs', thus supplementing the Covenant, and especially Article 16, through a series of preventive alliances. Ten years later one of Britain's legal representatives at Geneva, Alfred Zimmern, regarded his government's response as positive rather than negative in the light of the absence of the United States from the League. (Hankey would surely have endorsed this reservation.) A preference for replacing an unwieldy, large-scale Protocol which might not gain international backing with a small-scale 'consultative pact', regional by nature and thought more workable, was not hard to understand.[85] After all, Chamberlain had told the House of Commons in June 1925, 'We are involved whether we like it or not, and the question for us to consider is within what limits, upon what principles, and for what purposes we can undertake fresh obligations'.[86] The considerations, too, of the Dominions and of the Foreign Office advisors served to nullify further willingness to accept the Protocol.

The inappropriateness of the Protocol as an agent of change has been examined by Zimmern. Treaties may be revised only by a legislative process, not by an arbitral one. Rights cannot be surrendered by decree of an international body, however prestigious. Fundamentally, a weakness in the Protocol system seemed to be that it could 'only ensure the observance of the law and not its change, still less its growth'.[87] Philip Noel-Baker did not dissent from this point of view. Territorial or political change by means of force was to be proscribed. 'Is not the worst conceivable status quo better than resort to arms?' he asked. Moreover, 'the great need of the present hour is not for change, it is for stability . . .'[88] This seems to be an echo of the wish of Robert Cecil, addressing the Paris Peace Conference on 14th February 1919, for an international consultative organisation which could 'devise some really effective means of preserving the peace of the world consistently with the least possible interference with national sovereignty'.[89]

Vacillating governments, the obduracy and suspicion of the Great Powers had helped to splinter the Protocol foundations of arbitration and security; the third framework of disarmament was similarly broken. A Disarmament Conference was to be summoned for 15th June 1925. No Protocol was to come into force until this Conference had 'adopted' a disarmament plan. The marked attentiveness which Europe's Prime

Ministers gave the League of Nations by their attendance, particularly after 1925, was not enough to expedite the work of the Preparatory Committee for the Conference. A vast amount of paper work by representatives of more than 20 countries resulted only in the meeting of the actual Conference being delayed several years until 2nd February 1932. Unhappily, much of what was to take place in Geneva represented Machiavellian posturing, 'a system of détours' (as Count Grandi termed it) leading inexorably into the area of Great Power contest and disagreement. A fundamental question for a later commentator was whether Europe's leading nations would accept the responsibility of organised peace or whether they could still hope to enjoy security without paying the price.[90] Few discerning observers in 1925 or later can have looked with equanimity on the prospect of securing wide agreement on an important part of the Protocol preamble, namely, 'the reduction of national armaments to the lowest point consistent with national safety and the enforcement by common action of international obligations'. Divided opinion in Britain about the Protocol certainly blunted any governmental thrust. Misunderstanding and superficial perusal by Whitehall were seen by Noel-Baker, in a note to the Czechoslovak Edvard Benes in October 1924, as inimical to progress and, further:

'So far as I have been able to learn sections of the Conservative Party are strongly against it, while other sections are anxious to support it. The Liberals have not yet taken up any attitude, but I think Professor Murray will be able to persuade them to go straight. The Labour Party are divided and I believe the element of opposition is quite considerable.'[91]

Benes, he felt, 'a child of the League and one of its parents', could rally the faint-hearted to ratify the Protocol.

In the eyes of Whitehall, bilateral treaties were preferred to general ones such as the Protocol and 'non-justiciable' disputes should be submitted to a council rather than to arbitration. At that time how firm was Government opposition to the League declarations on security? Was it not likely, as was said of Sir Austen Chamberlain, that for all their interest in the League of Nations, critics had little notion of what it was all about, that they still lived in a world where the 'balance of power' was important, and that they were, 'still wandering in the trackless mazes of the old diplomacy'?[92] 'The great difficulty of Disarmament', Cecil put to Noel-Baker in February 1926, 'is to induce the nations to take the first step. Once that were done and no ill results followed it would be easy to get them to go further'. In that case, 'What should be the first step?'[93]

Whatever the influence of the supporters of the League, Noel-Baker, in later years, was to make much of the persuasiveness of 'hawks' in the Cabinet and of the predilections (or fears) of Services ministers. Yet in

Disarmament (1926) and elsewhere he indicates that some politicians and military chiefs were prepared to look squarely at the purposes of arms reduction and at its consequences. Baldwin's government, he believed, though 'ill-disposed towards arbitration <was> well-disposed towards disarmament . . .'[94] Clearly, then and later, this appeared as a contradiction not easily to be resolved. A failure to agree on arms limitation at the Three Power Naval Conference in Geneva in 1927 led to a frustrated Cecil resigning. The target of gradually bringing about a Demilitarised Europe seemed farther off than ever.

For Cecil and Noel-Baker, the voices advising the government against backing the League of Nations were influential and insidious. Nor had the Secretary General, Eric Drummond, any illusions about the same critics. Sir Maurice Hankey, Secretary to the Cabinet and to the Committee of Imperial Defence, had little faith in collective security or international arbitration. This was the 'hawk' who had whispered in the ear of Ramsay MacDonald and of Stanley Baldwin. Cecil was not deceived. His influence and scheming had been Machievelian. 'It is important I think to get rid of the Prime Minister', he was to assure Noel-Baker, 'but in my view it becomes essential to get rid of Hankey. As soon as you get back to England <in May 1930> I should like to have a serious talk with you as to what steps if any can be taken with regard to that object'.[95] Nothing, though, appears to have come of this conspiratorial move.

Had the League then not failed? Were the hopes of its supporters to be justified in any real way? Who could now declare that in Geneva moral authority and the prestige associated with it were established unmistakably? Early in 1922 Noel-Baker had written candidly to Drummond to deplore the lack of consistency and courage among permanent members of the League Council. Given this lack of commitment the achievements of Geneva might seem remarkable and give grounds for hope, although, the League itself, he believed, had been rather pusillanimous over territorial disputes such as Vilna, the Saar, and Upper Silesia. No Secretariat could be expected to accomplish much if among the permanent members impartiality and resolve were lacking.[96] This was emphatically a point which Arthur Henderson, MacDonald's Foreign Minister, between 1929 and 1931, was urged to declare through briefings that his Parliamentary Private Secretary, Noel-Baker and his Parliamentary Under-Secretary, Hugh Dalton supplied. Two generations later it is not altogether easy to make out in what way these three participants, together with Cecil, might have treated the old cynical proposition 'only the strong can afford to be impartial'. There is some evidence that Cecil spoke for all (echoing, too, Smuts) in the thought that Britain's imperial status both lent strength to the country's role and helped to buttress the fragility of the League. The suggestion, of course, would have been much less chauvinistic than anything Hankey uttered.

More than 60 years later it is not easy to be convinced that public opinion behind the League was as potent as both Cecil and Noel-Baker saw it. 'The great weapon we rely on', Cecil believed, 'is public opinion and if we are wrong about it, the whole thing is wrong . . .[97] Why, then, did the British and other governments do so little to educate the public as to the potentialities and limitations of the League? There are grounds for thinking, it has been suggested that, 'Britain stayed in the League not out of conviction but rather out of cowardice. The public believed in it, and to disavow it might be to court electoral disaster.[98] Politicians might see risks in informing the public but, nevertheless, Cecil and Noel-Baker were both agreed that had the Government been more definite about, for instance, Britain's responsibilities under the League Covenant the result might well have been more realistic expectations and lessened fear. Nor did His Majesty's Government feel the need to do anything to advance the claims of the smaller members of the League of Nations, many of them newly autonomous. The protest of Alexander Cadogan that Balkan peoples should not have behaved as Great Powers at Geneva, 'in spite of everything that Philip (Noel-) Baker might say' received assent all too often.[99]

Noel-Baker in the early 1920's clearly saw himself as a *provocateur* as well as a protagonist. A certain sense of frustration with the unadventurouseness of the Government is plain in his putting constantly to Professor Gilbert Murray, the Chairman of the League of Nations Union, subjects for the Union's agitation and representation to Members of Parliament. A conference should be summoned for 1924 to consider the growing menace of the production and export of opium. Cabinet ministers ought to be asked to state their international priorities unequivocally. There was a need to press for more government understanding of German and Japanese grievances. Noel-Baker, for his part, agreed to sound out German attitudes towards equal membership of the League of Nations. Murray was urged continually to publicise with undiminished vigour the need of disarmament and to ask Baldwin, the Prime Minister, and the Services chiefs to draw up a definite and detailed scheme for arms reduction. Above all, the League of Nations Union should deplore publicly the all-too-frequent resort of the League to 'tea-party' conversations rather than debate on the floor of the Assembly where it could be observed, for, 'Publicity and lime-light are the life blood of the League', Murray insisted. Noel-Baker pointed out that if the League of Nations Union was to be successful in securing full public backing for the League it must do a great deal more than 'emit discouraging and unoriginal generalities, which have of necessity been watered down to suit eminent individuals with professional reputations to safeguard . . .'[100]

Nor should the League of Nations Union fear divergence of opinion within its ranks. J. M. Keynes, discussing in one of their pamphlets the economic consequences of the Versailles peace was sure to upset some conservatives as would the airing of a number of minority questions.

No less than any other group of intelligent people, the L.N.U. ran the risk of schism. Particularly in 1927 differences came to a head as to how far the Union should be engaged in a disarmament campaign. Indeed, the Union's Secretary, Maxwell Garnett, appeared terrified, it was alleged, of the faction led by the formidable Mrs. Oliver Strachey and he went so far as to excise the term 'campaign' from the Union broadsheets. Robert Cecil felt he had to restrain the 'violent' protestations of Noel-Baker by diverting him to the task of keeping Clement Attlee and Hugh Dalton informed about the Union's programme and meanwhile lowering the flashpoint by substituting the word 'Committee' for 'Campaign'. Noel-Baker, clearly, was able to distinguish between the discordant views of members heard in open forum and the consensus they must have from 'the Left, the Centre, and more rational parts of the Right'. When it came to upholding the machinery and principles of the League of Nations and underwriting Union declarations of policy, clarification was at the heart of the matter and Noel-Baker spent many hours convening study-circles and summer schools and commissioning books and leaflets. For some time, he served as a member of London County Council's Education Committee.

Publicity as the life-blood of the League is something that Murray and Noel-Baker took very seriously. It had to be the right publicity. The *New Statesman* in Noel-Baker's view was 'quite beneath contempt. Opinionated, violent, prejudiced, not interested in peace, openly scoffing at disarmament . . .' A last rejoinder that the paper was 'crassly ignorant like Sharp' (Clifford Sharp, its Editor) compelled Noel-Baker's wife, Irene to add a postscript to a letter to Murray: 'P.N.B. is rather too hard!'[101] Rather, Noel-Baker put to his associate, radio talks could do much to stimulate interest in international questions (and Murray and Noel-Baker were to become capable exponents in the medium), reaching out to the business fraternity and the wider public. Publishers, naturally, must be approached positively. Gollancz, for instance, in 1927, had proposed to Murray that he edit a written symposium by experts on the nature of another world war. Would Gilbert Murray also include in such number, say, Robert Cecil and John Masefield? All in all, public discussion and the supply of impartial and authoritative information were regarded by both men as vital to underpinning the League, to reassuring those in political travail (such as Cecil who resigned office in 1927), and to preventing a government having 'the time of their lives' by relying on a secure majority and a compliant Foreign Office.

Not unexpectedly amid the confusions of the times there were differences of emphasis among those who promoted the work of the League. It was Murray who affirmed the need of the politician to 'have mind and a power of learning': Sir John Simon and Sir Herbert Samuel were thought distinctive in this respect. Noel-Baker, a rising man in the Labour Party as we shall see later, and 'all-sagacious' in Murray's estimation, saw as a priority the need of 'a great sanctions campaign in England in the near future'. This must be orchestrated widely and effectively and it was important that the Labour Party be 'tied up in a sanctions policy so tightly that it cannot possibly wriggle out of it if it should ever come to power'. Noel-Baker's comment is from the time when the Conservatives held power between 1924 and 1929. Murray's position seems slightly detached in putting more reliance on discussion across political divides.[102]

Clearly Gilbert Murray saw himself as a gadfly in the Socratic sense. 'Is there not a very distinct line between criticism and attack?' he had asked Austen Chamberlain in December 1927. 'In fact, if we are not to criticise, what good are we?' Chamberlain, then Foreign Secretary, would not have found a straight reply very easy. Murray had in mind, in correspondence with Noel-Baker, such issues as all-out disarmament, compulsory arbitration, the Geneva Protocol of the League of Nations, issues which engaged him intellectually and with which the Press was much concerned. To one chronicler, 'Cecil, the visionary, could go bald-headed for his goals; ready to disregard the government of the day in his first enthusiasm; ready – illogically – to ignore public opinion as represented by the L.N.U.: Murray's ear was always near the ground: he weighed and counter-weighed, conscious that the L.N.U. could only be effective if held together'.[103] The same writer believes that Murray recognised the difficult position of Robert Cecil as critic, needing to be loyal to his Cabinet colleagues (at least until his resignation from the Cabinet in 1927) and to be dissociated from any position of 'influencer' that his L.N.U. associates might wish for him. 'The League', Murray was to say in the mid-1930's, 'has ruined my Greek' but he continued resolutely on platforms and in *The Times* columns to censure aggression, political expediency, and deviousness wherever he discerned it.

Noel-Baker's optimism displayed publicly in lecture rooms and on platforms was basically imbued with disappointment and frustration in the estimation of Gilbert Murray. The Chairman of the League of Nations Union moved quickly to induce Noel-Baker away from Ramsay MacDonald, the 'swollen-headed' Premier, and his colleagues and on to the Executive Committee of the Union. (He was equally adroit in 'netting' members of the Labour and Tory Parties, groups seen by both men as essentially 'conservative'.) Perhaps Murray was doing some of the Labour Administration less than justice for Noel-Baker had been writing the speeches which Parmoor had been regarded as delivering effectively: indeed, both Parmoor and MacDonald impressed a wider audience than the Genevan with their candour and vision.[104]

For two years, between 1929 and 1931, Noel-Baker enjoyed a parliamentary vantage point as Member for Coventry. Hugh Dalton was his associate as Under-Secretary to the new Foreign Secretary, Arthur Henderson. Noel-Baker was now Parliamentary Private Secretary, for Henderson, it seems, according to Dalton, had arranged to have 'some clever and devoted intellectuals like Philip Noel-Baker about him who could stand up to the foreign equivalents and knew all about subjects like disarmament'. 'Perfect', it appeared to Dalton, diarist and raconteur, relating the way Henderson had informed his civil servants, 'My P.P.S. is a man of very great knowledge and experience' had been Henderson's introduction, 'I dare say you know him – Philip Noel-Baker'. (He was to take over responsibility for relations with the press among other things.) 'I could hear Lindsay's jaw drop' <Sir Ronald Lindsay, Permanent Under-Secretary>. 'I didn't know he was in Parliament', he said.[105] Other observers of the goings-on at the Foreign Office were less impressed. 'Sincerity, of a glib and superficial kind, was one of Philip Noel-Baker's most obvious characteristics' was one sharp recollection 25 years later. It went on:

'He was anxiously good-looking, with swift, nervous movements, incapable of appearing relaxed or at ease. He was an eager pacifist, a great pamphleteer on the wickedness of the arms trade, intensely emotional and a good deal of a prig.'[106]

Neither prophet nor pamphleteer can expect honour in their own country: Noel-Baker certainly did not.

Cecil, Murray, and Noel-Baker were well aware of the need to recruit across a wide spectrum those who could express and maintain belief in League principles. M.Ps. of all parties, members of the House of Lords, dignatories of the Church were approached. Of course, as Noel-Baker put it to Murray in 1927 the old war-horse David Lloyd George would need some weekend schooling to improve his pacific inclinations:

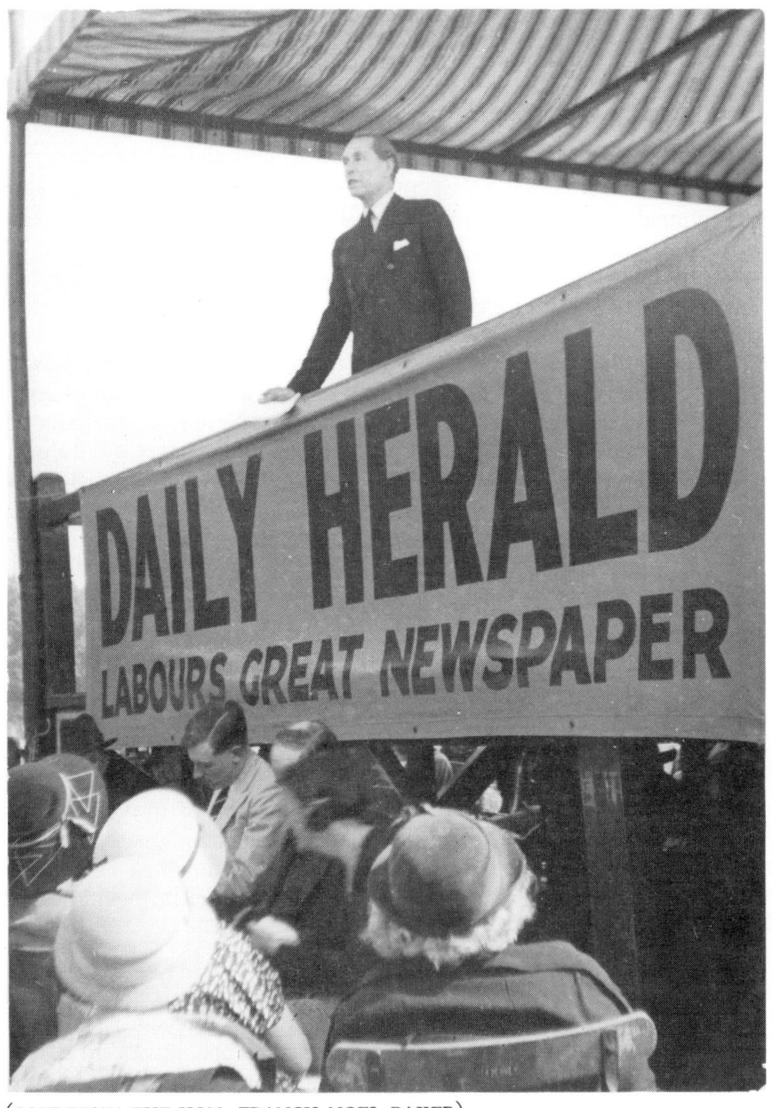

(COURTESY: THE HON. FRANCIS NOEL-BAKER)

Pl. 9. On the Hustings in Coventry, 1929

'It is just his stuff, if he would see it. He could denounce the Protocol to his Liberal heart's content; demand the closing of the gaps which Lord Robert so wickedly left in the Covenant; curse the great armaments which the Tories now keep up; laud pacific settlement by Arbitration, of which Gladstone is the legendary prophet. All his complexes satisfied in one campaign – what more could he want?'

Finally, 'He could surely drown his scruples about Russian frontiers (as I do), in the rivers of blood which will not be spilt in the next war!'[107]

Those in the vanguard of the campaign for peace and increased international understanding recognised the need to dispel illusions. Norman Angell's *The Great Illusion* published, rather tentatively, in 1910 sold a million copies world-wide and profoundly influenced Cecil and Noel-Baker. A number of Angell's principles greatly appealed to the young Quaker and were reiterated constantly by Noel-Baker down the years. First, there must be substituted for the illusory Balance of Power a 'Community of Power', an energising instrument to 'push for peace' by degrees rather than seek to impose it abruptly. Secondly, an 'unnoticed process of disintegration' (so it was put) was eating the heart out of Europe. It was economic in the failure to organise production, to redistribute wealth, and to deal fairly with national indebtedness. It was political in the quarrelsomeness and competition of a 'Balkanised Society'. Thirdly, we had to acknowledge that there existed psychological reasons for conflict, certainly lack of trust but, more generally, fears and anxieties. These latter were manipulated, all too often, by those in power – arms manufacturers, unscrupulous market speculators, and by those who became known as 'the Hawks'.

'Was the Left Turn Right?' mused Angell in his later autobiography. Noel-Baker must have asked himself the same question from time to time. For both men the Labour Party's international doctrine appeared to lessen nationalist pugnacity. Neither was blind, though, to the paradox that (socialist) nationalisation of wealth could harmfully reduce the economic interdependence of nations. Dogmatism of the Left allied with pacifist confusions could be as dangerous as the Blimp and the Bully on the Right flank.

Angell and Noel-Baker tried none too successfully to extend inter-party consultation between London and Paris on as broad a front as possible. Angell's diligence earned him a knighthood on the recommendation of Ramsay MacDonald in 1930. The conferring of a Nobel Prize for Peace five years later brought him fewer letters of congratulation but more pleasure. Noel-Baker wrote to his friend in delighted terms:

'It is, of course, 20 years overdue . . . If peace comes it will be more your doing than that of any man alive. Other people have battered on the walls of hell, but you have undermined the foundations, and the man who does that is the man who breaks them down.'

Leonard Woolf appreciated the influence of the case for dispelling 'illusion' when he commented that 'if you do not agree with it there is nothing left for you to do but lose your temper', an allusion, perhaps, to Angell's report that both Ezra Pound and Hilaire Belloc had invited the propagandist to a duel![108]

It must have appealed to Noel-Baker that Angell's prime media were that of the lecture desk and the press column. Part-publicist, part-educator, the lucidity and the wide-ranging concepts of 'Norman Angellism' were inseparable from the conviction and modesty of their presenter. Noel-Baker believed that Angell under-estimated his own influence on the Labour leaders of the day:

'To judge by his autobiography you would think that Angell failed to influence these powerful and brilliant men in any significant degree . . . But the fact remains that Angell could go uninvited to see MacDonald when MacDonald was Prime Minister; that he could put to MacDonald the argument for pooled international security guarantees as the price for world disarmament.'[109]

There is reason to believe that the dispeller of illusions was behind the thinking of MacDonald and Henderson in regard to the Geneva Protocol of 1924. Without doubt, Angell's liberal internationalism reached across political divides and made him want to move in larger circles than Westminster allowed. Noel-Baker certainly recognised this and said of Angell:

'He was, in fact, an outstandingly successful Member; but after two-and-a-quarter years, he himself decided that his work could be better done elsewhere.'[110]

Working 'elsewhere' entailed both for Noel-Baker and for Angell the risk that their espousal of the case for the League and for abolishing war would be seen as idealism, detached from hard realities, the product of the Enlightenment rather than of the world of Versailles and Wall Street. The risks were accepted and so was frequent misunderstanding and inaccurate misrepresentation. Angell and Noel-Baker clashed frequently with those who professed 'true' or 'pure' pacifism, who abhorred resort to force for any reason, and who could not bring themselves to follow through the imperatives and logical conclusion of empowering an institution to uphold international law. Not only was there a cleavage within the League of Nations Union where 'realists' inveighed against, or, at least disputed with 'utopians', there was in the country at large, or so these two campaigners believed, a need to look carefully without emotion at the case for defence as well as that for peace. One had to accept, if the necessity demanded it, the legitimate employment of a restrained degree of force, this was 'arming' the judge, not the litigant.

Angell's standpoint on defence seems logical enough if it lacks strength in political terms. Should a writer continue to describe himself as a pacifist when he had come to believe that a resistance to the legitimate use of force, in fact, played into the hands of the militarists? Noel-Baker seems to have been more straightforward in his declared convictions and to have had more success in dissipating illusions and misconceptions. The question no longer was, 'Should force be used or not be used?' Now the issue appeared to ask, 'How should force be organised?' And to this Noel-Baker's cogent reply was to assert the superiority of collective action over the old discredited 'Balance of Power'.[111]

Press attitudes towards the League of Nations in leaders and assembly reports were something that Philip Noel-Baker keenly eyed. Generally, the positions of *The Times* and of the *Daily Herald* were approved, while those of the *Manchester Guardian* were regarded as inadequate with a trace there of pro-German and anti-French tendency constituting 'a dangerous guide' and liable to spread 'dismay and disillusion'. In Germany, whatever our Press said, were there not two kinds of people Noel-Baker enquired. Those, 'who want the Conference <the projected Disarmament Conference> to succeed and bring disarmament and those who want the Conference to *happen* in order that if it does not succeed they may be able to rearm'. 'I am afraid', he confided to Robert Fraser, Editor of the *Daily Herald* in November 1930, 'the latter people are now in charge, which explains a good many things . . .'[112]

Despite misgivings in some quarters in the early 1930's Lord Cecil reckoned he was making good progress with proposals for limitation of armaments by means of a skeleton treaty which (he pointed out to Kathleen (later Dame Kathleen) Courtney of the L.N.U.) 'if filled up with adequate figures by the Conference, will produce a genuine reduction and limitation of armaments'. True, there were objections about budgetary limitations from the United States, France, and Japan, there were unhelpful reservations from the British General Staff as to the need of reserve powers for dealing with Indian insurrection, there was the tortuous nature of German resentment, but Cecil assured Noel-Baker, 'we have come marvellously well through the Preparatory Commission'.[113] In fact, Noel-Baker was much less sure that there was not an element of 'humbug' in negotiations that seemed loose in character and fragile without quite specific United States commitment. Especially, taking Cecil's point about enumeration, he saw 'the draft treaty, with figures to be filled in' compelling governments 'to convert rhetoric into real discussion about armaments'.[114]

Rhetoric was manifest in the summer months of 1929 as delegations from 53 nations met at the Tenth Assembly to celebrate a decade of the League of Nations. Rhetoric generally expresses hope on such occasions; it may admit of some frustration to things unrealised and reveal confusions undispelled. The basic necessity for the League was witnessed in speech after speech at Geneva. Future plans took account of a more favourable attitude in Washington, for the United States Senate had ratified the Kellogg Pact. Lying ahead were promising developments for agreement on the reduction of tariff barriers, the codification of international law, and for the calling of a world disarmament conference. Faith and hope remained strong.

A lack of uniformity in the League's successes, however, was admitted by Noel-Baker writing in 1928.[115] The case of the so-called 'Optional Clause' is an interesting one for it reveals Philip Noel-Baker as a tenacious upholder of a principle only grudgingly subscribed to by His Majesty's Government. Signing this Clause would demonstrate a country's preparedness to recognise the jurisdiction of the Permanent Court of International Justice at The Hague. Ramsay MacDonald's new administration in 1924 had seemed to favour ratification of the Clause, then had side stepped to pay more attention to the Protocol which had been tabled at the League's Fifth Assembly that year. At the end of 1924 an incoming Conservative government had time for neither Clause nor Protocol. Yet the Optional Clause and acceptance of the binding force of international jurisdiction had become a live issue and Noel-Baker, stomping the country, made sure it stayed in the public view. Five years of campaigning on platforms for the League of Nations Union, in the press, and in the Commons whipped up popular interest and Labour Party support for 'peace through law'. Ratification by a British Labour Government came at last in February 1930.

Alongside the difficulties and the significance of creating a revolutionary institution such as the League of Nations the realism of J. C. Smuts saw 'any small failures to live up to the great decision, any small lapses on the part of the League as trifling indeed'. In Smuts' belief a more hopeful and longer view of the situation confronting League members would encourage us to substitute for the 'Armed Peace' (a disastrous failure) 'the converse experiment of the "Disarmed Peace", coupled with a universal organisation in support of it'.[116] Challenges might lie ahead but as the century's third decade dawned there was still hope in many quarters that rhetoric might be converted into 'real discussion'.

CHAPTER 3

The Control of Arms: Pre-War Views 1926-36

SALVADOR DE MADARIAGA had put in a nutshell the requirement for securing peace through arms control when he wrote in 1929, 'Like the price of liberty, the price of peace is eternal vigilance, but also eternal activity'.[1] Philip Noel-Baker was vigilant and increasingly active in the cause of peace for well over half a century. Against the background of events in the 1920's and 1930's and amid the changing fortunes of the League of Nations he became recognised as an authoritative exponent of disarmament through international arms control.

In March 1926 a systematic examination of armaments limitation appeared under the title *Disarmament*. In this work Noel Baker proposed to explore an obscure and complex field and in so doing:

'to show the complexity of these problems to those who think them simple and to suggest solutions to those who think them insoluble.'[2]

Since the Preparatory Disarmament Committee of the League of Nations was about to begin its work, and was in session when the second edition appeared the following year, Noel-Baker saw his study serving as a primer (in every sense of that word).

In the decade that followed the drawing up of the League of Nations Covenant, Noel-Baker records, there was general approval of the spirit of Article Eight, namely, that armaments should be reduced 'to the lowest point consistent with national safety, and the enforcement by common action of international obligations'. A resolution of the League's Sixth Assembly in 1925 had set in being a preparatory study whose proposals would eventually be submitted to an international conference on the reduction and limitation of weapons of war. The formulation of British policy for this conference was, after an initial period of delay and some confusion over terms of reference, assigned in November, 1925 to a subcommittee of the Committee of Imperial Defence under the chairmanship of Lord Cecil, then Chancellor of the Duchy of Lancaster. Essentially, it had to be decided which matters should be referred to a Preparatory Committee in Geneva. Cecil can have had few illusions about the task he was undertaking. He and Noel-Baker must already have been aware of a shift in responsibilities which a later writer puts in these words:

'responsibility for the formation of policy was effectively [being] transferred from the elected representatives of the people to the Service Departments; by subordinating the political evaluation of disarmament to the technical, the Government gave the Services a *de facto* veto over any policy to which they took exception . . .'

There must, then, be some truth in the suspicion that Baldwin's Cabinet colleagues, other than Cecil, remained cynical, uncomprehending, and ill-informed.[3]

Joint will, confidence and action could reverse the advance of creeping militarism. Economic burdens could be lifted; the insensate competition of the armourers diminished. Events were to reveal these desirable ideals as a bone not easily dislodged from German throats. Were the strictures of the Versailles Treaty reducing Germany to impotence and inability even to defend its frontiers consistent with the general intentions of the Covenant provisions? The Preamble to the Versailles settlement declared that the imposition of restrictions on ex-enemy countries represented for the Allies:

'the first steps towards that general reduction and limitation of armaments which they seek to bring about as one of the most fruitful preventives of war, and which it will be one of the first duties of the League of Nations to promote.'

Nine years after the Preamble expressed this bland hope, Noel-Baker was able to detect already the first signs of disquiet in Berlin. The Draft Convention of the Preparatory Disarmament Commission set up after Versailles in 1926 seemed an 'unequal treaty'. There was speculation in the later opinion of Noel-Baker as German resentment grew even more bitter.[4] Why were we so unadventurous in understanding and exploring the German desire for equality of status in regard to the possession of armaments? How was fair treatment to be brought about? By a promise from all other states that they would disarm 'down' to the proscriptive limits of Versailles? Or by allowing Germany to rearm 'up' to the level of others? If the second approach were resorted to it veered away from qualitative control towards a measure of permitted rearmament. Did Britain have a better grasp than some other countries of the notion that equality does not necessarily involve rearmament? The point reads rather unconvincingly. A more plausible suggestion is that France, fearful of invasion across the

Rhine, may have wondered how an *entente* could continue to be effective as well as *cordiale*. The optimist in Noel-Baker takes a stand upon the notion that Europe's concern was with equality of status and not with equality of strength. The concept of 'qualitative equality' would, he feels, have appealed to Chancellor Brüning, and Weimar would have 'jumped at' honest proposals for arms reduction binding upon all. The pessimist in him though, sees Hitler's growing Nazi movement steering towards government and taking advantage, feeling 'our irresolution and her power, and her price goes up'.[5]

Stresemann's revisionist impulses about Versailles had to contend with rising nationalist fervour at home, thus, he sought to be placatory in two directions, towards Geneva and towards Berlin. Had the British Government, as Noel-Baker urged, seen the implementation of German 'equality' as a legal obligation rather than as a moral one, and so gone on to grant some visible concessions, they might have found the negotiations more conciliatory and the German Problem easier to contain. Consequent ambivalence in Whitehall did nothing to mollify fears among the French and resentment in Germany.[6]

The 'disarmament bottle thoroughly shaken' produces 'a precipitate of politics' claimed Madariaga.[7] Noel-Baker, in his book, agrees in the main. Nevertheless, the first step, is the establishment of committee and commission, however hamstrung they are likely to be by sectarian differences. Only through the continued and systematic work, technical and political, of an international institution such as the League of Nations does standardisation of method and approach to consensus stand any chance of realisation. Was it, though, quite realistic in the years of the infant League to maintain that through 'the machinery of diplomacy we could never hope to get results'?[8] Few Foreign Ministers of the day were prepared to work through any other medium at Geneva. 'Special difficulties' were said to dominate an international scene so recently demobilised after conflict. Cadres of war veterans would still be regarded as reserves of strength if not as willing recruits. Conscription was considered indispensable by many countries. New weapons were being developed, either in secret or openly. Overarching the whole arena was the structure of scientific and industrial strength which some states possessed more than others. Few of these factors were likely to be dealt with satisfactorily without, one would have thought, an element of compromise and bargaining, the stock-in-trade of the diplomat.

Noel-Baker goes on to deal in *Disarmament* with a universal requirement, the need to offer guarantees of security as a prelude to negotiated reduction. It will not be easy to reach a state of affairs where feelings of security result from the provision, clear and lasting, 'of reasonable safeguards by the joint and common action of the society of states against aggressive attack aimed at any one of them . . .'[9] The difficulties of offering nations even a minimum of assurance might have been stated more candidly by Noel-Baker. The reader is presented with the notion that 'no scheme for the reduction of armaments can ever be really successful unless it is general'. (The point was often reiterated in succeeding years.) Cecil had put the matter in similar terms to the Temporary Mixed Commission, an enquiry body of civilians and officer-experts set up in 1920, and he had seen the proposition accepted by the Third Assembly two years later. As Cecil saw it, in a scheme for a draft Treaty of Mutual Assistance:

'without an effective guarantee of security, there could be no hope of disarmament and [that,] without a reduction and limitation of armaments, a guarantee of security was impracticable.'[10]

Noel-Baker in the same context stresses that here generality has the double meaning of acceptance by all members and, also, that all aspects of military strength must be encompassed. There would be what might be termed 'exclusions by function' where a naval agreement would hardly need the approval of landlocked Switzerland. Conciliation of interests around Baltic or Bosphorus and negotiated lessening of tension there would not involve distant Japan or Ecuador in deliberation. Might general security be brought about through regional understandings and arrangements? Tentatively, the possibility of *continental* agreements to disarm is broached, to include European members or American states: the continental group is the one that holds hope of success. One wonders now how firmly this preference was held by the author. On another occasion, the same year, he had voiced at Chatham House the dangers of regional agreements which might be made up of overlapping or exclusive groupings.[11]

It is interesting to note that in 1926, the year *Disarmament* appeared, there were two broad, diverging approaches to the campaign for arms reduction. Madariaga was to distinguish them a little later as the 'Direct Method', essentially a frontal attack by way of legislating reductions without waiting for enhanced security, and the 'Indirect Method', which saw collective security promoted through guarantees and arbitration as a preliminary to effective arms reduction.[12] It would not be correct to see those who advanced these methods as established in opposing camps: the mutuality of approach was usually admitted. More fundamentally, both persuasions would have recognised the overriding importance of general disarmament. It seems that Noel-Baker was going further than Robert Cecil, when he displayed interest in regional or localised guarantees. The two men strove manfully, but without success, to convince governments that a Treaty of Mutual Guarantee and a Protocol, to energise the Covenant, would be milestones on the road to tangible security.[13] At the same time, and much more plainly than Cecil, Noel-Baker writes as one advocating direct, phased reduction doubtless because he recognises the consequences of inconclusive political factors fragmenting progress. In common with many other League adherents, he prefers inching towards disarmament, in the hope of agreement on security, rather than resorting to a general advance which might be swift but unproductive.[14] For most of his later life Noel-Baker remained consistent in this attitude.

A general scheme for disarmament, Noel-Baker suggests, must include all military arms by quantifying them; further, it is vital to attempt a calculation of relative military strengths. The Versailles Treaty had enumerated thoroughly every detail of manpower and material that the defeated powers would be allowed to maintain. Could not something be done with similar precision for, say, Canada or Hungary, making allowance for a degree of naval or land power that each might legitimately claim?

Quantifying measures of arms reduction must really depend upon defining ratios and units and having them generally accepted. Problems over definition of military strength had certainly bogged down talks in Geneva over which Cecil had presided. Was it not possible to distinguish between those means of warfare which existed only in peacetime and were limitable surely by agreement, and those which should be termed 'ultimate war strength' and which were calculable only after mobilisation? Two cardinal points here were clear to Cecil and to Noel-Baker when, as usual, they compared notes about these issues.[15] First, an attempt to limit peacetime effectives would have to take account of the fact that some countries, like France for instance, might be held to have a 'high war potential' with trained reserves that could be mobilised rapidly, whereas, say, Italy or Belgium were rated as having a 'lower' war potential. Setting a threshold of limitation too high would discriminate unfavourably against states such as the last named. Secondly, there was the interdependence of armaments to consider. Should the different arms of the military establishment, land, sea and air, ever be treated separately in devising a programme of limitation? If they were, though, the maritime nations might regard their fleets as hobbled to a disproportionate extent. Correspondingly, a continental power would grow anxious over losing the advantage of land forces. To get arms limitation off the ground, was there not some way at least, of arranging a programme 'across the board' (to use a modern phrase), with the hope, subsequently, that further discussion might eventually resolve disproportion and disadvantage?

In *Disarmament*, Noel-Baker recalls a bold attempt in 1922 to systematise reduction. It was the work of Lord Esher, a retired civil servant and a long-time member of the Committee of Imperial Defence, celebrated for his reconstruction of the War Office and of the army hierarchy. The size of peacetime standing armies was to be restricted numerically according to a scale and this diminution was to be phased over 10 years. A fixed ratio would be based on a unit of 30,000 men of all ranks. Thus, Belgium, Italy, Portugal would have 'entitlements' of 2, 4 and 1 unit respectively. The forces so measured were peacetime effectives and excluded both reserves and colonial troops. Esher, it was believed, had contrived an innovation by distinguishing between what he termed 'Period A', in which belligerents field only their standing armies, and 'Period B', when reserves and new recruits are deployed after training. A limit on Period A ought to put a brake on the juggernaut of battle; moreover, it should give time for arbitral measures to swing into action. One has to remember that such proposals were tabled in an age when conflict was customarily signalled through diplomatic protocol, the donning of uniform, the flourish of trumpets, and no scrambling of aircraft. Esher's scheme was submitted to a number of League committees which regarded some features with great interest but finally threw out the submission. One reason for rejection may well have been the judgement, gaining ground among strategists, that future conflicts were likely to be foreshortened by military innovations; thus, the 'artificial coefficients' of Period A followed by Period B were not really tenable. Noel-Baker was certainly of this mind. Already in 1926, he, too, foresaw an intensification of latent conflict (today, it might be termed 'cold war') when a Period A might incorporate bouts of sharp, severe hostilities with no very obvious result.

Unacceptable in the main, the proposals of Lord Esher are seen to have provoked lively disputation. Viscount Cecil had joined a group of international officers in a committee scrutiny of the Esher proposals. It was not so much the principles occasioning controversy as the fact that limitation was applied only to men called to the colours. Any future war, Noel-Baker reminds the reader would be:

'the clash of nations in arms, of entire peoples making use of all the resources which the whole of their economic and industrial systems could bring into play.'[16]

(How true this was to be within the space of 13 years!) Necessarily, there should be taken into account the maximum *potential* of each signatory power and, of course, this went far beyond the calculations of Lord Esher. A very significant point, too, already in 1926, and certainly 10 years later, was the development of new weapons and tactical devices.

Counting heads is thought of less consequence than an assessment of the wealth and technical expertise which gives some nations an 'edge' in preparation for war. Computing ratios may be seen as an arbitrary exercise, taking insufficient account of alliance and simmering dispute – Madariaga's 'precipitate of politics'. Computation had led successfully to demilitarisation, Noel-Baker suggests, between five Central American republics in 1923, when geographical cohesiveness and poverty-in-common had encouraged *détente*. Another example was that of the Treaty of Versailles (Part V, Land & Air) which had carefully disassembled the military existence and potential of a vanquished enemy. Compacts such as these demonstrated the possiblities of painstaking enumeration and careful accord.

Noel-Baker's argument for a comprehensive scheme of arms reduction only holds water if one assumes that a Disarmament Conference is able to agree about ratios and then goes on to decide upon a way of implementation. This is a daring assumption to make, admittedly. Equally daring, and really rather contradictory, is his statement that the specificity of the Peace Treaties provides a model for the adoption of similar measures. Punctiliously drawn up they may have been in 1918 but resentment over the generality of their application was to lead to 20 years of heightening hostility. The observance of a number of basic principles, however, is thought in *Disarmament* to give a tentative, international contract to disarm land forces some chance of success. First, numerical 'ceilings' must be sought for standing forces; whether front-line, auxiliary, or reserves. Secondly, there ought to be some attempt to restrict the service-time that conscripts perform if not to remove it entirely. Thirdly, methods of budgetary limitation, to include totals, appropriation, and procurement, should be subjected to experiment. Fourthly, states should consider the prohibition of those weapons which are costly and very destructive such as bombers, tanks, chemical and biological agents.

Budgetary limitation agreed among contracting states had something of an appeal in the 1920s after four years of war had demonstrated the profligacy of military systems. Noel-Baker had participated with his father in discussions of such limitations at Inter-Parliamentary Union meetings before 1914. The first directive would require budgets to be curtailed. There would have to be some standard means of monitoring to take account of varying methods of accounting by national exchequers. The factor of different standards of living, that is, the relative cost, e.g. to Greece or France of an enlisted soldier, must be allowed for. There could even be a device for basing a ratio of expenditure on the status quo of some given year like 1913, before the great surge to arms, and, then, to get all states to agree to spend only a certain fixed proportion, the same for all, of their military and naval budgets related to the selected ratio year. Technical difficulties apart, Noel-Baker fears, the very directness of the commitment might predispose governments to reject such a scheme. (He does not mention the inflationary problem.) We were probably back, he admits, to those root fears about security and 'outside' intervention, and into the technical problems of distinguishing the function and the potential of particular weapons and systems. Suppose, though, the writer asks, a degree of budgetary limitation could be negotiated as an interim measure – it might be as large as 30% – pending the institution of some general disarmament scheme? It would relieve state budgets, do something to reduce tensions, and offer a harbinger of success to the international conference anticipated around 1926.

Naval limitation is seen as easier to effect than control of land arms. The warship has a finite existence of its own and there is no difficulty in reaching comparisons. Noel-Baker regarded the twin successes of Versailles and the Washington Naval Conference of 1921 as pointing the way forward. Precise limitations as to the composition, numbers, and replacement of the *Kriegsflotte* had been enjoined by the Treaty.[17] In two respects the Washington Naval Conference is regarded as remarkable by Noel-Baker. For the first time the world's leading naval powers had resolved, quite voluntarily, to end their rivalries at sea. Then, 'the old League problems of security' examined under the aegis of a power which had refused to join the League of Nations was, in fact, something which led to four-power accord. An Anglo-Japanese alliance (of respectable ancestry) worried United States admirals. A hostile coming together of British and Japanese fleets would menace American coasts. On the other hand, an association at sea between Washington and London would generate alarm in Tokyo. Mutually offsetting these alliances removed fears to some degree, enhanced security, and brought about a Four-Power Treaty using, indeed, 'the machinery of diplomacy'. The outcome of the deliberations was a Washington Convention which laid down quite specifically the limits of strength in 'big ships' which signatories might retain. Additional construction would not be permitted. An attempt was made to scale down the displacement of capital ships and the calibre of their guns. Reserve vessels were not to be kept and a 'naval holiday', lasting 10 years, would restrict replacement of front-line ships. An important principle underscores the agreement of 1921 as Noel-Baker sees it. The status quo of relative strength at sea is recognised and encoded. A simple formula establishes the permitted ratio of tonnage between Britain, the United States, Japan, France, and Italy in the order of 5:5:3:1.75:1.75. There was thought to be an interesting significance for would-be disarmers in such a calculation, namely, that a theoretical arrangement could be so readily acceptable and, furthermore, that it was based upon the facts of existing disparities of strength.

Another conclusion of Noel-Baker bearing upon stabilising the status quo remains as applicable today as it did half a century ago, namely, that the essence of such a measure as the Washington accord is not so much reduction in itself as the prevention of increase in number and armament of, in this case, warships. This was arms control rather than disarmament. There is always the risk (as subsequent negotiations were to show) that the limitations are only temporarily observed. A further point made in *Disarmament* is that reductions in 'strength', however they are negotiated, can not rely solely on general limitation of the total tonnage allowed every naval power: a supplementary restriction on tonnage in the most important classes of fighting ships must be agreed. Otherwise, a nation with a preponderance of major or minor craft might consider itself as having to make a disproportionate 'sacrifice'. Discussions in Washington did not find it easy to deal with this complex factor of differing strength. The distinction between what was an 'offensive' vessel and what was a 'defensive' vessel proved inconclusive as did the proposal in some quarters that the submarine be abolished.

The author of *Disarmament*, finds 'the problem of the ratio' an awkward nut to crack. Given that states, differing so widely, could not be treated equally in regard to distribution of military strength, two crucial questions arise. In Noel-Baker's words, 'On what *principle* can the strength of each state be settled relatively to that of all the rest? And by what *method* can agreement on the subject be achieved?'[18] If, to take the second issue first, the method of disarmament employs an agreed ratio then what factors could be considered for establishing the weighting a country should be given? One set of criteria might relate to fixed points, for instance, size of population, or the *status quo ante bellum* of such years as 1900 or 1913. Alternatively, there might be an objective appraisal of the military potential of each nation – the maximum military strength which it could develop during a prolonged and all-out war. Related criteria might be geographical situation, difficulty of terrain, vulnerability of frontiers, and the significance of borderlands traditionally disputed. All these factors could lead to an allocation where:

'each nation will have a moral right to have under a disarmament scheme a strength proportionate to that which its maximum effort would allow.'[19]

Whether this 'capability' (to use a more modern term) is proffered as evidence to an international organisation by its members or whether assessment is the task of an impartial body of military experts the result is likely to be the same, namely, the propping up of ceilings rather than the lowering of them. Putting the brake on naval construction and deployment is one thing; the limitation of 'military hegemony' is a far-reaching target not seen as easily reached.[20]

In regard to principle Noel-Baker constantly circles back in his thinking to the status quo. Is this not, he asks, the least artificial of all possible principles in that it is based upon actual, concrete, defensive efforts of nations and also that these explicit efforts have already taken into account those other individual circumstances of position, terrain, and frontiers? Even so, negotiations will be protracted. There needs to be determined 'what the status quo in the selected year really was'.[21] There has to be some allowance for change in circumstance; initial ratios may have to be modified. The modern reader, with the benefit of hindsight, will acknowledge the pitfalls obvious so far and will appreciate that at least two of the consequences of this principle have not helped progress. Determining ratios will call for direct inter-governmental dealing, that creaking 'machinery of diplomacy' the disciplines of international communion seek to replace. Some general standards must be agreed, for, we are reminded:

'the ultimate ratio to be established between the various participatory countries must be in one sense a single whole, since it must cover all the countries with whose armament the treaty deals.'[22]

If this was not difficult enough (and abortive negotiations over more than half a century illustrates the hindrances to agreement) the generality must take account of the local significance of one armed country abutting another. We seem to have returned to the theory of utility of regional conference where Balkan or Scandinavian states appraise that local significance. Noel-Baker, as we have seen, had doubts about regional associations which so often led to overlap, or fragmentation, or ossified alliance.

If arguments such as those outlined above seem circular, particularly nowadays, and are not very helpful, at least one new factor presented itself to the author of *Disarmament*. How could we retain the status quo of 1913, as a stabilising measure, when the advent of air power was skewing a delicate balance and was growing in military significance? Noel-Baker, in his book, devotes a long Chapter 12 to aerial disarmament. Like many commentators of the time he cites the speculations of 'experts' as to likely developments in air warfare, and their effect on conventional land and sea operations. Characteristic of those days was a fear that a state possessing large numbers of civilian aircraft might be able to convert them to military use. Uncertainties about armament in the air predisposed the generals and admirals assembled in Washington, for instance, to find reduction 'almost insuperable'. For Noel-Baker in 1926 (and it was a firm stance to last him very many years into the nuclear age) this point of view was 'equivalent to saying that one must wait for a foreseen disaster to occur before a way to avert it can be found'.[23] A new principle, a two-fold one, could be employed. First, ban aerial bombardment altogether since it is 'repugnant to the general conscience of mankind'. Second, recognise that certain functions of air power which are auxiliary to land and naval forces are legitimate (and not abhorrent), and use that position to contrive for each participating state a certain strength of air force proportionate to the army and navy it is allowed. Limitation of air strength would be measured in 'air effectives and air budgetary appropriation'. This is a very complex proposition and one wonders how far it takes account of the criteria relating to a status quo and to the identifiable and calculable resources of a state.[24]

The 1920s recoiled at the prospect of extending hostilities into the skies. Equally fearful was the prospect of large-scale chemical warfare. Was it conceivable that any earnestly drafted convention could diminish or get rid of research and development in surreptitious, small-scale units? Monitoring the multifarious activities of the chemical industry in many countries would be a task of enormous difficulty. It should be possible, Noel-Baker believed, for international action to set up investigatory and control mechanisms under the aegis of the League of Nations to scrutinise particular branches of chemical production. As with the bomber, promotion of the public interest demands a ruthless and radical approach:

'Against the claims of freedom, against all national prejudice and hesitation, the paramount and overriding international interest of all nations should prevail.'

If doubts remain about the effectiveness of measures to control and limit, 'about the end itself there can be none'.[25]

In the decade after the first World War two proposals were frequently made by servicemen and civilians that carried conviction and showed the glimmerings of practicality. Prime place of suggestion went to the abolition of those newer weapons which seemed to encapsulate offence and indiscriminate terror. These were the submarine, the tank, the bomber, and 'super-heavy' artillery. Indirect limitation through restrictions on budgetary appropriation ought to be possible Noel-Baker thought in 1926 and he was to continue to urge this in the face of European rearmament. Sadly, the chance of prohibition (if there ever was one) was lost and militarist lobbies were to prevail. Secondly, there was an interest in the definition and maintenance of demilitarised zones. The recent treaties of Versailles and Laussane had provided for such arrangements between Germany and France and between Greece and Turkey. Frontiers of North

America and Scandinavia had long been recognised as effective. The idea of neutralised territory had some attraction, too, for Noel-Baker since, he was writing after all at a time when an international pact had set up a *cordon sanitaire* along Europe's eastern flank. He was writing before geopolitical forces violated the concept. He does, though, record the dislike of His Majesty's Government for neutrality at sea. The strait, the enclosed Black and Baltic Seas, should always provide absolute right of entry for British merchantmen in unlimited numbers, but then, of course, maritime access had always been held sacrosanct in contrast to the expected impediments to free movement by land. In regard to land-based demilitarisation, at least two reservations are apparent in Noel-Baker's view, the one explicitly stated, the other implied. Removing defences from mountain frontiers or from thickly-populated salients is likely to increase the vulnerability of a community. Again, a demilitarised zone may be no more effective as a frontier than a river. Everyone wants to cross it. Neutralising the Black Sea would not be possible until such time as Russia had decided 'that a policy of disarmament and cooperation with other nations is in her own true interest'. At this point he might have added that certain areas for which Versailles made provision could not be guaranteed as sacrosanct given the conflicting interests of West and East for most of the present century.[26]

Public disarmament for Noel-Baker must certainly involve intervention in the nefarious, private trading of arms and ammunition. Article Eight of the League of Nations Covenant had castigated the 'evil effects' of such enterprise and charged its Temporary Mixed Commission with investigating means of regulation. Noel-Baker himself was devoting many hours and much labour to assembling an indictment of private munitions manufacture. It would clearly be necessary to reduce both private arms production and trafficking. Inspection by independent observers, some system of licensing, publicity and auditing, proscription by convention, could all be applied – in theory – to a private sector which was auxiliary to a public sector which, again in theory, might be regulated by international agreement. In practical terms, it is not easy to see how certain League members would reconcile the nationalisation and scaling-down of the armouries of Essen, Le Creusot, and Tyneside with their legitimate rights to promote industrial growth and sustain certain aspects of independent foreign policy. A possibility explored only tentatively in *Disarmament* is in some way to work from the fact that the heavier weapons require relatively long production cycles so that a reduction in the first stages of development will effectively reduce potential and restrict deployment. This argument is an extension of the purpose of Lord Esher's 'Period A', the stage of readiness of standing forces before mobilisation brings in reserves, a period when the League of Nations could arbitrate or organise joint resistance by way of intervention.[27] Noel-Baker might have done better, in 1926, to separate private production and private trading. Of course, these two enterprises overlap but some sort of self-denying ordinance might have been easier to agree and enforce in the matter of trading rather than that of manufacture. Rather surprisingly, Noel-Baker makes no mention of the political attitudes that motivate both individual and state arms sellers.

Some years before *Disarmament* was written, Norman Angell had stressed that to show good faith you needed to accept risks. A state which is prepared to disarm expects at least a degree of assurance against betrayal by those signatories who may become disloyal. Trust and feelings of confidence will only accrue if there is some system of impartial investigation and restraint; they are not likely to flourish just because 'High Contracting Parties' formally sign a convention, for Madariaga, 'one of the forms that nothingness may take . . .'[28] What the Geneva Protocol termed 'enquiries and investigations' must be grounded in full, free and mutually-accorded information. For Noel-Baker the conducting of enquiries would give Geneva a paramount role. Crucial to the success of this system would be an empowering of the League 'to end an irregular and perhaps a dangerous situation' and to deal with definite violation of a disarmament treaty and a resulting threat to peace.

'First things first,' as a maxim, convinced Noel-Baker in 1926 that disarmament would come only through patient exploration in committee – isolating the factors of military strength, agreeing on their separate control, drafting a model treaty to substantiate regulation, and only then proceeding to reduce to order distributively by means of ratios. Step by step, disarmament could be brought about if there was will, confidence and action: the elements of pacific settlement and open, cooperative dealing between nations. Noel-Baker's reliance upon the driving power of intention and goodwill appeared excessive to one of his book reviewers in 1926. It seemed to this commentator that frontiers in Scandinavia and that between the United States and Canada were the result of 'a generous spirit and determination to settle little in evidence today'.[29] Noel-Baker was doubtless well-aware of this; indeed, in an accompanying review he considers a recent pamphlet by Will Arnold-Foster on arbitration and agrees that more frank international communion would lessen the loopholes for evasion and confrontation. Today's world, in his view, was 'retaining only too many opportunities for influencing judgement by political pressure, for intimidating those who differ, and for suppressing inconvenient issues'.[30]

More reality and a sense of sadness were plain in the Noel-Baker of 1934, eight years after the appearance of *Disarmament*. The insidiousness of the

Nazi emergence in Germany was becoming clear. After two years of tortuous debate in Geneva the World Disarmament Conference, on which such high hopes had been placed, was collapsing in bickering. Where, indeed was the hope and resolve expressed in June 1932 by Edouard Herriot defining the verb 'to disarm' in grammatical terms? This verb, he declared:

'is conjugated only in the future tense. The task of the Conference is to give it a present tense and a first person: to transform "Thou shalt disarm" into "We are disarming".'

However, there now seemed little prospect of 'transforming the incantations into action'.[31]

Britain, in Noel-Baker's eyes, could have given a stronger lead and had lacked the persistence and courage to follow through what the Foreign Secretary, Sir John Simon had told the Conference on 6th February, 1932: 'Let us give defence supremacy over attack'. International initiative, returning to first principles, could surely contrive measures of quantitative and budgetary limitation which would reduce dramatically the capacity of any possible aggressor without weakening legitimate means of defence. Those who opposed disarmament, had not won the day, so Noel-Baker thought; rather, it was 'the disarming politicians who had failed under the pressure of forces stronger than themselves'. They and their Services advisers had not understood that force should no longer be used as a unilateral response. There was now an international organisation which could regulate force and, if necessary, employ it (or redistribute it) to restrain a threat to collective peace. 'We must,' he wrote, 'clear up our thinking; and we must clear up our loyalties.'[32] That way, 'security resting on balance' would supersede 'security resting on preponderance'. At this point, it is worth remarking that in later days, Noel-Baker would draw a distinction between 'balance' and 'parity' bringing to his support the axiom of Lord Grey that parity really meant competition.[33] Public opinion, in any case for this optimist, could be a great force for pressure, if effectively marshalled: the results of the Peace Ballot in Britain would demonstrate that.[34]

It was also in 1934 that a group of prominent writers set themselves the task of enlightening the public about the danger to world peace arising (as one of them put it in terms typical of the time) from 'the rising tide of mendacity subverting decent people'. Their collective response was published that year as *Challenge to Death.* Disrespect for rationality, the 'irritant poison of Versailles', contempt for an international organisation such as the League of Nations, all must mean in the view of Cecil writing the Foreword, that the people must be 'consulted'. Pens for peace were, then, held firmly in the hands of Rebecca West, Mary Agnes Hamilton,

J. B. Priestley, Storm Jameson, George Catlin and his wife Vera Brittain, Philip Noel-Baker, Julian Huxley and Vernon Bartlett.

The contribution of Noel-Baker raised a familiar issue: the seduction of public opinion by the 'Official Mind'. If, after 1918, demonstrations and one's own observations reveal that 'the peoples no longer accept the shibboleths of the past' how is it that so many governments have 'failed' their peoples? Allowances must be made for bureaucratic inertia, for the mystique of the British Fleet in popular perception, for the understandable role of General Staffs, for the alliance of armourers, and for the reservations and escape clauses to which diplomacy habitually resorts. Yet, determination and respect for tradition seemed employed for the wrong ends. Chauvinism and tension have reared out of a morass of economic crisis but was all this sufficient to blunt and deflect the thrust of a positive and public desire for concord? Must this state of affairs continue? Fifty years later, this reads, and reads poignantly, as a conjecture in broad terms. At the heart of the issue there was the German Problem as Noel-Baker had noted in *Disarmament* eight years earlier. Britain, as Europe's 'natural leader', should make up its mind in regard to the twin issues of equal treatment of Germany and of improved collective security via a strengthened Covenant. It was, and is, a matter of balance he declares. Buttressing the League Covenant is for Noel-Baker and several of his fellow-contributors the only way to subvert the 'visceral pull' of nationalism. Only under some system of collective security, 'when national resources are pooled and the strength of all becomes the defence of each', will belligerent motives shrink and arming become unprofitable.[35] Those, who, unlike himself, declared themselves to be 'pacifists', must face up to the need to incorporate force into common protection against a common danger.

In *Challenge to Death* Noel-Baker assembles a case for replacing national air forces by an international body, under the auspices of the League of Nations. It might be called the International Air Police Force, the I.A.P.F. In the eyes of many at the time, and certainly since, such a proposal has seemed rather fantastic. One has to pause and think back to 1934. In Noel-Baker's own words, 'bombing, not as an incidental aid to the operations of other forces but as a direct means of military pressure' was here to stay.[36] No longer would civilian populations be immune. For many, this realisation, and the fact that the destructive potential of aircraft and weapons was increasing fast, meant that the best means of defence would be attack. To rely upon an interceptory defence alone, it had been authoritatively stated, would be 'the first stage of defeat'.[37] 'The bomber will always get through any defence you can visualise today,' the Prime Minister had warned the Commons and M.Ps. knew that Baldwin's government accepted the obligation to expand an offensive potential by way of response. There followed, in Noel-Baker's thought, the conclusion that the world could no longer tolerate members of a civilised community owning individual means of destruction on such a wide scale. Air force squadrons should be disbanded progressively. A Permanent International Disarmament Commission would be authorised to inspect ground facilities and workshops. Some system of international licensing would not in itself, though, ensure demiliterisation of civil aviation – this called for international policing. Members of the League of Nations must decide, as with all nations of peace-keeping forces, whether the I.A.P.F. were to consist of national contingents subordinate to the authority of their own national states or whether, as an alternative, a single, homogeneous corps would owe allegiance to the League alone, a truly international force. It was likely that the second alternative would be adopted, and, a sign of the emphasis of the times, that it would be confined initially to Europe.

Confidence in the concept of such a peace-keeping force would be enhanced if its commander were a national of one of the smaller powers. The High Command would recruit only the finest staff and commission the best possible types of aircraft. Moreover, a design and research department would make sure that the force had the benefit of technical innovation. Careful budgeting would provide 1,000 aircraft for perhaps a fifth of what Europe was then spending on its national air forces. The technical problems of supply, maintenance, and deployment across Europe were surmountable. The difficulty, he thought, 'lies in getting the Governments to decide they want it'.[38] Intervention to deal with aggression was not the only role for the I.A.P.F. It could be a useful agency to develop standardised practices to assist civil aviation (in the days when airport facilities and long-distance routes were still rudimentary). Meteorological and scientific report and research might be promoted. Whether in helping to prevent smuggling, effecting air-sea rescue, acting as agents of liaison and arbitration in times of crisis, an international air force which had the benefits of swiftness and surveillance could be an invaluable medium of collective security.

For Noel-Baker, force in the air must be the prerogative only of a collective and responsible agent like the League of Nations. An institution such as the proposed I.A.P.F. would 'take the mark of Cain from the most thrilling triumph of human genius in our modern age'.[39] The scheme was Utopian in many respects Noel-Baker admitted, yet he believed it had political and non-political support in very many countries. He had been utterly convinced about that after 18 months attendance at the Geneva Disarmament Conference. Fellow-countrymen who shared his view of the possibilities of an international air force were, he claimed, two former

Chiefs of Air Staff, Lord Trenchard ('Father of the R.A.F.') and Sir Frederick Sykes, Colonel J. T. C. Moore-Brabazon (later Lord Brabazon), a valiant aerial pioneer, and the influential columnist, Vernon Bartlett. In reality, there can have been few who subscribed to a campaign for disbanding national air forces. One would not expect much enthusiasm for shackling the legitimate expansion of defence measures against aerial attack or of restraint upon the soaring prospects of civilian air transport. Considerations of protection, prestige, and of commercial gain must have been paramount. Too many countries were flexing their muscles and building up investment to have their entrepreneurism shackled by collective interventionist control. Such understandable reservations, ought to have been obvious to the well-informed observer of the 1930's.

Challenge to Death ends on a note of robust humour from J. B. Priestley. Disdaining cynicism, he believes that during years of bewildering decline, disillusion and tyranny, 'people only see peace as an attractive state of things actually during a war . . .' 'When we have a better peace, we can simply appeal for its unbroken reign . . .'[40] Talking less about peace and more of the evils of war will never be done most effectively if serious and excoriating terms are used. War must be ridiculed as 'colossal idiocy', as farce rather than Heart of Oak. Laughter kills the ideas of the jingo as finally as shrapnel. The message of a 'sour' pacifist, the 'dull dog' is not widely attractive. Sober vehemence may not always triumph. It was a hint that Philip Noel-Baker might have taken.

Altogether, for Noel-Baker, the following year (1935) was somewhat irksome. His wife, Irene, had detected the signs of some sort of impending collapse while they were staying with the Trevelyans near Corbridge, Northumberland. This was no Spring Fever. Irene did her best to get doctors to deal firmly with someone who had been overworking consistently for a great number of years and they agreed to prescribe a complete rest for four months. 'Rest' for such an unwilling invalid included earnest conversation, the mailing of book parcels after a two-mile trudge to a village post office, several hours each day reading, and note-taking for a substantial account of the arms trade. Each week there were up to 100 letters to pen or read, bundles of newspaper clippings to sort and annotate and, always, concern for potential constituents in the Midlands. Philip should finish that book on the arms trade, Irene told Zilliacus in late summer:

'and when he wastes the whole afternoon in distributing prizes at a Coventry carnival I could weep. It won't matter a bit whether he gets into Coventry or not if the League is killed in the meantime . . .'[41]

A period of peaceful convalescence was not easy when Philip's wife fretted about their being 'not at all well off'. Postage, subscriptions, journeys by rail all ate into their income at home while receipts from Irene's Greek estate were often erratic and delayed. Philip's concentration can not have been helped by the constant need to deal with correspondence from an Athens Ministry, reluctant, rather surprisingly, to facilitate a sale of Noel-Baker acres to estate employees.

The year 1935, through taxing for the Noel-Bakers, brought Philip much encouragement when the Government set up a Royal Commission to review the whole enterprise of private arms manufacture. His written evidence to the Commissioners was over long and repetitive he conceded: better to put matters straight-forwardly to them in person. Noel-Baker went on to do this. There was a two-fold force in his argument. Primarily, the main case against private enterprise in munitions was on political rather than on moral grounds and in opposition to:

'the steady pressure of an elaborate organisation and financially powerful vested interest against policies which make for peace and in favour of the increase of armaments, whether there is political justification for such increase or not.'[42]

In the second place, he felt the need to blame governments rather than individual manufacturers. Political considerations underpinned commercial instincts; these were the complex and extensive aspects of disarmament that were so much more difficult to resolve than the technical problems. He went on to warn the Commission that complex issues demanded elaborate and dynamic strategies to deal with them for:

'it is an illusion to think that the "simple" plans are easier to work in questions of armament . . . although it sounds like a paradox, the more drastic solution is always in reality by far the simpler . . . when you try to get a compromise or a half-solution which goes a little of the way, it does not create confidence and, therefore, in fact, it will not work, probably will not even be accepted. It is the drastic solution that is likely to be accepted once you make the decision and which will give the results when you have got it.'[43]

The argument above appears to show one or two inconsistent threads. The protagonist of the League may be impatient with conventional diplomacy, even dismissive of it, yet prudence suggests a need to allow and permit compromise at an international gathering. If the 'drastic' solutions appear more straightforward and less hedged about by reservations than others, their very audacity is unlikely to ensure easy acceptance. More progress may well be made by proceeding in short stages after preliminary agreement has been secured. The point Noel-Baker makes is debatable, of course, and it depends upon an appeal to governments to act promptly and resolutely in regard to the supply and trade of weapons.

It is very much Noel-Baker's belief that the 'drastic' step of banning, say, heavy weaponry or capital ships or chemical warfare failed to succeed because complete abolition seemed a threat to security. Only multilateral disarmament, then, had a chance of winning through: any other way would upset those delicate balances that maintain the individual securities of nations. Indeed, he had told the Commission that he had never been, as he put it, 'a unilateral disarmer. I think government rests on a certain measure of force'.[44] No realist, he thought, could dismiss the legitimate concern of a government with the defence of its territory. No realist taking seriously 'the further future' could see civilisation as other than menaced by hawking in weaponry. The drastic step, moreover, would be both realistic and humane and, 'on a balance of considerations' would abolish private supply and dealing in arms.

Twelve months after he had appeared before the Royal Commission Noel-Baker brought out *The Private Manufacture of Armaments*. Ten years of patiently accumulating facts produced, in 1936, a 'temperately stated' argument (Robert Cecil's phrase) with little that was surprising. The prime focus of attack is evident again, namely, that it is the public sector of government which allows and often encourages entrepreneurial dealing in weaponry. States have reneged on their obligations under Article Eight [Five] of the League of Nations Covenant; they have failed to prevent the proliferation of a noxious enterprise. Against this void, political and moral, the motives and methods of arms dealers are clear enough. They resort to solicitation, bribery, lobbying, engineered rumour; their reliance is upon orchestrated xenophobia and espionage. Careful documentation by Noel-Baker builds a case but to do so through 570 pages is, one might think, to do it in an unwieldy and repetitive fashion. A 'robust agitation' such as the Mulliner panic of 1909, when untrue statements about the extent of German Dreadnought building fuelled a profitable rearmament drive, is detailed in 60 pages. The edge of disputation is dulled in this way though the central message is clear and consistent. It is: first, disarm your government through vigorous and informed attacks on ministerial fatalism and inertia. Second, restrain and control the manufacturers and traders through scrutiny, disinvestment, and inspection. Although a second edition of the book appeared in 1972 the presentation of the case is rooted in the circumstances of the 1930s. It is worth taking a closer look at it in the present chapter.

Part I deals with a network of contributing and conflicting motives and values which underpin a *system* creating and inflating a demand. As always, Noel-Baker's imperative is founded in a revolt of conscience and an intellectual conviction that the objective is 'to substitute fact for feeling; to establish truth where truth too often has been obscure'. Thus, in print (or on the floor of the House of Commons) 'we must seek the answers without bias or pre-judgement of any kind'.[45] It is hardly going to be easy, one might think, to 'prevent', in the words of the League Covenant, the 'evil effects' of the arms trade by disclaiming pre-judgement. Factual concern, though, is to displace emotional or over-theoretical response. The basic question asks: how are we to deal with the difficulty of reconciling the moral values of patriotism and defence with those of gainful enterprise? The feelings in both quarters are understandable; the facts resulting from them, again in the words of the League Covenant, are open to 'grave objections'. In Noel-Baker's view:

'Governments and peoples are still actively engaged in developing the system, although they know it is founded on principles, and that it leads to practical results which are at variance with the ideas of morality and civilisation which all enlightened persons today accept.'[46]

A description of armaments manufacture goes into great detail, in Parts II and III, about the individuals and agencies that promote dealings in weaponry. The 'paradox' of man's peaceful intent being subverted by destructive sectional interests lies deeper and more extensively than the superficial indications of wickedness or hypocrisy reveal. Self-deception and short-sightedness ramify through a Cabinet office, the ministerial sanctum and lobby, the boardrooms of the Press. Brasshats leave the Active List to take up positions in defence establishments. Strident nationalism is bolstered and neighbourliness sapped by the canvassing of 'patriotic' societies. International obligations are evaded by a Hands Off Britain posture and by playing off one 'customer' against another. The 'action of popular opinion in its demand for disarmament and peace', vibrant in so many quarters one and a half decades after an enormous war, was being 'paralysed' by vested interests and unremitting persuasion towards immoral and destructive ends.

In 1936 the blame had to go where it belonged – to the governments whose 'defeatist certitude', even more insidiously than hesitation, helped to prop up the wavering fortunes of those who profited from conflict and uncertainty. It was still possible to restrain and divert destructive energies. Accords reached in Geneva, Locarno, Washington, and London pointed to that. A group of states recognising that private gain in armaments was irreconcilable with public peace, could affirm intentions, initiate proposals, construct a programme, and bring about a progressive abolition of, at least, some sectors of weapons manufacture and exchange.

Very clearly, *The Private Manufacture of Armaments* is a child of its time. There is, however, a poignant significance about the publication date in the 'troubled atmosphere' of June 1936. A further volume was promised for the winter of that year that would go on to deal with 'the true problem of Private

Manufacture', namely, that many people admitted the evils of the present system yet reluctantly believed it to be essential for National Defence. The attention of readers would be directed to considerations, in factual terms, of scale, productivity, and economy, all criteria related to the question of whether private enterprise should be replaced by state production under rigid accounting controls.[47] There was certainly in the earlier volume already the proposition that governments and their electorates could exercise some leverage upon 'irresponsible' dealing. The second volume, in fact, was never to appear.[48]

Was putting an end to private manufacture of weaponry a Lost Cause soon after 1936? There is every reason to think that it was. Noel-Baker, never the man to admit defeat, contrived to attack a nefarious enterprise which was actively encouraged by governments. Worse, the tacit condoning of what the League of Nations had termed 'evil effects' in the days of Baldwin and Chamberlain had given way to reinforcing a heinous business where 'super salesmen' were appointed by governments. Considerations of 'strength', 'balance', 'influence', and 'enhanced stability' were advanced by governments to justify an arms sales drive and injection of capital and war materials into a market lucratively yawning all over the world. Behind the commercial front, research and development continued to expand prodigiously.

Noel-Baker saw the events of the 1930s as vindicating his judgement that only general, staged disarmament could put an end to a system which was part-private and mainly subsidised by governments. Arms control, he reminded his audiences, was not unpatriotic. It was not impractical. Thousands of men and women would not lose their jobs: their energies and productiveness could be transferred to more peaceful and constructive fields. Real defence was based on the informed and willing participation of all who subscribed to a covenant designed to prevent war.[49] Indeed, the price of liberty and peace was eternal vigilance and activity.

CHAPTER 4

A Time of Challenge 1931-1936

'IT IS A THOUSAND PITIES THAT THE LEAGUE is called to such an ordeal in its very infancy.' The voice is that of J. C. Smuts, in 1931, thinking forward to the heavy task of convening international discussion of the processes of disarmament.[1] However much optimism had been engendered by 10 years of steering covenants, securing arbitration, making progress and making mistakes, too, there was no doubt that critical decisions to do with arms control and reduction, the furtherance of collective security, the more equitable treatment of Germany, all confronted an immature organisation with its greatest tasks. Clearly, it might take a generation yet before the League of Nations was 'sure of itself'. More ominously, a decade of hopefulness would be succeeded very likely by a time of challenge, even of conflict. Three notable developments overshadowed the emerging 30s leading to hopes frayed at the edges if not torn by cynicism. A prime challenge to the League itself was the strident quarrel between Imperial Japan and Republican China soon to flare into open warfare. In the second place, a relentless surge of pugnacious nationalism underlay tensions in the Far East and in part of Europe. Thirdly, the world-wide economic calamities of a slump in industrial production and in trade coupled with violent fluctuations in currencies were leading to rancour and hostility. Amid circumstances that were far from promising, the League of Nations decided to arrange a Disarmament Conference for February 1932. Eight years had gone by since the League Assembly had resolved to hold the event.

The first World Disarmament Conference of 1932-34 was surveyed retrospectively by Noel-Baker over 40 years later. His purpose then was to show that international disarmament negotiations had not failed because of inherent technical difficulties but because 'men in positions of authority or influence have wanted them to fail, and have striven successfully to make them do so . . .'[2] If there were substance in this contest of 'hawks versus doves', there was far less clarity about how to create sufficient support and affirmation for arms reduction. A general demand for disarmament among the survivors of the Great War had to face tensions and suspicions, a German claim to equality of treatment, and a preoccupation among many politicians with the concepts of 'parity' and 'strength'. To make arrangements for the Conference, a Preparatory Commission was set up in Geneva and its members, among them Lord Cecil, Philip Noel-Baker (the Foreign Secretary's Parliamentary Private Secretary) and René Massigli, worked hard to reconcile the preferences and instructions showered upon them with what they construed as the realities of the European scene. Generally, as Noel-Baker had pointed out several years previously, their task was, 'to explore obscure problems, demonstrate their complexity, and suggest possible solutions'.[3] By this means 'consideration' hopefully would give place to 'action' provided the Commission members worked (in Hegelian terms, it seems) 'stage by stage, from first principles, from the general to the particular, from the simple to the more detailed'. As Parliamentary Private Secretary to Arthur Henderson, the Foreign Minister, between 1929 and 1931, Noel-Baker was able to talk with Robert Cecil and with Hugh Dalton about the drawing up of a scheme for budgetary limitation of land and naval forces bearing in mind the problems of distinguishing between front-line and reserve *matériel*. Two groups of technical experts advised the diplomats, consisting of serving officers and experts in economics and communications. A draft Disarmament Convention was to elaborate and codify the proposals.

Delegations from 64 countries came together in Paris on 2nd February 1932. Arthur Henderson, now no longer Foreign Secretary, had already been nominated as President (Dr. Benes had been an earlier contender), together with Thomasis Aghnides, former Director of the League's Disarmament Section, as Secretary. Disillusioned by British politics, Henderson certainly was but he felt buoyed up by his hopes for common resolve and progress at Geneva. To aid him he had Philip Noel-Baker (dubbed 'the memorandum king' by Robert Vansittart) and Hugh Dalton.[4]

Moves to enlist public support for the Conference had been organised by the League of Nations Union since 1929. Robert Cecil and Noel-Baker formed a national Disarmament Committee and held a great Albert Hall meeting in July 1931 with MacDonald, still Prime Minister of a Labour Government, Lloyd George and Baldwin as speakers and with a Field Marshal in the Chair. Meanwhile, Henderson sought to recruit European socialists and sent Noel-Baker to a Vienna congress to move a disarmament resolution. Nervous then before speaking as he always was, Noel-Baker felt that 'for me the speech had been like an Olympic final: I had had to give it everything I had'.[5]

At the outset of the Conference Henderson in the Chair allowed an innovation in that representatives of a number of non-governmental organisations were allowed to attend and address the Conference. Their speeches to the assembly, their petitions and manifestoes sounded the idealism and pledged the cooperation of, it was said, 1,000 million subscribers.

For France, André Tardieu introduced a new and elaborate scheme proposing that all the most powerful weapons should be reserved for use only on the orders of the League of Nations or in self-defence; that the League Council should have an international police force; and that general security should be strengthened by mandatory arbitration, identification of aggressors, efficient sanctions, and their extension to cover breaches of the Disarmament Convention as well as of the League Covenant. Yet, there was no mention of the German Problem so traumatic to France and little chance anyhow that such sweeping commitments would be acceptable. Sir John Simon, Britain's spokesman, countered with the suggestion (owing much to Cecil) of 'qualitative disarmament', namely, that heavy weapons for attack rather than for defence be reduced or abolished. Germany, seconded by Italy, pointed out – Heinrich Brüning was the speaker – that qualitative limitation already applied to Germany and thus it could be generalised; meanwhile, his country called for equality of treatment. Litvinov for the U.S.S.R. would have nothing to do with the French plan and pleaded for abolition of heavy arms as a first step towards general and complete disarmament. There were signs that qualitative disarmament was a notion appealing to the majority of members if only French insistence on strict adherence to the Versailles Treaty could be reduced along with modification of British reluctance to take on advance commitments. Specific tasks were allotted advisory committees. Both Brüning and Tardieu, however, were distracted by impending domestic elections. All too frequently, conversations in hotel bedrooms and corridors by-passed assembly debate.

Reconvening in April 1932, the Conference received fresh impetus from the readiness of the United States, Britain, and Italy to proceed with abolishing all tanks and all mobile guns over six inches in calibre. Corresponding decisions in respect of naval and air weapons were anticipated. Tardieu, however, was not ready to approve of reduction without improvement first in security provisions; further, he was not in favour of easing the military constraints on Germany imposed by the Versailles Treaty beyond allowing them under a new Covenant to retain some arms for their own defence.

The transactions of services committees looked like sterile manoeuvring concerned to uphold the military strength of the member countries, with the high-ranking officers who manned the committees finding it difficult to relinquish some offensive capability, and blaming inertia on the political power of General Staffs. Impotence such as this, America's Henry Stimson confided to Chancellor Brüning, was 'like the unfolding of a great Greek tragedy, where we should see the march of events and know what ought to be done . . . powerless to prevent its marching to its grim conclusions'.[6] Simon, the Foreign Secretary, as Noel-Baker has related, found giving a United Kingdom lead that summer 'an appalling job' in consequence of the new National Government under MacDonald being divided over Stanley Baldwin's proposal to scrap all military and naval aircraft and the stout opposition to such a plan from Lord Londonderry, Secretary for Air.

In June 1932 President Hoover tried to cut through the impasse by advancing along the path the Kellogg Pact had blazed, namely, the principle of weakening the power of attack and of strengthening the power of defence. Was it not possible to abolish offensive arms such as tanks, bombers, large mobile guns, and chemical warfare, and to forbid aerial bombardment? Land forces additional to a certain minimum for maintenance of order – and numbers allowed Germany under the Versailles Treaty were a model – would be cut to two-thirds of present strength. Fleet tonnage and numbers would be pared drastically. 'The American proposals', in the view of Frank Walters working in Geneva for the League, 'revived for a space the almost imperceptible pulse of the Disarmament Conference'.[7] Almost predictably though, Herriot put with heartfelt conviction the need of France to be assured first of security from invasion, all the more necessary in view of the ominous advent of Nazi power across the Rhine. British reservations, above all from admirals and air marshals, were uttered more laconically but with emphasis. Simon, in the eyes of Noel-Baker, failed to face down the hawks both in Whitehall and in the Commons. 'Platitudinous and tame' his words sounded at Geneva. Imperial responsibilities, always the guiding light of Hankey and his school, ruled out the acceptance of additional obligations under Article 16 of the Covenant. In addition to this was it ever conceivable, Noel-Baker wondered, that the United Kingdom, in the spirit of Kellogg or Hoover, would submit 'justiciable disputes' to the International Court (by subscribing to the so-called Optional Clause)?[8] Whenever would Britain be prepared to reveal its defence deployments to a multi-national committee? A candid view of more than one observer was that in Ramsay MacDonald's attentiveness to Conference proceedings there was a measure of self-interest, for the Premier knew 'that the consequences of failure at Geneva would not only be grave for the future of international peace: they would be disastrous for his National Government'.[9] Madariaga in vain put the irritated protests of many smaller powers at the indecision of the Great Powers. A cotton wool resolution was received unhappily. 'I vote', concluded Litvinov, 'for disarmament but against the resolution'.

German rearament now became a real threat to the Conference. In one opinion Berlin 'posed as innocents, who had carried out their part of the <Versailles> Treaty in good faith prejudicing their own security by denying themselves those armaments forbidden them at Versailles, only to be cheated of their reward, the disarmament of the other major powers. It was a performance which won them a good deal of sympathy . . .'[10] Baron von Neurath, with a combination of elegant condescension and increasing impatience, insisted that if Germany were to remain a delegate, then equality of treatment was indispensable. More directly, his successor Nadolny, reiterated this demand and walked out of the meeting, indicating, not only his country's resentment at its unfair treatment but also the possibility that the growing chauvinism of Germany might be highly aggressive if Hitler succeeded the fragile Weimar Government. It was December 1932 before the anger of the German representatives was mollified and this was by means of a formula to grant German 'equality of right in a system which would provide security for all nations in return for solemn assurances signed by all that no resort to force should ever be used to settle disputes'.[11]

As the spring of 1932 gave way to summer, Noel-Baker felt strain and loneliness surrounding him in his Genevan apartment. Tensions infiltrated what had been pleasurable social occasions: excuses were proffered rather than ready acceptances. Communications from Irene in Achmetaga sounded forlorn and he hastened to reply:

'Your letter has made me so unhappy. I simply hate to think of your going to Athens all alone when you can't bear it and feel so nervy and miserable about it. I simply hate not being there to help. I couldn't have got there in time, as you didn't telegraph: and I'm afraid I c'ldn't have come. MacDonald, Tardieu, Brüning, Grandi, Stimson are all here: and the Conference has got into the very heart of the problem: and there's nearly been a gt. English-French squabble; and I have had to be active on the inside – and Uncle <Henderson> isn't really well yet, tho' much better; and he c'ldn't possibly get thro' a single day without me. I hate to say it, but it's true: and for me to have left him at this crisis wd. have been to let the whole Disarmament thing down at the crucial moment . . . I have been making a speech for JRM <J. Ramsay MacDonald> and sending it via Drummond – I don't know if he'll do it, but I hope he will . . .'[12]

A week later, following a brief visit from his wife, Philip wrote a warm and reassuring note from a Swiss railway train, intimating that while, of course, he would like to have gone on to England with the wife he loved so dearly, the pressures of work, prevented it. He was glad and relieved that her health was so much better.[13]

The second year of the Disarmament Conference began in January 1933 with delegates worried at the failure of a World Economic Conference held in London to sort out problems of war debts and trade tariffs, and at blazing disputes between Bolivia and Paraguay, and Columbia and Peru. Six weeks of fruitless discussion reflected growing French unease over Italo-German campaigning for treaty revision. Elsewhere, across the Pacific there was tension between militaristic Japan and Roosevelt's United States. A British initiative in the hands of Eden and Cadogan, suave diplomatists both, outlined a draft Convention. This, for the first time, listed in bold detail actual figures of effective forces on land and in the air, and went on to prescribe limitation of mobile artillery by calibre (4-inch), and of tanks by weight (16 tons). Naval limitation was based on a continuance for the next three years of the Treaty of London, so tardily negotiated in April 1930. Germany would be allowed a short-service based army. A Permanent Disarmament Commission would supervise and investigate should breaches of the agreement be detected. (Even the United States was enrolled cleverly in a consultant role.)

It might be thought that if only this draft could have taken the place of the mouse produced three years previously, after five years of debate by the Preparatory Commission, generalisation might have been elbowed out of the way by specific enumeration. Yet, as Noel-Baker wryly points out, the recommendations were left high and dry by a requirement that the Commission submit its report after a period of five years. Stanley Baldwin insisted that MacDonald and Simon should go to Geneva in mid-March 1933 escorting, as it were, the draft papers. As Noel-Baker saw it, MacDonald's visit, 'produced a profound moral effect and everybody believed for a few hours that the Conference was going to succeed'. The initiative, though, faltered because of tardiness and indecision.[14] Wariness among the other delegates was compounded with cynicism when Britain's representatives entrained for Rome to meet Mussolini. (The assignation had been arranged by Robert Vansittart and approved by Hugh Dalton, the last a circumstance that his erstwhile colleague Philip Noel-Baker never forgave.) Four powers, Britain, France, Germany, and Italy, met in Rome to bind themselves to the maintenance of peace, to work for treaty revision within the principles of the League of Nations, to facilitate Gemany's achieving equality of rights, and to act together in all economic and political affairs. 'For what purpose do we meet?' Edouard Daladier, Premier of France, is reputed to have asked. Well might he have enquired, considering the breadth of ideological differences. Within four months of the Four

Power Pact being initialled, Germany had petulantly withdrawn from the League, and the Little Entente, led by Benes and sandwiched between Germany and the U.S.S.R., showed implacable distrust.[15]

The satisfaction with Conference progress felt by Noel-Baker in the autumn of 1932 gave way six months later to sadness yet not resignation. Replacement of the existing quorum by a smaller body was not to be entertained, that and an adjournment seemed 'quite chimerical'. Events outside – he was referring to financial clouds and political defeatism – were 'beating' an international gathering which lacked men of the calibre of Pierre Cot, Anthony Eden, and Salvador de Madariaga. Even at this late stage, could British public opinion, now 'so strongly favourable to disarmament', not back the government and help, too, the French radicals struggling against their militarists? Was private dealing to be preferred to open public debate? Henderson appeared to believe that personal soundings might usefully replace or at least preface discussions in public and Noel-Baker was realistic enough to see that more movement might possibly be gained that way for 'it is no good being patient until the flood of international destruction has swept the whole Conference away'. It is doubtful whether anyone in Geneva was more optimistic than he in June 1933: at any rate, he took care to interleave personal memoranda with the more objective sheaves of report sent regularly to contacts in Whitehall.

The waning confidence of the Conference, led with dignified frustration by an ailing Henderson, once more received an injection of hope from across the Atlantic. Franklin Roosevelt, scouting for a New Deal at home and possibly abroad, appealed on 16th May 1933 to the delegates of 54 countries through his ambasssador-at-large, Norman Davis. If the British plan for reduction of offensive weapons were accepted, America would put her weight behind League recommendations for dealing with a breach of the Kellogg Pact. In this respect, Roosevelt was facing Congress more doggedly than did his predecessor, Herbert Hoover. The very next day, Adolf Hitler endorsed the United Kingdom draft as a basis for a future Disarmament Convention. The message from Berlin, a mixture surely of conscious and unconscious deception, seems to have been successful beyond anything that might have been expected or feared. German assurances may have served as a bromide in some quarters among those who were still hoping, against their own instinctive convictions, that a new Germany might become part of a peaceful Europe. Elsewhere, the French, in alarm, tightened their stipulations for control of German armaments. Now at a plain disadvantage compared with the London plan, Berlin rejected the proposals from Paris and reiterated a preference for what after all had emerged earlier from London. The autumn of 1933 revealed an uncompromising France, a

Germany smarting from humiliation, and 50 ill-informed and helpless other delegates. Eden and Simon did not find it easy to deal with the vacillations of their own government, which, in Liddell Hart's opinion, signalled a green light to the dictators. Henderson still refused to give up the battle, 'pacing the empty lobbies of the disarmament building like a captain pacing the bridge of an all but abandoned ship', threatening to resign unless governments kept their top ministers in Geneva.[16]

Neither rhetoric, nor Washington's influence, nor the intercession of 'neutrals' could mend the obvious disunity among the major powers. Committees were, indeed, set up to examine specific technical matters like arms traffic, air disarmament and security guarantees but they did so fitfully. Chief delegates left disconsolate for Europe's capitals leaving subordinates behind them. Yet, nobody was prepared to vote for a coup de grâce, believing that an international organisation such as the League of Nations must always be ready to try again. In the words of Frank P. Walters, 'This characteristic was a joy to its critics, an embarrassment to its friends, a problem to its servants. But the persistency with which it recurred proved that its roots were deeper than was generally understood'.[17] Henderson, with only a year to live, sadly realised by early June 1934 that the uncoordinated labours of committees, indeed the tabling of reports, however finite their recommendations, could lead to no effective result in default of a Disarmament Convention. Mutual suspicions had wrecked the fragile possibilities of negotiated disarmament, were fuelling now an armaments race, and raised as urgent and inescapable the drawing up of guarantees of security by the League. 'Safety First' had become the all-important consideration: Stanley Baldwin did not mind saying that, though he was less forthright about the consequences of the Conference breakdown, doubtless sharing the view revealed in the Foreign Secretary's report to the Cabinet on 29th October 1934 that 'while it was clear that there was no immediate prospect of securing a Disarmament Convention, the results of saying so publicly might be very serious . . .'[18] A close observer has declared that the Disarmament Conference, 'was never at any moment of its eventful history a League Conference in the true sense of the word. It was not conducted under the sign of international cooperation. It was a political Conference centring round the problem of the balance of power in Europe'.[19] Moreover, after five years' frustration in the League's Disarmament Section, Salvadore de Madariaga had pointed out that a disarmament conference sooner or later was bound to degenerate into an armament conference, for disarmament was a political question rather than a technical one from first to last.

Shorn of the United States, Japan, and now Germany, the League of Nations had looked increasingly insubstantial by the middle of October 1933. Yet, in England it seemed necessary to demonstrate a confident front, at least in public, and Sir John Simon hastened to reassure the House of Commons in a debate on 7th November 1933 that 'At a time like this, when the international system set up since the war is in jeopardy, we declare ourselves, without any qualification, believers in and upholders of the League of Nations as the best available instrument of peace'.[20]

The summer of 1933 had, in fact, also brought Noel-Baker to the point of crisis. Were there not a number of plain reasons why he should now terminate his association with Henderson and back away from the Genevan imbroglio? The position had to be made clear because of the assurance he had given his chief that the last thing he wanted to do was to let him down. In the first place, the restrictions of private secretaryship were felt to be onerous and defeating, particularly now that, with Henderson out of government, the close and useful links with Whitehall were severed. Then, his public work – writing, speaking, committee work in London – had all markedly suffered. Recently, in Geneva, at least five-sixths of his time had been given 'to doing jobs which any intelligent young man of 25 could do well . . .' A married man of 44 had considerations of family and career that could come to the fore legitimately if he were 'free'. Plainly involving a measure of 'sacrifice', the position of private secretary was not to be preferred to that area of greater opportunity and responsibility lying invitingly away from Geneva. Cecil, it will be recalled, had put the matter in similar terms to his associate. Although, in Noel-Baker's mind, this was not to be a letter of resignation, since he hoped for a continuation of association, Henderson's receipt of it and further discussion of it clearly revealed the Conference President in ambivalent mood, compounding what seems to have been uncertainty on the part of Noel-Baker.[21] Doubtless going through Henderson's mind were doubts about whether he himself should persevere with a Conference visibly falling to pieces or tender his resignation in a decisive and, of course, dignified manner. Konni Zilliacus, in notes to Hugh Dalton and to Philip Noel-Baker, urged a double objective if the Conference were aborted. Throw the onus on the governments! Let the disappointed electors realise what is going on! And devise 'some means of extricating Uncle from the noisome job of the disarmament conference'. (There was strong feeling among Labour Party members in England about this, he reported.) Zilliacus' further comments did little to raise the spirits of Noel-Baker:

'I believe the key to Uncle's psychology is that he is dominated by his emotions, which in his mind have combined into one: (a) He is passionately anxious to get disarmament; (b) He is mortally afraid lest if he resign the blame will be put on him, and the stigma of failure attached to him. Perhaps also he fears and dislikes the prospect of the tough, struggle ahead of him when he comes back and gets on the job here . . .'[22]

A turning point in the career of Noel-Baker was clouded by personal consideration. Financial worries were relieved temporarily by an increase in salary but there were the poignant letters from his wife Irene missing him, wrestling with bureaucratic demands from Athens ministries over estate matters, and convalescing from dysentry. Facing 'complete confusion' in Geneva, should Philip not take Hugh Dalton's advice and find some means of escape without offending the Conference President? On the other hand, there was Robert Cecil sadly contemplating his own political career disfigured by resignation which, he admitted candidly, had achieved little and warning Noel-Baker against becoming, 'a resigning man'. The Conference, Cecil thought, surely ought to adjourn and neither Henderson nor his assistant would incur blame over that. Might a compromise be that Noel-Baker would ask for three months' leave, during which time he would think things over, help Irene at Achmetaga, and, when he felt more rested, go on perhaps to an unofficial disarmament conference being arranged in Canada?

Disappointed hopes naturally fed public protest in Britain and elsewhere. In London on Monday 16th October 1933 Arthur Henderson received a deputation headed by Lord Cecil. A resolution from a mass demonstration the previous evening moved the former Foreign Secretary to give his visitors a message:

'the struggle for disarmament must go on and <. . .> the Covenant will not be treated as a scrap of paper . . . To you who represent public opinion I would say – nail your flag to the mast of the League. Make the will to peace stronger and more steadfast than the will to war.'[23]

Towards the end of 1933 Philip Noel-Baker had made up his mind about where the Conference was sagging most alarmingly. 'How can we ever talk about the "democracy of the League" again,' he asked Konni Zilliacus, 'when Uncle simply pushes everybody on one side and talks only to four Great Powers, three of whom he knows to be dishonest?' It was as bad as Austen Chamberlain's 'tea-parties' in the years 1925-29, something Henderson himself had censured. In the full light of day, Conference participants must be required to table the minima acceptable to them. If this revealed British procrastination then Henderson should not hesitate to resign as Conference president.[24] Eighteen months later, Noel-Baker urged the editor Kingsley Martin to see that, 'it was clear that with almost mathematical precision the conference did well when meeting in public, and badly when it adjourned into private, or so-called "conversations" . . .'[25]

The hesitations of Noel-Baker were augmented by declarations he read in letters from his wife in the summer of 1933. Her political judgement, she reminded him, was not considered worthwhile by her husband although others valued it, nonetheless, she felt she had to put it strongly to him:

'But darling I do boil with rage that you should have to work so hard and so unceasingly for such a stupid old creature as Uncle is. And I resent terribly that you can't now be working for yourself – something then really would happen. The futility of Uncle trying to butter idle people in the lobby without knowing what to say, is devastating. But what a beast Ramsay is!'

Warming to the theme she continued, 'And after <sic> July you persist in sticking to Uncle and in deluding yourself that you will get something done – I shall despair of you!' Pushing disarmament 'from the outside', she felt, was the only thing to do. One week later, she was questioning, not her husband's reckoning of the future of the tottering Conference – that was plain – but his motive in delaying departure. Was it fear of annoying Henderson, of harming his own career? 'Then what in Heaven's name keeps you to Uncle?' Philip would help Henderson best by proceeding independently. True, Cecil might not favour such a permanent rupture but further indecision would only appear to be 'diplomatising' Henderson and surely, 'There is enough goodness and straightforwardness in Uncle to deserve straightforwardness on yr part'.[26] Henderson by this time, began to suffer from frequent bouts of sickness. He felt assailed by doubts as to the National Government of Ramsay MacDonald and its standing in the assemblies of the League at Geneva. Despite these uncertainties, Henderson made up his mind to stay even though his close colleague might leave. According to his biographer:

'He [Henderson] was sorry when this summer Philip Noel-Baker asked to be released; he sympathised entirely with the bitter and impatient disappointment Noel-Baker felt, although he did not at all agree with the general views which had, even in 1932, caused him to urge the President to resign as a protest. They travelled back to London together and there parted.'[27]

Exasperated and sad, Noel-Baker was to begin work on his *Private Manufacture of Arms*, to collect and submit evidence to a Royal Commission on the same subject, and to commence preparations for a League of Nations Union project, the Peace Ballot. Geneva, all too obviously, had revealed strategic madness and political betrayal. 'Vibrant hopes inspired by the Hoover Plan became a mocking memory' yet, 'the hawks had only won narrowly'. For him questions of disarmament remained psychological ones, as they did for his former League of Nations colleague John Wheeler-

Bennett who had asked 'Can the nations of the world renounce wars with their minds as well as with their lips and pens, subconsciously as well as consciously? Renunciation must precede the devising of ethical codes and systems to sustain them'.[28] Dismayed Noel-Baker may have been, despairing most certainly he was not for he still believed, as he had put it 10 years earlier, that the Covenant corresponded virtually in every sentence to real needs and pointed to real possibilities and to that extent represented an irreducible minimum for men to implement if they had a will to do so.

In the light of the breakdown of the Disarmament Conference at Geneva and the general disappointment voiced in the British Press and on platforms was there any possibility of a legislative thrust to disarmament proposals? A Peace Bill laid on the table in the Commons perhaps? Konni Zilliacus, busily moving between Switzerland and London in October 1933, broached the scheme to Hugh Dalton. The aim, he wrote, would be 'to prevent any possibility of a situation arising in which citizens feel torn between their duty to peace as believers in the League, and their duty to their Government, in time of grave national emergency'. Reaffirmation in this manner of Britain's adherence to the collective peace system should strengthen that system, reassure the electorate, and encourage ministers.[29] Given such an imaginative idea, Henderson did not dismiss it as unfeasible, rather, he asked an informal group, consisting of Stafford Cripps, Philip Noel-Baker, Will Arnold-Foster and an international lawyer, Hersch Lauterpacht, to explore the technical and legal aspects of the proposed legislation and draft a text for it. At the outset, though, who should organise a public backing: M.Ps. in their Labour constituencies or the League of Nations Union, supposedly an energising group, but in reality piloted by a secretary, Maxwell Garnett, unhappy about charges (or even hints) of political partisanship?

'I am in two minds', Noel-Baker confided to Zilliacus:

'whether I really want the Union <League of Nations Union> to take up the Peace Act; particularly whether I want them to get in first before the Labour Party has produced the Bill. My own view is that it would be far better to bring the Bill in first, and then force the Union to support it. As we have not begun to draft the Bill in the Labour Party Committee, there is no violent hurry!'[30]

The last, faint reverberations of this legislative attempt, and of the aftermath of the collapsed Disarmament Conference, are discernible in a note from Noel-Baker to Arnold-Foster dated 2nd November 1934. 'It is frightfully difficult to get everything in, but do let us both try to see that we get a real result in the early future!' The advice of Leonard Woolf, a seasoned campaigner, was to be sought. Nothing more is to be found in the record: presumably, the project was still-born, for we know nothing of the definitive text of the Bill nor is there any evidence of its progress.

By way of a coda, and a sad one, it is worth remembering that when in 1926 a reinvigorated League Council had set up a Preparatory Commission to stage-manage a Disarmament Conference there was optimism and forward thinking on every hand. Germany had been admitted (not too patronisingly) to Geneva and the comity of nations; the Locarno Treaty, criticised by some but applauded by most, appeared to offer hope of more secure European relationships. Noel-Baker at that time had little doubt that the omens were propitious:

'Great Britain should give the lead. America stands ready, ardent if doubting; Germany, eager for the equality which only our disarmament can bring; France, democratic France, ready to take a risk for reconciliation; Russia, using fair words, fairer than could have been expected; all the smaller powers enthusiastic for results for which they have been waiting long. The influence of the British Empire, in every quarter of international affairs, is almost infinitely great; in this grave matter, if it were wisely, firmly used, who doubts that it would be decisive?'[31]

Fair prospects such as these, exaggerated and arguable in some eyes, did not materialise eight years later.

On 11th June 1934 the Disarmament Conference broke up at Geneva morosely aware that it was unlikely to reconvene. By the end of the month Sir Eric Drummond had left the Secretary-Generalship (although his departure was not a direct result of the shattered assembly). Arthur Henderson's name was being submitted to Oslo for a Nobel Peace Prize. With the shutters in place at Geneva it seemed to Noel-Baker that 'seeing it <disarmament> through' might need a less formal and wider public forum.

The collapse of the Conference in 1934 was, of course, a severe disappointment but it was not the end of the matter. Here, certainly, was an area where the compulsions of nationalism collided with pacifistic intent all too publicly and the League suffered. At Geneva, wrote Zimmern in 1936, there were two organisations: 'The League of theory and the League of fact were simply in separate worlds'.[32] President Wilson's ideal of arms reduced to 'the lowest point consistent with national safety' was being translated as the minimum force needed to maintain autonomy. National self-sufficiency in the view of some had to be allowed, otherwise, as Adolf Hitler told a Party meeting on 7th November 1933, 'The League of Nations will never see us again until the last vestige of discrimination is removed'. These years of what Litvinov had termed 'a time of shifting sands, of verbal promises and declarations' were for Noel-Baker a period of intense and far-ranging activity. As a Member of Parliament and assistant to Arthur Henderson between 1929 and 1931, 'Phil <had> come into his own' as Hugh Dalton recalled during the hard bargaining of the London Naval Conference of

1930-31.[33] There was little disposition on the part of the governments of the United States, Britain, France, and Japan to go below the minima they considered essential to safeguarding survival. Power and rivalry ousted peace and cooperation. In such circumstances, Noel-Baker and Cecil in particular felt they had to move beyond a Covenant codifying rights and obligations, which became so easily the victim of evasion and indecision, to the field of action where a static reliance on code was confronted by a dynamic set of forces. A linkage of disarmament and guarantee would attempt to bridge the 'pacifist' and 'realist' approaches and square up to the undoubted vigour of nationalism and the visible longing for peace in so many quarters. This conjunction of resolution, scheme, and effort appealed to Salvador de Madariaga who had, after all, wrestled with vacillation in the League's Disarmament Section. 'Peace there must be', he asserted, 'by an ever-reiterated act of will and reason.'[34]

Philip Noel-Baker, in common with those who campaign for 'peaceful coexistence', constantly had to come to terms with nationalism (more or less chauvinistic) and with pacifism as motivating forces. In regard to nationalism there is the optimism, revealed in most of his speaking and writing, that 'problems commonly shared' and the instinct for survival will together make for a replacement of selfish autonomy by a search for international accord and decision. Equally, there is every sign of a realism and of the statement of it that Noel-Baker seemed satisfied to find in the writing of C. K. Webster, F. P. Walters, W. E. Rappard and, much later, F. H. Hinsley. (At least the first three of these men had worked beside him.)[35] Noel-Baker and his father, it will be recalled, were aware of the competitive jousting for power that launched the Armageddon of 1914. Philip, posted to the 'neutrality' of Geneva in 1919, sensed there the forcefulness of national points of view as they emerged in response to the inequity of the Versailles Treaty, and in the wake of the collapse of Hapsburg, Romanov and Turkish Empires. Self-assertion stood vigilant, if not armed, around Baltic and Bosphorus, in Warsaw, Prague, Athens and Delhi, while the delegates of those states gathered in the Salle des Nations. In the search for unanimity and resolution of conflict that arose in the Middle East and in the liberated Baltic States there seemed little profit in ignoring ethnic and cultural and political differences. On the other hand, as both Noel-Baker and Madariaga saw it, the idealism of Wilson and Smuts at the League's creation had been spoiled by the 'realists' who whittled down Genevan powers by 'reducing it to a mere club of fully sovereign nations, a league and not a society'.[36] A League which attempted to restrain nationalism would probably prove ineffectual: if these forces were encouraged, though, they would almost certainly sink the League.

There are indications, after the internecine war of 1914-18, of a shift in the concepts of national security away from aggrandisement and material preoccupation towards a more civilised responsibility for positive international relationships, concepts voiced by Cecil, Briand, Stresemann, and Masaryk. Tensions at Geneva over the limits of autonomy appear to have divided the Assembly, as both Madariaga and Noel-Baker have recounted, into a 'power party' of larger states and a 'moral authority' party made up of smaller states – Belgium, Czechoslovakia, Switzerland, the Scandinavians – the last trying to exert independent influence. The exercise of power in this way appeared to both men to have odd effects. An instance of this for Madariaga was the Locarno Treaty which Britain's Austen Chamberlain appeared to have advanced 'as a line of policy deliberately outside the League . . . as a balance of power contrivance instead of a moral-power forum'. Should such a manoeuvre fail, as when the Nazis reoccupied the Rhineland and Mussolini invaded Abyssinia, then the balance-of-power people 'came hurrying back to the Covenant for an injection of moral power'.[37] Cynicism apart, had not Austen Chamberlain, the Foreign Secretary in 1924, epitomised the limits beyond which His Majesty's Government was not prepared to go when he acknowledged the League of Nations as a useful adjunct to his country's foreign policy provided it were, 'firmly restrained from doing too much'? Ten years later, the reservations of Sir John Simon, despite his declarations, seem to have been cast in the same mould.[38]

'Why', Noel-Baker once asked a conference, 'should an idealist not be a realist? Why not a patriot?' He and others would then go on to agree that conversion to the League ideal from the narrower perspectives of raison d'Etat required, in the mix of peace-makers, elements as various as faith and objectivity, candour and rational detachment. Above all there was required of statesmen and of their electorate a systematic and reasoned preparation (some kind of educational programme borne on the shoulders of campaigners), and an attempt to enumerate common, concrete objectives.

After a week of inconclusive League debate the question about nationalism was for Cecil, 'When will the organisation at Geneva become the League of Nations and not the nations of the League?' With Madariaga there was a need to enquire of nationalism, 'who led it?' Neither of these two, nor Noel-Baker, could reconcile the separateness of the Locarno agreement with fulfilment of the aim of universality: they were well aware then and later that 'certain issues' were not raised and settled in the public glare of Geneva. Chamberlain's anticipations about a 'spirit of Locarno' in a Guildhall speech in October 1924 irritated Noel-Baker and Cecil. In any event, the blinkered self-interest of Britain was to force Cecil's resignation in the summer of 1927.

The particularism of French nationhood was not hard to understand whether it took the form of opposition to German reinvigoration or refuge in the illusions of the Maginot Line. Britain's imperial tradition had to be allowed – and so it was by Cecil and Noel-Baker – as a formative and compelling force. Die-hardism must not, though, occlude dispassionate discussion. Even when nations reined in their self-sufficient instincts room for manoeuvre was limited. Pacifying the French with proposals to enhance security and preserve frontiers would not appeal to English parliamentarians preferring to disengage from Europe at not too great a cost. Approaches to the weak German government of Weimar, in response to the straight sincerity of Gustav Stresemann and Chancellor Brüning, would doubtless bring about consternation in Paris. Quite evidently, earnest attempts to placate Ramsay MacDonald, at heart a pacifist yet less objective in his Cabinet Room, earned for Cecil and Noel-Baker cool regard if not hostility when stress was laid on the arbitration formula of the Genevan Protocol or on those broader economic functions the League was expected to serve. An instance was the opposition of Philip Snowden, Chancellor of the Exchequer, to the mollifying proposals of Noel-Baker, delegate to a reparations conference at the Hague in 1929. On hearing about the results of the conference Cecil confided to Noel-Baker, 'Snowden has no warmer supporters than the English Die-hards!'[39] In the halls of Geneva or in European chancelleries, national leaders, it seemed to Madariaga, 'still wore their nationalism like the Crusaders their armour'.[40] A final point about nationalism in the early 30s is one that both Noel-Baker and E. H. Carr were to agree on, namely, that the credentials of nationalism were under attack, as E. H. Carr puts it, 'from the standpoint of idealism and from the standpoint of power'.[41] Totalitarian excesses and the inadequacy of small foci of economic and military sufficiency were leading increasing numbers to question a future characterised by a lack of coherence internationally. In turn, there was growing speculation as to the appropriateness of pacifism as a response to militarists so clearly preoccupied nationalistically.

There were many beside Philip Noel-Baker who saw the unrolling of the 1930's as a succession of timid responses to a number of brushwood fires. Unity, resourcefulness and decision would have stemmed the onrush of the flames if not quenched them. Certainly, in Noel-Baker's view, it was not so much the League of Nations failing the civilised world as the failure of its delegates to employ its machinery loyally and constructively. An experienced member of the League Secretariat later deplored the inability of states to come to terms either with the League as a union of Force and Law (its supra-national moral entity) or with the League as a consortium of national powers (greater and smaller). Either way, principles might be evaded and rules regarded as elastic and variable. All too often, decisions resulted in paralysis and confusion.[42]

One of the earliest instances of international procrastination was the Sino-Japanese crisis of 1931. When a force of Japanese infantry crossed into the Mukden Province of North China on 18th September few can have supposed that the 'Manchurian (or Mukden) Incident' would lock Japan and China in battle for a further 14 years. Some would argue, Noel-Baker among them, that the audacity of a militaristic imperial power and the failure internationally to contain it were to lead to further rapacity and ultimately to the trial-by-strength of European-Asian conflict between 1941 and 1945. It is doubtless significant that at the time of the initial challenge from Tokyo – to China and beyond to opinion internationally – the Western World was preoccupied with the repercussions of economic slump, with uncertainties in the United Kingdom and the United States over recent or impending governmental change, with French anxieties about revanchism across the Rhine, and over the withering of democracy in Italy. Thus, over the Mukden invasion, it is not surprising that contestants' appeals to the League of Nations met with a mixed reception. Moderately enough, China sought League action under Article 11 of the Covenant, which conferred on members the right to 'bring to the attention of the League circumstances threatening peace or good understanding'. Although China had never really accepted Japanese succession in the neighbourhood of Manchuria after Japan's victorious conflict with Czarist Russia in 1904-5 she was prepared to abide by an arbitral decision from Geneva. The Japanese case rested on evident anarchy among war-lords in China's northernmost tract necessitating a defensive response to provocation and attack. Their Empire, so it was asserted, had no territorial designs in Manchuria, merely the safeguarding of legitimate and (it was blandly urged) mutually beneficial trading links. There were those in Europe and North America who recalled the excesses of Chinese nationalism in the time of the last Manchu Dynasty, who recognised the extra-territorial aspirations of a crowded Japan, yet who supposed that careful negotiations would rule out intransigence and lead to settlement and evacuation. In some Western quarters there was an acknowledgement that Japan's imperial and commercial interests felt menaced by the revolutionary nature of China's Kuomintang regime.

On 30th September 1931 the League of Nations called upon both sides to settle their quarrel peaceably and on 24th October approved a Resolution requiring evacuation within three weeks. The optimism of those who framed this statement was to be fatefully cut short. In Washington the lack of a firm political response doubtless owed something to the separation, often enfeebling, of executive and legislature; more certainly, Capitol Hill listened to the assurances and reservations of commercial interests. Threats to peace were naturally deplored in the United States but a policy of 'concerted international protest' was favoured rather than too close an association with League resolutions. Britain's point of view was hardly more clear though her envoy in Tokyo had sent cables home distinguishing, on the one hand, between protectionist strategies which in an island state were understandable and on the other, the aggressive designs of a militarist faction contemplating a coup d'état. Given the explosive propaganda potential of the 'Incident' it was necessary to reckon the balance between a League of Nations response which was firm, united, and consistent (and based on the Covenant) and a collective action, or expression of intended action, which would appear to the Japanese Government to be intolerable interference. Points such as these formed the substance of a memorandum to the Cabinet from Sir John Simon, Foreign Secretary, in November 1931. Noel-Baker pressed home 'the issues in Parliament' and elsewhere at the time, confident that if Britain took a vigorous lead in addressing the Asian situation then smaller nations and even the United States would feel bound to follow. 'At present', he confided to Gilbert Murray 10 weeks after Mukden, 'we are using neither of the two weapons which make up the strength of the League, that is, public discussion and the supply of impartial information.'[43]

Japanese reluctance to accept an enquiry commission was deplored in two letters Noel-Baker wrote to *The Times* in November 1931. Three months later a group including Sir Arthur Salter, A. D. Lindsay (later Lord Lindsay of Birker) and Gilbert Murray (all staunch champions of Geneva) wrote in the same columns urging a special meeting of the League of Nations, pressures from the United Kingdom of an economic kind, and diplomatic initiatives by the United States 'to secure from Japan respect for the collective system and the sanctity of treaties'. Fifty years ago, of course, reporting and commentary about international events lacked the comprehensiveness and immediacy accorded them by the 'media' of today. Eye-witness accounts and photographs did much to corroborate the views of those who condemned the aggression and intolerance of Japan as they were explained away by Japan's delegate at Geneva. Noel-Baker and his colleagues felt sharply the attacks of those who interpreted a call for restraining Japan as a policy fatal to peace. Particularly galling to liberals was the fact that Japan had given the League good support in the previous decade. Now some sections of the press were ridiculing the idea that the

League might usefully intervene; for them there were to be no economic sanctions nor moral condemnation even though, inconsistently it seems, this might appear to condone warlike enterprise.

Early in 1932, after a good deal of prevarication, the League of Nations decided to despatch an investigatory commission to survey the disputed Manchurian territory. The length of the sea voyage, the difficulties of the terrain, and the complexities of survey all led to delay in publication of the commission's recommendations, but when these did appear in September 1932 the Lytton Report (named after the British chairman, the Earl of Lytton) was straight to the point. Military intervention had gone beyond the limits of self-defence. Colonisation of a backward province was an untenable proposition since it would not advance internal order, economic progress or human rights. Moreover, if autonomy were to be encouraged it should take account of the needs of the inhabitants and of the interests of several Powers, namely, China, Japan, and the U.S.S.R. Pronouncements such as these were badly received in Japan. The Imperial Court proclaimed the constitution of a new state, Manchukuo, in February 1932. The Japanese Diet rejected the Lytton Report, branding it as containing 'gross errors both in the ascertainment of facts and in the conclusions deduced'. Enunciating, it seemed, 'inapplicable formulae', the Report sadly demonstrated an irreconcilable divergence between members of the League and an outraged and isolated Japan. Inevitably, Japan, long a stalwart League supporter, would be minded to withdraw from Geneva.

The outcome of the Lytton Report had been awaited in Britain with confidence rather than apprehension. Noel-Baker at first saw resolution of this Asian conflict as 'the vital test for the League and the greatest opportunity it has ever had, especially in view of U.S.A. cooperation'. He went on to suggest, in October 1931, a tactic to Gilbert Murray, 'Lord R. <Reading> is to be there <at the Geneva League Council> so the only problem is to terrify Reading <by?> accepting his advice when he proposes bold courses!' Adopting the thought Murray replied, 'I will write letters about Manchuria to every one I can think of and do my best to frighten Lord Reading . . .'[44] The optimism of the classics professor, at this time every whit as buoyant as that of Noel-Baker, led him some months later to echo the initial confident stance of Sir John Simon who had succeeded Reading at the Foreign Office:

'it does look as if the public opinion of the world, which was so outrageously falsified in the first weeks <of the Manchurian crisis>, eventually got expressed and proved, in conjunction with other things, irresistible.'[45]

Philip Noel-Baker's impatience shows in a letter to Robert Cecil about this time. He blamed squarely the Secretary General of the League of

Nations, Sir Eric Drummond, for the 'quite lamentable' delays in regard to the Lytton Commission. Drummond was almost as Japanese as the Japanese and had pressured the Chinese consistently to give in, ceased speaking in a hostile manner of the Japanese, and had been a spokesman for Simon's later back-away policy. A trifle acidly he remarked that Drummond need not follow an intended resignation from Geneva by rejoining his country's diplomatic service, rather, he should be awarded a 'bonus' by being asked to keep himself ready for future League work.[46] It was the lawyer in Cecil that counselled circumspection and patience. Many years later he recalled that at this time two crucial points occurred to him and presumably were discussed with Noel-Baker. In the first place, the obligation to take action against an aggressor rested on each League member individually, in other words it was an *individual* duty to adopt *common* action. The implications of this must have been clear then and in retrospect to those who were similarly well-informed about international affairs. Secondly, action should be preventive rather than penal and would be obligatory only if there were good prospects of its being successful.

The eventual appearance of the Lytton Report was greeted with some hesitation. There were those who saw its findings as abstract and too conciliatory. The more pacifist among Liberals may have been relieved that Lytton did not advocate armed collective intervention. Conservatives and, indeed, many others feared involvement and the extension of any obligations which might be required by adherence to the League Covenant. Where Sir Austen Chamberlain considered collective impotence to be lack of power in an as yet immature League, Winston Churchill robustly advised against requiring the League of Nations to attempt 'tasks beyond its strength and absolutely outside its scope'. By 'scope' Churchill appears to have had in mind the limitation of League influence to the Continent of Europe, a curious limitation in one who constantly and readily affected a global vision.[47] At about the same time, in the Commons and elsewhere, Leo Amery was attacking 'the amiable generalities' and 'the make-believe machinery' of the Genevan institution.

Within the Foreign Office there was a realisation that Britain should exert as much diplomatic influence as she could, given that the country's defence weaknesses dictated a strategy which must not involve a conflict with Japan. Yet Japanese threats not only to the Chinese northern province but also to the international settlement in Shanghai should be met by something more than bluff and vague aspirations though this would risk heightened irritation in the United States. Only a strong policy would deter Japan, Noel-Baker told Gilbert Murray in 1932: such things as withdrawal of ambassadors, a refusal to approve loans, and an embargo on the sale of armaments. The apparent inclinations of the British Treasury rather than the Foreign Office to seek Anglo-Japanese rapprochement and disentanglement from too close an association with the United States must be resisted: 'let us have', he urged, 'no more of the intolerable device of putting the blame on Washington without ever asking what they will do'.[48] Nevertheless, as he confided to an Oxford friend some months later, 'mere protest, of course, leads nowhere . . . *Constructive* protest, therefore, with special emphasis on the responsibility of H.M.G. . . .' was to be preferred. A positive policy must look carefully at issues and situations in the light of what was required in conformity with League principles. The Manchurian Incident, he felt, was a case where we had to look beyond the 'paper argument' and the evident doubts about who had attacked whom. A very clear decision, and a two-fold one, firstly, requiring the combatants to disengage and, secondly, to submit to further enquiries in the wake of Lytton would do much to clarify international protest.[49]

Half a year after leaving the wreckage of the Disarmament Conference of 1932-34, Noel-Baker still proclaimed a faith in the principles of the League of Nations and an implicit reliance upon a British ability to lead in Europe and in Asia, though he now cast these beliefs in more speculative terms. In the *New Clarion* of January 1934 he wrote:

'But . . . no one who has seen it can understand how the United Kingdom, when it leads the six democracies of the Commonwealth in the support of League principles, that is to say, in support of peace, world law and international justice cannot dominate the international situation and secure the international decisions which it demands.'[50]

A month later in the same publication he seems more sure but rather over-eager in his conclusions:

'I say without a moments hesitation that France, Italy, Germany – Brüning's Germany – as well as 50 smaller powers – would all have followed a bold British lead. I have myself no doubt that with courageous statesmanship, the cooperation of Stimson's America could have been obtained.

'I heard Litvinoff make numerous speeches in which he plainly said that Russia would cooperate in economic action against Japan. A bold British lead would have united the world so that even the militarists of Tokyo would have seen that their adventure was hopeless from the very start. It was always a bluff. By prodigious efforts Sir John Simon succeeded in insuring that it was never called.'[51]

Two years after the Mukden Incident there appeared wide divisions within the Labour Party where the Right and Centre were moving, albeit reluctantly, towards more forceful 'constructive' protest while the Left, uncompromisingly opposed to rearmament, showed uncertainty about the implications of collective security. In the House of Commons on 13th November 1933 Stafford Cripps, something of a nonconformist on the Left, had called for abandonment of the idea of being able to support peace with armed strength and urged therefore the country to adopt the policy of 'collective security short of war'. This was in line with a resolution adopted at the Labour Party Conference in Hastings the previous month, in which the party had been required 'to pledge itself to take no part in war . . .'. On behalf of the Labour Party Executive, Philip Noel-Baker and Hugh Dalton had accepted the motion, though not at all willingly, since the former had regretted that the mood of the party paid scant attention to the Kellogg Pact and Dalton had deplored a lack of firmness as to economic sanctions against Japan. Neither of them would have seen the resolution as having any teeth; neither could have been termed a pacifist in the sense used by George Lansbury and his followers though, of course, they stood unwaveringly for the peaceful resolution of conflict.

Pacifism as an explicit component of the public life of the 30s has been much discussed. A recent account of a rather complex constellation of attitudes distinguishes between *pacifism,* a personal conviction that it is wrong to take part in war in any way and *pacificism,* the search for non-aggressive solutions to disputes, accepting that as a last resort the controlled employment of armed force may be necessary.[52] A similar distinction (and one much easier on the tongue) is that between *pacifism,* the condemnation of all war and a refusal to be involved in it, and *pacific internationalism,* which reserves the right to self-defence provided all arbitral and mutual disarmament measures have been tried.[53] A point common to both distinctions is that after 1930 or so there was evident a broad shift away from perfectionist (if not absolutist) faith towards a more pragmatic, less idealistic readiness to accept, reluctantly, a legitimised use of force. Certainly, elements of confusion, irresolution and rationalisation resulted in a welter of attitudes which were generally disparaged and misunderstood. The term *pacifism* and the label *pacifist* (often a perjorative one) were frequently employed by those who were unaware of the distinction or by those who for some reason sought to be derogatory.

Where did Philip Noel-Baker stand in respect of the distinction just outlined? Both he and his father were heirs to the Individual Resistance standpoint of the Society of Friends yet each, it might be said, were 'collaborative pacifists' and thus '*pacificist*', their witness and their resolve acknowledging pessimism about the effects of war on civilised values, combined with optimism that political progress had made internationalism a realistic possibility for the first time. A readiness to explore the bounds of non-violent action led to participation in the Hague Conference and to fervid parliamentary work for the elder, on the son's part it was to lead to 60 years of striving for action where, in the light of moral imperatives, a resort to forcefulness, even rearmament, could be justified. It is clear that Noel-Baker was asked frequently about his standpoint on peace, where the concept of opposition to violence was thought pre-eminent. There is every indication that the realist had to stress very firmly the political relevance in a violent and prejudiced world of having a covenant and an arbitral organisation and, in addition, appropriate means of enforcement. It is in keeping with such principles that Noel-Baker rounded on the timid, the defeatist, and the isolates 'safe with their consciences' in the troubled years between the wars. Forthright speaking such as this, particularly over rearmament and disarmament, was to lose him a number of followers particularly among the Society of Friends and in the Peace Pledge Union.

Whatever the inclinations of the political Left may have been in regard to the issue of non-violence, a united front was slow to materialise. For some, a principal concern was a vigorous anti-imperialism and in the case of many trade union members, a preoccupation with domestic concerns. Hitler's assumption of power in Germany, and particularly the Nazi harrying of German unionists, loomed larger than the distant Asian threat. A more constructive note, though, from radical Socialists was sounded by Konni Zilliacus writing to Noel-Baker:

'Sino-British relations will become more and more important in the next two or three years for events in the Far East are obviously shaping for a conflict . . . Uncle <i.e. Arthur Henderson> has accepted the view that a lot of useful spade-work can be done in the next year or two to establish good personal relations and mutual understanding, sympathy and trust between the leaders of the Labour movement and important Chinese . . . So do please get busy laying the foundations of a Kuomintang-Labour Entente!'[54]

The importance of creating a forum for the discussion of international relations and the practicability of building collective security referred to earlier, was a constant preoccupation of Noel-Baker and his confederates. There were those who preferred to work within the domain, and the restrictions, of an international network such as the League of Nations Union. Others opted for the pen and the platform. Noel-Baker, by reason of multifarious experience, was able through public meeting, academic seminar, press and journal articles, to rise to the challenge the League increasingly faced.

A man such as Noel-Baker, 'with his vast knowledge and flame-like enthusiasm', as Mary Hamilton put it, was expected to enter the political lists. True, he never showed any reluctance to do this nor any resentment at the grape-shot directed at him. With Viscount Cecil it was different despite the reputation of the lords of Hatfield for political finesse down the centuries. First-rate as a chairman, skilled in dissecting argument and in marshalling a case, Cecil represented his government and led the League of Nations Union within bounds frequently defined by the more orthodox and timorous. Zeal, lucidity, conviction in the make-up of Cecil were to lead to his going beyond limits preferred by the more conventional and to taking up a candid position in the 'never-quite' reaches of political life. He was proficient at establishing priorities. 'I am afraid I do not have to think of what I want', Cecil had assured Noel-Baker at the outset of their partnership in 1918, 'I have to think of what I am going to be able to get'.[55] For Cecil declarations must be simple and realistic. You did not use a text that might be read ambiguously; you never reneged on your principles. In June 1921 J. C. Smuts had invited Cecil and Murray to be two of the three South African delegates to the League Assembly in Geneva. Madariaga many years later applauded their zest and devotion, commenting humorously that these scions of the imperial tradition discovered the world to be full of foreigners.[56] Cecil's undoubted power (he modestly attributed it, rather, to the French), 'of stripping off Anglo-Saxon nebulosity and showing facts as they really are' startled many in Geneva and upset Whitehall.[57] Philip Snowden, once more Chancellor of the Exchequer, complained in June 1929 to the Prime Minister about this Tory Peer congratulating MacDonald's 'Peace Ministry':

'I cannot for the life of me understand why he is allowed to represent our Government. His position in the League of Nations Union – which under his influence is a most harmful organisation – ought of itself to deter him from an official position in the Government. He is on the official staff of the Foreign Office as you know. Philip Baker has been his colleague for years and the two together ought not to have the influence they have. Cecil is just a Tory Jesuit.'[58]

The partnership of Cecil and Noel-Baker within the League of Nations Union reached its zenith in the Peace Ballot, an enterprise they undertook in 1934. Some 39 non-governmental organisations met in coordinating committee in October 1934 in response to threats from 'hawks' who were pressing MacDonald's government to leave Geneva after the shambles of the Disarmament Conference and to devote energy instead to rapid rearming. Over a period of six months Britain's electors were to be asked six questions about the League, disarmament, and the prevention of aggressive war. Large quantities of leaflets were prepared, public meetings arranged, and newspapers 'primed', for the Ballot was seen not merely as an opinion poll but as, 'an intense, sustained effort of public education about the issues which the six questions involved'. In 600 parliamentary constituencies ballot committees were set up and funds collected. Canvassers, numbering more than half a million, voluntarily distributed ballot papers to those aged 18 and over in every home in the land, and prepared at the same time to distribute literature and answer questions. Finally, national results were declared by Lord Cecil in the Albert Hall at a meeting chaired by the Archbishop of Canterbury. Surprise and delight greeted the returns, for there were 11 million replies, nearly thrice what had been expected. Nine out of 10 respondents believed that their country should remain a League member, that economic and non-military sanctions should be employed collectively in the face of aggression, that private arms manufacture should be prohibited, and that there should be an all-round reduction of arms by international agreement. Some 85% favoured the proscription of warplanes. Hesitation showed in replies to the last question, as to preparedness to use, if necessary, military measures against an aggressor. In this instance, 74.2% were in favour.[59]

Robert Cecil, not surprisingly, was attacked, ironically, as a warmonger, by the Beaverbrook-Rothermere press and critics of this kind tried to disparage the intentions and methods of the promoters and the validity of results. Allegations such as these irritated workers for peace but did not discourage them. 'We were ridiculed as cranks . . .' wrote Gilbert Murray some years later, 'as unpractical pacifists when advocating general disarmament, and as warmongers when demanding the fulfilment of the obligations of the League against aggressors.'[60]

For its originators the Ballot demonstrated the strength of popular feeling on critical international issues and members saw it as indicating 'the extent of public knowledge'. An electoral dividend may have been gained in significant by-elections at North Lambeth and Swindon. In September 1935 Cecil was able to assure Eden that a strong backing for the League of Nations would command very obvious support. The administration of Stanley Baldwin, then only three months old, could not in public disregard the thrust of interest in international action-and-agreement. Baldwin, MacDonald, Eden, Hoare, Churchill, at least perceived a need to speak up vigorously for Genevan initiatives, although their country and the dictatorships had embarked on an arms race and feelers were being put out to test the preparedness of Berlin and Rome to negotiate and compromise outside the ambit of the League of Nations. Undeniably, Cecil and Noel-Baker were right to see the Ballot as a successful trial bore. What, of course, they could not foresee at the time and were rather reluctant to admit later is that the communication of public opinion lacked potency. It is clear that the implications of campaigning for peace were not easily understood among the electorate at that time and crucial issues were clouded all too often by epithets flung at those who raised them. Speaking up for the League of Nations was frequently assailed either as 'defeatist' or as 'war-mongering'. Cecil was quick to recognise the *double-entendre* in the assertion that the L.N.U. was keeping the nation out of war. 'I am', he later declared in May

1938, 'unable to agree that you can secure peace by pacifism; I am bound to support rearmament'. For him the Peace Ballot had been a probe, a consultative attempt to ginger up the government. Peace would come of readiness. 'Of all the miserable slogans', he said some years later, 'that the necessities of party politics have ever invented I think that slogan "We have kept you out of war" is probably the worst. It has produced the most unfortunate results.'[61]

In 1934 the foci of international anxieties became located in Europe and in eastern Africa. Some two months before Italian forces set out to occupy the Abyssinian monarchy of Emperor Haile Selassie it was obvious that preparations for annexation were afoot. After a border clash at Walwal in December 1934 General Emilio de Bono was given extensive powers as High Commissioner for East Africa. Elaborate mobilisation arrangements were not disguised, almost as if Italy had reckoned the divided counsels of Geneva to be an asset in its enterprise. 'I am sure', Noel-Baker warned a colleague, 'Mussolini is imitating the Japanese Technique, and that he is meaning to put over a big show in Abyssinia . . .'[62]

It is now more generally apparent than it was at the time that French response to Mussolini's colonial aggression was coloured by the desirability of maintaining the alliance of Italy against likely German expansion in central and southern Europe. At the 1934 Stresa Conference between Italy, France and Great Britain, the latter two had tacitly agreed to accept Italian colonial expansion in East Africa in return for close collaboration with respect to eastern Europe. Had not Pierre Laval emphasised at Geneva the conciliatory rather than the coercive role of the League of Nations? And did not Sir Samuel Hoare five weeks later, urge the House of Commons not to imperil the prime objective of unity, implying that an unwise intervention in eastern Africa might fragment accord? Hoare as Foreign Secretary doubtless had in mind the appeal to Baldwin's electorate of a stand (at least verbal) against unprovoked aggression, nevertheless, the coercive potential of the League had to be used in such a way as not to torpedo the positive hopes of an anti-German front. It was debatable, whichever way the Italian military enterprise developed, whether Britain's own strategic interests in the Horn of Africa would be menaced. Yet, in the summer of 1935, the dilemma of the United Kingdom seems clear. Baldwin had succeeded Ramsay MacDonald as Prime Minister of the National Government and Sir John Simon was replaced at the Foreign Office by Sir Samuel Hoare. Conciliation was tried by offering Mussolini a strip of Somaliland to facilitate Italian access to the sea, demonstrating, as Hoare put it, our understanding of the Italian 'desire for overseas expansion' (short of legitimating war). It was unavailing. On the other hand, a firm British stand was tempered by Cabinet fear of the likelihood that other nations might not fulfil their moral commitments in practice.

In the background in London there were the 11 million votes in the Peace Ballot, the enterprise so carefully directed by Philip Noel-Baker and Lord Cecil. This plainly demonstrated public opinion as being in favour of stopping an aggressor. Perhaps as an admonition it may have impressed Baldwin's colleagues: it did not, however, activate a firm response despite Hoare's assuring the French ambassador on 22nd September 1935 that at Geneva attention had been drawn to 'the recent response of public opinion in this country <showing> how completely the nation supported the Government in the full acceptance of the obligations of League membership, which was the often proclaimed keynote of British foreign policy'.[63]

Support for the Government, indeed also opposition to it, was not evenly spread between political parties. A meeting of parliamentarians in April 1935 had gone on to consider some form of neutralising Abyssinia at least until the contending claims of that country and of Italy could be examined objectively.[64] Elsewhere, in London and in Paris, there was emerging a clear reluctance to anger Mussolini, perhaps even a measure of understanding in regard to defence of interests, and reservations as to the legitimacy of third-party intervention. Noel-Baker sensed the lack of certainty among a number of Labour Party colleagues and communicated it to Lord Cecil:

'I have Abyssinia more and more on my mind. My horror: Dalton (sic) inclined to say that Hitler was so great a danger that we must not quarrel with Mussolini or drive M. into alliance with H. lest worse disasters follow in Europe. I am certain, however, that it will not be the attitude of the Party and, indeed, I think Irene and I persuaded Hugh out of it.'[65]

A lesser degree of deference had been displayed by Konni Zilliacus, active as ever in producing newspaper articles and broadsheets and at whipping-in those he regarded as timorous. As Italian troop deployments were observed in early spring 1935 his feeling was that procrastination made out 'a pretty damning case against the Government over Abyssinia'. 'I hope', he told Noel-Baker, 'you will find ways of giving 'em hell publicly over it!'[66] A six-page commentary, 'Britain, Italy and Abyssinia' accompanied 'Zilly's' urgent letter.

There are two political considerations of great significance in regard to the League's influence on the deteriorating situation in Africa. In the first place, an unreadiness to see the Abyssinian conflict in international terms led to the assumption that it was a quarrel between Italy and an African Kingdom, not between the League and its accredited Italian member.

Myopia to this extent failed to bring the situation before League jurisdiction at an appropriate time, and it distanced the victim from international inspection and negotiation.

The declaration by the United Kingdom that it was prepared to fulfil obligations in the event of hostilities lacked credibility since it seemed to depend upon not only Britain's material ability to discharge responsibility but on the preparedness of League members to recognise a corporate obligation and to give effect to implementing it. Secondly, the voice of Britain in the Salle des Nations, that of Anthony Eden, while it did not lack conviction, seemed somewhat short of authority. Madariaga has attributed the shallowness of British assurances to the bifurcation of responsibilities whereby Sir Samuel Hoare headed the Foreign Office and Anthony Eden was given a subsidiary portfolio as Minister of League Affairs. This, Madariaga observes, 'kept Eden under the authority of a politician who was an outsider and institutionalised the false idea that League foreign affairs were just a special section of general foreign affairs . . .'[67]

Given the limitations of Hoare's position and indeed, the pressure exerted upon him by interests peripheral to Whitehall, the initial efforts of Britain's Foreign Minister were recognised by Noel-Baker as commendable to some degree. Firm British support for the League was announced in Geneva on 11th September 1935 amid expectation that this would entail the application and maintenance of a rigorous system of economic and other sanctions. The Covenant must be upheld in its entirety. Hoare had gone on to refer to the 'vicious circle of insecurity' then gripping men's attention and he did not refrain from lamenting 'too many empty chairs', since the effectiveness of League action must be hampered by the non-membership of the U.S.A., Japan and Germany.[68] Philip Noel-Baker did not join those who readily applauded Hoare more uncritically. 'Tories have no intention of working the League, even if it were possible' he wrote to Walter Layton, Editor of the *News Chronicle,* the following month, 'and Hoare's speech last night <not at Geneva evidently> clearly indicates selling the pass on Abyssinia. If this happens – as happen it will if the Tories are returned – goodbye to the League and all that'.[69] A further point urged was that if a Labour Government was returned at Westminster there would be a firmer line against the dictators in association with a more secure ally in Paris, the Front Populaire. A stronger bond with the Front Populaire would certainly help to support the British position at Geneva. Noel-Baker wrote a long letter to Léon Blum, the Socialist leader, begging him to use all his influence to ensure that the French Government would press London to stand by the Covenant. Diplomatic initiatives of this nature might be the last chance of getting Great Britain on the side of collective security and such an achievement would make France 'one hundred per cent safe'. French bitterness over the Anglo-German Naval Agreement, seen as condoning German rearmament at sea, was acknowledged, but the Agreement 'and the other follies which the present Government have committed are of no real importance in comparison with the opportunity now presented of making the Covenant work in a serious aggression'.[70] Two weeks later he wrote in similar vein to Anthony Eden, wishing him luck in the arduous public sessions at Geneva, alluding to the caveats he had encountered in France and in Belgium, and expressing the thought that one should have some regard to too obvious a hurting of Italian pride. The last point, one not at all widely shared, seems a trifle mysterious.[71]

Already towards the end of June 1935 informed sources in Britain were realising that offers of mediation and the suggestion of territorial concessions in Abyssinia were being received contemptuously in Rome. League of Nations arrangements for a committee of conciliation were meeting heavy weather. Meanwhile, Italian troop transports were bringing reinforcements to Massawa. A resolute approach by London seemed necessary and Philip Noel-Baker put a list of suggestions for this to Cecil. Pierre Laval, French Prime Minister that August, was unreliable and leaning increasingly towards Italy. Laval must be the target: he should be pinned down, straightforwardly reminded of the obligations of France's membership of the League, and not be treated deferentially just because he was an ex-Premier. The new Minister for League Affairs, Anthony Eden, it was intimated, should side-step the Foreign Office conventions of Sir Samuel Hoare and declare roundly for the Covenant. Private consultations had their place, although Noel-Baker had condemned them 10 years previously. In public, and especially with Litvinov in the Chair at special meetings of the League Council, French objections could be displaced and the delegates of that country isolated if Eden did not speak 'in semi-tones'. Britain's new Prime Minister, Stanley Baldwin, with a policy in his pocket, could come to the League of Nations Assembly to put weight behind a call for sanctions. And Downing Street might bear in mind that in the Peace Ballot of 1934, 11 million voters had proclaimed faith in the League of Nations.[72]

Meanwhile, with an eye on the publicity-value of their annual autumn conference, the Labour Party was gathering together its forces. The Party Executive, in mid August, asked Noel-Baker to prepare a resolution for public debate. In the light of Mussolini's peremptory dismissal of Franco-British concessions, the situation had worsened and the Labour tactic must be to promote at all costs the League ideal of settlement by arbitration and to speak out against the weakness of Whitehall's 'drift to war'. Konni

Zilliacus, and from Party headquarters, William Gillies, saw to it that the Party printing presses were active and solicited material for leaflet and pamphlet from Cecil, Noel-Baker, Leonard Woolf and others. Gillies sent unequivocal instructions to Noel Baker. He should go to Paris at the beginning of September to speak more forcefully than the pacifist George Lansbury. He must be aware (the message reads patronisingly) of what was happening in Paris for, according to a recent visitor, Clement Attlee, the French were condoning the Italian aggression. Was this not because public opinion had been misled deliberately? If so, the situation ought to be rectified. No Frenchman would back a naval engagement by allied fleets; they might be led, though, towards some preventive action to bolster collective security if the idea were put carefully. Noel-Baker, however, must stop talking about his scheme to close the Suez Canal with sunken capital ships: the project was scarcely feasible and its consequences might be irreversible.[73]

For five days at Brighton 'we talked of nothing else than Abyssinia and sanctions', Noel-Baker told Frank Walters. Total rupture of diplomatic relations was expected. They had discussed his plan for sealing Suez with concrete-filled blockships. They had pored over maps. Sporadic bombing by Italian aircraft would not loosen such a blockade of oil and freight supplies, only a land sortie which was inconceivable across Egyptian territory. An undertaking such as this, admittedly intimidating to its creator, would put to shame the irresolution of British trade unionists and, in time, overcome the hesitations of Paris. Italian depots would become unusable, East African quays be emptied, and the possibility of conflict at sea reduced to a minimum. There is no evidence that the blockship scheme was ever considered seriously by Chiefs of Staff; they were more interested in the views and policies of politicians in regard to imposing economic sanctions.[74]

At the beginning of October, Italy had invaded Abyssinia. The outlook for an agreed policy on sanctions appeared bleak during the autumn of 1935. Only very slowly did a body set up by the League frame proposals for sanctions. This was the so-called Coordination Committee. Their scheme was thought too restrained and too hesitant by Noel-Baker. Eden, himself, in a broadcast of 12th October 1935, recognised that 'Action must be swift and action must be effective if the League is to achieve that end for which it was set up.'[75] The overwhelming majority gained by Baldwin's National Government on 14th November 1935 seemed a promising augury, for the election had focussed significantly on the parties' championship of the Covenant. Noel-Baker, sensing, perhaps an eventual repudiation of intent, urged Cecil to use the moment and publicise the need to stand absolutely for the Covenant and for the application in practice of its principles as in proposals for effective sanctions.[76]

In December 1935 representatives of Britain and France tried to settle the East African conflict – at Abyssinia's expense. Almost half the Emperor's territory would be ceded against a narrow outlet to the Red Sea. The consequent storm of protest cost both Hoare in England and Laval in France their government seats, more importantly, it torpedoed the moral authority of the League of Nations. The immediate aftermath of the Hoare-Laval settlement, for one observer, was 'a week of doubt and demoralization – a week of misery . . . all over the world came tidings of the disastrous effects of the Paris plan'.[77] Forty-eight hours after the signing of the Pact the indefatigable Zilliacus was despatching long letters to Noel-Baker, to Hugh Dalton, to Robert Cecil, and to the *Manchester Guardian*. What would happen if the League failed? We should be back to flimsy alliances and international anarchy. Now the Labour Party had to make 'crystal clear' its stand on loyalty to the League. Empty rhetoric was not enough. We must call a halt to calling the Government 'naughty boy' otherwise the rank and file 'will fall more and more into the hands of woolly-minded pacifists and Bolshevists!'[78] Yet the fulcrum for effective action was pitifully insubstantial. Noel-Baker and numerous liberal-minded parliamentarians had lost their seats in 1931 and, together with those grouped around less conservative newspapers and public platforms, they were very much outnumbered by the solid core of government loyalty. Flagging spirits revived spasmodically in response to public meetings in London and the provinces. 'Well', declared Zilliacus to Noel-Baker, 'we'll have to go on fighting with our brains, as best we can'.[79] Moreover, the expertise and contacts of his associate would be invaluable in London and in Paris.

Last minute attempts to retrieve something out of the crumbling front at Geneva were made by Noel-Baker in May 1936. His views of the effectiveness of sanctions, of the robustness of Eden's position, of the difficulties for Italy on the Home Front do not really match reality as they are expressed even in correspondence.[80] Pressures applied earlier in Geneva by a cautious band of states were now beginning to separate and lift. There was hope in France perhaps as a coalition of Socialist, Communist, and Radical-Socialist parties thrust Léon Blum forward on a stronger-sanctions platform against the floundering opportunism of Pierre Laval. Three weeks before Blum indeed gained the premiership, Philip Noel-Baker and Clement Attlee tried hard in Paris to resuscitate French optimism as to the effectiveness of extended sanctions following Mussolini's victory. They had scant success.[81] Franco-British distrust was being aggravated by Hitler's reoccupation of the Rhineland and by Mussolini gravitating toward Berlin. The League's functions as an instrument for keeping the peace seemed discredited in many quarters. Neville Chamberlain in London felt the need to make the most of waning credibility. Might it not be wise, the Chancellor of the Exchequer asked a London meeting, 'to explore the possibilities of securing peace by means of regional arrangements which could be approved by the League, but which should be guaranteed only by those nations whose interests vitally connected with those danger zones?'[82] The plea appeared to represent a devaluation of concepts of collective security, to hedge about the desirability of more universalist approaches to war and peace, and to reintroduce the chimera and dangers of 'vital interests'. After all, his critics answered, why did sanctions fail over Italy? Was it not because of the regionalisation of vital interests and, in consequence, a lack of wider, positive agreement? Maxim Litvinov was to go on to criticise publicly the reluctance of League members to apply the provisions of Article 16 of the Covenant. Fifty-two nations, led by three of the most powerful, had been unable to protect the weakest in their midst from destruction. They had turned their backs and isolated the wan figure of Emperor Haile Selassie who stood at the Geneva rostrum on 30th June 1936 putting with dignity and desperation to the Assembly that international morality was at stake and asking, 'What reply shall I have to take back to my people?'

Inevitably the Labour Party's recriminations over the shame of Abyssinia took a political turn in sharpening their differences. Customarily spearheading the critics, Zilliacus sent copies of his observations to Noel-Baker, Attlee, Dalton, and Herbert Morrison. War in the life-time of the National Government appeared well-nigh inevitable. The Government, he declared, had finished with the League 'except as a hypocritical camouflage for a new Balance of Power maintained by alliances and an arms race'. Getting the Government out and 'ourselves in while there is still time to save peace' would be a form of war-resistance in the fullest sense of the term.[83] Another proposal from Zilliacus, which he put about energetically, was that Attlee and Noel-Baker deliver to Blum – 'in an impossible position, poor devil' – a straight, private message saying that the Labour Party would reject any treaty signed with Fascist Italy as null and void and inconsistent with the League Covenant. Indeed, so long as Italy was represented at Geneva, the League was 'nothing but a cynical humbug'.[84] Philip Noel-Baker was certainly one of those who continued to lament the fashion in which Britain and France pursued the 'will-o'-the-wisp' of permitted Italian membership of the League. Over the next three years there were frequent questions from the Member for Derby, as he had become in 1936, about the treatment of Haile Selassie, about the reported use of mustard gas and other atrocities by Italian troops, as to the possibility of aiding Abyssinia's stricken economy through loans, the rehabilitation of refugees admitted into England, and the potential threats to Egypt, the Sudan, and Libya of Italian colonialist expansion. Optimism that some life might be restored to the writhing corpse of the East African Kingdom remained apparent in Noel-Baker's letters to *The Times* on 6th and 24th September 1937, a position which appears ill-judged, for there was little to substantiate the proposition that 'Abyssinia is not yet conquered' or that Italian pacification remained threatened by stubborn resistance.

The conflict in East Africa threw into graphic relief the anxieties of those who voted Labour and Liberal as to how far their country should support international obligations with committed physical force. Was it legitimate to join the collective action of other League members in this way? Would the effecting of such action necessitate rearmament? In general terms the Labour Party's basic stand on rearmament is plain. They recorded their opposition because they considered the government was not following a policy of collective, pooled security. Admittedly, it would be premature if not unrealistic to found Britain's armed strength upon what could be contributed to a collective security system not yet in operation. A vote in favour of the Cabinet's Defence Estimates, though, could be used as a lever to force Britain to turn to collective rather than independent defence. The General Election of autumn 1935, just after Italy attacked Abyssinia, had revealed Labour reservations about rearming to uphold the principle of shared security. Half a year later, Noel-Baker attempted to reconcile the understandable conflicts and dilemmas in a constructive way:

'I have met no independent observer who has followed the recent meetings at Geneva who is not convinced that a strong Anglo-French proposal to maintain and strengthen sanctions would have rallied the entire League *More Firmly than Ever Before* . . . There is only one path to peace. It lies in the Labour Party's plan of international disarmament on equal terms, controlled by international inspection and guaranteed full Collective Security and above all, by a Preventative Boycott against any State which breaks its undertakings and prepares for war.'[85]

Commentators more recently have seen the Labour Party of the 1930's as splitting with growing width over the issue of lending firm physical resolve to upholding the principles of the League. Pimlott (1977) has described the 'insensitivity' of those on the Right who were equivocal in regard to preparedness to defend international agreements and who failed, as he puts it, to channel the frustrations of a depressed electorate and to give them any sense of wider purpose. Correspondingly, on the Left there was support for pacifist aims and non-interventionist policies which led to its advocates, Stafford Cripps, Aneurin Bevan, D. N. Pritt, being termed disruptive and disloyal. A closure of ranks in the Labour Party in response to evident dissension and its unfortunate political image resulted in a *mélange* of those who professed extreme pacifism and those (remembering the distinction) who were more down-to-earth. By the mid-1930's the party echelons were roughly quartered into (a) a liberal-internationalist leadership believing in the League (Attlee, Dalton, Henderson, Noel-Baker), (b) the 'straight-realism' of the union hierarchy (Bevin, Citrine), (c) worker/intellectual-internationalists opposing arms whether for the League or for capitalist governments (Stafford Cripps, Bevan), (d) unswerving pacifists (such as George Lansbury).[86] At Annual Conference the platform thundered to the impassioned rallying of the first three sections identified above. Sanctions must be imposed. Right had to be reinforced. Justice had to be seen to be done. Force to be effective must be 'pooled'. Noel-Baker, Dalton, Bevin, as members of the Labour Party National Executive had an uphill task in 1937 persuading the Bournemouth Conference, 'to resist any intimidation <by means of strongly equipped defence> by the Fascist Powers designed to frustrate the fulfilment of our obligations'.[87] Indeed, in the previous year, Conference 'dissenters' were not only opposing the rearmament intentions of the National Government but were rejecting any element of bipartisanship on the part of their Executive.[88]

Placed on the periphery, isolated and vulnerable, were the followers of George Lansbury, 'the unrepentant, whole-hearted pacifist' as the *Manchester Guardian* had once called him. Their blend of emotionalism and political acumen sustained socialist loyalty but began to fragment when, confronted by the proclaimed need 'to face up to the Dictators', Bevin felt he had to out-manoeuvre the 'peace people' in 1935 and proceeded to savage Lansbury, the Party's grey eminence, at the Brighton Conference that year. Noel-Baker among others, while regretting the public drubbing of the leader, nonetheless was satisfied that Brighton marked the height of Labour devotion to League ideals as well as to the need to confront fascism. Within a year, though, Leonard Woolf was to detect obvious 'fatuousness cutting the heart out of the League'. Yet, the League could be 'resurrected' through government initiatives.[89]

Where Noel-Baker and others were now able cautiously to allow for collective security relying on an association of national rearmament and judicious alliances, the bulk of the Party appear to have felt that this increased the risk of war. On the one hand, there were those who saw any rearming of Europe as playing into the hands of private arms manufacturers whether they were the Underdowns of Shaw's *Major Barbara* (who had some humanity) or the fantasies of cartoonists. Noel-Baker's *The Private*

Manufacture of Armaments was a detailed 'catalogue of guilt' much thumbed by those on the Left of the Party. Its central theme, was that profit motives eclipsed moral and moderate considerations in the minds of governments and industrial 'lobbies'.[90]

Undoubtedly effective on the platform and in print, Noel-Baker could not always rely upon the unquestioning support of the Labour Party's National Executive Committee, let alone the majority of the movement, during the agitated years of the early 30s. His personality was rather tightly etched. Not for him was the back slapping camaraderie of union members nor the calculated thrusts and recoil of political gamesmanship. At an early stage in his career, for instance, Beatrice Webb had picked him out as 'an accomplished intellectual' and a representative of the old 19th century governing class. He was, she felt, 'singularly free of the assumed evils of political life'. Charm he had, too. There was the occasion in February 1930 when she had had to dinner M. Maisky (the Soviet Ambassador), Mme. Maisky, George Bernard Shaw, and Philip Noel-Baker. Neither of the Maiskys was fluent in English, 'but owing to G.B.S.'s wit and Noel-Baker's French, we had a successful evening'.[91]

The ranks of miners, railwaymen and steel workers understandably were not instantly converted to broader perspectives by an ex-professor. Fifty years later it is still not clear how much muscle they were prepared to put behind campaigning for peace based on arbitration and deterrence. Ramsay MacDonald, speaking on the Draft Treaty of Mutual Assistance at the League of Nations Assembly in September 1924, had presented the instincts of his country (and particularly of his party) in guarded terms: 'Our interests for peace are far greater than our interests in creating a machinery of defence. A machinery of defence is easy to create, but beware lest in creating it you destroy the chances of peace . . .' Yet the intellectuals Dalton and Noel-Baker were calling then and over the ensuing years for Britain to make specific commitments as to the character and extent of military aid to be forthcoming to buttress Protocol and Treaty. Pointedly in relation to all this Noel-Baker had called for 'a system of security of joint defensive action by the signatory states in support of anyone among them which may be aggressively attached'. Would a firm commitment on the part of the United Kingdom and an endorsement by the country's Labour Party have demonstrated understanding and resolve? The likelihood of this is not easy to judge since the Labour Government fell before it might have ratified the Protocol and the succeeding Conservative administration did not ratify. Possibly Noel-Baker's rationale for upholding the Protocol in terms of collective strength, as he developed it in his 1925 book, was outlined with the Labour Party 'faint-hearts' in mind. There must have been in the author's reckoning the consideration that a Covenant which sought to abolish 'the right of private war' was hardly likely, as some might put it, to go on to substitute the licence of corporate war-making.[92]

In some quarters, campaigners for collective security were seen with misgiving as being too ready to fraternise across political boundaries. In February 1934 Hugh Dalton, Ernest Bevin, Philip Noel-Baker, and George Lansbury had published a manifesto under the sponsorship of a widely-representative group, the Liberty and Democratic Leadership Group. When Liberals and some Conservatives began to converge with interest on this group the Labour leadership advocated cooled ardour yet Philip Noel-Baker retained his interest in cross-bencher activity and became associated, 12 months later, with Harold Macmillan's Next Five Year Group, composed of leading people 'of all parties or of none'.[93] A more vigorous pursuit of the 'collective peace system' was to be looked for through firm support of the League of Nations. In Britain a 'mixed economy' would incorporate increased public control of transport, electricity supply, and arms manufacture. More than 150 prominent men and women signed a manifesto aimed particularly at upholding the League of Nations. Noel-Baker and Dalton, though much in favour of many Group proposals, appear to have felt the constraining relevance of their Labour Party membership, and were able to sign a first manifesto in February 1934 but not a further one in May. 'The old arguments between individualism and socialism seemed to us irrelevant', wrote Macmillan of the time of totalitarian challenge yet within two years the effectiveness of this broad grouping had petered out. Hugh Dalton began to doubt whether such a group could readily become active as a Popular Front. They were, he wrote, 'like officers without rank and file, better known to each other than to the general public, moving in select and narrow circles, carrying almost no political weight'.[94] It is possible that Philip Noel-Baker would not have denied this assertion. Apart from this stricture of Dalton there is no doubt that as the European scene became more sombre, Dalton perceived a chance to attempt at least detachment of Tory 'rebels' from loyalty to Neville Chamberlain. Mainly in secret (a favourite style of his), as his biographer, Pimlott, relates, he explored the chances of combining forces against the government that had brought about the infamous Munich agreement.[95] The enterprise was not to prosper.

Noel-Baker's interest in cross-bencher activity was more theoretical than that of Dalton, less calculating in the sense that he did not share Hugh Dalton's fear, post-1931, of the risk of losing his place possibly for ever in the ever-moving Parliamentary queue for preferment. The Quaker had a more instinctive grasp of pacifist concepts; his historical awareness was better informed than that of his fellow Kingsman. He seems to have felt no qualms in responding to Robert Cecil's report of a letter dated 9th April 1936 from Winston Churchill who had spoken for 'Arms and the Covenant' in declaring, 'I believe we still have a year to combine and marshal superior forces in defence of the League and its Covenant'.[96]

The summer of 1936 saw a mustering of those, there were 100 of them, who supported a proposal for a 'Focus for the Defence of Freedom and Peace'. This was to be a small assembly of like-minded individuals, in the eyes of its founder, Eugen Spier, a German Jewish emigré, 'swimming against the tide – not only of government policy but of the prevailing public attitude and mood'. Members included Winston Churchill, Lady Violet Bonham-Carter, Wickham Steed, Sir Archibald Sinclair, Norman Angell, Gilbert Murray, Walter Citrine, Duncan Sandys, Philip Guedalla, Philip Noel-Baker, Sir Robert Mond, Sir Walter Layton, Sir Robert Waley-Cohen, Oliver Locker-Lampson, Kingsley Martin, Wilson Harris, the Duchess of Atholl, Vyvyan Adams. Here was a broad spectrum of parliamentarians, trade unionists, industrial managers, academics, journalists. A close-drawn constitution was thought unnecessary but frequent informed meetings there had to be, whether around a Savoy Hotel luncheon table (press excluded) or in members' apartments. Large public gatherings at the Albert Hall and in the provinces were envisaged. Churchill was regarded as the fountainhead of the Focus, desiring, in his own words, to make, 'an all-party effort, create a source from which unbiased and objective information will constantly flow to the government and to the whole country . . .'[97] Through contacts with Eden and Sir Robert Vansittart at the Foreign Office, through Sir Austen Chamberlain and numerous M.P.s, by working closely with Sir Walter Citrine of the T.U.C., and with Steed and Kingsley Martin in Fleet Street, the Focus would urge and direct the government to stand up for the authority of the League of Nations. A Focus Manifesto of March 1936, signed by all, deplored the infamy of Hitler's reoccupation of the Rhineland and proclaimed a need to arouse public opinion before it was too late.

Focus members saw themselves at a fulcrum of opportunity. On the one hand they were able to sound out Whitehall over luncheon (once Anthony Eden and Austen Chamberlain were assured of confidentiality). Indirectly, through their parliamentary connections, some of these soundings might be amplified, again discreetly, in discussions behind the Speaker's Chair. Further, the experienced journalist and the industrialist could contribute flair and authority to broadsheets and public platforms. Above all, it was crucial to keep up the momentum, as Winston Churchill put it to Robert Cecil on 21st October 1936:

‘I wonder if Noel-Baker gave you any account of the private luncheon which some of us, who are deeply alarmed, considered what steps could be taken to mobilise the moral as well as the material forces available at the present time in Europe, to resist the potential Aggressor . . . When you have talked with Noel-Baker and received his report, perhaps you will write to me again . . . There is no question of the eclipse of the New Commonwealth Society nor the League of Nations Union, but only for a fusion of practical working effort and for united advance . . .’[98]

Noel-Baker appears to have been the sole ‘front-runner’ in the Labour Party to have identified his association with the Focus. Though evincing understanding and sympathy the others – Dalton, Attlee, Morrison, Alexander – kept their distance in public. Noel-Baker readily signed the Focus Manifesto in November 1936, regarding it as an instrument for welding people together and for galvanising effort. Some indication of Noel-Baker’s infectious animation about this time may be drawn from a comment of Virginia Woolf. Robert Cecil, over tea, had related how a wide band of associates was responding to Churchill’s alarmed appeal and to the sense that Britain (and, unhappily, Eden himself) were failing the League. Noel-Baker was wearing himself out she thought:

‘Phil Baker should do half what he does, & should drink wine. Everyone loves him – the boys at the Treasury will do anything for him. But he dictates letters as he drives.’[99]

Throughout 1936 and 1937 Churchill canvassed support for the Focus in many quarters. Men of all opinions must sign up to support the League Covenant, ‘that is our root’. They must have ‘some Tories to show up the others. We can certainly now get – after the decisions taken by the Labour Party – large numbers of their leading men’. This proves to have been rather an optimistic assumption. It is possible that Attlee, following an approach from Lord Cecil, had agreed that members of the Labour Party who wished to associate themselves with a Focus working group on the Covenant and rearmament should be regarded as ‘unofficial’ participants.[100]

The accounts of the Focus activities given by both Spier and Gilbert, Churchill’s biographer, make interesting reading, considering that so many of those who joined the group were doing so in uneasy political alliance. An ambitious programme of approaches to government (public and covert), of relaying information widely through press and platform, of compiling information sheets and speakers’ notes was undertaken by those possessing oratorical and didactic skills who could employ them without too many political constraints. Noel-Baker’s competence at assembling figures and drafting argument was much in demand. Generally, there was a substantial amount of disagreement with the extent of Chamberlain’s appeasement and, of course, the perfidy of the dictators’ assurances. Leanings towards excusing Nazi excesses on the part of Dawson's *The Times* and the *Financial Times* were deplored. Noel-Baker and others, churchmen particularly, were anxious to stress the ideological gulf between the active Nazis and the traditional culture and humanity of 'good Germans'. Many of them joined Lord Allen of Hurtwood's 'Anglo-German Group'. Nor was there disunity over the clear tactical need to isolate Chamberlain and to support Eden (who was to resign from the Government in February 1938) without putting the latter into the position of being arraigned for disloyalty by a suspicious Cabinet.

In retrospect it is not easy to see exactly why the cross-benching of Focus collapsed as it did after two-and-a-half years. Dissipation of effort there was perhaps but would such a varied and experienced group really neglect journalistic and Cabinet contacts? It is true that there were so many agencies (including German ones) justifying appeasement that public opinion was largely tranquilised and political influences to some degree dampened. Undoubtedly, there were those like Harold Nicolson who found the Tory-Liberal-Labour group, 'a mysterious organisation . . . one of Winston's things' and so as suspect as the *enfant terrible* himself. Most certainly, as one scans the membership of Focus, Spier's list of names came from 'the alternative elites'. They were not likely to have opened many doors in Whitehall.[101]

There is, in any case, an interesting sequel to the Focus affair. When in 1953 Eugen Spier thought of publishing an account of the Focus he approached Winston Churchill for permission to quote from the Prime Minister's pre-war addresses and correspondence. Permission was refused. Letters between the two men followed and it was not until June 1957 that Churchill was prepared to leave the matter to the judgement of Spier, stating his preference for posthumous publication. Eventually, the book appeared in 1963, two years before Churchill's death. Shortly before the book came out Spier and Noel-Baker discussed the obstacle to publication of Churchill's opposition. One wonders whether there was a fear that former political adherences would now be regarded as discredited. Could it have been difficult for a man outwardly so robust but privately so easily hurt to admit that he had not stood up to the Foreign Office in 1937 when they had forbidden him to meet with Yugoslav anti-Fascists and when Noel-Baker's arrangement for a visit by Léon Blum to London had been circumvented?

Avowedly non-political, the Focus campaign had tried, as its name suggests, to bring attention to bear upon the critical issues of preserving democracy in the face of totalitarian threat. Eugen Spier saw the movement making the public 'cause-conscious'; Winston Churchill regarded it as a spread of 'crackling flames', not easily quenched by government disapproval. Given the inflexible policies of governments such as the British and the French, the response of the voting public to a decade of challenge was in many respects ad hoc and bumbling. For Noel-Baker, 'the Focus was a splendid effort in its attempt to encourage discussion and to recruit widely'. By every possible means, he felt, loyalty to the principles and work of the League must urgently be promoted. We must not fail the League of Nations.[102]

CHAPTER 5

The Years of Defeat 1936-1939

Over something like three years, 1936-39, the foundations of the League of Nations, so earnestly built in faith and hope, were undermined to the point of collapse. The superstructure had withstood the challenge of totalitarian states and the apathy and neglect of some of its members. What finally brought about failure was a persistent reluctance on the part of two long-standing members, Britain and France, to allow the League Assembly or the League Council to deal with crises arising in Spain, Austria, and Czechoslovakia. The effects of this deviation from loyalty to the Covenant were bitterly corrosive and irreparable. Disciples of the League such as Noel-Baker fought hard and resourcefully but to no avail. An account of their failure and that of the League to stem the hole in the dyke makes a harrowing story.

Two weeks after the League of Nations Assembly in silence and gloom had put an end to sanctions against Mussolini's Italy, a Spanish civil war erupted on 18th July 1936. Essentially, the contest in Spain was between syndicalist, and liberal elements on the Left and militarist, commercial, land-owning groups on the Right. In Madrid a coalition of socialist and moderately liberal republicans had taken office in April 1931 and somehow since then clung to power despite the political indifferences of the countryside and the quarrelsome allegiance of miners and factory workers. A phalanx of dissatisfied conservatives – the Falange led by General Francisco Franco – saw themselves as arbiters of Spanish politics in bringing about the end of socialist administration. To this end they sought Italian and German aid and prepared to launch a 'Nationalist' crusade against the despised Republican Government in Madrid. The enterprise took five years to prepare and ultimately a formidable insurrection was to use Morocco as its springboard. Underestimating the extent of popular resistance, the rebels saw their hopes for coup d'état turning into a war of attrition. Within a month they were appealing to the governments of Germany, Italy and Portugal for aircraft, artillery and military experts.

At Geneva in the first instance there was a disposition among League delegates to see the Falangist uprising in Madrid as an internal matter. Impassively, if not complacently, their instinct was for a call to all foreign troops to leave and for a policy of non-intervention to be applied. French and British inclinations were in line with the position as stated by Anthony Eden in October 1936: 'However tragic the civil strife in Spain may be, it in no way absolves us from our duty to make every effort to confine that tragedy within the boundaries of the country where it is being enacted'.[1]

The bloodstained excesses of the Spanish Civil War impelled Noel-Baker to muster his Labour Party colleagues for an appeal to the government:

'It is intervention in violation of the Covenant of the League of Nations. It is aggression by a new technique . . . And do we believe that if it succeeds in Spain, it will not be repeated in Romania, in Czechoslovakia, perhaps in Belgium too? How can the present drift to war be stopped? The guarantees of Article 10 have become the lifeline of civilisation today and I believe it is not too late for a British Government which means business to save international law and to save it without another war.'[2]

Noel-Baker felt it his duty to make the position of the Parliamentary Labour Party very clear. 'We are not urging the Government to intervene . . .' he told the House of Commons in July 1936. 'We urge them to give to the Spanish Government every facility which the practice of international law allows . . . We urge them, above all, to use their influence to prevent other Powers from intervening on the side of the militarist dictators'.[3] Six months earlier, indeed, and in the same House, sensing an impending threat to Madrid, Noel-Baker, had called for Spain to be allowed an arms 'facility' which his country should help to secure. Mindful that his colleagues on the Opposition benches around him were receiving urgent appeals from union members and constituency workers as to the need for calling for something more effective than passive neutrality, Noel-Baker spoke out for a more realistic approach. 'Is it seriously suggested', he asked:

'that if, as a reply to the German and Italian aggression, we sold arms to Spain, Hitler would declare war upon us? I am certain that this is a fantastic suggestion. Indeed, I am certain that the best hope for averting war lies in stopping this continual encroachment of aggression spreading from continent to continent – Asia in 1931, America in 1932, Africa in 1935 and Europe in 1936. And now Hitler is preparing to spring another mine in Austria . . . Czechoslovakia is on the list. Let the Government make a stand while they have a chance of stopping one of the aggressions without war by peaceful means.'[4]

Spain's Republican Government occupied a seat on the Council of the League of Nations and at an early stage, in September 1936, naturally had raised the issue of foreign intervention as being 'incompatible with the maintenance of open, just and honourable relations between states' as was provided for in the Covenant. In the view of Madrid, League members should have reacted more positively, at least in respect of an appeal under Article XI, which held any war or threat of war to be a matter of concern to the whole League. It is understandable that there were doubts among members as to the applicability of Article X, which dealt with external aggression.[5] Added to reservation and hesitation was the fact that all decisions were being taken through the medium of independent diplomatic negotiations between the nations concerned. Whatever might be thought in Geneva in August 1936 about a non-intervention agreement, it was certainly Foreign Ministers in London, Paris, Rome and Berlin who exercised influence on the situation in Spain.

Ten weeks after the beginning of Spain's internal contest the Labour Party met in annual conference in Edinburgh. Delegates were tense amid discussion and recommendations. There was pressure from Philip Noel-Baker to secure the end of any embargo on arms purchase by the beleaguered and legitimate government in Madrid. His argument was carefully weighted, though to some it must have sounded slightly contrived in proclaiming a faith in non-intervention at the same time as it appealed to the British Government to allow private firms under contract with Madrid to fulfil orders and export their products.[6] In the back of Noel-Baker's mind may have been some confidence that this appeal was likely to succeed for at about the same time he had approached Lord Cranborne, one of Eden's Foreign Office colleagues, and found the United Kingdom Government prepared to grant export licences though not if the arms were to go to Franco's insurgent group centred on Burgos. A 'handful of adventurers' had violated international codes and sought to defeat a properly-elected government. Noel-Baker believed that such a situation could give Hitler a pretext for international war. Not all were to agree: Hugh Dalton, sitting on the same platform, saw Labour attitudes 'wallowing in sheer emotion, in vicarious valour'.[7]

Remembering the hiatus over Abyssinia, Noel-Baker lost no time in sounding out the French in early August 1936. Now M.P. for Derby, he went over to Paris to confer with Léon Blum, whose Socialist administration had been installed (with multi-party support) since the summer, and with Pierre Cot, the indefatigable worker for the International Peace Campaign. Blum asked him, as Noel-Baker was to note, 'to do whatever I could in the British press to keep the true nature of General Franco's revolt, and the true democratic character of the Spanish Government before the British people'.[8] In return, the English visitor proffered the decision of Cranborne as an inducement to Paris to approve expedited delivery of Spanish aircraft orders. Might more be done, though, nearer London? Was it possible that His Majesty's Government might take a more benevolent view of the Republican régime if they were to heed strategic considerations rather than ideological ones? News reaching Noel-Baker from people within the Conservative Party gave him reason to believe that the government might be elbowed into acting firmly: 'If Eden', he minuted in early 1936, 'is not convinced that the powers he most dislikes is <sic> interfering, then he ought to resign for incompetence!'[9] Some months later Noel-Baker was assured by Winston Churchill that in general terms the Government would most certainly stand by the League. However, the Spanish contest had been 'boiling up for a long time and Franco was going to win'.[10] No British Government, in Churchill's view would back an insurrection.

At the same meeting in Paris, Blum took Noel-Baker aside to describe how a Franco victory, aided by anti-Comintern if not anti-democratic elements, would clearly endanger both French and British interests in the Mediterranean. How might Whitehall best be convinced that this constituted a real threat? In reply, Noel-Baker felt he had to point out that, in an English August, Members of Parliament and also Cabinet ministers were on holiday and that the only person who might be able to convene an emergency meeting at Downing Street, was the Cabinet Secretary, Sir Maurice Hankey. The best approach would be through the Admiralty. Blum then despatched the Chief of the Navy, Admiral François Darlan, to London to meet his opposite number, Sir Ernle Chatfield who was found, however, to be curiously unresponsive and disinclined to intervene. The French government, hoping that the days of Laval's defeatism were over now felt increasingly isolated.

From every side, though more often from the political Left, came resolutions, meetings, appeals, and deputations aghast at the threat to liberty in the Iberian peninsula. Noel-Baker found himself speaking widely in Britain and in France and, naturally as chief spokesman for the League of Nations Union. It is interesting to look at the make-up of the Union in these years. Viscounts Cecil and Grey were Joint Presidents (the latter until his death in 1933); Stanley Baldwin and David Lloyd George were Honorary Presidents. There were among the Vice-Presidents a number of world statesmen such as J. C. Smuts, Sir Robert Borden, J. B. M. Hertzog. The Executive Committee, apart from Gilbert Murray, the Chairman, included Sir Austen Chamberlain, Sir Norman Angell, Philip Noel-Baker, Lord Lytton, Lord Eustace Percy, two retired admirals and six former army 'brasshats'. Ordinary membership of the Union had doubled from 514,789 in 1926 to 1,000,000 in 1933. The monthly *Headway* had a circulation in

1933 of 94,500, about half that of *The Times*.[11] This influence could not be negligible. As Gilbert Murray, Chairman for 15 years, saw it, 'The power of the League is all-pervading . . . all-puissant, if it is given the time'.[12] If this were an excess of optimism there was no shortage of energy in Noel-Baker's case. Broadsheets, memoranda, letters, the inevitable suggestions for the speeches of others, all flowed from his pen as autumn 1936 brought a war in Spain increasing in severity on land and sea. 'The Labour Party opposes Baldwinism' was a sentiment winning him applause. Not by any means, however, would a majority have endorsed his conclusive sentiment that 'we are prepared to *risk* war for the collective system and Democracy'. Noel-Baker, often in the minority, saw Baldwin's antecedents and now Baldwin himself wanting to 'keep the country out of war' by preferring short-term settlements in the style of Locarno to support for the Protocol and the Optional Clause or to the offer of guarantee to threatened states. The disarmament proposals of Coolidge and Hoover had been rejected. Baldwin, Eden, and Neville Chamberlain appeared unable to hold an unwavering and positive line over Abyssinia and Spain. Understandably, there is a Labour Party thread to the commentary and suggestions of Noel-Baker and there is more than a tinge of idealism (if not wishfulness), but generally one detects a broad, liberal and humane concern that Franco's insurrection is a threat to the codes and the existence of civilised communities.[13]

Yet, how was keeping out of the conflict, by way of non-intervention, likely to promote the Covenant principles to which 'the whole League' subscribed? In realistic terms, and given the very real possibility that the conflict might escalate, was non-intervention an action, to quote Article XI, 'that may be deemed wise and effectual to safeguard the peace of nations?' The presentations of Noel-Baker apparently made up for the deficiencies that Konni Zilliacus detected in others. They had 'no guts and no revolutionary spirit . . . You've got both', he wrote, 'and a clear head to boot, although from my point of view you're too liberal and optimistic . . .'[14] Material aid was to be collected for Spanish refugees and prisoners and perhaps sent most expeditiously through a League High Commissioner for Spanish refugees. Yet, as noted above, Noel-Baker saw the main thrust as a political one bearing upon the problem of non-intervention. Twenty-seven countries were accepting a dual obligation, French inspired, of August 1936, namely, to refrain from direct or indirect interference and to proscribe the export of war material. London was to be the seat of the Non-intervention Committee. Anomalies, loopholes, delay, complicated arrangements at sea and on land for intercepting gun-runners all combined to bring to a halt after two months measures for preventing illicit interference. The Labour Party, at its Annual Conference met the concept of non-intervention head-on. 'I believe in non-intervention . . .', Noel-Baker had asserted. 'But in this dispute there has never been non-intervention from the first day onwards . . .'[15] There seemed little point in being content with ineffective non-intervention. Ernest Bevin, realist and moderate, felt few qualms in growling, 'I am afraid, however, that we may have to go through force to liberty'.[16] On the Left of the Party – though the clamour moved increasingly centrewards – there was a clear rejection of the Government's stance of 'let's see how things develop' and agreement that Fascist determination to aid the Falangist rebels and the difficulty of preventing arms imports undercut hopes for non-intervention. At all costs the danger of a defeated Republican government had to be prevented even if for some this might bring about the concomitant peril of a more general war. Labour could only support the Government if non-intervention were to be made effective for all sides Noel-Baker pointed out in the Commons. Improved measures of control would have to grip harder than a tame sea blockade which, in his view, showed Britain standing in fear of a Spanish fleet for the first time since 1588.[17]

In carly 1937 there were moves to focus attention on the way in which the Spanish situation was eroding observance of the League of Nations Covenant. Konni Zilliacus put the tactic in these terms to Noel-Baker:

'The general idea, as you will see, is to confront the Government's Spanish policy with the obligations of the Covenant. I think genuine "non-intervention" applied all round from the outset would have been compatible with the Covenant. But "non-intervention" as a camouflage for tolerating Fascist intervention is certainly not . . .'[18]

This seems to have been a repetition of a tactic which had gone off at half-cock the previous summer. 'The end of non-intervention must not mean *neutrality*', Zilliacus had told Noel-Baker. 'Hope you agree', he added, '& will stir up Clem & the party on these lines'.[19] Apart from this, the Union of Democratic Control had asked Noel-Baker to press for an extended parliamentary session: the attempt was unsuccessful. Research by the Labour Party's International Department and by its Spanish Campaign Committee, messages from the Spanish Red Cross, and from the Spanish Embassy in London, consultations with the International Federation of T.U.C.'s, and with the Socialist International all pointed up the gravity of the situation. Zilliacus pressed his point in similar vein when he wrote to Attlee, Dalton, Morrison and to the U.D.C. Generally, copies were sent to Noel-Baker, now elected to Labour's National Executive Committee. Others, though, in the Party were putting less reliance on the Covenant as an instrument for enhancing the security of states. Leonard Woolf and Ivor

Thomas submitted a memorandum in early summer 1937 to the Labour Party's Advisory Committee on International Questions expressing their doubts, calling for a clear recognition of shortcomings and suggesting an early review of the Party's entire peace policy. Noel-Baker, who had been ill for several months, read the statement with consternation:

'If I may say so with all respect, it seems to be founded on a total disregard of the true history of international affairs in the last six years . . . If the memorandum were to be adopted by the National Executive or the Annual Conference as the official policy of the Party, I should not have the slightest hesitation in resigning my membership of the Party and of the House of Commons.'

He added that he had talked to other members of the Parliamentary Party who had shared his view.[20]

In Britain parliamentary opinion as to the effectiveness of the tattered Covenant provisions was discordant: it had to be canvassed. If Labour was moving leftwards to reject the fragility of non-interventionist policies and if the United Kingdom Government clung to them timorously then the inherent strength of the League of Nations must be stressed. The feeling, if not the charge, that Geneva had lost momentum irretrievably since the Abyssinian 'surrender' was discounted in a retort of Noel-Baker in the House of Commons in October 1937:

'In fact its <the League's> membership is exactly the same except that Egypt has joined. Mussolini then <in 1935> was already an aggressor, but now he is an aggressor exhausted by two long and bloody wars. Russia's membership then was a far less solid factor than it is today. The hope of American cooperation is enormously greater, as Mr. Roosevelt's speech makes clear. Potentially <even> if our Government ceased to lead it, the League is far stronger today than it has ever been . . . We are now entitled to count in 130 million Americans, who are in favour of upholding the sanctity of international law, and who would give us all the practical cooperation that we should require, and if we do that we have 160 million people in the League against less than 200 million people of Germany, Italy, and Japan, who seem inclined to challenge the League and its authority today.'[21]

In retrospect, such a degree of optimism seems markedly naïve since American isolationism that autumn was clearly already blunting the Washington zeal for dealing with an 'epidemic of world lawlessness' and the dictator powers were making the running both in Europe and in Asia.

Zilliacus, particularly, was more level-headed: the authority of the Covenant must be upheld. He saw public agitation in fairly clear terms when writing to Noel-Baker in the November of 1937:

'My idea is that you <as "the past-master on the League"> may be able to use something like the enclosed in order to confront the Government with the fact that it has at Geneva pledged itself to respect not only the territorial integrity, but also the political independence of the Spanish Government and to recognise that foreign intervention exists in Spain and that such intervention is incompatible with Article 10 of the Covenant.

'There is a very marked discrepancy between the Government's constant pretence that there is no difference between the rebels and the Spanish Government and its references to respect for the integrity of Spain without mentioning the country's political independence on the one hand, and the attitude to which the Government were constrained to commit themselves in the Council and Assembly of the League on the other. Has not the time come to bring out this discrepancy and to rub it in?

'Incidentally, that will also help to show up the mendacity of Eden's assertion that the League cannot or would not deal with this matter because it is rent by the "ideological" conflict . . .'[22]

It is tempting to speculate, in the light of his moral standing, how adamant Zilliacus might have remained had the Madrid Government been a Fascist one and the rebels a left-wing cohort.

At any rate Zilliacus' intention seems straightforward in seeking Noel-Baker's alliance. In some haste to leave for the United States where his mother was seriously ill he added three weeks later:

'I have sent copies to Clem <Attlee>, Herbert <Morrison> and Ellen <Wilkinson>, but not to Hugh <Dalton> because the central feature of the enclosed is the suggestion of how to put teeth and claws into Labour's Spanish campaign, & I know Hugh has never cared a damn about Spain, & thinks the Spanish campaign is all rot.

'My hope is that you will read this thing on your way to Spain, & perhaps if you feel like it, discuss it with Clem, & Ellen . . .'[23]

Not unexpectedly, the exertions of Zilliacus, Noel-Baker and others occasioned both misunderstanding and opposition. For the more conservative there were political risks in taking on the cause of the Basque minority in addition to that of Republican Spain and in lamenting loudly the tightening blockade of civilian communities along the Spanish coast. An instance of the care which was felt necessary is Noel-Baker's enquiry of Herbert Morrison some time later in July 1937 as to the advisability of accepting an invitation to preside over the Westminster Spanish Relief Committee. The reply was to keep clear of an affiliation which contained elements of the Communist Party.[24]

There is little doubt that Philip Noel-Baker took the Spanish Civil War very much to heart. Compassion for the suffering of civilians is demonstrated by a letter he and other members of the Society of Friends wrote to *The Times* on 29th June 1937 appealing for financial aid. A visit to Spain in December 1937 in the company of C. R. Attlee and Ellen Wilkinson revealed the unevenness of a contest between primitively equipped Republicans and the Nationalists deploying German dive-bombers and artillery from Italy. Villages and towns were being pounded into dust amid the rigours of winter, more than that the crisis represented a crumbling of democracy and a fight between Good and Evil. Strong feelings, indeed, a conviction about the nature of this struggle and about its likely consequences did not lead Noel-Baker to uncharacteristic petulance or intolerance. Nearly every week he wrote objective appraisals in letters to *The Times* and elsewhere joined battle in correspondence columns and in public halls. He may well have found amusing one criticism from Hampstead in July 1937:

'The chief aim of this letter however, is to ask you to consider whether you do not speak too much in parliament? As a regular reader of parliamentary discussions, it is monotonous to find the same persons chattering day after day . . .'[25]

'Chattering' (with effect), of course, was in his blood and it can not be denied that Noel-Baker represented a more vigorous political species than did his comrades, Murray and Cecil. Writing shortly before the former's return to Westminster in 1936 Murray noted of him:

'If the League of Nations is to be the keystone of British policy, Philip Baker ought to be in the House of Commons. This seems to be quite obvious and though I do not belong to his party – I should certainly vote for him.'[26]

Two years later Murray, Chairman of the League of Nations Union, is not so sure: Philip is seen perhaps as an institutional risk for he gnaws at the fabric of Chamberlain's foreign policy:

'I used to wish Philip to succeed me as Chairman and spoke to him about it some years ago, but I do not think he would be a good choice now. His judgement is not good; he is now practically the most prominent and trenchant leader of the hostile critics of Eden . . . We are rich in opponents of Eden already, and poor in supporters.'[27]

A constant area of conflict between Government and Opposition in the Commons was over the Italian commitment to supply aid, a partisan gesture which clearly went against any principle of non-intervention. Deliberations within the Non-Intervention Committee and ambiguous policies in several European Foreign Offices had not gone beyond tentative acceptance of Italian assurances as to volunteer withdrawal. Noel-Baker in the House of Commons castigated the 'pitiful and dilatory' diplomatic exchanges where under the cover of 'the much-advertised' negotiations in the Foreign Office, Mussolini had been applying non-intervention in his own way . . . beginning with the despatch of 6,500 'volunteers' at the end of 1936 and ending with the Italian 'victories' at Malaga, Bilbao, Santander and Gijon. During this whole time the British Government was negotiating the setting-up of, 'that wonderful control under which not a single shipment of arms has yet been found, although everybody knows the war has been conducted with foreign arms!'[28] For the best part of a year, keeping an ear close to the ground, Noel-Baker had learned of deepening Italian involvement in Spain. Pierre Cot had told him about this in August 1937 and a month later Alvarez de Vayo, the quietly persuasive Foreign Minister of Spain, had described the ambiguous position of Yvon Delbos, his French equivalent, in trying to shift blame for ineffective remonstrance on to the British, altogether, 'a diplomatic manoeuvre for dodging responsibility'.[29]

If negotiations failed, clear government pronouncement could put an end to interventionist sallies if there were consensus and especially if the latent potential of the League of Nations were employed according to its best-known publicist, Philip Noel-Baker:

'We believe that even today by far the best chance of getting rid of foreign troops in Spain, and of ending the dangers which the presence of these troops involves, would be to have a League plan, drawn up in public, impartial and fair to all, administered by impartial League agents responsible to no government but to the League alone, and to present it to the two other parties. If either refused it, let it take the consequences of that refusal. Cut off arms supplies to that side by more effective measures of control; give arms to the side which accepted the plan, and supplement that action with whatever economic measures might be required.'[30]

There was a predicament for the British Government, as there was for France, in that however they sought to put an end to an inflow of mercenaries from the dictatorships they had to reckon with the not inconsiderable contribution their own nationals were making to the Republican forces as members of International Brigades. Moreover, in regard to Italy, there was basic Entente agreement to try to separate Italy from German influence through rapprochement wherever it was judged practicable. Successive Anglo-Italian agreements of January 1937 and April 1938 sought to press for evacuation of Italian forces although, as Eden foresaw at his resignation in February 1938, there would be something required in return namely, the British recognition of Mussolini's annexation of Abyssinia. From time to time the situation forcibly struck Noel-Baker as dishonest in its intention and presentation and as demonstrating partiality (a sign of weakness) and indifference towards the League.[31] A Government statement by the Prime Minister, Neville Chamberlain, in April 1938 was criticised severely for its negativeness. Noel-Baker and other Labour members pleaded for a firm position on allegience to the League of Nations, indeed, 'a revitalisation of it, and an unambiguous commitment to the "rule of law"'. Britain must act, not drift.[32] Never had the constant visitor to Geneva seen anything 'so half-hearted, so tepid, so frigid' as the reception given there to the Anglo-Italian Agreement. It was not approved certainly in the legal sense, and hardly either in any moral sense. Most distressing was the fact that Britain, had failed to use this opportunity to strike a blow for the maintenance of international law by recognising that non-intervention in Spain should be ended and that there was now an overwhelming case for giving the Spanish Government its rights under international law to purchase arms.[33] To some this criticism may have appeared diffused to an extent; however, the Labour Opposition lost no chance of expressing clear dissatisfaction with Conservative foreign policy. When Government ministers were already beginning to suggest that reliance might be placed upon Italian assurances and intentions these remarks aroused fury on the Labour benches. Was this really a demonstration that the Italians would be 'keeping faith' with us?[34]

Situations such as the Anglo-Italian one evincing apparent timidity and double-dealing in Whitehall swung many of the Left and Centre in Britain into attacking Chamberlain's government, no longer mainly for pacifist reasons on account of a deplored militarism, but on anti-Fascist grounds because they opposed what they regarded as appeasement of the dictators. Straight-speaking came from the veteran H. N. Brailsford in April 1938. (He had tried to enlist in the International Brigade some 18 months earlier.) Recognising the finality of the appeasement issue, he went off to have a talk with Labour's leader, C. R. Attlee, and came back to plead with Noel-Baker for immediate action: 'You may care to have some idea of what is in our minds before the National Executive meets tomorrow. If it doesn't act', he warned, 'the rank and file will'. In Brailsford's view the Anglo-Italian Pact effectively scrapped non-intervention since it tacitly authorised Mussolini to keep his troops in Spain until victory. Accordingly, Labour should repudiate interventionism and 'volunteers' should be recruited openly and sent to Spain with munitions with the full responsibility of the Party clear to the public. Labour, and perhaps Liberal leaders, might accompany the volunteers to their embarkation. Further, sanctions against the government might call even for a one-day General Strike.[35]

As a member of the Socialist International, Philip Noel-Baker was asked in 1938 to endorse an invitation to a prominent Spanish Republican to speak at their Paris conference that year. Dolores Ibarurri, a Communist miner's wife, was dubbed 'La Passionaria' and was an intense, devoted, yet unostentatious symbol of revolutionary faith. Feeling uncertain as to the propriety of such a gesture Noel-Baker consulted Cecil enquiringly:

'The Communists have given us their usual demonstration of helpful loyalty – they have brought the "Passionaria" as at Brussels! If we let her speak – an international scandal on the Right. If we don't, an international scandal on the Left. Which do you prefer? Should we beg the President of the Cortes <Spain's Parliament> to smuggle her out of Paris now at once? Or what? De Bouchère <of the Socialist International> thinks she had better speak – but at Brussels she cost us most of our success.'

Cecil's reply was terse: 'Let her speak somewhere else in Paris – after the conference is finished'.[36] This incident and others demonstrate the extent to which a public figure such as Noel-Baker felt the need of discretion during the 30's however committed they appeared to be to any particular cause.

On another occasion Noel-Baker incurred the wrath of C. G. Grey, Editor of *The Aeroplane.* Parliamentary questions about the aerial bombardment of British ships in Spanish harbours asked by this Member had been commented upon with acidity. Grey found fault with the shipowners 'bringing supplies to the Reds' and the complainant went on to add:

'I have followed your questions and your speeches in Parliament for a considerable time and I am still puzzled whether you are (a) a Communist, (b) merely anti-Fascist, or (c) merely constitutionally opposed to everything progressive.'[37]

Danger to British shipping off the coasts of Spain had received attention in the newspapers for some time and brought about a flurry of anxious letters to M.P.s. It was the excesses of 'pirate submarines', as Winston Churchill termed Italian harassment, that led to the calling of a naval conference at Nyon in September 1937. Much to the fore was the delicate question of belligerency rights. Put briefly, Powers outside a civil war are able best to protect their nationals and their legitimate maritime operations by conceding to insurgents the power to searching ships for contraband. 'Right of belligerency' may be granted to enable them to do this. Force must not be employed. A mere declaration by insurgents that they constitute a 'Provisional Government' is insufficient to justify recognition. Consideration has to be given to the length of time the insurrection has continued, the number, order, and discipline of rebel forces, and whether external relationships can be sustained. Two consequences are of importance, firstly, that a recognising state becomes entitled to neutral rights and these are to be respected by rival parties, and, secondly, that belligerent recognition, while 'normalising' rights and duties does not *ipso facto* confer recognition as a legitimate administration on either contending party.[38] Moreover, as Noel-Baker had pointed out to readers of *The Times* on 5th July 1937, Britain did not usually grant belligerency rights as a traditional policy. Only once since 1824 had the British Empire conceded the rights and this was when a Greek rebellion against a Turkish overlord had presented a *fait accompli.* During the American Civil War, he went on, blockading and a threat to British mariners had forced the hand of London. To recognise these rights in Spain while German and Italian troops were there would 'legitimize by implication what everyone agrees to be a Covenant-breaking invasion'. If Whitehall followed the preferences of its naval advisers this would seem to signify in general terms that the United

Kingdom Government regarded both belligerents in the same light and it would do much to advance the legal status of the Fascist insurgents.

While all governments having interests in Spain were, as *The Times* put it, 'pawns on a diplomatic chessboard', it was noticeable that in Berlin and Rome there was much agitation for granting belligerency rights to both Spanish contestants. Britain and France regarded this as unacceptable since they believed that such an apparent impartiality would disguise, in fact, partiality in material terms and might lead to a loosening of naval controls.[39] A further warning in customary terms from Noel-Baker was despatched to *The Times* on 10th July 1937. Granting belligerency rights to Franco would condone violation of 'the most important and most solemn of all treaties'. We had no right to adopt an attitude of neutrality when the Covenant was broken. Recognition would be another blow at the rule of law. Many months of discussion were to ensue in London between politicians and the Crown's law officers where both were mindful of Franco's appeal for recognition. The strictures of international law and the precedents of history were one thing, yet Franco undeniably needed to keep sea lanes open in order to receive aid from Germany and Italy and thus augment his strengthening campaigns. As the reality of an overwhelming Nationalist victory grew along with the withdrawal of Republican volunteers the administration of General Franco was granted recognition after all on 27th February 1938 though belligerency rights, as such, were not granted. A consequence of this manoeuvre was an escalation of public protest in Britain over the high-handedness (and collusion) at the expense of legitimate mariners.

In the early summer of 1938, Noel-Baker and others decided to enlist the help of the so-called Committee of British Shipowners Trading to Spain in bringing pressure to bear upon a slow-moving government. In the event of there being raised in the Commons the possibility of paying compensation to British shipowners engaged in Spanish commerce the Committee should be invited to proceed further viz.:

'A number of powerful organisations led by the International Peace Campaign are hoping to have a large-scale propaganda campaign against the granting of belligerent rights to General Franco. They are hoping to start their work by flooding the country with five million or more leaflets, which on one side will state the case against belligerent rights and on the back will contain an appeal to Members of Parliament to oppose any such grant with instructions that recipients of the leaflets should send them to their respective Members. The whole machinery for launching this campaign is ready and they are hoping to get the thing over the country well before 23rd November when the Prime Minister and Lord Halifax go to Paris.'

However, the Secretary of the Committee was informed that the campaign was held up by lack of funds and a contribution of two to three thousand pounds from the shipowners 'would be marvellous'.[40] A generous response was indeed forthcoming and in an expression of thanks, Noel-Baker told the Committee that 10 million leaflets could now be distributed; further, that meetings in Trafalgar Square and at Friends House, London, together with a powerful delegation to the Prime Minister from the League of Nations Union, all would surely impress the House of Commons and influence Chamberlain in his dealings with the French Government. There is no evidence, though, that this soliciting of public opinion was to surmount the party loyalties of members of the legislature.[41]

In the minds of both shipowners and readers of newspapers, one question loomed large: what happens if British vessels are damaged or sunk? His Majesty's Government were declaring in October 1937 that they could not intervene should a ship go within Spain's three mile limit. On the other hand, if such a ship were in distress, vessels nearby must be able to effect aid and any prevention of this would be a plain violation of international law.[42] Six months later, Franco's bombing of east Spanish harbours (probably using Italian aircraft) impelled Noel-Baker to press the Premier in the House of Commons. Would not the Government take action to protect British seamen? Must Britain meekly be content with a Spanish-Italian assurance of ultimately desisting from these raids?[43] R. A. Butler, Under-Secretary for Foreign Affairs, applied an instant emollient in saying that a policy of non-intervention with all its difficulties had averted a major war but his rejoinder the following month that claims for damage to vessels must await the outcome of the civil war was unlikely to reduce alarm.[44] A further parliamentary question from Noel-Baker raised the possibility of arming British freighters going about their lawful occasions with anti-aircraft guns. 'I do not consider', was the reply, 'such a measure would be expedient'. It would be difficult to establish any protection where a merchantman riding at anchor opened fire on an approaching aircraft, however certainly and quickly the planes were identified. In these circumstances, too, the ship would become part of the defences of the port and a legitimate object of attack.[45]

In similar fashion to the vulnerability of merchant ships the issue of unprotected civilians in Spain aroused great anxiety internationally. Indiscriminate bombing must be stopped, Noel-Baker stated in a letter to *The Times* in March 1938, for conventions observed in the general field of warfare as to the illegitimacy of attacking civilian targets must be observed in any particular sphere of warlike operations, whether on land, sea, or in the air. Otherwise, we could see here the shape of war in the future. 'Guernica was a portent: Barcelona is the writing on the wall'. Three months later the same writer was to recall in *The Times* work done in

The Hague in 1923 by a group of jurists attempting to draft a Code of Air Warfare. Bombardment of civilians was forbidden as also attacks on military objectives when an 'overspill' of non-combatant damage was probable. Indeed, to secure the upholding of these principles, more than protest would be needed he felt. The inference of this remark was not elaborated.[46]

Within a year, on 27th February 1939, the British and French governments were to acknowledge Franco's administration as the *de jure* Spanish Government. Another Fascist 'leader', the Caudillo, had joined the Führer and the Duce. Anger and dismay of liberals were obvious in the warning of Noel-Baker, 'In effect he <Chamberlain> is giving him <Mussolini> a free hand in Spain, and saying, "Do what you like. I shall not trouble you any more about it".' Recognition seemed to follow on the heels of inadequately supported League of Nations resolutions. Some Genevan delegates doubtless might have agreed with an earlier comment of Noel-Baker that governments still wedded to power politics and secret diplomacy were incapable of understanding any new international order founded upon the rule of law. They might have been slower to extrapolate the consequence, as Litvinov put it, that sheltering behind a flimsy, non-interventionist role, hoping vainly that mediation might be practicable, nations such as Britain and France had allowed an international struggle to become a war between Spain and two other countries, in effect, a developing international conflict.[47] It was one of Noel-Baker's former academic colleagues, J. L. Brierley, who spoke for many in expressing greater bitterness against His Majesty's Government for their share in bringing about the collapse of Spanish democracy than for the mere process of translating *de facto* acknowledgement of Franco into *de jure* recognition of his conquest.[48] Lassitude and unpreparedness to act collectively were eroding inevitably the fragile basis of Europe's democracy.

Amid the alarums of Europe in 1937 and 1938, the festering conflict in the Far East could hardly be overlooked. By the summer of 1937 the 'undeclared war' in Asia had lengthened and deepened into a conflict with major political and economic implications. Japan seemed intent on colonising ruthlessly a 'Greater East Asian Co-prosperity Sphere'. The China of Chiang Kai-shek was not prepared to give major concessions. Britain, in some commercial jeopardy, was not unwilling to mediate. The United States had put up a somewhat uncertain proposition that, as F. D. Roosevelt saw it, America would seek to curb an 'epidemic' of world lawlessness by leading law-abiding nations in an organisation to 'quarantine' aggressor states. The relation of this to the League of Nations was not at all clear. What was beginning to interest public opinion in a number of European countries was the possible effectiveness of trade boycott to stem Japanese expansion. Unanimously, the Bournemouth Labour Party Conference of 1937 called for economic boycott and shortly afterwards this was followed up by Noel-Baker in the House of Commons when he focussed attention on interruption of the supply of oil to Japan. Such 'quarantining' could bring effective results, for he went on to conclude that 'Should she <Japan> dare to attack Hong Kong, Britain could merely wait six or nine months until Japanese oil was finished'. Japanese arms, 'would be useless encumbrances to troops who sought to use them. They would come out of Hong Kong as they went in, without a shot being fired, and Hong Kong would be ours again'. Optimism such as this did not engender a spontaneous response among his fellow-countrymen. A China Campaign formed in London and with Harold Laski as its Vice-President had to work hard to whip up solidarity among dockers handling cargo bound for the Orient. Gilbert Murray and other intellectuals associated themselves with the boycott campaign and drew adherents in the cause of China Relief from a narrow circle in the main.[49]

At the outset of 1938 Noel-Baker perceived a need to reactivate the protest mechanism of the Peace Ballot so successful three years earlier. With this in mind he wrote a long letter to Robert Cecil. An international consumers' boycott of Japanese goods would be sponsored by the International Federation of League of Nations Societies. An army of half a million volunteers would carry through a house-to-house canvass, as they had for the Peace Ballot, this time asking people to pledge themselves not to buy the products of Japan so long as Japanese aggression continued. Posters and letters would be sent to companies and shopkeepers. Cecil, he knew, would approve of such an effort to bring strong pressure to bear upon the government. 'My 20 years of propaganda for the League', he told Cecil, have convinced me that something of this kind is required, and the immense success of this movement in many countries on the continent has added to the strength of my conviction . . .'[50] The very next day he was able to reassure Cecil as to the Labour Party's preparedness to resuscitate the Peace Ballot method of working.

Noel-Baker clearly was careful enough to sound opinion widely as the effectiveness and propriety of boycott. He talked with Anthony Eden now and then and with the I.L.O. and managed also, with the help of Cecil, to secure a donation of $10,000 from the Rockefeller Foundation. Urgency was vital, for the effort of the boycott campaign, he assured Harold Butler, his old League colleague, was 'Lord Robert's last desperate attempt to make the public save the League'.[51] Coordinating efforts could best be carried out in the opinion of Noel-Baker by some type of popular front to effect liaison among groups and individuals determined to press governments into positive and resolute action. He had in mind the International Peace Campaign. He can hardly have overlooked the fact that not everybody would consider the I.P.C. as necessary or legitimate or non-partisan.

The origins and development of the International Peace Campaign are well worth looking at in some detail. To launch it in the summer of 1936 an Anglo-French group assembled: Robert Cecil, Philip Noel-Baker, Norman Angell, Edouard Herriot, Pierre Jouhaux, speaking for French trade unions, and Pierre Cot. Motivated by anxiety over the excursions of the Fascist dictators and by a retreat from the Covenant, the I.P.C. set out to reinvigorate League powers, insist on international mediation, the halting of the arms race, and the abolition of private arms manufacture. An international Congress to be held in Brussels in September 1936 was to be coordinated through steering committees in many lands. Delegates would come from 40 countries representing trade and professional organisations, ex-servicemen, womens' movements, and the churches. Much discussion would centre on the issue of how far the League of Nations should be *coercive* or remain fundamentally consultative. Noel-Baker in October 1937 assured a friend in Canada, Brooke Claxton, that the I.P.C. was not an organisation aiming to rival others but it was, he said, simply a means of establishing liaison among existing organisations and of securing common effort. With Cecil and Cot as Presidents (Noel-Baker as Vice-President), this rallying point was gaining rapid ground in various parts of Europe, exercising influence on Genevan delegates and arousing, to some extent, the frenzy of conservative opponents. 'It would', said Noel-Baker, 'be the biggest possible instrument for stopping Hitler's dreams of conquest.'[52]

The Campaign was designed to stress the salience of Four Points, viz. (i) recognition of the sanctity of treaty obligations, (ii) agreed limitation of armaments and suppression of profit from private manufacture, (iii) strengthening of the League of Nations through more effective coordination of measures for collective security and mutual assistance, (iv) establishment of League machinery for conflict resolution. Promulgation of these Points, in a non-partisan fashion, would provide a blueprint for groups with aspirations in common. A danger here that Noel-Baker recognised was that the Campaign might become anti-German and anti-Italian specifically where it should more profitably seek to deal with generalised aggression and conflict. Kathleen Courtney, back from a Geneva I.P.C. Congress, in September 1937, raised the point that to be more anti-Nazi or anti-Fascist rather that pro-peace and pro-international cooperation might conceivably discredit their undertaking. To this Noel-Baker replied:

'I think our right line is to say we are going to make the League succeed, whatever they <the Fascists> do, that it is always open to them, to come in, and that, in fact, there is no solution for economics and other troubles except in cooperation with us.'[53]

However impracticable this may have seemed as an affirmation it was, as he told Louis Dolivet of the French Socialists, better to do this than risk the allegation that all the Campaign wanted to do was to divide the world into two opposed ideological camps. Meetings held subsequently at Cecil's home, in Paris and in Geneva attempted to tread warily within the frontiers of existing organisations and in London there was a careful delineation of the Campaign's central cadre, separate from the L.N.U. but in close cooperation with existing resources.[54]

Outside the secretariat of the L.N.U. in London (which had its good and lean years) the daughter branches in the provinces struck Noel-Baker as often 'very weak and unrepresentative'. As the international situation worsened in Europe, with Spain in flames and Austria menaced, was there really time to fall back in protectionist fashion on the slow resuscitation of bodies frequently moribund or lacking in articulation? To those who asserted that the establishment of a new umbrella organisation, the I.P.C., would obfuscate objectives, skew allegiances and generally duplicate effort, Noel-Baker and Cecil replied that a broad force would bring pressure to bear on wavering governments with a new, enforced power and passion. This would not be vague advocacy of peace as some critics had suggested. The two men agreed in letters and memoranda that the Campaign would depend upon carefully coordinated spadework by its constituent bodies. Cecil was insistent on avoiding 'stunt elements' and 'a splashy international effort'; Noel-Baker wanted to see an end to 'hesitancy' and a determined effort above all in Britain and France to mobilise the understanding and vigour that an enterprise like the Peace Ballot had revealed.[55] London and Paris were key sites for the I.P.C. organisers to harness the energies of thousands of rank and file members and to establish offices and funds. The Campaign's momentum increased visibly through 1937 and 1938. 'Do you know that you have a tremendous gift of energising people?' a Scottish lady enquired of Philip Noel-Baker in October 1937. 'Perhaps', she added, 'it is because you live at about six times the normal intensity'. Certainly, his enthusiasm bestrode the arrangements for the Brussels Congress in September 1936. The following year he was active in organising peace weeks and meetings about Spain in Glasgow, Manchester, Blackpool, and Chesterfield. At the Paris International Exhibition the same year the *Rassemblement Universel pour la Paix* (R.U.P.), as it was known in France, would have a special Peace Pavilion and package holiday deals would be set up with travel agents for British visitors.

Despite impressive progress with lacing up European peace-worker groups, Noel-Baker felt frustrated with what he saw as a League of Nations Union prevaricating if not back-tracking. Their indecision had prevented him from taking up latent but rather inert trade union collaboration, although Clement Attlee and others were willing to orchestrate it. Moreover, the Secretary of the L.N.U., Maxwell Garnett, and certain members of the Executive Committee were raising the spectre of the Third International haunting the Paris office of the I.P.C. Since these earnest people were prepared to work alongside Communists, the best tactic appeared to be that of assurance that the I.P.C. was neither directed by subversives nor funded by Russian roubles. They ought to be told, at least, that Noel-Baker had managed to get $10,000 from the Rockefeller Foundation.[56] It is an interesting fact, and one not without irony, that a modern commentator claims to have found evidence in the Public Record Office:

'that the British Government had people in France reporting back to the F.O. on what Angell <Sir Norman Angell> and Noel-Baker were saying and doing – they apparently regarded their activities in Paris as subversive.'[57]

Noel-Baker's energies, extended on so many fronts, were inevitably the subject of comment from his Labour Party comrades and brought from the Party Leader, C. R. Attlee, some reproof. In November 1936 Noel-Baker felt compelled to meet these observations:

'I do mean to follow your instructions and to be extremely religious about my parliamentary duties. In particular, I mean never to miss the Executive, the work of which I think extremely important and in which I am very proud to share. But I am sure you will understand that before this change came into my life, i.e. becoming an M.P. again, I had some other arrangements which I cannot break.'

He must have been referring here to his regular obligation to attend I.P.C. Executive Committee meetings in Brussels.[58]

There is a special significance in the reply of Noel-Baker that November. In the summer of 1936 he had fought a by-election in Derby with keen anticipation for the seat he had won at Coventry in 1929 had been lost in the debacle of 1931. It was necessary to walk gingerly in view of a Labour defeat by 12,000 votes at a preceding election. He felt, after all, that his status as a member of Labour's National Executive would be enhanced if a parliamentary seat were to be his. He would take his stand as a League Man he told Cecil, keeping international affairs in the forefront of the fight, as for the Campaign, he was at pains to put the issue plainly to a critic:

'I have purposely refrained from mentioning the International Campaign in this election, as I do not want to make it a political issue. If we should win this election the Tories will, of course, try to make the utmost capital out of our dragging the

League into Party politics. This would be greatly intensified by the letter of support which Lord Robert has sent me, about which they are already making a great fuss. If I brought the I.P.C. in they would certainly make the same attacks and I think this would be extremely undesirable, especially in view of the doctrines about its strong Left character.'[59]

The last point was one which cannot have appealed to some of the candidate's colleagues. Here was the idealist singing small to the realist – a charge made with some fervour in the 1930's by members of the Society of Friends, the more radical followers, and many of a liberal-humanist-pacifist complexion. In the context of Derby, Noel-Baker might well have elaborated the tactical advantages of cooperation with the Liberals, though not with Lloyd-George, for him a 'vote-loser' in Coventry's disappointing alliance the previous year. Was there not, too, a strategic need to check the strident excesses of voices belonging to the Independent Labour Party and the Communists? In a word, discretion over international positions was necessary.

Noel-Baker evidently did not feel the importance of a similar degree of circumspection at L.N.U. headquarters. Maxwell Garnett, the Secretary, urged in January 1937 a right to go through I.P.C. files, and to be allowed to see all letters written by other L.N.U. executives. Such a preposterous demand would cut more ground away than had been lost already. There must be 'full-blooded support for the I.P.C. and such an accession of strength was not to be neglected'. Noel-Baker went on with some heat:

'We do need something new to say and a new drive. This you could get out of the I.P.C. and I believe only out of the I.P.C. Depression about the League results principally from the belief that all foreigners are devils. The I.P.C. can show that this is not true . . .'

Warming to the theme he concluded:

'Personally, if we go on with this same atmosphere as we have had in the last three months, I shall soon reach the point where I shall resign from the Union and devote myself to other things.'[60]

A week later, Noel-Baker wrote to Garnett to deplore his unhelpful delaying (the Disarmament Campaign of 1929-30 and the Peace Ballot of 1934 were instanced) though he acknowledged that a reluctant Secretary had gone on nevertheless to work generously and wholeheartedly. Now things were different. Time was being lost. Executive decisions were flouted. The alienation of smaller subscribers was not compensated for by placating the rich. Communist 'lies' must be exposed: the Campaign looked to the promotion of peace, not to the disruption of society. The British National Committee of the I.P.C. (Irene was a member) was progressive in the broadest sense; to oppose it (he also told Murray) would be illogical and divisive. Noel-Baker's reply does not seem to have dispelled the anxieties of Garnett as to the competitive role of the I.P.C. in relation to that of his own organisation. Lord Cecil, to judge from correspondence, was less troubled about the autonomy of a 'Ginger Group' but would prefer it to be 'a semi-autonomous committee of the L.N.U.' and in these circumstances he was prepared to contribute funds from his Nobel Peace Prize.[61]

Most organisations from time to time go through the travails of partisan accusation. On occasion members of the L.N.U. Executive had shaken their heads over the promotion of material they viewed as 'radical'. In October 1934 the dismissal of an official responsible for study circle literature had been called for. Firmness and tolerance should be the mark of the Union, Noel-Baker had assured Gilbert Murray, then a Chairman undecided about the matter, for, as he put it, 'I hate hunting people out of their jobs because of their political views, but it is obvious that the ordinary Communist in this country is ex-hypothesi violently against the League, and I do not see, therefore, how any of them can possibly work for the Union'. In fact, anxieties over radicalism at L.N.U. headquarters were to be felt for a number of years. Again, at the end of 1936, Noel-Baker told Murray that there was evidence of an 'understanding' between Jesuit circles and Italo-German Fascist organisations to attack the I.P.C. because its adherents included numerous well-known Communists. Particularly among L.N.U. members there were Roman Catholics who, while they resented the intolerance of their Church, could not bring themselves to support the Campaign and so the Union in explicit affirmation.[62] Were there not also behind headquarter's desks officials now openly hostile to the Campaign?

At Christmas 1937 matters of division came to a head. Was it merely a coincidence that a sketch at a seasonable staff party had lampooned Robert Cecil and others (including Philip Noel-Baker)? Those such as Maxwell Garnett and John Eppstein, a colleague, were not culpable solely for Hogarthian humour: they were responsible for disloyalty and dissension and should be impeached. The future of the L.N.U. itself was in doubt.[63] Gilbert Murray hastened to quieten the row by soothing the bruised feelings of Robert Cecil and by 'carpeting' the accused. The Executive Committee was aware by now of the tempest aroused and apprehensive that its top officials were pulling in different directions. But would a purge help a broadcloth organisation? Too drastic a cauterising of the wound would force the half-declared intentions of Cecil and Noel-Baker to resign. Murray's instinct and his policy was to parry the thrusts of Noel-Baker's exasperation (fierce letters were received but not always promptly attended to) and to deflect the anxieties of Cecil into discussion as 1938 dawned over the next positive step for L.N.U. promotion, say, a second Peace Ballot or public agitation over His Majesty's Governments' floundering in regard to Spain and to Japanese aggression in China. The whole incident now seems a fierce storm in a quite large teacup although one has to allow for the suspicions and frustrations of Noel-Baker, increasingly alarmed by the impotence of organisations to which he belonged. Cecil is milder mannered, offended certainly, but anxious not to let the indiscretions and inadequacies of an organisations' officers rive its membership, nor blunt the sharpness of what pressure on government it could still bring to bear. Cecil and Murray were surely right to give priority to righting the buoyancy of their organisation rather than to sweeping up the mess occasioned by internal squabble. Murray put it bluntly:

'We are no longer a Peace Party opposing a Jingo Party. We are a 'League of Collective Security' party opposing Pacifists, Isolationists, pro-Germans etc. We are actually for a spirited foreign policy.'

Cecil, three days later, agreed that something must be done about 'serious signs of loss of vitality'.

'Spirited' and 'firm' policies to stand behind an impregnable League were advanced by Noel-Baker, Cecil, and Murray as unfolding events revealed to some the dangers of weak 'appeasement', and to others the risks of military involvement. Members of the L.N.U. Executive showed some adroitness in moving in more than one direction towards associates now plainly adopting differing views as to 'force' and 'peace'. As European decks became awash with a menacing tide of hostility, Cecil stood by his statement of 1923, that persuasion must be substituted for force. Within 10 years, as many questioned his 'realism', he was telling Noel-Baker that 'sacrifices' would be necessary to maintain peace. His country could not afford to lose faith or courage, nor avoid a readiness to stand up to challenged principles. The search for arms control and for disarmament must not be sabotaged by wavering or 'unilateral' disassociation.[65]

For numerous peace groups, financial prospects began to fluctuate coincidentally with the darkening of the European scene. In the autumn and winter of 1937 Noel-Baker, Angell, and Cecil had organised a 'Peace Penny Plan' to secure a plethora of small donations, using the slogan 'A Penny for Everyone and Peace for Us All'. Cecil certainly gave some Nobel Prize money to underwrite organisational costs and he remained confident, as he assured a querulous Honorary President (and Prime Minister) Neville Chamberlain, that the appeal would support two interdependent and mutually respecting groups, the L.N.U. and the I.P.C. Prominent Jews such as the Rothschilds and Sir Montagu Burton were approached. Irene Noel-Baker tried unavailingly to raise cash from the publisher Edward

Hulton, whose weekly *Picture Post* was so graphically and pointedly illumining the course of international affairs. Partly it was a drying up of resources, but largely it was the exigencies of wartime London and the severance of communications with Europe that was to lead to the British National Committee ceasing to function during 1940. The last flickers of controversy were evident in correspondence between the remnant of the international secretariat of the Campaign, then housed in St. Martins Lane (and virtually impoverished) and the Chairman of the British National Committee, A. D. Lindsay, where it was conceded that separatist (and Communist is implied) tendencies had led to suspension of activity, nevertheless, there was room for *ad hoc* movements to collaborate with the L.N.U. There is, though, no clear sign that these suggestions were straightforwardly put into effect.[66]

Very plainly during the autumn of 1938, amid the shame of Munich and near-despair on all sides, Noel-Baker made his position clear in regard to what he saw as 'pacifism' (the distinction earlier in Chapter Four will be recalled, also the change in public position of Viscount Cecil in the May of that year). He appears to have felt more and more worried about the significance of his Vice-Presidency of the National Peace Council. One week before the Munich agreement was signed he wrote to the Council's Secretary of his inability to endorse a letter of theirs to the press:

'The present crisis seems to me so fundamental to the whole future of civilisation that I could not sign any declaration that did not deal with what I regard as the basic problem . . . the letter goes too far towards tacit approval of Chamberlain's main <sic. 'tame'?> surrender to force . . .'[67]

In October, three weeks after the *Wehrmacht* had occupied the Sudetenland in Czechoslovakia, Noel-Baker knew the time for severance had come. He told the National Peace Council:

'The truth is that we have reached a point where nothing can succeed unless we first solve the problem of stopping aggression by collective security and thus establishing the rule of international law. Until this is done, I don't believe in the practicability of any proposals for armament reduction, economic cooperation, the removal of minority grievances, the change of frontiers or anything else. So long as world affairs are dictated by the threat of force, no constructive international cooperation will be taken seriously either by Government or people, and if by a miracle plans were made they would be violated or evaded at once.'

Noel-Baker, obviously and very firmly, had reached the end of the road:

'Since that is my view I am sure you will agree that I ought not to be connected with an organisation which says that it is working for peace which leaves out what I regard as the starting point for peace.'[68]

As one onlooker has expressed it, the national and international peace campaigns were 'a great and gallant effort born too late to exercise any decisive influence upon the main course of events'.[69] Henceforth, the armourers would be taking over from the diplomats.

Throughout 20 years of recurring crisis the volume of criticism of the League of Nations inevitably grew. Just as vocal were the claims of the 'rationalists', among them Noel-Baker and Gilbert Murray, concerned in the words of the last-named to nail the old lie, spread by the Press, that old-style diplomatic methods were to be preferred to League discussion. Tolerance had to take the place of prejudice and narrow nationalism; reluctance and fatalism must give way to readiness and consensus. A recent American commentator still seems to blame the inadequacies of the League *qua* institution more than the irresolution of its members:

'Its dismal failure to take effective action when confronted with Japanese aggression in Manchuria seemed to confirm British doubts about its usefulness in this particular role <viz. conflict resolution> and the disastrous collapse of its efforts to halt Italian aggression in Ethiopia, after the British had played a leading role in instituting economic sanctions to serve that end, was a most disheartening experience.'[70]

That this critic belonged to a nation which failed to support the League may strike some as a telling irony. As a familiar argument since 1931 it was often combatted by Noel-Baker, Cecil and others with the charge that to retire from, admittedly, a disheartening experience without a vigorous insistence on international action was to leave the field open for half-truth, evasion, and demoralisation. In many quarters, eyes were now open to the urgency of firmer conviction and moral leadership. The pity of it is that all too often the ideals and the recommendations remained on the abstract plane and were thus not readily intelligible to common men and rational men. Gilbert Murray, classicist and L.N.U. Chairman was not oblivious of the need to recruit, convince, and lead. By 1935 the theoretical Murray was giving way to the pragmatic and resolute observer of Mussolini's challenge over Abyssinia and to the indications of Hitler's obduracy about the Polish Corridor and the Czech Sudetenland. His Majesty's Government, he told B. H. Liddell Hart, must be consistent about treaty obligations and not wavering or disunited. The letter was written after hearing from Robert Cecil a call for the pre-eminence at all costs of the Covenant of the League of Nations. Vacillation must be contained at the eleventh hour of impending war. 'I believe', exhorted Murray, 'there is material for regaining our lost sheep – especially the more formidable rams among them – by a clear exposition of our own policy and more emphasis on the need for toleration . . .' Murray's cutting edge was reserved for those politically timid creatures he frequently met who embodied, 'the subconscious dislike of the League and all such new-fangled, idealist fads in the mind of the average British Philistine . . .'[71]

There were many in Britain who had hoped that Winston Churchill would provide leadership for those who believed in the League and in defending democracy. Maverick to many Conservatives, Winston Churchill was St. George to those who stood against appeasement. Of recent years there has been re-examination of the shifts in understanding of the term 'appeasement' as it has been used over half a century. One of the latest statements sketches a move between, say, 1865 and 1939 away from:

'a positive policy based upon certain optimistic assumptions about man's inherent reasonableness and the practicability of negotiated settlement towards a negative element of fear and horror of conflict.'[72]

One might perhaps detect something of the shift in the 'classic' approach of Cecil (heir to a great family tradition in this mode) and in the rational-realist humanism of the Quaker Noel-Baker. As the 1930's revealed futility piled upon futility, the lauded perspective of Palmerston became the despised weakness of a Chamberlain administration and 'appeasement' acquired a pejorative sense. Attempts to bestride the diverging paths of an increasingly isolated Right and Centre and an ever-more critical Left helped to crumble the bases of moderate groups such as Focus. A last desperate stand had somehow to be made and Noel-Baker's mail in 1938 and 1939 brought by each post appeals from constituents in Derby and readers of newspapers elsewhere for a united staunchness. Sensing the urgency, Irene Noel-Baker wrote earnestly to Winston Churchill on 16th March 1938:

'16th March 1938 In the Simplon Express to Athens

My dear Winston Churchill,

Your speech on Monday in the House was quite magnificent and is the one hopeful thing that has happened in these last disastrous days. I feel that I must write to thank you for it & to beg you – as *thousands* of men and women now want to beg you – to take up the fight for the League and collective security with *all* the great intelligence and marvellous compelling force that you can give to it. Why must we leave all initiative and courage to the two madmen of Europe?

'You, Ld. Rbt., Eden, Archie Sinclair, Attlee, Alexander, my Philip and Lloyd George are a band of warriors in the House & in the country who surely ought to beat that miserable middle class businessman with no scrap of imagination, who to our immense misfortune is now Prime Minister of Great Britain.

'Wherever I go it is the same story – despair and amazement among the people of every country at the complete feebleness of British policy. And, as you say, this is our last chance, & the people everywhere know it and are passionately longing for us to act. Ask Philip to tell you of my long talk with the conductor on my part of this train – most indicative at this moment & all the conductors-waiters on the train think as he does, he tells me.

'For God's sake lead now and put an end to this most ghastly nightmare in which we are all living.

Most sincerely yours,
Irene Noel-Baker

I *do* hope you agreed to speak in Paris, or if you haven't, you *will*.'[73]

Who, in the wider international scene, would provide leadership in the struggle for peace? Not the United States, isolationist behind its Monroe Doctrine, not France, gripped by Germanophobia and prey to domestic political intrigue. Why not Britain? Noel-Baker's writings in the 1930's advance the case for British initiative and by the spring of 1938 the point is urged hard. *The Manchester Guardian* of 14th March 1938 reported his argument thus:

'What the British Empire and its Dominions should do was to go to Geneva, summon all the 56 nations of the League, work out plans for the prevention of aggression, and at the same time offer the dictators what they had not been offered before – real equality and real justice and help to rid their countries of misery and poverty. If then Germany, Italy and Japan refused to cooperate for the common peace and prosperity they should be told plainly that the other nations with the population of 1,500 million and their absolute command of money and raw materials, would see that peace was kept.'

One week later, this strategy of peace-through-pressure assumed a tactical move of interesting proportions in holding, of course, to understanding and tolerance but reserving the right to use *force majeure* and the advantages of alliance. Noel-Baker, speaking in a Commons debate, saw the government's resolve as proving effective:

'If they were to make a definite, concrete, binding alliance with France, Czechoslovakia, and Russia, they would, as I believe, have a chance by the balance of power, of keeping the peace for a considerable period of time. What we want to do, and what we believe can be done, is to revitalize the Covenant of the League of Nations, to stand against aggression, to stand for law, and to put British power behind it.'[74]

At this point it is important to remember that Noel-Baker was an influential member of the Labour Party. He and Leonard Woolf had worked with great resourcefulness as members of the Party's Advisory Committee on International Questions. With Woolf as Secretary, the Committee saw itself, in its own words, as reporting to Party leaders and helping them 'in the formation of an instructed, coordinated and democratic Foreign Policy – a thing that Great Britain has never yet possessed.[75] To some extent the hold of the Foreign Office might be reduced. Party rank and file might reach a fuller comprehension of foreign and imperial problems. Yet the Committee's influence on the higher echelons on the Labour Party and certainly on the Foreign Office never quite matched the expectations which accompanied its setting up. Membership of the Committee had at least afforded Woolf and Noel-Baker the chance to talk round the table with Ramsay MacDonald, Arthur Henderson, Ernest Bevin, and Philip Snowden. The Committee's task grew more difficult as tensions in Europe increased. We advised, wrote Woolf many years later:

'the Executive Committee and through it the Parliamentary Party by a stream of reports and memoranda, explaining, often intellectually in words of one syllable, complicated situations and problems, warning about approaching crises, continually suggesting ways in which . . . general policy should be applied practically to these situations and problems . . .'[76]

Midway through the 1930's it was obvious that many in the Labour Party and in its Advisory Committee were at odds over the nature of a 'general' foreign policy (as it was termed). The traditional pacifist repudiated any attempt to back the League Covenant with a readiness to employ force: rearmament was inadmissable to them, while, on the other hand, those who held sacrosanct the obligations of the Covenant and of its collective security system put forward arguments for swift and drastic mobilisation of resources to halt further aggression. For a minority of ardent pacifists the dilemma was anguishing though this found scant sympathy in some quarters.[77] Woolf and Noel-Baker had 'bombarded' the leaders of the Party with candid assessments of a deteriorating scenario. For them there was no moral turmoil – rearmament was necessary. In urging a firm stand the two appear less blind than many of their colleagues, to the inconsistency between demands for standing up to the dictators and a refusal to contemplate national rearmament. Articles the two men wrote in the *Political Quarterly*, in *Nation*, and in the *New Statesman* were looking to the resurrection of the League as the only hope for Europe.

Labour, it seems, were so determined to oppose the Government's Defence Estimates until they felt they could approve of its foreign policy, that they virtually ignored the bad impression these tactics were making in the country. Not surprisingly, in the Commons on 21st July 1937, the Parliamentary Labour Party had overruled its Executive and decided to abstain on the vote rather than support the Estimates. It was Hugh Dalton, supported by Philip Noel-Baker, A. V. Alexander, F. Pethick Lawrence, Arthur Greenwood, and by Walter Citrine (a prominent union leader) who repeatedly pressed the Party's Executive Committee to think urgently through its position on rearmament. How could Members affirm the need to preserve democracy if they failed to support a gathering of resources in its defence? Narrowly the prospect of party schism and more glaringly the frailty of members' convictions was averted by a closing of ranks – 'a silent revolution had overtaken the Labour Party'.[78] Yet it was not until the summer of 1938 that the Parliamentary Labour Party could unequivocally endorse Whitehall's arms estimates.

Despite their differences of opinion, Noel-Baker and most others in the leading Labour ranks remained close to the Leader, Clement Attlee and to the Deputy Leader, Arthur Greenwood. There were times when the 'ordinariness' and dogged will of the Leader appeared less attractive to many than the 'cockiness' of such as Herbert Morrison, offering vigour, and oratorical flourish. Morrison had shown great industry and ingenuity in the dire days of 1930-31 by formulating schemes for the advance of national recovery and re-employment. From 1934 to 1940 he devoted formidable energy to the leadership of the London County Council. There seemed every reason why such a courageous and convinced political figure should be groomed for leadership of the Labour Party. Philip Noel-Baker favoured a ruse for finding Morrison a parliamentary seat 'because he was the ablest and best speaker and had a wide range covering not only domestic but foreign policy, too'. Morrison's support for collective security through the League of Nations and his condemnation of armaments was warmly approved by his sponsors.[79]

In contrast, the distance between former colleagues, Philip Noel-Baker and Hugh Dalton had widened. There is no doubt that the latter acknowledged the beliefs and persistence of the other. 'Phil', he remarked in his diary of April 1938, 'has transferred all his eager enthusiasm and credulous optimism from Geneva to the Spanish front . . .' There seems to be meaning, moreover, in the words used. Dalton's own very confident position admitted neither credulity nor over-optimism. Superior political *nous,* as he saw it, was 'good judgement' and Party allegiance all along the line. Noel-Baker's constancy was for him never quite 'reliable' enough. In May 1929, for instance, 'Phil Noel-Baker ran away and did not vote . . . Uncle cursed him soundly'. Two years later, privy to the confidences of others, Dalton had noted that Ramsay MacDonald appeared unready to bring into the Foreign Office, 'Phil who has wonderful knowledge, but perhaps not much judgement'. Nowadays, also, the peace campaigner appeared to be too thick with the Mosleys and others to whom he 'listened'. As for Noel-Baker's view of Dalton, it was 'tinged with regret about a marked degree of shortsightedness in international problems'.[80]

The annexation of Austria by Nazi Germany in 1938 entrenched the division between cynics and idealists, between those who 'wrote off' the League and those who remained hopeful. Noel-Baker, always in close contact with the Secretariat and committee rooms of Geneva certainly preserved his faith though privately he owned to qualms about the future of the League. He was comforted perhaps by a note from Harold Butler in Geneva:

'In spite of the signs of dissatisfaction which appeared during the Council, I am not quite so pessimistic as you seem to be about the future of the League. I believe that we have recently passed the turning point and that the dictatorial powers are beginning to crack . . .'[81]

Viewed across the span of the last 50 years, Butler's judgement from 'the listening-post of Europe' seems astonishing. Noel-Baker, cheered certainly but perhaps not keyed to the same pitch of optimism, arranged some three weeks later a mass I.P.C. lobby of M.P.s. If he had tried without success for two years to get the whole-hearted endorsement of Walter Citrine and the T.U.C., he was determined to lay siege to the minds and conscience of his fellow Members. Four cardinal points were urged. First, the Italian conquest of Abyssinia was not to be recognised as permanent. Secondly, as a consequence, the economy of Italy must receive no financial alleviation from British sources. Third, His Majesty's Government should press for immediate withdrawal of foreign troops and war material from Spain. Lastly, no fundamental change in League policy was to be approved without submitting it to the electorate.[82] The feasibility of the last point is not easy to see clearly.

In regard to Austria, informed opinion looked back to 1922 when a hopelessly impoverished Austria was being left to bankruptcy and social chaos by an inter-Allied conference and the League of Nations Council had stepped in, put together a rescue plan under the leadership of Britain's Arthur Balfour and Edvard Benes of Czechoslovakia, and in almost three years of hard work salvaged both Austria and the credibility of the Genevan institution. The peacefulness of Austria was endangered within 15 years. A sustained barrage of German propaganda amplified the Nazi plan to absorb German-speaking minorities within the Third Reich and for Adolf Hitler it became imperative to incorporate his Austrian homeland. Orchestrated from Berlin and by Nazi sympathisers in Vienna the movement for *Anschluss* gained momentum among elements that were pan-German or anti-Marxist or anti-Semitic. The thrust of the campaign borne forward by German threats and incitements rode over the objections of divided Socialist and nationalist groups. In July 1934 the Austrian Chancellor, Engelbert Dollfuss was assassinated. A *putsch* associated with this deed failed but it was only a temporary respite – the annexation of Austria was to come in 1938.

There was little about the impending disaster in Austria that could be concealed after 1935. Some years previously, in July 1933 and again in February 1934, the British Government had rather mildly communicated to

Berlin their 'serious concern about subversion in Austria'.[83] Whitehall was apprehensive about an Austrian appeal to the League over harassment by Hitler. They had in mind the dangers of arousing German and Italian hostility and, as Noel-Baker recalled, it was considered that representation might be made less provocatively through ambassadors rather than in the open councils of the League.[84] The machinations of Nazi followers in Vienna using explosives, riot, and 'spontaneous' demonstrations were witnessed, for example, in the correspondence that Noel-Baker received from informants in the Austrian Trade Unions and the Austrian Socialist Party. Occasionally, a delegation of Austrians would bring fresh news to Westminster and from time to time there were meetings in London, to pass resolutions and sign petitions protesting about the harsh treatment of Austrians in general and of its Jewish citizens particularly. 'It is no longer possible for a Jew to exist', a Viennese student told Noel-Baker in April 1938. 'The Jewish people are trembling for their lives'.[85] To judge from his filed memoranda, it appears that Noel-Baker had little faith in the protestations of the British Government that the integrity and independence of Austria were honestly and consistently an object of London's foreign policy. More specifically he had concurred earlier in the reckoning of Sir Eric Drummond, the former Secretary General of the League of Nations and now Britain's Ambassador in Rome, that France showed a high degree of concern for Austria, Italy a low degree, and that the United Kingdom was somewhere, never too clearly, in the middle. The most that Whitehall might venture would be some diplomatic pressure on the periphery.[86] This posture might be seen by many as expedient neutrality.

Deserted, it seems, by civilised Europe, the courage and resilience of a once-great capital impressed Noel-Baker strongly. It is interesting that he kept closely in touch for some years with Austrians who had emigrated to London after 1938, though eventually his war-time government commitments were to prevent a continuous association. Five years later he was assuring one of his closest contacts that:

'I should have wanted to revive my vivid memories of the greatness of Socialist Vienna and of the magnificent struggle which your comrades in the Austrian Social Democrat Party made between the wars in the cause of Democracy and freedom . . .'[87]

The spring of 1938 brought intense activity among those concerned with international affairs and among politicians confused by the Central European debacle and the resignation of Anthony Eden. For Noel-Baker the new phase of crisis was a chance to stand up straight for the Covenant, 'wherever and whenever it may be attacked'. The attack on Austria struck against Article X guaranteeing the independence of League members. One reads perhaps an extra significance – the thought is in a letter to Edgar P. Young – that any League policy must take account both of 'absolute justice for all law-abiding minorities' and of the need of a highly developed economic cooperation among members of the League. 'This applies with particular force to the states of Central Europe', was his concluding rejoinder. This was perhaps a recognition that the preservation of democracy depends and clearly depended then upon assured and effective economic underpinning with the corollary that international intervention (or subvention) might be required to further this.[88]

Equally as forthright as Philip Noel-Baker, was Leonard Woolf in March 1938. Hitler's annexation of Austria was going to call for a dramatic change of policy by the Labour Party. The Party's Executive Committee ought to call together Westminster's Labour Members and instruct their leader to state publicly the need of drastic action, even the possibility of entering a coalition government should Winston Churchill be able to form one. There would be a resort to immediate conscription and rearmament. Two catalysts in the process were identified by a group of Labour Party élite meeting hurriedly: A. V. Alexander and 'Phil Noel-Baker'. Unfortunately, Alexander failed to enlist support and the latter was in Paris. 'Nothing was done', Woolf later recorded '– and the herd, Europe and the world, continued downhill all the way . . .'[89]

German troops crossed into Austria on 12th March 1938, pre-empting the results of a plebiscite hastily arranged 48 hours previously when already the columns had begun moving. The amalgamation of institutions in the two states, Germany and Austria, the process of *Gleichschaltung*, was set in train.

Autumn 1938 brought the agreement of Munich after Britain's Prime Minister had paid two visits to assuage Nazi Germany. Was it possible that British public opinion might still do something? It was agreed by the Focus Group that a telegram should be dispatched urgently to Chamberlain, then in Munich, to be signed by representatives of the three political parties and demanding that no further concessions be made. Lady Violet Bonham-Carter and Sir Archibald Sinclair signed on behalf of the Liberal Party. Cecil willingly acquiesced but not Eden, on the grounds that this would be seen as hostile to his government chief. Philip Noel-Baker agreed to represent the Labour Party though the result was an unsatisfactory one, as Lady Bonham-Carter records:

'Attlee, with whom Noel-Baker pleaded urgently, refused to sign without the approval of his party, who were meeting at some watering-place a fortnight hence . . . <The result was predictable, it seems> . . . Leaden despair descended on us as we realised our helplessness; and when we parted there were tears in Winston Churchill's eyes.'[90]

Helplessness was felt also in Geneva by those watching the disintegration taking place there. Axis powers inexorably attacked the League; the democracies steadily abandoned it. Moscow, never consulted in four-power negotiations, withdrew into resentful isolation. Late appeals in several quarters for a preventive alliance of East and West to stop Hitler met little response either from those who feared the Russian component in such an accord, or from those who somehow hoped the League was inextinguishable. Association among Britain, France and the U.S.S.R. was necessary, granted Noel-Baker, but, 'if the League were utterly destroyed, if it were disbanded and broken up, the Labour Party would be compelled by the very logic of events to recreate it.'[91]

The impotence of Britain's democrats was revealed in unsuccessful attempts to prevent the victimisation of the German Jews and to do something tangible for Czech and Austrian refugees. Eugen Spier, the initiator of the Focus Group and himself a refugee, wrote a letter to *The Times* as war loomed, outlining a scheme for mutual transfer to and from the German homeland of Aryans and non-Aryans. Spier felt heartened by the support he received from many directions. Philip Noel-Baker, who was then much concerned with refugees, thought the plan thoroughly sound with no insuperable administrative difficulties. It seemed to him, 'to have the supreme advantage of providing a really strong bargaining point against the present German government. Once Aryan refugees started arriving back in Germany, I believe the expulsion of refugees might cease at once . . .'[92] However, either bureaucratic inertia or political wire-pulling restrained Whitehall from doing anything at all in this regard.

Very typically the trauma of 1938 did not at all discourage Philip Noel-Baker. For much of the time he was an indispensable committee man at the L.N.U., his efforts unstinted for such groups as those concerned with Amendments to Covenant, Covenant Revision, Mandates and Minorities, Disarmament Campaign, International Law, the Future of the L.N.U. Frequently, Irene Noel-Baker took her husband's place on the Executive Committee and on the Administrative Committee. Writers, clergymen, lawyers, admirals, generals were brought in to his working parties. Syllabuses for study circles were drawn up; conferences, lecturers, seminars arranged. He perfected over the year a network of 'lines-out' to Government and Opposition. Legend had it that this fierce upholder of Geneva had tunnelled his way beneath one or two publishing houses in London.[93] Towards the end of 1938 he put thoughts together trenchantly in a memorandum to the International Peace Campaign:

'Many people believe that the events of 1938 have proved that the policy of collective security has failed. I believe that the exact contrary is true. The policy of collective security was tried against Mussolini in 1935-6. It was amply succeeding within the measure of the action taken when sanctions were unhappily called off.

'It was tried at Nyon against the piracy of Franco. It succeeded beyond all hopes.

'It was tried on May 21st when Herr Hitler attempted his first lightning strike against the Czechs. It was tried on September 11th in a statement by the British Government. It prevented Herr Hitler from declaring war in his speech at Nuremberg.

'On September 28th the public opinion of the world had created so strong a combination that many of the best judges believed that Herr Hitler would not have been able to begin a war. On none of these occasions was the policy of collective security more than a pale shadow of what it should have been. It was called in at the last moment, it was used in a hesitating, half-hearted manner, but nonetheless it did not fail.'

For Noel-Baker the argument as to the usefulness and effectiveness of the League depended upon the proposition that any dismal failure resulted from members' irresolution for, as he put it in the same memorandum:

'Unhappily there have been many more numerous occasions when no attempt has been made to use it at all. The result of this abandonment has been the chaos in which the world now finds itself today. There is no hope for peace unless real collective security can be built on the foundations of international law. I still believe that this can be done. I believe it because on September 28th the peoples of the world had spontaneously shown that they were prepared to stand against aggression if their Governments asked them to do so. It is in the public will for real peace that our hopes must lie. Every effort now made to strengthen that will is of inestimable service to the future generations of mankind.'[94]

This judgement would not have been endorsed by many observers of the heightening European drama. Neither the forceful oratory of Maxim Litvinov nor the behind-the-scenes efforts of small and middle-sized powers was sufficient to stem the hastening decline of the League whatever popular agitation may have wished. For F. P. Walters, after all a Deputy Secretary-General, the League 'as guardian of the peace was on its death-bed'. This is a retrospective judgement and we do not know how far the former colleagues might have agreed at the time, he and Noel-Baker. Both of them must have been aware that Britain and France saw negotiation with dictators as achieving more than anything the League could offer. Noel-Baker's informants ought to have convinced him also that neither Austrian government nor people as a whole 'wished to offer forcible resistance to annexation by Germany, nor were any of the other European powers willing to run any risk to prevent it'.[95]

Liberal-minded Europeans at this time were well aware of the dilemmas of Anthony Eden (at any rate the publicly demonstrated ones) while he remained in office – a man schooled in classic traditions of diplomacy, which some critics viewed as archaic, yet by virtue of his experience in Geneva, a man seized of the possibilities of international arbitration and agreement. 'Eden will not be allowed to carry through League policy', Noel-Baker confided to an Oxford friend. Those Tories who had reservations would probably abstain rather than vote against their government.[96] Eden himself, 'symbol of the League' corresponded privately with Noel-Baker, contacts were maintained but too covert an association with Labour's voice in the House would put his own Conservative allegiance in some jeopardy. Labour, anyway, scarcely presented unison on its benches: 'they have cut a miserable figure', wrote J. M. Keynes to his friend Philip Noel-Baker, urging him to speak even more often at Westminster.[97]

As Hitler's demands on Czechoslovakia intensified, it occurred to Noel-Baker that he had to see for himself what was likely to happen in Prague. Asked if he would like to accompany him, Harold Nicolson felt he could not assent, constituency engagements were pressing, and in his own mind there were doubts:

'Naturally I agree absolutely that the domination of Czechoslovakia by the Nazis would mean absolutely the complete control of Germany over Eastern and South-eastern Europe. Naturally, I see that such control would within a terribly short time give them such strategical and economic advantage as would render then the most formidable opponent that we have ever faced in our history. I feel certain, however, that the present Government would not, when it comes to the point, give any firm assurances to the Czechs.'[98]

There must have been the thought in the mind of both correspondents that both in Chamberlain's Cabinet and among the public at large the notion 'not a single British life for Czechoslovakia' would be urged with emphasis. If it were true, as one contemporary observer put it, that in the face of the unequalled brutality and intemperance of Nazi Germany, Anglo-French influence 'was used not to steady that intemperance, but rather to secure capitulation before it' there seemed little that could be done to divert the policy.[99]

Visiting the Czech capital in May 1938, Noel-Baker held talks with Wenzel Jaksch, leader of the Sudeten German Social Democrats. The conversations were to be resumed six months later, when Jaksch might briefly come to London. It seemed plain, as Noel-Baker told Lord Noel-Buxton, that:

'there is no sense in which it can rightly be said that Germany is making an effort for her "co-Nationals" in Czechoslovakia. Sudeten-Germans never have been German nationals and many wars have been fought by the Bohemians to keep them out of the combinations which have now become the German Reich.'[100]

The writer had made the point in the Commons in March 1938, suggesting that an international commission made up of neutrals should be sent to the disputed border.[101] In regard to this visit, some controversy was occasioned by a Mr. Geza Szullo, a member of the Parliament in Prague, who represented the Hungarian minority. Szullo, visiting the Labour Party's London headquarters in May, had then organised a rally at which he affirmed that the British Labour Party was in agreement with the justice of Nazi claims on his country. Szullo went on to accuse Noel-Baker of continued interference in Czech elections, and one outcome was a letter written by Szullo to *The Times* a week later, where the Englishman was said only to visit the Czech Socialist Party and never to mix with minorities other than German. Noel-Baker set out to refute these allegations by stating that Szullo and others had acted impulsively and without authority in misrepresenting the Labour Party attitudes, further, that as a visitor he had been careful to consult with all shades of opinion in Prague.[102]

The situation in Czechoslovakia became ever more dangerous as reports of German troop movements coincided with anxious appeals from informed Czechs, who believed that their British correspondents and visitors wished to make a distinction between those Germans who were anti-democratic Fascists and those who were not.[103] It was important to aid those nationals who were still able to leave their country as refugees and to this end a Czechoslovak committee was organised in London. Wenzel Jaksch wrote frequently from Prague to Noel-Baker soliciting help for those who wished to leave his country, many of them intellectuals from the universities, professional people and Jews. One of the escape routes was through Rumania and a possible destination was Canada. Perhaps, it was suggested, some of the English Quakers might be persuaded to have some of the homeless immigrants? Alec Cadogan at the Foreign Office was the target of an appeal in October 1938 for more visas to be granted and for the families of refugees to be admitted.[104]

There arose in autumn 1938, an outcry over what appeared to be concessions to Nazi Germany in the wake of a hasty visit to Czechoslovakia by Lord Runciman, an emissary-investigator from London. 'After a few weeks of feverish investigation', one description has it, 'under totally abnormal conditions, he produced a report which the British Government chose thenceforth to consider, without any discussion with the country chiefly concerned, as an authoritative basis for the most far-reaching decisions'.[105] It was left to diplomatic conversations in capitals to by-pass the constitutional procedures of the League Council; far-reaching decisions were reached between Whitehall and Berlin at Hitler's mountain retreat of

Berchtesgaden. 'If war is to be averted', the National Council of Labour proclaimed in London, 'and civilisation secured, the peace-loving nations must make an immediate and concerted effort to restore the rule of law'. On Chamberlain's return from Bad Godesberg on 24th September 1938, Labour indignation was voiced by Noel-Baker and others. The British people they pointed out, were bewildered because they had been left deliberately ill-informed and without any strong moral lead. The Prime Minister, according to Clement Attlee, had been the dupe of the dictators.[106] Governmental evasion if not confusion was plain to see. From one of Britain's foremost authorities on eastern Europe, Professor R. W. Seton-Watson, Noel-Baker received confirmation that the four-power Munich Agreement (that is, Germany, Italy, France, the United Kingdom), as interpreted by the draughtsmen charged with 'rectification' of frontiers, was not different from the Godesberg proposals which Neville Chamberlain had rejected as unacceptable and as an ultimatum rather than a memorandum. The Munich Conference of 29th September, called partly at the behest of a Mussolini anxious to placate his fellow-dictator, saved the peace for the time being at the expense of the dismembered entity of Czechoslovakia. Neither the Czechs nor the U.S.S.R. were ever to forget that they were never consulted. The exclusion of the League of Nations and negotiations over the heads of the frightened Czechs was hardly any surprise to those who had been able to draw deductions from the forcefulness and speed of German deployments and obvious inadequacy of any collective response from other powers. Members of the House of Commons on all sides, deplored the secrecy of diplomatic initiatives and the lack of parliamentary discussion.[107]

From Jaksch in Prague came an agonised appeal. If only 'our Allies' would stand beside them! The Czechs were ready to fight! Was it really necessary for their country to resist in isolation (as the editor Wickham Steed feared might happen) and for Prague and other towns to be sacrificed 'to press upon the indifferent world that only such nations <viz. the resisters> have the right to an independent existence'? Despite the contempt of Göring and his like, Czechoslovakia had a splendid cultural inheritance, and to leave it to its fate would be a victory for intolerance everywhere. British attitudes were unlikely to change overnight. Somehow the danger of defeat-in-isolation must be proclaimed. Noel-Baker should not reveal the identity of his informants, but present it as the cry of one (already aged 70) who would feel neither vanquished nor cynical and who felt a need to speak 'to future generations'.[108]

Noel-Baker thought it best to pay another visit to the threatened capital of the Czechs, and President Benes and he discussed the German ultimatums being despatched to Prague. On his return he lost no time in expressing to his host and former associate in Geneva by means of a short note, 'the feeling of shame which we have experienced at the proposals which have been laid before you by the British and French Governments'.[109] There was little optimism among the Czechs that their country would not be overrun. Some last hopes are to be found in a letter from Professor J. B. Kozak, a Czech delegate to the I.P.C., written after Bad Godesberg but before Munich, conveying a sense of being cheered by what appeared to be French and British resolve and praying that Chamberlain might advocate an ultimatum in case of a German attack. He added, 'Even a revival of collective security through the League of Nations seems possible now'.[110] In his reply, Philip Noel-Baker treads realistically and just short of disillusionment in saying, 'I am not yet sure how it is possible to recover from the fearful disaster that we have allowed to occur. My one conviction is that the magnificent Czech people have still a great future before them, and that in no distant time'.[111] Similar feelings were expressed in the House of Commons on 6th October and a day later, Noel-Baker reiterated his concern to Jaksch and to President Benes. 'I want you to know', he asserted, 'that vast numbers of people in this country, and I am certain throughout the world, are feeling bitter shame at what has happened and bitter misery at the sacrifice which the treachery of others has forced upon your gallant people . . .' He had attempted to convince fellow Members that Benes had proved himself the greatest man in Europe, towering over Hitler, like a moral giant beside a despicable dwarf. 'I believe', declared Noel-Baker, 'that in the end Fascism simply cannot triumph . . . the Czechoslovakian republic will live again.'[112]

Straight-speaking questions from Czechoslovakia reached Noel-Baker's desk as Parliament was about to resume in October 1938. First, what was His Majesty's Government going to do to safeguard the self-determination of their menaced land? Secondly, would an association of Britain and other powers agree to underwrite a guarantee against German occupation? Thirdly, what were the chances of international pressure securing an indemnity apropos the German demands for railways, building, and finances in the disputed Sudeten borderland? Fourthly, – and here the question is put in realistic and forlorn terms – how far was the United Kingdom prepared to negotiate with Germany over colonies and access to raw materials and markets if the price at the beginning of the process was the dismemberment of Czechoslovakia? 'Tell the world', was the plea. 'We hope Chamberlain will himself advocate an ultimatum to Germany in case of an attack. Even a survival of collective security through the League of Nations seems possible now'. Tomorrow the British Parliament would meet in a crucial session. 'Stand firm – we are standing firm, too' was the cry from Prague.

As matters came to a head in Whitehall, a firm stand by the British Government appeared less and less likely. Noel-Baker could have inferred from his Czech correspondents and from the knowledgeable assessments, say, of Seton-Watson, that the Runciman Report would be used as justification for rather precipitate ceding of territory. A hope that Hitler might have been prepared to negotiate had he not found Chamberlain irresolute and so 'manageable' was probably unfounded. In a most dramatic sense, the year 1938 saw the end of Czechoslovakia for at least seven years and the beginning of defeat for the League of Nations.[113]

Throughout Europe there was growing concern that the 'Czech question' was being manipulated secretly and hastily in the chancelleries of the major powers. Replies to Noel-Baker's parliamentary questions did not throw much light upon events. 'Was His Majesty's Government consulted by the German and Italian governments about the establishment of a new frontier between Czechoslovakia and Hungary?' The answer was 'No'. 'Is the new frontier between Germany and Czechoslovakia arranged by the International Commission in Berlin in accordance with the provisions of the Munich Agreement?' To this the reply was 'Yes, Sir'. A rather earlier question had sought to prize open the truth of the extent to which the Munich Treaty defined frontiers and embodied guarantees as to the integrity of those frontiers by Great Britain and other powers. Related enquiries looked for an explanation of how far the obligations of the German Reich within the ceded territories were recognised and laid down in print. Ministerial replies rather lamely anticipated further discussions between Germany and the East Europeans, Czechoslovakia, Hungary and Poland.[114]

By way of postscript to the Czechoslovakian affair it is worth recording the attitude of Philip Noel-Baker towards recognition by Britain of Hitler's annexation.

In March 1939 he had argued the case for a *de facto* recognition of the German administration in Czechoslovakia and not a *de jure* one. This does not seem a very satisfactory position from an ethical point of view if such an obligation is judged in relation to Article X of the League Covenant. Member States, under this convention, were required to respect and preserve, that is to say, to defend the territorial integrity and existing political independence of other members. In political terms *(Realpolitik)* this is a far-reaching undertaking. In legal terms (as a recent authority puts it) *de facto* recognition is purely a non-committal formula whereby the recognising state acknowledges that there is a legal *de jure* government which 'ought to possess the powers of sovereignty, though at the time it may be deprived of them' but that there is a *de facto* government 'which is really in possession of them, although the possession may be wrongful or precarious'.[115] In a realistic perspective, foreign governments in 1939 could not avoid the issue of recognition by leaving the situation in a vacuum. Support for witholding recognition as a collective act was contemplated by Noel-Baker and others loyal to the League.[116] Czech emigrés would have given the gesture warm support. In the absence, though, of a moral forum in Geneva or elsewhere, since the League of Nations was being allowed to collapse, it is scarcely disputable that there was any alternative to the sad one of *de facto* recognition of German-occupied Czechoslovakia.

The rape of Poland followed the investment of Czechoslovakia. Ironically, in view of the Western abandonment of the Czechs there was a last-minute attempt, in March 1939, to offer Poland a far-reaching guarantee of assistance in the event of a threat to her independence. Britain, followed by France, reversed a policy of avoiding involvement in eastern Europe, and sought to undertake obligations, so it was declared, in conformity with the League Covenant. More a measure of expediency than of moral resolve the alliance failed both to deter Nazi ambitions and to reduce criticism at home. By September 1939 Europe was at war. The first seven months of the conflict was a period of uneasy quiet, save for the invasion of Finland by a Soviet Union feeling spurned by the Western democracies and menaced by Hitler. Nothing the League of Nations was able to do could prevent the evaporation of confidence in collective security, and in the possibilities of positive, collective action to secure peace.

At the beginning of 1940, Britain's Labour Party, led by Clement Attlee, was asked by Finnish Social Democrats to send a goodwill mission of those who would be able to make known the *extremis* of a small democracy. Citrine was to represent the T.U.C. and Noel-Baker the Parliamentary Labour Party. The two braved an unusually severe winter to travel in discomfort and to see the Front Line for themselves. They were present at the interrogation of starving, demoralised Russian prisoners. They were privileged, too, to be received by the Commander-in-Chief, Marshal Mannerheim, in his schoolroom headquarters and to be able to discuss long and profitably the furnishing of aid from abroad. It seemed a useful exercise to trace a return through Paris to explore French sympathies and there, 'Phil Baker and <Léon> Blum rattled away in French so fast', according to Citrine, 'that my head fairly ached in trying to understand them'.[117] Their reception in Whitehall brought less productive results. Although Lord Halifax, then Foreign Secretary, was able to tell the Cabinet that the visitors to Finland 'evinced the strongest hostility against the Soviet Union', there was little preparedness to go as far as Paris wished. Almost half a century later it is not difficult to appreciate the strategic considerations which put a brake on British involvement in the Winter War, domestically, too, there were political factors which blunted the edge of sympathy for the Finns or, at least scaled down a practical demonstration of it. Citrine, it is true, was straightforward enough to urge Chamberlain to set up a special committee of supply chiefs to speed munitions to the Finns. This was the least he had promised Mannerheim. Noel-Baker did not disguise his anxiety as to the extent of British initiative. 'With one squadron of Hurricane fighters about to be sent to Finland . . .<there was> a certain nervousness on this point in some sections of the Labour Party'.[118] War reporters' despatches, on the other hand, certainly brought a public response in many parts of Britain. The Noel-Baker family were prominent in organising a large-scale relief exercise: Philip and his wife addressed meetings and helped staff collection points, their son Francis and fellow-undergraduates solicited funds in Cambridge market place using as receptacles a Russian trench boot and 'tin hat'. Concerts were organised to raise money.

There seems to have been less sympathy for the Finns among those on the political Far Left. Willie Gallagher, member of the British Communist Party and writer of editorials in the *Daily Worker,* deplored the orchestrated demeaning of the intentions and effectiveness of the Red Army. Gallagher's view of Noel-Baker's mission was plain:

'Philip is a kindly, generous soul, with a Quaker upbringing and a desire to help his fellow men. But he's "nice people" and he has lived his life amongst "nice people", with no real association with the working class.'[120]

German and French forces were poised uncertainly on opposite sides of the Rhine, yet the spring of 1940 brought no end to the months of immobility known as the 'phoney war'. In knowledgeable quarters in London there was a growing feeling that Paris might be 'soft at the centre' and difficult to depend upon. There might be some point in manoeuvring outside the languid government circles in the capital, and to this end Attlee, Dalton and Noel-Baker went to Paris in February 1940 to confer with French socialists. The experience was a depressing one. 'Most of those whom we met', concluded Attlee, 'were either pacifist or defeatist. Leon Blum and Grumbach were the outstanding exceptions'.[121] Political accord, if not alliance was prospected for nearer home. An instance of it about this time is recorded by D. N. Pritt, a well-known Socialist lawyer. The National Executive of the Labour Party had convened a group to attempt a draft of war aims. It was widely felt that such a task, difficult as it surely must be, was something that had to be addressed if the British public, confused by wartime rumours and stalemate, were to grasp the moral imperatives of the struggle. How objective, though, could any political party be? Could the term 'Socialism', for example, be incorporated into the desirable shape of a post-war world? According to Pritt, Noel-Baker had whispered to him in the working party on one occasion that the word 'Socialism' had indeed been left out of the preliminary draft in the hope that Liberals might find themselves able to associate in spirit with the declaration they were seeking to fashion.[122]

May and June 1940 ultimately brought chaos in the Low Countries as German *panzer* forces swept to the English Channel. In a bomb-battered London, political forces regrouped under the indomitable vigour of a new Premier, Winston Churchill. Amid feelings of a nation with its back to the wall, little room was allowed for public expressions of appeasement or fatalism. Yet there are now on record the intentions and tactics of some who thought about a possible negotiated peace with Hitler's Germany. Among this number evidently were David Lloyd George, George Lansbury, C. E. M. Joad, Sydney Silverman, Liddell Hart (surprisingly), and members of the House of Lords, like Lord Allen of Hurtwood, the Astors, and Lord Londonderry. On one occasion in September 1940, Kingsley Martin convened a meeting of the group and the flow of argument convinced those present that an outside political opinion was now necessary to enable the next step to be decided. 'I'll ring up Philip Noel-Baker', Kingsley Martin told Joad. Martin's biographer recounts what happened:

'The others then heard one side of a telephone conversation, a monosyllabic side. Kingsley put the receiver down . . . and he said, "Well, that is really most preposterous. Philip says *of course* we must go on with the war. He says the object should be to restore freedom to Poland, for one thing. We shall *never* be able to do that. I don't see how we can possibly win." Then there was a long pause. And then quite suddenly: "But perhaps he's right after all!"'[123]

Being 'right after all' is an affectation of many pundits; it was not so with Noel-Baker. As a careful observer of what F. P. Walters has termed a parallel process of general political degeneration and 'the ceaseless activity of nationalist diplomacy' he continually pointed out with anxiety, yet moderation, the inevitable outcome of crisis mismanagement.[124] Though he would scarcely have found accord with E. H. Carr on numerous points the two would surely have agreed on one thing: the fateful outcome of renewed crises might have been avoided had there been more rigorous and concerted scrutiny of feasibilities, of possible compromises 'between the utopian conception of a common feeling of right and the realist conception of a mechanical adjustment to a changed equilibrium of forces'.[125] Noel-Baker and others of his ilk were too right and too late.

CHAPTER 6

Noel-Baker in the Ministries 1942-1951

PHILIP NOEL-BAKER returned to Whitehall in 1942 as a junior member of Winston Churchill's Coalition Government. When the war ended three years later, he was to go on to last out the decade as a Minister in Attlee's Labour Administration. At six p.m. on 14th May 1940 the new Prime Minister, Winston Churchill, asked Hugh Dalton whether he would take the Ministry of Economic Warfare. The appointment suited the informed economist – daily conspiracies with the like-minded and confrontations with Whitehall's 'stuffed-shirts' were not displeasing to his ever-present sense of farce. Buoyancy, originality and courage had gained him recognition ahead of his Quaker rival, Philip Noel-Baker but when the latter also joined the Coalition, in 1942, Dalton was anchored in the calmer reaches of the Board of Trade Presidency.

The early war years were times of stress and changing opportunity for anyone in the swirling circles of government service. Chances came and went. Shortly after Churchill came to Downing Street on 10th May 1940, Clement Attlee took Noel-Baker aside to explain that a desirable balance between the political parties placed a limit on the number of Government vacancies. There was, he stressed, no lack of appreciation of his colleague's qualities. Inevitably, some of those who might have been included in a purely Labour administration had to be omitted.[1] For a Labour Party leader a balance had to be maintained between bourgeois and working-class members on promotion. One cannot exclude from the reckoning the influence of personal anecdotes reaching Attlee as to his colleague's 'enthusiasm' (not highly esteemed by Attlee); he may have concurred with the political commentator (an anonymous one) who saw the Member for Derby as too frequently oscillating 'between a mood of buoyant optimism and heavy despair'.[2]

There is another possible explanation of Noel-Baker's missed chance. If Hugh Dalton is to be believed (and allowance has to be made for variations in his impartiality) then Attlee left Noel-Baker out of the Coalition because the younger man was 'too unbalanced in his judgements, increasingly so these last few months'.[3] Dalton's liking for political intrigue at this time emerges in his wartime diary with touches of irony and condescension. He had called on Attlee, then Lord Privy Seal, in mid-December 1940 to make suggestions:

> 'I press the claims of Noel-Baker to any No. 2 job other than the Foreign Office. It would do him great good to get his mind, now soddened with lost hopes, frustration over decades, falsified appreciation of every recent war from Abyssinia through Spain to Finland, and personal relationships gone stale, on to some quite remote Department – either Treasury or, better still perhaps War Office.'[3]

Two months later, Dalton was still ruminating over his scheme:

> 'I speak again <to Attlee> of Noel-Baker, who is getting wispier and wispier, though still very good in many ways, the longer he is left outside. Attlee says he is going to push him for the next suitable vacancy – almost anywhere outside the Foreign Office.'[4]

Noel-Baker's eagerness to enter a government was not rewarded until almost two years had elapsed. He was sure, though, that administrative experience was what he now needed. Cecil was consulted. Ever since 1918, the elder statesman pointed out, his younger friend had acquired that experience in diverse ways, though, granted it had been 'usually that of a lieutenant or under secretary rather than that of a Minister'. Was it not possible for Noel-Baker to keep himself free to continue, somehow, his vital work for peace? This answer probably did little to quell the natural instincts of a rising politician.[5] Although he had been denied office Philip Noel-Baker had been coopted to a number of committees and working parties. He and Leonard Woolf served as secretaries to a sub-committee of the Central Committee on Post-War Reconstruction Problems, chaired by Emanuel Shinwell. Hugh Dalton and Harold Laski were members. Noel-Baker was given the task of reporting to the Party's Annual Conference to meet in London in 1941. Delegates, it was believed, would want not just general statements but concrete, practical planning. Within six months an interim report, *The Old World and the New Society,* was elaborating the prospects of collective security promoted ultimately, as these authorities saw it, by some sort of supra-national body. Neutrality and unilateralism would be obsolete. In retrospect, it is not at all clear how far the transitional difficulties of moving from national to international sovereignty were convincingly examined in print or in discussion. Noel-Baker had been pondering these difficulties for some time.[6] Discussions were going on with

Harold Butler, Leonard Woolf, and Will Arnold-Foster. Resolutions put before the 1942 Labour Party conference, again held in London, bore all the marks of the co-authors, Woolf and Noel-Baker, and were incorporated, two years later, in the Party's pamphlet *The International Post-War Settlement*. Reliance on public opinion influencing the action of states was as strong as ever and just as idealistic. There was perhaps the recognition – it was to grow firmer after 1945 – that the influence of the Great Powers would transcend that of other nations. More weight than in previous decades was now given to what Hugh Dalton termed the coordination of 'Force and Fairness' in the statement:

'Experience shows that, for any period with which we are concerned, pacifism is an unworkable basis of policy. There must be sufficient armed forces readily available and properly organised to prevent any repetition of this bitter experience . . . It is better to have too much armed force than too little . . .'[7]

Noel-Baker, in anticipating these statements to a Conference audience must have had in mind the shuttered halls of Geneva and the need to harness realism where theorising was seldom popular. He had elaborated the theme to a transatlantic audience two months previously. 'We have listened to the realists', he said, 'for 20 years; on every serious issue they have been wrong'. Nansen, he added, had never believed 'realists':

'They were wrong for the narrowest and the meanest reasons; because they thought evil more real than good; because they believed in the folly and cowardice and greed of human beings more than in their courage, their generosity, their love of justice and their common sense.'

Behind the heave to overthrow the dictators was the deep, fervent determination of Britons to fulfil the pledges of the Atlantic Charter. After this war, stronger international institutions must be built.[8]

While Noel-Baker was waiting in the wings, Hugh Dalton felt himself being edged off-stage. He had been accorded a responsibility for setting Europe ablaze with subversive warfare through the Special Operations Executive. This was work much to his heart and he master-minded it creditably though not without incurring hostility in the Services and at the Foreign Office. Within 18 months he was to be leafing gloomily through memoranda on the rationing of clothes and sweets. 'How dreams fade when one wakes', he mused in May 1942. Though, all might not be lost. 'If I went out the right way, I might greatly strengthen my position in the Labour Party'.[9] How long should he stay in Whitehall? On hearing from Irene Noel-Baker that Philip was considering retirement to become a 'publicist' Dalton asserted that it was a 'lousy' life and that only politicians mattered. Noel-Baker and he would be serious aspirants for power at only one more election and the need to help Labour win that contest was pre-eminent. If the chance were lost, 'we should be too old, by the time the next one came, to do much'.[10] Like many other Labour men, Dalton realistically doubted the chances of the Party ever breaking through electorally. Would not their best chance be to join a reformed coalition? Rather than uprooting the Tories, Labour would endeavour to influence and persuade them. Labour M.P.s who were members of Government seem to have been more wholeheartedly behind this position than their backbencher colleagues.

Dreams did not fade for Philip Noel-Baker: he followed Dalton into a sandbagged Whitehall office on 4th February 1942. It was the Ministry of War Transport, set up under Lord Leathers to combine the Ministries of Shipping and Transport. To Dalton, his colleague's appointment seemed an appropriate niche far removed from the Foreign Office. 'It will do him a lot of good', he believed. The Colonial Office had been suggested it seemed, but for Dalton, 'Phil was a bit too viewy for that, as for the Foreign Office'.[11] For Britain the time was a terrible one. Japanese troops swarmed through S.E. Asia. The Mediterranean was now closed to Allied shipping. At sea maritime losses were immense.[12] As Parliamentary Secretary Noel-Baker was detailed to join a section responsible for allocation of ships. It was an extraordinarily complex task. Leathers himself, was vastly experienced in everything to do with marine freight. Forecasts had to be drawn up of the needs of military theatres for weapons and foodstuffs. Available tonnage must be assigned to a careful balance of import and export so that while strategic imperatives came first the obvious importance of sustaining the Home Front was borne in mind. Convoy movements were coordinated through Admiralty liaison.

For three years Noel-Baker laboured on shipping and inland transport, sometimes staying all night at the office and using a camp bed near his desk, often going home through streets ankle deep in broken glass and snaked with fire hoses after an air raid. On occasion the Minister and his aide steered past blitzed ruins on cycles, he wearing a Russian 'tin-hat' (a souvenir from visiting the Finnish front) and she the ministerial steel helmet.[13] He had always been a reasonably methodical worker, quick to grasp detail and he found the programming of ships' movements not uncongenial. Particularly interesting and pleasurable were his consultations with representatives of Allied merchant fleets – Norwegian, French, Belgian, Dutch – for this was work in international relations in the context of coping with constraints and observing, multilingually, a number of rules of thumb. He and his colleagues, a curious assemblage of civil servants, ship owners, lawyers, actuaries and dons, became a community, so the record states:

'conscious of its corporate existence, proud, by the end of the war, of its traditions of six years' standing, and with its own ways of doing things that were often highly unconventional.'[14]

Pragmatism, flexibility, patience (very much the personality of Noel-Baker, indeed) were applied to the insatiable appetites of war theatres and to the task of contriving those other human strategies, the arts of management, for dealing with inter-personal rivalry, ambition, and secrecy to be found among both Service personnel and civilians. It can never have been easy. Again, the record attests that:

'At headquarters in London and often abroad people lived in an atmosphere of perennial crisis: they worked themselves to the bone; there rarely seemed time to reflect on, still less to record on paper, the lessons taught by experience, or even to preserve a proper order among the files or to ensure that functions were not duplicated . . . There was no denying it; no other civil department in the world had so vast and intricate a task, or notwithstanding, a greater record of success.'[15]

From time to time there were involved discussions with Hugh Dalton, in 1942 President of the Board of Trade. In mid-1942 coal needed to be rationed and the Ministry of War Transport was to follow the line of Sir William Beveridge (charged with initiating rationing schemes) that 'rationing is distribution even more than restriction'. A formidable programme of civilian procurement was in prospect.[16] War in the Middle and Far East was leading to a serious shortage of oil and rubber, reducing road transport and aggravating the burden on the railways. Noel-Baker's energies in early 1943 were directed to overseeing the institution of a road haulage scheme, directed from London but with regional transport allocation committees. 'Operation Torch', the invasion of North Africa, was under way and his Ministry could just about manage to deal with the traffic which this immense tactic involved. Adding to the delays and difficulties of inland transport was dislocation from frequent air raids on railway junctions and port installations. Nor was it always certain that Noel-Baker could leave his desk in the evening without a flurry of notes marked 'ATTENTION THIS DAY' from 10 Downing Street. The task might be to reply to an observation or a question, for example, 'The Prime Minister considers that the Ministry of War Transport is showing undue relish in banning the rail transport of flowers' or 'The Prime Minister wants a report on bus queues in London and other cities and on what measures are being taken to reduce them'. In consequence, Noel-Baker had to scrutinise rail tallies and to assemble an overview of road safety measures in the wartime blackout.[17]

In late 1942 and early 1943 the Ministry of War Transport became more closely concerned with Anglo-American collaboration. This was partly the consequence of alliance forged after Pearl Harbour which brought the

United States into the war; it was also the concomitant of importing American supplies under the Lend-Lease Agreement of 1941. Payment for imported arms and raw materials was to be deferred and this necessitated very careful accounting in Whitehall. The summer of 1943 brought some faint signs of a turning in the tide of Allied fortunes. There were victories at Stalingrad, in the Pacific islands, and in North Africa. The major powers meeting in Casablanca, Washington, and Quebec were almost certainly devising the D-Day liberation of Europe. Some future planning on a wider front could be tentatively undertaken. Noel-Baker took part in the preparation of a White Paper outlining schemes for replacing when war ended, the tremendous losses of the British merchant fleet.[18]

On 14th July 1943 Noel-Baker outlined to the House of Commons, proposals agreed between the Government and the General Council of British Shipping. There was, he stated, a national obligation to repay a debt to those in the Merchant Navy who had done so much for the United Kingdom. Three basic principles must underlie the process of restoration, viz., first, that Britain should continue to have a large and efficient merchant fleet, second, that international cooperation was vital, and, third, that merchant seamen deserved the best conditions obtainable. Wars and slumps must never again damage the Merchant Navy. Cooperation among nations must take the place of competitiveness. When the war was over it was hoped to make the sea 'a calling worthy of its loyal and gallant men, and shipping, under Britain's leadership, an instrument of deep and lasting international friendship'.[19] National interdependence would be proclaimed if allied ships wore their national flags at sea. It was perhaps a sign of faith in the future that the autumn of 1944 brought into being, an International Merchant Shipping Agreement where representatives of the British, United States, Belgian, Canadian, Greek, Dutch, Norwegian, and Polish Governments signalled their desire to collaborate in the building and deployment of maritime transport. Noel-Baker had a hand in the preparation of the drafts and, of course, this was work very much to his taste. On 1st November 1944 he laid before Parliament, proposals for the improved training of crews and for the provision of better working conditions at sea.

The war situation changed remarkably with the onset of 1945. Nazi Germany, squeezed remorselessly between West and East, was beginning to make faint peace overtures through Stockholm. The Yalta meeting of the Big Three leaders in February indicated the shape of post-war Europe with its 'modifications' and 'concessions'. Europe's war was over on 8th May 1945. Two weeks later the Coalition Government came to an end as a result of Labour's decision to leave it. On 23rd May 1945 Winston Churchill formed a 'Caretaker' Government which was composed only of Conservatives and National Liberals. The administration lasted a bare seven weeks until Attlee's party swept the country resoundingly in July 1945.

There has been much discussion of the frame of mind in which the new Labour leaders found themselves the day after their sudden accession to power. Programmes for domestic reform in industry, finance, education, distribution of resources, had to be framed in practicable, carefully-costed terms. No longer would vague, eclectic, gradualist aims and methods suffice. It is, though, worth remembering that, apart from the prescriptions of Keynsian advisers, the post-war shape to planning was composed during the period of the wartime coalition when it seemed that some sort of combined administration might be the only possible political solution. Britain's foreign policy must no longer be regarded as diverting attention from issues at home nor could it be left to the persuasions of nationalists, moral rearmers, nor vague internationalists. This was the candid pronouncement of the men at the top of the new administration. Fundamentally, the consensus for progressive government would depend upon an educated sense of reform in Parliament and country and this must oust an essentially passive and negative rejection of 'all that was bad before'. Prime Minister Attlee's first appointments seemed to flesh out the intentions to ameliorate contained in his party's manifesto *Let Us Face the Future*. Ernest Bevin and Herbert Morrison brought vigour and candour respectively to Foreign Office and domestic affairs. Hugh Dalton became Chancellor of the Exchequer. Noel-Baker returned to the Foreign Office he had left a quarter-century previously, this time, as Minister of State. His 14 months there were very much occupied with assisting at the birth of that successor to the League, the United Nations Organisation.[20] He was disappointed not to get a full ministerial post and membership of the Cabinet, but his almost immediate promotion to the Privy Council (unusual for someone not of full ministerial rank) provided some consolation. Later, on 4th October 1946 he moved out of the Foreign Office and across Whitehall to the Air Ministry to be despatched once again to the United Nations, this time wearing a new departmental hat.

The appointment as Secretary of State for Air surprised and upset a number of Philip's Quaker brethren. Was a member of the Society of Friends to have responsibility for the R.A.F.? The new appointee, perhaps by way of explanation, advanced the point that the new post would give him unparalleled experience of the way the Services operated their planning, procurement, and deployment.[21] This would be invaluable information for a 'disarmer' to acquire. A further point of some relevance was that recent

(COURTESY: THE HON. FRANCIS NOEL-BAKER)

Pl. 10. Minister of State, the Foreign Office, 1946

appointments on the 'defence side' of Government were envisaged as holding appointments pending rationalisation of the 'Service Ministries' when Parliament would ratify the merging proposals of a recent White Paper. Thus, the three Service Ministers (War, Air, Admiralty) would be working more closely than hitherto and there would be less 'exclusive' information to be ascertained. These Ministers would not sit in Cabinet but they would be summoned when the agenda needed their presence. They would, of course, constitute the core of the Downing Street Defence Committee. Exclusion from Cabinet was a source of desperate disappointment for Noel-Baker. He had assumed, when agreeing to the post, that he would be a Cabinet member as his predecessor had been. Attlee, most probably inadvertently, and in the flurry of Cabinet changes, had not explained the new arrangement to him.[22]

Noel-Baker was 'doing very well' at the Air Ministry, so Kenneth Younger, his P.P.S. both at the Foreign Office and at the Air Ministry, thought in the New Year of 1947. 'He looks well and seems in good form. He attends many cabinets at the moment so I hope he may be feeling less depressed at this job.' As Minister Noel-Baker was involved in the spring with departmental proposals to be embodied in a National Service Act. Initially, the Government planned to increase the period of military service from one year to 18 months in 1948 and to extend it to two years by September 1950. There was strong opposition to this scheme among the Government's supporters and Ministers were forced to keep the statutory period of enlistment at 12 months 'in the interest of balancing the needs of defence and national economy'. Noel-Baker being no strong militarist, readily accepted this measure. Parliamentary questions about the R.A.F. were handled with authority and his P.P.S. was impressed by this:

'March 1947. The Air Estimates debate was very quiet. Philip made quite a good speech. He also wound up the Defence debate, and certainly made the best speech in any of the service debates. The competition I am bound to say is not very hot. However, I think it has probably done Philip some good in the House and he is quite pleased with himself.'[23]

On another occasion, on 14th May 1947, he deftly anticipated criticism of the way in which the R.A.F. had handled statistics during the 1940 Battle of Britain. The British estimate of 2,692 Luftwaffe aircraft destroyed must now be revised downwards to an actual total of 1,733. 'This retrospective correction of claims', the Minister gently stated, 'which were honestly put forward does nothing to diminish the achievements or dim the glory of the men who fought so bravely against great odds.'[24]

Unhappily, for Kenneth Younger, there was no disguising the fact that he was dissatisfied with the pace and scope of work at the Air Ministry just as he had been at the Foreign Office. He wrote in his diary to this effect in the summer of 1947 and included Philip Noel-Baker in a rather pessimistic observation:

'11th June. Air Ministry work has been almost negligible. I do nothing in the department, and even Philip, I am afraid, is not doing a great deal . . . letting the department run itself. There is no doubt that Philip will have to have a change of work within a year or two if he is to do any good. He cannot be expected to get enthusiastic over a service department with his background of Quakerism and the U.N. . . . but there is no place for him to go except the Dominions Office, which is a backwater. There is a possibility that he might be able to become permanent U.K. representative at the U.N. . . . He would do it well and would enjoy it, but I am not sure whether he would be offered it.'[25]

Though not much seems to have been happening in the ministerial corridors of Adastral House there were things to do elsewhere. Several trips were arranged to R.A.F. stations in West Germany. According to Younger his Minister made 'an excellent impression. Full of life and interest and talked to everyone he met.' A visit to Czechoslovakia saw Noel-Baker greeting his old friends Edvard Benes and Jan Masaryk. There was no hint in their discussions of anything other than confidence in the continued survival of an often-threatened republic. A threat to existence was to become real only eight months later. There was less cordiality in a meeting arranged with the Communist Premier, Klement Gottwald. The Minister first saw it as 'a rather useless formality – what on earth have I to say to him?' The reluctance is understandable given the anti-Communist inclinations of Benes, Masaryk and other contacts in Prague, nevertheless, the interview passed off successfully. Yet another visit was to Yugoslavia, another country undergoing the trials of Stalinist displeasure, indeed, the prospect of a final rift with Moscow was at hand. Marshal Tito received the Englishmen very cordially. 'During the whole visit', commented Younger:

'Philip has been in remarkably good form. So far as I can judge, he has done the business end of the job excellently . . . he had no authority to negotiate but handled the various questions with tact and polish. At the parties he was of course in his element and could never be dragged away from the dance floor.'[26]

By July 1947 the relationship of Noel-Baker and Younger was falling apart it seems. Kenneth Younger put a disconsolate pen to paper:

'There seems little that is worth doing at the Air Ministry . . . Philip isn't sufficiently in the swim to be really well informed except in so far as he sees Cabinet papers . . .'[27]

The criticism then acquires momentum as a private opinion:

'I never seem to get anything of much interest out of him. Indeed much as I like him, I find my respect for him steadily dwindling. He seems to have very little grip on reality. I never want to know his views on current problems because I have no regard for his judgement. He seems to be able to convince himself of practically anything.'[28]

A number of considerations underlie a criticism such as this. An ambitious politician nearing his 40th birthday feels fretful in a backwater, especially if preferences for methodical working are hampered by lack of challenge and evident laxity in the office. Then the year 1947 had been traumatic for Government with crisis after crisis: a harsh winter, fuel shortages, Cabinet reshuffles, a grave balance of payments situation, conflict over nationalisation, dissension over the Downing Street succession – all these alarums served distraction in Whitehall. And, of course, there was an intellectual air about Noel-Baker which he never quite lost.

There were mixed feelings at home, at 12 South Eaton Place, when Noel-Baker received an offer of mere membership of the British delegation to the U.N. Assembly for 1947. Should one accept a U.N. posting, returning to London for consultations, say, every two to three months, or would he be better placed by staying nearer Whitehall? The Foreign Secretary was much occupied in Paris with the American Marshall Plan for European reconstruction and with Soviet attitudes to it, but what sort of offer was it that put Hector McNeil at the head of delegation and an old League hand trailing behind? Cecil's opinion was sought. There had to be a clearing of the air he thought but it would be imprudent, above all politically, to offend an influential (and sensitive) senior minister. For a month Noel-Baker pondered, then on 23rd August 1947 replied to Bevin with, naturally, a copy to the Prime Minister:

'I am afraid I think it would be wrong for me to go to this Assembly under the arrangements you propose. Hector and I have always been close friends. But I think the plan suggested would make difficulties of various kinds. It is nearly 20 years since I was first a delegate for H.M.G. to the Assembly <ie. 1929>; I have dealt with many of the leading men who will be in New York ever since then. Last year, as Secretary of State for Air, I was in charge when you could not be there yourself.'[29]

Most certainly the position of second string would prove embarrassing and strange, and would go far to undermine his influence in the General Assembly and, by implication, his political status should a Government reordering be on the cards. Kenneth Younger had also received an invitation to join the U.K. Delegation that August. For him it would not mean demotion and he readily saw the point of view of his former chief:

'. . . there has been a contretemps over Philip, who was asked to go but not as head of the delegation . . . It was altogether too much to ask Philip to serve under Hector McNeil who was his P.P.S. only two years ago. I think it would have caused comment and embarassment in a milieu where Philip is so very well known. He wouldn't go on those terms and I think he was right.'[30]

What a pity the replacement would be, too, for Younger found McNeil shrewd and competent, certainly, but 'so cynical that there is none of the "lift" which Philip certainly gave, even if he was often wild.'[31]

Two months later, Kenneth Younger finally left his Minister and joined the Home Office as Parliamentary Under Secretary. It had been a long and cordial association and Younger wrote down an appreciation of the man he was leaving:

'He is one of those to whom one feels loyalty and I should have found it difficult to break away without a very good cause . . .'

At the same time he confessed, 'I did not feel I was close enough to Philip to do him much good personally.'[32]

Clement Attlee, in early October 1947, finally made up his mind about a Government reshuffle, reduced his Cabinet slightly, and admitted to it a new Secretary of State for Commonwealth Relations, Philip Noel-Baker. This appointment appeared to Younger from his Home Office vantage post, a much more congenial one for a declared internationalist:

'Philip goes to Commonwealth Relations which now includes India and gives him a seat in the Cabinet. I am delighted about it, and so, I gather is he.'[33]

The three years of the new tenancy were at a time of momentous events in the history of the Commonwealth. Mountbatten had presided over the dissolution of the Raj, assisted at the birth of India and Pakistan, and succeeded in keeping the two 'within the family'. Burma and Ceylon achieved independence, the former giving up its old British association. Territories previously mandated to Britain or to a Dominion, like Tanganyika, Western Samoa, Nauru, South West Africa, British Togoland, were placed under the impartial trusteeship of the United Nations. In south-east Asia, Singapore, Sarawak, Labuan and Penang were given a status which envisaged their transition from colonies to units in a Malaysian Federation (actually achieved in 1963). New Guinea fused with Papua under U.N. trusteeship and British North Borneo relinquished Protectorate status, to link more securely with the Colony of North Borneo. Surveying needs and resources, preparation of inventories and development programmes, consultation with advisers and 'interested parties', conferring in negotiation, visits to 'scheduled territories', attendance at Cabinet, the process of Parliamentary report – all these made the 'C.R.O.' (Commonwealth Relations Office) an exceedingly busy and exciting place of work.

The new Minister also walked into an institution undergoing quite far-reaching structural reform. In July 1947 the Dominions Office, once part of the Colonial Office, was renamed the Commonwealth Relations Office. This institutional reorganisation is an interesting process reflecting the emergence of the Dominions after the first world war when, in 1925, Leo Amery had persuaded Prime Minister Baldwin to hive off Dominions from

Colonies in ministerial terms. One commentator sees the transition of 1947 as 'more than just a change in terminology – it represented, so to speak, a departmental coming of age'. He adds, '19 years later (in 1966), reflecting the continued and rapid evolution of independent nationhood in the Commonwealth, the Department <C.R.O.> was able to absorb its erstwhile progenitor, the Colonial Office'.[34] There had taken place in August 1947 a reform signalling the emergence of newly-independent India and Pakistan. The India Office closed and yielded its functions to the C.R.O. which remained, nevertheless a relatively small department. (Burmese affairs went across to the Foreign Office.)

What might be thought of as foreign affairs aspects of Commonwealth relationships, continued to present some administrative overlap. Nominally, there was reasonable liaison between the 'F.O.' and the 'C.R.O.' given that the major work of the C.R.O. related to Commonwealth constitutional development rather than to external relationships. While this linkage may have facilitated an appreciable exchange of views, it has to be borne in mind that individual members of the Commonwealth were free to pursue their own foreign and defence policies, thus a Minister like Noel-Baker was partly concerned with counselling and with an attempt to reach some measure of coordination where possible. At least one observer has pointed to the difficulty the Foreign Office had, liaison notwithstanding, in recognising any common policies distinct from those of individual members.[35] Again, a Minister had to be careful how he dealt with international bodies. This was made easier when a sub-department of International Relations replaced the twin desks of political and economic affairs. Noel-Baker had to tread warily at home for as a committed 'international organisation man' he faced in Parliament a dilemma put, by one observer, in these terms:

'If they announce their policy to Parliament beforehand, then they will be unable to participate fully in the give-and-take upon which these organisations depend. If they do not, they may be accused of entering into commitments behind the back of Parliament from which it is now too late to withdraw.'[36]

From the point of view of the junior partners in the Commonwealth there was often some resentment that they had been inadequately consulted, for instance, in regard to end-of-war settlements. Henceforth, their sense of autonomy had to be allowed for, indeed, it has been said, 'many found it easier to accept obligations to the U.N. rather than to the British Commonwealth and were anxious to avoid any appearance of 'ganging up'.[37] Matters perhaps came to a head at the end of 1948, when the 'F.O.' requested the right to communicate directly with Commonwealth governments in matters of foreign affairs. While the F.O. regarded this as a reasonable facility, Noel-Baker's C.R.O. viewed it as an unwarranted intrusion into departmental responsibilities. The controversy was referred to Attlee who smoothed ruffled feelings.

It is interesting to look back for a moment to Noel-Baker's earlier involvement with the matter of Commonwealth members' external relations. Already in the 1920s, as Professor of International Relations at the London School of Economics, he was considering the question of how far, as mother country of the Commonwealth (Empire), Britain had a particular role to play in imperial foreign and defence policies. London may have held to this: there was far less assent to the notion of 'indivisibility' in Cape Town and Ottawa and markedly less in Dublin. Noel-Baker was asked in June 1926 to draft an official statement about the matter in time for an Imperial Conference scheduled for October 1926. Under international law, he held, the Empire was a single unit. Constituent members must stick together observing 'a unified foreign policy in different questions as they arise'. The enthusiast for the League regarded the Geneva Protocol as something that would reassure members about matters of security and generally provide a mechanism for reducing conflicts of interest. The complex task of expediting the formulation of policy, would be managed through a Commonwealth Secretariat built up 'on the lines of the League of Nations Secretariat'. Ramsay MacDonald approved of the draft but seems to have been uncertain, as he told Robert Cecil two years later, whether the Dominions could be persuaded 'to think in terms of unity . . .'[38] Twenty years later, of course, Noel-Baker had to reckon with several latter-day developments, first, a disinclination on the part of Commonwealth members to trail passively behind Whitehall, secondly, wariness in many quarters (not least on the part of Noel-Baker) as to the advisability of setting up regional defence pacts, and thirdly, an incidence of 'little Englanderism' in Britain which put in prime place a difficult and costly programme for erecting a Welfare State.[39] Domestic preoccupations were understandable in 1947. There was rationing of meat, bread and potatoes. A harsh winter had grievously affected industrial production and supplies of fuel.

How did his colleagues at the C.R.O. see Noel-Baker as Minister? Lord Garner who worked closely with him as a senior official, has drawn a portrait on full lines:

'Noel-Baker (who) came to the Office after long experience in political and diplomatic life . . . He had limitless compassion, unquenchable faith and courage and inexhaustible energy. Above all he had a great heart. He was an idealist with all the virtues of the pure in heart – but also some of the drawbacks. He reached for the stars, but was not one to calculate nicely and under-rated the art of the possible. Often he appeared to direct his energies over too wide a field of interest. The very sweetness of his nature prevented him from showing the ruthlessness that politics sometimes demanded. He was unfortunate, too, that his passion was for international pacification but that in this field he was over-shadowed by the burly figure of Bevin, of whom he was a great admirer. Noel-Baker did not always show a firm grip on administration or the capacity to give a decisive lead; he pursued his own individualistic line too enthusiastically to be able to make the best use of his staff and, although the blame sometimes lay with others, he did not enjoy the full confidence of his senior advisers. But whatever frustrations his methods may have caused, he was recognized by all as one of the kindest of men and one always inspired by the highest motives.'[40]

What of Noel-Baker's association with the permanent civil servants in his ministry? Another writer throws a revealing light on certain developments:

'Noel-Baker, despite his supposed 'lack of ruthlessness', was one of the few Ministers who succeeded in removing his Permanent Under-Secretary. He had inherited Sir Eric Machtig, who had made no effort to treat India and Pakistan as on a par with the old white dominions, and kept them separated into Divisions B and A respectively. One of Machtig's colleagues has described him as "completely unhelpful" to the Minister. At the end of 1948, after discussions with Sir Edward Bridges, the Head of the Civil Service, and with the Prime Minister, Noel-Baker secured Machtig's removal and replacement by Sir Percivale Liesching, who after earlier service in the Dominions Office had become Permanent Secretary to the Ministry of Food.'[41]

Liesching's arrival improved the allocation of responsibilities, for now the former A and B Divisions were amalgamated. It did not, however, result in departmental harmony – for the new broom, though less autocratic than Machtig, cultivated firm views which precipitated many a head-on clash with the more flexible Quaker. Garner has described the outcome:

'Basically they were not interested in the same things, and each thought that the other did not give him the help that was his due – Noel-Baker was obsessed with the search for a solution in Kashmir which Liesching regarded as futile; Liesching was concerned with the practical job of producing an efficient machine in the Office and resisting F.O. claims; such matters held little interest for Noel-Baker. More seriously they disagreed on the question of colour; Noel-Baker abhorred colour prejudice to an extent which Liesching regarded as unrealistic. Their differences came to a head over the plan for a Federation in Central Africa which Liesching supported and Noel-Baker resisted. Temperamentally they were poles apart – Noel-Baker regarded Liesching as a racialist and thought he was disloyal. Liesching considered Noel-Baker an ineffective busybody and relished repeating a comment that he was an "intellectual mosquito". The partnership did not last more than a year. Noel-Baker always suspected that Liesching influenced his removal. If so, it would be ironic if he removed one P.U.S., only to appoint another who succeeded in removing him!'[42]

Liesching appears to have been adept in 'using' his Minister and very likely monitored to some extent the material that went to Noel-Baker's desk. A point of some significance is that the Minister's unpunctuality must have severely irritated Liesching and others. Colleagues relate how Noel-Baker would frequently give time-without-stint to a caller, regarding the business of that moment as of overwhelming import. Any sporting visitor would gain undivided attention. Such behaviour would be seen as destructive and unprecedented in the offices of Whitehall.[43]

Within two weeks of taking office, Noel-Baker was plunged into a situation in south-east Asia that threatened the whole fabric of Commonwealth relations. India and Pakistan, new Dominions formed when India was divided, were at each other's throats. Twelve months earlier, a three-man Cabinet mission sent out by Attlee, had had to wrestle with the separatist instincts of Mohammed Ali Jinnah's Muslims, the conservatism of the India Office in London, and with the protectionist interests of Hindus towards their dispersed minorities in Kashmir, Hyderabad, and other princely states. Mountbatten, in March 1947 had been given the task of bringing about independence for the separating halves of India, by using compromise and a perilous containment of violence both latent and explicit. Within 12 weeks a partition plan had been hammered out, and amid a welter of charge and counter-charge, the India Independence Bill was rushed through both Houses of Parliament in July 1947. There was an element of haste in the British Government's intention to bring about independence as soon as possible. The laconic minute from Attlee in June 1947 – 'Accept Viceroy's proposal' reflected the unwavering firmness of a Prime Minister who had been a very useful member of the India Round Table Commission before the war. Attlee was determined to push ahead and in this respect Noel-Baker, his Secretary of State three months later, could have no other option than to follow 10 Downing Street to the letter.[44] The day's telegrams from Delhi indicated the danger of delay – they reported the suspicions of the Muslims that Britain was indifferent to them, they evinced the impatience of Jawaharlal Nehru with slow moving discussions at the United Nations, partly 'an American racket' as he wrathfully observed on one occasion. Mountbatten himself was realistic. 'If the Viceroy had not transferred power when he did', records his biographer, 'there could well have been no power to transfer.'[45]

A quarrel over the princely state of Kashmir was destined to bring feelings to boiling point in Delhi and Karachi. Largely a Muslim state with a Hindu ruler, Kashmir was almost surrounded by what was to become Pakistan. The indecisive Maharajah procrastinated during the summer of 1947, delaying an accession to Pakistan which might have found favour in most places, even reluctantly among the Congress Party. As the new Secretary of State took up his post the reports of impatience in the sub-continent were ominous. A plebiscite seemed the only way to prevent intervention from outside. The United Nations, Mountbatten thought, should supervise the plebiscite, possibly despatching a peace-keeping contingent. Nehru wanted to persuade Mountbatten to legitimise a temporary accession to India, and so make an Indian 'armed rescue' possible; Jinnah, autocratic and suspicious, saw this eventuality as an unjustified seizure of territory. Noel-Baker, though anxious about the heated debate in the two Dominions, was naturally most anxious to facilitate the Indian presentation of the case in New York.

There was a chance to show that the United Nations machinery really could work, and the Minister embarked at Southampton in the 'Queen Elizabeth' along with a team of advisers. Three months of torrid debate and mounting piles of paper convinced not only conservatives that a solution by consensus was nowhere in sight by Easter 1948. Britain was prevaricating in New York, too, in some views, and this, Kingsley Martin told Mountbatten in February 1948, reflected the personality of Philip Noel-Baker, an intelligent and charming man, but 'on matters of high policy weak as water'.[46] Mountbatten (now formally Governor-General of India and not Viceroy) replied that Britain's irresolution might only encourage Muslim irridentism and according to his biographer, went on to declare:

'it must be made clear to Noel-Baker that the British attitude was "endangering the whole structure of good will between Britain and India". He had already done his bit to bring enlightenment to the errant Noel-Baker by giving a visiting junior minister, Patrick Gordon-Walker, a brief prepared by his staff extremely critical of British policy towards Kashmir. Noel-Baker was offended and asked Ismay (later Lord Ismay) to warn Mountbatten that this was a most improper way for a constitutional Governor-General to behave.'

However, relations between Minister and Governor-General were not soured and the latter typically seems scarcely to have noticed the rebuke.[47]

Attlee instructed Noel-Baker to take urgent measures to resolve the Kashmir dispute by direct representation in New York, or behind the scenes, even if it were to take several months. The redoubtable 'Pug' Ismay, who already had first-hand knowledge of the situation at Srinagar, was recruited to the Minister's staff. Noel-Baker, an admirer and friend of Nehru, was anxious to strive for objective resolution but felt constrained to try to be fair towards Pakistan, such was the fatalism of London and the stone-walling of Delhi. Ministerial neutrality was not easy when telegrams flooding across the Atlantic showed the C.R.O., of course, responsible for equable relations with two dissenting parties looking for progress, while the Foreign Office rather self-consciously played for time as instructions were sent to the United Kingdom delegation. Lord Garner, a close observer of the goings-on, has described it thus:

'The differences between the F.O. and C.R.O. came to a head in New York when Noel-Baker was constantly pressing for action in the Security Council which Cadogan sought to postpone or avoid altogether. In the list of those who laboured in search of a solution, special tribute must be paid to Noel-Baker who devoted his energies with passion to the problem and on more than one occasion felt, thanks to his close collaboration with Bajpai <of India> that he was on the point of reaching a settlement.'

Garner adds to this comment a final sentence, whose meaning is not clear and one which would have disconcerted his chief, namely that the Minister's intense 'and successful efforts to associate the U.N. with the principles of a possible settlement by plebiscite, eliminated any slender chance of reaching an agreement by negotiation'.[48] Face-to-face discussion between the contending parties seemed particularly difficult to bring about on both sides of the Atlantic. Rapid demoralisation was in prospect. Noel-Baker's message to Attlee in March 1948, declaring that only a 'summit conference' of three days or so could bring about a breakthrough, was despatched, seemingly by a Minister run off his feet and frustrated at having to 'pick up the bits' of a never-ending dispute.[49] Yet, as he well knew, the process of U.N. consideration must take its course since the matter had been referred formally to them.

In July 1949 Noel-Baker went down to the House of Commons. No Minister, however isolated, worn, and baffled he may be, can fling away the political card of confidence. His statement must have disguised feelings of failure and gave no hint of discomfiture at lack of support in Whitehall, of disagreement with Machtig in his department, or of insufficient liaison between Delhi and London. Referring to the contestants he said:

'I am confident that both Governments still desire that the matter shall be settled by the inhabitants in a plebiscite conducted under free and fair conditions. His Majesty's Government have always believed that the Kashmir dispute could best be settled by such a plebiscite, and that in this way an early solution of the problem can be found, which will in future be accepted as just and lasting by the peoples of India and Pakistan.'[50]

In retrospect, it is arguable that Noel-Baker, the idealist, found it difficult to reach the point where the realist attempts to square arguments. Apart from his own dejection, the Kashmir issue remained unresolved and some 20 years of squabble and of military foray by India were to ensue.

The political bones of contention in the Indian sub-continent were clear enough: another source of division was the constitutional question of whether India and Pakistan could remain within the Commonwealth. Was it possible for India to accept any longer, the traditional doctrine of unity 'in common allegience to the Crown'? It was known that Pandit Nehru and most of the Indian Congress Party were thinking to begin with in terms of secession although Nehru through 1948 and early 1949 was considering the retention in some institutional manner of the principle (and the advantages) of 'free association' with other Commonwealth nations. London, too, was willing to explore the possibilities of modified membership for a new republic within a former imperial unit.

A rupture with the Commonwealth appeared to Indian leaders to be undesirable if it led to a countervailing strengthening of Pakistan. The issue was to be tabled at the Commonwealth Prime Minister's Conference scheduled for April 1949. Intensive diplomatic footwork took place some months before this, and emissaries were despatched to Commonwealth governments to take soundings. Patrick Gordon-Walker, the Under Secretary at the C.R.O., found himself being sent to Delhi, Karachi, and Colombo about the same time (November 1948) that the Indian Premier was formally requesting His Majesty's Government, that a republican India be entitled to remain within the Commonwealth. Noel-Baker, as the Minister responsible, had done his best to accommodate the varying views of nationalist leaders, conservative British politicians, and cautious constitutional lawyers. Attlee's Cabinet had already set up a Commonwealth Affairs Committee, which conducted long and not always harmonious meetings at Downing Street. Ernest Bevin put to this Committee in January 1949, the readiness of the Foreign Office to release India from Commonwealth membership and to allow them 'most-favoured nation' status, their ambassador working closely with Whitehall. Others attacked him for this – Attlee, and Cripps, with first-hand experience of 'the Raj connection' regretted such severance and, according to one observer, 'Noel-Baker gave a child's guide lecture on the Commonwealth.'[51]

In the view of one recent historian, Noel-Baker's ways of dealing with a difficult and fast-changing situation did not always find favour among his colleagues:

'Noel-Baker's activities at the U.N. had threatened the prospects of keeping India in the Commonwealth. India had raised the question of Kashmir at the Security Council, and Noel-Baker sponsored a resolution calling on both India and Pakistan to agree to a referendum of the people of the state. This was acceptable to both parties, but there was no mention in Noel-Baker's draft resolution of the need for the prior withdrawal of the raiders from the North West frontier. The Commonwealth Affairs Committee realised the dangers of this: Cripps even thought it would cause India to leave the Commonwealth at once. Attlee himself was annoyed that the resolution was being put forward without the Whitehall committee being consulted; he spoke sharply to Noel-Baker on the transatlantic telephone in order to get its terms altered. As Gordon-Walker put it in his diary, Noel-Baker's desire to execute an exercise in abstract peace-making came near to wrecking the Commonwealth.'[52]

Commonwealth Prime Ministers reached agreement later in 1949. India as a 'sovereign independent republic' would recognise the King as 'Head of the Commonwealth' (Gordon-Walker laid claim to originating the title) and would continue to be a full member. Alienation had been averted. The new relationship (an abstract device to some eyes) recognised a changed and idealised concept of Commonwealth.

Not all the papers arriving on Noel-Baker's desk related to high-level issues. In September 1948 the Prime Minister noted that he had been approached by the M.C.C., suggesting a cricket match between India and Pakistan at Lords. But would rival Dominions consent to field their elevens? Sports enthusiast and idealist though he was, Noel-Baker thought it unlikely at that moment that agreement could be reached on representation or finance. The match, indeed, never took place and the Indian Dominions later played England at Test and invitation matches separately.[53] Sports affairs took up quite a proportion of Noel-Baker's time with preparations for the first post-war Olympics scheduled for London. It seemed appropriate for a Minister preoccupied with overseas affairs to effect liaison with the Olympic Organising Committee. Only three years were allowed to arrange for an event attracting over 4,000 competitors from 59 countries. Here was an opportunity to engage the minds of people in cooperative activities and to release them from the recent trauma of conflict and fear. Working parties, long-distance telephone communications, visits of inspection to Wembley Stadium kept the Minister away from his office. But it had been worth it he wrote:

'The Games are not a faked antique – they answer something universal and eternal in the human heart, something which very visibly has touched the athletes and nations of the world . . . the flame is out but the Olympic spirit lingers and it leaves us a vision and a hope!'[54]

Also in 1948 there took place the Berlin Airlift, a knife-edge confrontation between East and West which occupied ministers' minds a great deal. Herbert Morrison links Philip Noel-Baker with the original ideas as to the feasibility of supplying the beleagured Berliners:

'My recollection is that the idea of the <Berlin> airlift originated with Philip Noel-Baker, who was confident that the job could be done . . . Noel-Baker had never forgotten the inspiration Henderson had given him to work for peace and the League. His idea of an airlift was not regarded as practical at first. However, as a possible solution of a seemingly insoluble problem it was put to the Americans. And, of course, it was a triumphant success – one up to Philip Noel-Baker.'[55]

This attribution is a most unlikely one. The main impetus for putting what was already operational practice into higher gear, probably came from the interface between military government contingency planning and the

Foreign Office in a whole series of informal discussions at different levels and over a period of some months. It would not be fair to give the credit for the notion to any one person. Noel-Baker, of course, would have been aware of discussions in the Cabinet Room and may himself have elaborated the idea in an unminuted moment, perhaps in the corridor outside. Bevin was unwaveringly in favour of the operation and one may speculate as to whether Herbert Morrison, who detested Bevin, displaced the credit not too skilfully.[56]

Altogether, the year 1948 was not an easy one for Commonwealth relations. Apart from the Indo-Pakistan quarrel there was another constitutional crisis over the future of Newfoundland. That island's pre-war financial difficulties had led to its constitution being suspended. In 1946, with an improving economy, review of the situation was desirable. Would not Newfoundland, sparsely peopled and rather deficient in resources, gain from federation with her Canadian neighbour? Ottawa was disposed to ignore an inconclusive referendum organised by islanders. However, a vocal group of Newfoundlanders succeeded in asserting a claim to independence and found a London champion in A. P. Herbert, vigorous parliamentarian (an Independent Member) and writer. Petitions were organised to the Houses of Parliament and to the Judicial Committee of the Privy Council. Herbert, for his part, deplored Westminster's interpretation of an island referendum which showed 78,000 favouring confederation and 71,000 wanting independence, for he doubted very much whether valid generalisations from those figures were possible. Herbert was affronted, so it is written, by Noel-Baker's refusal to receive a delegation representing the island's interests. He had, it seems, to 'slip a remark' to Attlee over lunch, and a hint, if not a command, from 10 Downing Street appeared to have changed the Minister's mind. It may have been a coincidence that the delegation was invited into the office a day or two later.[57] Notwithstanding this gesture, the objective of the independence group was not attained and Canadian federation won the day. Had local autonomy been steam-rollered by an intolerant Minister, despite his reputation for tolerance?[58] Noel-Baker spoke to the British North America Bill on 2nd March 1949, 'pale and precise', the speech '. . . an extremely clear and competent and conciliatory speech . . .' Federation was urged, the feasibility of appeal apparently dismissed. The Minister, in Herbert's eyes, 'became a little waspish and was evidently determined to rub my nose in it'. 'Mr. Herbert', he proclaimed, 'had shown a certain bias against Canada. The Third Reading went through, as expected, without a division'. Afterwards in the corridor Noel-Baker and Herbert smiled together: 'Thank God, that's over'. 'I expect', concludes the vanquished but unabashed Member, 'they had a happy bonfire of files and papers in the office of Commonwealth Relations. No more bother with Newfoundland.'[59]

Another affair, part-constitutional, part-political was to dog Noel-Baker's footsteps in his last four months in office. The case of Seretse Khama brought a shower of odium upon the Labour Government and, in particular, upon Patrick Gordon-Walker, Noel-Baker's successor from March 1950. Critics on all sides of the House and throughout the country held neither Minister free of hypocrisy and double-dealing. In September 1948 Seretse Khama, son of the ruler of Bechuanaland (now Botswana) married an Englishwoman, Ruth Williams, and went on to complete his studies in London while his uncle Tshekedi Khama was acting as Regent. Tshekedi opposed the marriage and managed to rally the Bamangwato tribesmen to his side. The High Commissioner of what was then a 'Trust Territory' recommended to London that Seretse should not be recognised as Chief. A judicial enquiry following his report agreed.

A general assembly of the tribe accepted Seretse and his white wife after all and dismissed continuation of Tshekedi's rule. Which way was London to turn? If they implemented the official recommendations from the Territory they would incite hostility, at least in Bechuanaland and inflame liberal opinion in Britain. Leniency towards Seretse, on the other hand, would incur the wrath of Cape Town's new Nationalist Government, succeeding in 1948 the more liberal regime of Smuts and endanger vital economic and defence links. Noel-Baker's first impulse had been to agree with the recommendations but the issue could not be left at that. He had better invite the young Seretse to London in New Year 1950 to discuss 'the future administration of the Bamangwato' and to see whether 'a further attempt might be made to persuade him to relinquish voluntarily his claim to the Chieftainship'.[60] Seretse accepted the invitation and flew to London, without Ruth his wife in mid-February 1950. Noel-Baker and his predecessor Viscount Addison, now Lord Privy Seal, both urged their visitor to renounce his chieftainship claim, indeed, to leave Bechuanaland. Addison added that direct British rule over the reserve was probably the best solution. Seretse suspected the worst. His actions then gravely embarassed Noel-Baker whose resolve may not have been too firm. The London Press was told on 7th March 1950 by an outraged Seretse, that he felt himself tricked and double-crossed. His Majesty's Government had offered him £1,100 a year tax-free to relinquish the succession claim and to reside in England. This had been rejected out of hand. The Minister, he felt, had been secretive and asked his visitor not to go to the Press. Was Noel-Baker, if not devious, too timid over the Khama issue? The evidence is inconclusive. London, of course, had to reckon with the attitudes towards miscegenation of South Africa and Southern Rhodesia and with the likelihood that if Seretse and Ruth were installed in Serowe, the capital, that Cape Town would demand incorporation of an 'unstable' Bechuanaland and even threaten blockade. It is not clear how far the Minister accurately assessed the views of Central African white settlers. He may have underestimated the degree to which their discomforture and hostility, might prove more damaging to the lands north of the Cape than anything the South African Government might do. Certainly, some of his advisers would have advised caution and it seems significant that Whitehall neglected to publish much in the way of explicit policy and accompanying documentation. Doubtless worn down by worry, Philip Noel-Baker fell suddenly ill and his Under-Secretary, P. Gordon-Walker succeeded on 1st March 1950. The unresolved Khama problem fell flaming into his lap.

Only as M.P. was Noel-Baker further involved with Bechuanaland. He cannot have been happy at Gordon-Walker's more brutal approach of banishment (initially for 10 years) for Seretse, and it is almost certain that he would never have agreed to it. His ears must have burned listening to the Liberal censure motion of 8th March 1950 and when he read the smooth, official denial of South African pressure in a following White Paper.[61] For well over a year both Houses considered the matter from time to time. It was to go on to a vote of confidence on 26th January 1951 when the Liberals called for rescission of the banishment order. Things might have been simpler and more justice secured, they said, if Noel-Baker and Gordon-Walker had paid more attention to what looked like a restriction of human liberty and, organisationally, had been able to fuse to a greater extent the supervisory functions of two ministries, that of Commonwealth Relations and of the Colonial Office. A narrow majority disposed of the Liberal motion and Noel-Baker was one of those who voted against it. A mid-summer debate in the House of Lords actually brought a two-to-one defeat for the Government. It was notable for a remark from Lord Harlech, a former Secretary of State for the Colonies and High Commissioner in South Africa, that the way in which Philip Noel-Baker and Patrick Gordon-Walker 'have personally treated Tshekedi is one of the blackest spots in the history of the treatment of the African people . . .'[62]

A happier phase of Noel-Baker's last days at the C.R.O. was the furtherance of positive relations in South East Asia. The ending of war in 1945, had been followed by a period of post-colonial break-up, with nationalist forces challenging and overthrowing the suzerainty of Britain and the Netherlands. Ceylon and Burma had achieved independence. Several thrusts to British policy were evident at this time in respect of south-east Asia. One might be thought of as politico-economic in that it sought to restore 'viability', as it was termed, to territories shattered in war and to restore the foundations of internal and external trade, agricultural and industrial production. If there was a moral imperative here, it was puny alongside the dictates of British self-interest and wider economic criteria. During 1948 and 1949 the Finance and Foreign Ministers of the Commonwealth had conceded the need to act mutually to plug gaps in a world of falling gold and dollar reserves and scarce raw materials. When the Labour Party in January 1950 detected 'a new confidence and a new energy (are) springing up throughout Britain's territories overseas', the Government knew that it must be planned and exported from London.

In the second place, an overall design for regional development depended crucially upon coordination of resource. Noel-Baker, as Minister, was thus playing a key role in bringing about consultation and planning between nine or so different Dominions. This called for constitutional sleight of hand and it was not inappropriate that the Secretary of State at the C.R.O. was author of *The Juridicial Status of the British Dominions in International Law* some 18 years earlier.

An over-arching concern for the economist and the politician, the third impulse, was strategic. 'Some kind of regional security arrangement' was what Bevin was looking for. Noel-Baker, naturally, subscribed to the concept of shared security. If, in the eyes of ministers, the solidity of S.E. Asia had to be buttressed, if instability (in Malaya, Indonesia, Borneo) must be contained, if Communist penetration of former dependent territories were to be limited – and all these factors made for a maintained communal peace – then a bloc had to be built, partly economic, partly defensive. An intangible successor to imperium would not do. Something like the Marshall Plan might offer positive encouragement by offering technical assistance, capital aid, and improved living standards. Military alliance on the lines of N.A.T.O. would be seen by Nehru and other nationalists as aimed at restoring Western power – there would be a shape of finality about it, although Noel-Baker had told the Commons in May 1949 that the pact was only a stop-gap until a real collective security arrangement was achieved. A possible model for Bevin was the Point IV collective assistance plan launched by President Truman in December 1948 and which had struck the Englishman as an imaginative, well-ordered scheme for 'collective benefit'.[63]

Colombo in Ceylon was scheduled to be the meeting place for the conference on south-east Asia. Bevin's heart was troubling him sorely and there was doubt whether the Foreign Secretary was up to a long journey by cruiser in December 1949. As ever, he was determined to trample over obstacles to achieve a worthwhile planned objective, and on arrival a press conference showed both Bevin and Noel-Baker 'groping for something to put flesh on the bones'.[64] As expected, Bevin 'did most of the talking for the British delegation and Noel-Baker . . . very little'.[65] Indeed, Noel-Baker was having to push his Prime Minister into recognising his standing at times. In April 1949 he had written a rather blunt note to 10 Downing Street declaring that when C.R.O. business came before the House it was he, as the Minister concerned, who should speak to it and not Herbert Morrison, deputising for Attlee.[66] Six months later he had to press Attlee that the responsible Minister should accompany Bevin to Colombo for 'it would really be derogatory to the office which I hold, if a meeting of this kind took place without my being present'.[67] There would also be a further opportunity for him to visit India and Pakistan. One wonders why Attlee needed an approach in this way. The outcome of the Conference was a programme of economic assistance, the Colombo Plan, envisaging a total spending of over £1,800 million, to be translated into action through collaboration between newly independent Asian nations and the older ones of European-settler origin. For Noel-Baker the auspicious launch of a collective programme to aid the peoples of South-east Asia was an exercise in planning and in the application of generosity, wisdom, and tolerance. As he told a special convocation of Queens University, Ontario in October 1949 (he was receiving an honorary Ll.D.), the Commonwealth had still to reach its full stature of greatness in world affairs. What they had achieved in unison, other nations in the world could do together in the United Nations.[68] He had spoken in similar vein on 12th January 1950 when the University of Ceylon had awarded him a honorary degree of Doctor of Laws.

On 28th February 1950 Philip Noel-Baker succeeded Hugh Gaitskell as Minister of Fuel and Power. This appointment meant leaving the Cabinet, a move that looked like relegation if it was not rejection. 'He has not advanced his reputation', Attlee said of the new appointee, 'he was talkative but not illuminating in Cabinet'.[69] 'Poor Philip N.B. has got pushed out of the Cabinet', Kenneth Younger wrote, '– it was only after much coming and going that he was offered Fuel and Power where he has now gone. He is of course much upset.'

Younger, by this time, had succeeded to the Minister of State, responsibilities previously exercised by Noel-Baker, with the difference that an ailing Foreign Secretary was forced to delegate much more important work to his assistants. The diary entries are now candid about his former chief:

> 'I cannot blame the P.M. for not wanting him in the Cabinet. I myself never really want to know his views on difficult problems. There is something unreal about his whole personality and process of thought.'[70]

(COURTESY: PAUL POPPER LTD.)

Pl. 11. As Minister of Fuel and Power Noel-Baker tears up petrol coupons, 1950 – petrol rationing ends

Within the Labour Party there was controversy over the timetable for nationalisation of the country's fuel resources. The terrible winter of 1946-47 had led to a grave shortage of coal, had bogged down rail and road transport, and crippled electricity power stations. Ministers grappling with domestic obstacles to a planned economy were aware of the grim international significance of decimated export trading and 'a run on the pound'. A new Minister at 'F. and P.' had to work with colleagues minded to compromise with a call for all-out nationalisation of steel, gas and transport for instance, in the reckoning that the State must collaborate with private employers. The euphoria that followed the 1945 electoral victory gave way to grudging realisation that the pace of legislation would be slow. At each Party Conference and, indeed, in many committees, Ministers, wearied by long hours and innumerable tasks, had to face querulous criticism from both Left and Right flanks of the Government's supporters. The Government itself was balanced on a knife-edge parliamentary majority of six after the election of February 1950. Those further away from Ministerial corridors found it difficult to understand – to take one example – why, when Government passed the Iron and Steel Act in the 1949 session, it then took well over a year to reach the vesting date of 15th February 1951 and a further two years to set up (via one more Act) an Iron and Steel Board. There was little doubt that party followers, possibly some ministers, underestimated the technological and financial difficulties of consolidating an idealogical approach. Less consideration than was necessary had been given to ways in which structures of public management would take over from and develop out of the conventional hierarchies of the private sector. Hugh Dalton, some years later, looking back with pessimism at this point saw the 'Forceful Forties' giving way to the 'Fading Fifties'.[71]

Apart from domestic controversies, Noel-Baker faced the contentious issue of economic cooperation with other European countries. Proposals coming from Paris were presented to London in May 1950 after a rather brief period of discussion. What was proposed was an international authority to control West European coal and steel, in the French view it would be an authority exercising real power over member countries, and not just another institutionalising of inter-government collaboration. The authors of the plan, Jean Monnet and Robert Schuman, saw political advantages where Britain more readily recognised benefits to the economy. Attlee already in mid-June, was warning the House of Commons that Paris envisaged a supra-national entity whose decisions would be binding, consequently, His Majesty's Government would be forced to reject the French proposals. Labour Members, two weeks later, rebuffed an Opposition charge of faintheartedness, and called for Ministers to press for a planned inter-government programme of resource management, for 'positive, imaginative British proposals as alternatives to the unacceptable plans put forward by the French'.[72] There are some indications that feelings within the Cabinet and perhaps among some Members, were beginning to ride over initial emotional reservations. The movement for closer economic ties (on the plane of economic commonsense) was a slow one. Noel-Baker, in October 1950, clearly thought that a cautious allusion to struggle and valour and resilience, even an admission of some impeded progress, was the right note to strike in addressing the populace. In the course of his presidential address to the Labour Party assembled at Margate, he said:

'We know and the nation knows that a hard struggle lies ahead. But thanks to our controls, to our nationalisation of finance and coal, to our legislation, to our conscious, systematic economic planning and above all to the sanity and courage of the British people, we have made a new start.'

Progress on the Home Front <a familiar phrase to delegates then> was slow but sure; abroad a Labour Government must strive 'to establish a new relationship of equality, confidence and trust between the European and American peoples, and all peoples in the world' and, perhaps rather more specifically to attempt 'to stop Europe being split in two as it already has been twice in our lifetime . . .'[73]

Two particular doubts were aired in respect of a closer European association. Might closer connections with the heavy metal industries of France, Germany and the new Benelux structure, jeopardise slow and unsteady recovery in the West Midlands and South Wales? Could initiatives originating across the Channel frustrate or skew planning of production and distribution as it was seen from the British boardroom? Was there not a case for retaining a degree of participation which voluntarily surrendered limited sovereignty on the basis of recognised self-interest – a device, not dissimilar, certainly in Noel-Baker's view, to membership of the U.N. where a nation retained some degree of protection for national interests? The danger was, of course, whether in Europe or at the U.N., that a member of such a community would find it difficult to judge the extent of their obligations. Then, there was Britain's peculiar and precious Commonwealth relationship. On both sides of the House, there were those who saw in the European movement a sheer towards federalism, and thus a step to be resisted while Britain was linked with her Dominions. A closer European association would be incompatible with economic and defence obligations towards the Commonwealth family. The usefulness of protective tariffs, it might be added, was not lost on some minds: the preservation at all costs of a Commonwealth ring-fence was a convenient position in which to take shelter and await eventualities.

Redevelopment of the coal industry occupied the first half of Noel-Baker's 20 months at the Ministry of Fuel and Power. In those days 90% of Britain's energy was derived from coal. The National Coal Board, set up in 1946, was doing its best to centralise a structure which still contained a multiplicity of uneconomic units. Since nationalisation, successive Ministers had attempted to coordinate the varying practices (and physical problems) of a number of mining regions. Their policies were subjected to keen scrutiny by 600,000 members of the N.U.M. Despite improvements in productivity, equipment, and manning, when Noel-Baker took over, manpower was declining steadily and coal stocks were correspondingly lower than anticipated. A recurrence of a hard winter of 1947, Dalton's '*Annus Horrendus*' or an upsurge in export demand would result in the narrowest of margins. Misjudgements in management would soon be criticised by the new consumer councils.

The Labour Party decided to publish a pamphlet in September 1950 before Parliament reassembled. Noel-Baker, invited to write it, told his readers very clearly that it was absurd to say either that nationalisation had succeeded or that it had failed. Who could possibly assess the balance if the scale of the enterprise and the great difficulties of post-war transition were taken into account? The Government had taken over a dilapidated estate. Without such an investiture, coal would have been scarcer and quite possibly dearer, now, with nationalisation, the policy of full employment was promoted, labour relations in the pits and miners' training had been greatly improved, and there were adequate funds to re-equip technically and to sponsor research. Nationalisation in the long-term would aid the recovery of the nation and that would strengthen our influence in the world.[74]

In November 1950 Noel-Baker was ready to announce a Plan for Coal. Over 15 years increased investment would help to produce more and cheaper coal. Output was to grow by 20%. Working conditions, still notoriously bad in some areas, would improve overall. Industrial reconstruction would be an ambitious scheme, the Minister had reminded Parliament on 13th July, not a rigid one but the first cross-section of a gradually evolving process. Alongside a commendable intention to modernise the industry there was an underlying concern to effect economies in something approaching a state of siege. Speaking at St. Helens on 25th November 1950, Noel-Baker warned that unless 'a lot more coal' was forthcoming from British mines, the country's position in the near future would become 'very serious indeed'. Shortly a 'big campaign' for fuel economy would be launched. It is interesting that already the Ministry of Fuel and Power was envisaging the employment of considerable quantities of oil to take the place of scarce coal. Such an alternative cost dollars but it did get around the problem of absenteeism (running at 11%), inadequate mechanisation, and restrictive labour practices hampering extraction. The next few months were difficult ones for Noel-Baker. On 12th December 1950, the Opposition tabled a motion of censure and were pressing for an enquiry into the failure of the National Coal Board to provide sufficient coal. Somehow the Minister's evident honesty saved the day. Regrettably, he admitted, there had not been the improvements anticipated in production yields and productivity. Government estimates of the availability of manpower were, alas, 'seriously wrong'. Imports would have to bridge gaps. Rigid economies were now vital. There was a chance of recruiting workers from Eire and Italy if the N.U.M. would agree to it at a Downing Street conference. The resignation at this time of Sir Eric Young, the sole remaining production member of the Coal Board, was an awkward coincidence and might have provoked an explosion. Sir Eric declared himself dissatisfied with the Board's structure and ways of working. Informed by the Minister that his contract would not be renewed but that he would be considered for an alternative post, he went on to assert that this was 'an unsubstantiated and unexplained reflection' on his services. Noel-Baker's understanding and tolerance were held in doubt as the publication of a none-too-friendly correspondence showed. There was no political significance in the matter retorted the Minister, and this and other reassurances carried the Government unharmed through the debate.[75]

Two months later, on 1st February 1951 Noel-Baker's straightforwardness and optimism appeared yet again vindicated. It cannot have been easy to announce a cut of 15% in industrial coal deliveries and the raising of the price of coal and coke. For the Conservatives, Brendan Bracken deplored the 'contrast between Ministerial promises of adequate supplies and stocks and the present shortages . . .' Robustly, he charged the Minister with 'reckless complacency'. Noel-Baker disarmed his critic with his customary suavity which exuded politeness, yet always fell far short of a ruthless 'edge'. Yes, the situation was critical he agreed, but the Government's 'vigorous steps' afforded good hopes of avoiding dislocation and stoppages provided all elements in the community cooperated.[76] A grim compulsion in the background, much emphasised in the months that followed as Noel-Baker faced a harrying Opposition, was the 'greatly enlarged and accelerated rearmament programme' (doubled defence spending) that Korea had brought about. Lumbered with a 'stupendous' home demand for fuel, faced with a worsening of the balance of payments internationally and with ineradicable push-pull inflation, Britain's fuel and power resources were scarcely dependable and those whose responsibility it was to coordinate them were highly vulnerable politically. In August 1951, a bare two months before the Labour Government was to be despatched at a General Election, Noel-Baker appointed a committee:

'to consider, in view of the growing demands for all forms of fuel arising from full employment and the rearmament programme, whether any future steps can be taken to provide the best use of Britain's fuel and power resources, having regard to present and prospective requirements in the light of technical developments.'

Broad representation was sought: there were delegates of local authorities, industry, trade unions, universities, and a housing manager. The challenge to the fuel industry was stark, for coal demands had increased by over 20%, gas by 25%, electricity by 50%, and oil by 90%.

Even more dramatically than a flickering grate, the shortage of electricity was discouraging to the Government's supporters. Despite its share of the national capital investment programme (the largest after housing) the British Electricity Authority saw a situation developing, that was not only serious but one that might be dangerous or even disastrous. A reduction in voltage, to industry to some degree but principally to domestic consumers and known as 'load shedding', would have to be enforced partly to conserve coal stocks at power stations and generally to prevent shut-down of factories and unemployment. His critics made much of Noel-Baker's rarely-cheerful style of public announcement and accused him of being the one man since the wartime 'black-out', to be responsible for dousing the fountains in Trafalgar Square and for dimming shop windows. More than 1,500 cross-country trains were to be cancelled. It is not recorded how far an audience in his Derby constituency, very likely in a barely-heated room, were convinced by the Minister's assurance that 'in electricity, as in coal, nationalisation has rendered outstanding service to the nation'. Moreover, he concluded, 'Any Conservative who will face the facts must admit that this is true'. This assertion came from one who, as a member of Labour's National Executive Committee at the 1944 Annual Conference, had asked that a composite resolution to introduce large-scale public ownership 'be neither accepted nor rejected today'. At the 1947 Margate Conference, Noel-Baker as Chairman, had 'protected' the platform in denying it to a critic of steel nationalisation. Events such as these did not endear the Minister to his Left of Centre opponents.[77]

There was also in the power stations a problem in another dimension: that of political sectarianism. In August 1950 Lord Citrine, then Chairman of the British Electricity Authority, complained to his friend Noel-Baker (the two had visited Finland in 1940) of Communist-led agitation in the Electrical Trades Union. Could not Downing Street do something about this? Noel-Baker thereupon urged Attlee to remove 'active and suspected

Communists in key positions in power stations and, further, 'to take action against any sympathetic strike action that might follow'.[78] At this time, moreover, certain other unions, notably the T.G.W.U. (Bevin's old union) and the A.E.U. were removing more radical figures from their executives. There is no sign that Attlee ever considered making a pre-emptive move on the lines suggested, and if he had done so there would have been censure from the Left flank of his own Party. We have noted earlier that Noel-Baker's well-known tolerance seems to have deserted him when he encountered Communists; in this instance, his advice to the Premier does not appear well-judged.

Foreign affairs were to impinge on Noel-Baker's time at 'F. & P.' as they did in the Foreign Office. Parliament in Iran on 30th April 1950, announced their intention to nationalise the Anglo-Iranian Oil Company terming it 'a dragon lying on the Persian people's hidden treasure'. Britain fearing, of course, repercussions elsewhere in the Levant sent the case to the International Court of Justice at the Hague. Iran's premier, Dr. Mossadeq, issued a shrill denunciation, refused all recourse to arbitration (even that of the Security Council) and intimated that the Company's main refinery at Abadan might be seized. Herbert Morrison, a newly-appointed and far from confident Foreign Secretary, was in a quandary. What could he do now that Iran had rejected both mediation and a compromise on compensation? Thought too 'United-Nations-y' by some of his parliamentary colleagues, was it possible to risk President Truman's displeasure over any unilateral and destablising move? United States and British emissaries came back empty handed, and Morrison wanly calculated the electoral consequences of his private inclination to despatch an expeditionary force to Abadan. The restraint shown in Whitehall at the point of crisis – and Iran had pushed things to the brink – was justified when an incoming Churchill administration on 25th October 1951 found that it, too, must play for time. Desultory discussion ensued at the Security Council for the quarrel had been seen as a threat to world peace. The matter was to remain unresolved and the Iranian pipelines choked up for another two years. The episode had presented an irony to the Left for as one commentator puts it, 'a Labour government which had nationalised 20% of the industry in its own country, could hardly raise objections if a poor third-world government did the same to its central economic asset'. The same viewpoint sees neither Labour nor Conservatives resisting the 'siren effect' of imperial pretensions, an observation which perhaps is rather dramatically stated.[79] In the view of Kenneth Younger, towards the end of 1950, Noel-Baker was 'the only Minister who has a really clean record in the matter, having poured out warnings at least since January.'[80]

Noel-Baker's tenure as Minister of Fuel and Power finished with the Conservatives regaining office on 25th October 1951. He was to sit on Opposition front or back benches until he went to the Lords in 1977. For a quarter of a century he was to witness varying political fortunes as the Tories reigned for half that time under Churchill, Eden, Macmillan, and Douglas-Home between 1951 and 1964, followed by Wilson's four years, the Heath regime of 1970-4, and Labour's return under Wilson and Callaghan thereafter until 1979. During all those long and troubled years, Noel-Baker kept lamps trimmed and a steady flame burning. There were global and domestic issues and crises in plenty with which to tax Tory and Labour administration. His speeches in the House reflected the authority of the ex-Minister, confidante of so many prominent international contacts. He remained an unflinchingly faithful member of the Labour Party though standing out on its periphery in power terms. The country and the world knew him as a titan for the cause of arms control and disarmament, and as an indefatigable campaigner for concepts of collective security and detente. A scrutiny of all that he did in those wide-open and controversial areas is the concern of the chapters that now follow.

As a Minister, how does Philip Noel-Baker measure up to the standards a critic would normally employ? The evidence has to be garnered from those who worked with him and from citation in published memoirs. Indispensable to the manager of a government department is skill at what is generally termed 'information retrieval': the Minister recalls, compares, analyses, and understands. Noel-Baker was good at that. The skilled government executive displays a political instinctiveness combined with flair in manoeuvring, that yields an aura of decisiveness together with the capacity and judgement needed to cover ones tracks if necessary. Noel-Baker's ability in these respects was only moderate. He clearly placed a good deal of reliance on the humaneness of personal encounter. He may have been nice when he should have been harder; tolerant when there was a need for sharpness and a more calculated appraisal. Can a Minister depend upon the imagination, courage and trust of others to work towards solution of problems? Is it sufficiently down-to-earth to adopt as he so often did, the position that 'We were repeatedly within inches of the crucial breakthrough: if only so and so had done this, or listened to that, I believe we should have pulled it off'?[81] Integrity, patience, and willingness-to-listen may have inspired affection among his departmental staff: they did not necessarily earn respect among his fellow-Ministers. A blend of humour, deep seriousness, and intellectual vigour were doubtless as misunderstood or as unwelcome in Downing Street as in Parliament with Noel-Baker, as *The Guardian* put it, 'looming over the Commons like an apparition or uneasy conscience, nagging them with a kind of moral migraine that refused to go away'.[82] Earnestness in political harassment is not easily tolerated, however well-intentioned or modulated it may be. Cabinet colleagues do not appreciate lectures even if they have a place in the front row of the audience.

Something perhaps that pointed to his colleagues' estimate of Philip, was the incident of being passed over ministerially when Harold Wilson formed a government on 16th October 1964. Patrick Gordon-Walker was appointed to the Foreign Office and an accompanying post of Minister of Disarmament, or more exactly, a Minister of State with such a responsibility, was expected. Philip was just the man for the onerous task it was widely thought. In the event, a former Defence Correspondent of *The Times*, Alun Gwynne-Jones, was enobled as Lord Chalfont and given the job. One of Noel-Baker's devoted secretary's, Helen Armstrong, has commented on her employer's reaction:

'It was a farce and a hard blow . . . Philip would have given anything for one more chance, from an official position; to make a dint on the hideous momentum of the Arms Race.'

The assignment would have been an appropriate recognition of unparalleled knowledge and background.[83] However, he was, after all 75 years of age and mature enough to realise that in politics, quite aside from the consideration of age, few things can ever be taken for granted. At no time then or later was the disappointed man embittered. He was sufficiently down-to-earth to allow that others might not possess quite such an extent of vision yet see themselves, and be seen by others, as more confident and hard-headed. With the poet he unquestionably believed that:

'Ah, but a man's reach should exceed his grasp: Or what's a heaven for?'

In the wider public world there was so much to do and not every much time in which to accomplish it. And at the end of the day there was music, conversation, dancing, or the flinty ridges to tramp above Buttermere.

CHAPTER 7

In at the Creation of the United Nations

A ROLLING SUCCESSION OF CRISES and challenges during the 30's already prompted internationalists to consider reform of the League. In what ways might the principles of the Covenant be sustained most effectively? Noel-Baker became a member of a consultative group which met in Geneva in 1936, to survey what might be done following the failure over Abyssinia, to check aggression and to preserve the territorial integrity and political independence of a League member. Discussion was purposeful but little of substance seems to have emerged.

Some three years later this group held a conversazione at which papers were considered by Professor C. K. Webster, soon to be a recognised exponent of League reform, Professor Gilbert Murray, Maxwell Garnett of the League of Nations Union, and Philip Noel-Baker. The League had had an astonishing success in the first 12 or so years of its existence until 1931, Noel-Baker argued. Handicaps, of course, there had been – the absence of the United States, difficult economic conditions worldwide, the reluctance and internecine jealousies of states which had become independent following the Treaty of Versailles – yet, achievements were clear. More than 100 disputes had been dealt with, mostly satisfactorily. Problems in regard to refugees, public health and economic cooperation had been handled competently by Genevan institutions. International law was gaining respect. Germany had joined the League in 1926, Italy was remaining loyal despite the quarrel over Corfu and there was a growing spirit of reconciliation among former enemies. Neither the United States nor the Soviet Union wanted to be excluded from international conferences summoned from time to time, and President F. D. Roosevelt was clearly showing more of a benevolent disposition than had his predecessors generally. Reasons for success, Noel-Baker believed, depended upon an acceptance, largely a tacit assumption, that international law would be translated into covenants, League articles, mandate agreements, and the statutes of the Permanent Court of International Justice. Correspondingly, challenges to that law would be identified and dealt with in formal and precise terms. Theoretically, the obligations of members would be reinforced if necessary by impartial judgement. Fundamental to the efficiency of the League was the international loyalty of its Secretariat and the continuous publicity given to corporate enquiry and debate. For Noel-Baker the troubled year of 1939 seemed an appropriate time to look back and to look forward:

'It is extremely unlikely that in the panic improvisations we are now making, we shall devise anything better than the systematic work of 12 or 14 years . . . It must be our object, therefore, to work from the improvised peace alliance we are now making, to the system of a real League which includes all the factors of success. In other words, while it may be necessary to see what has been wrong with the League as it was devised in 1919, it is still more important to see what was right and to ensure that it will be restored.'[1]

What then had gone wrong after 1931? Noel-Baker was quite sure that the larger powers had retreated into suspicious indifference and smaller states into a defensive preference for the status quo. With the United States absent ('neutral' if not 'isolationist') and with the Soviet Union, Germany, Japan, and Italy falling away from Geneva, no world organisation could function successfully in the long run if it consisted only of the British Empire, France and a group of less influential states mainly in Europe. France he saw as continuing to be resentful, and in its over-protective instincts against a German 'threat', believing League assurances to be weak safeguards rather than inherently strong ones. Japan and Italy had 'rebelled', taking umbrage at the censures of Geneva. Too many nations understood 'collective security' in narrow, limited terms. (This judgement of his is not elaborated and in some respects begs a question or two.) The Genevan Secretariat came in for extensive criticism. They could not have realised the importance of making budgetary policies plain to members. Thus, any delegation and the national press behind them were prone to censure, on occasion what appeared to be irresponsible expenditure. The complexities of debate were not always adequately clarified to a wider public which was entitled to know more of what went on in the Assembly and in committees.[2]

War's darkest days impelled Noel-Baker to think ahead to the return of normality. He had had long experience of international peace-making at Geneva as Secretariat member, as unofficial observer, and as P.P.S. to Arthur Henderson between 1929 and 1931. His contacts with figures in the Foreign Office and in Churchill's Coalition ministries were now many and various.[3] There were undoubtedly those who regarded the enthusiasm of Noel-Baker, Dalton, and others for the League of Nations as 'a kind of harmless eccentricity', otherwise, there were the beginnings of attentive interest in institutional resuscitation.

Noel-Baker, the premier eccentric, planned a deliberate campaign of persuasion.[4] A careful memorandum entitled *'What Kind of a League?'* was circulated in certain Whitehall corridors in early 1941. Nothing was to be rushed. In the autumn of 1941, Noel-Baker button-holed Alexander Cadogan and others, and broached the idea of an investigative group on the lines of the Phillimore Committee a quarter-century earlier. A paper was to be expected from F. P. Walters, an authority on the workings of the League, and it was believed possible and necessary to recommend this eventually to a Cabinet committee chaired by Sir William Jowitt, the Solicitor-General, with Richard Law as Vice-Chairman. However, it seemed that the Deputy Premier, Clement Attlee, with more time on his hands for 'civil matters' than the Premier, Churchill, was inclined to wait awhile until consideration could be coordinated with the Americans. Noel-Baker, unusually, seems to have been impatient with the need to await transatlantic discussion. This attitude is rather surprising since he well knew of American interest in promoting a successor to the League. The Foreign Office certainly envisaged the United States as a vital founder member of such a body.[5]

Walters, two weeks later, was encouraged to present his paper as a set of 'forward schemes', even though some Foreign Office people might term it 'an inquest on the failure of the League'. An agreed tactic was that Jowitt would ask Arnold Toynbee to prepare a preliminary document setting out the history of the League, and drawing attention to the prime questions for discussion. The Phillimore Committee had recruited historians and international lawyers in 1917; a new committee would seek people with experience of Geneva – Alfred Zimmern, Arnold Toynbee, Professor Manning from the London School of Economics, and Noel-Baker himself. There was a danger, though, that the historians might be too academic. Possibly Sean Lester, acting as Secretary-General of the League from 1940 (until its formal dissolution in April 1946) could attempt the task alongside, say, Henri Vigier, an outstanding documentary draftsman and French member of the Secretariat. Particular emphasis, Noel-Baker felt, should be placed upon League achievements in encouraging economic collaboration and in working towards a system of collective security buttressed by law.[6]

Discussions with the United States Government were under way by the summer of 1942 as to the nature of post-war reconstruction, and regarding the central function that might be discharged by a successor to the League of Nations. Noel-Baker, now Parliamentary Secretary to the Ministry of War Transport, talked long and fully with Richard Law of the Cabinet committee and with Harold Butler, a former Secretariat colleague and a man who had directed the International Labour Office before the war. Law's attitude and consistency heartened Noel-Baker. 'He is, of course, like Eden, 100% in favour of a highly-developed international system, 100% of collective security, and is thoroughly anti-militarist in every way'.[7] Why, then, did there seem to be an element of delay in codifying what might be understood as a new Covenant and fresh institutional procedures? Might procrastination even be traced, Noel-Baker wondered, to a wartime coalition having to reckon with reactionaries in its midst, men perhaps coolly disposed towards international collaboration (apart from ad hoc alliance)? Equally, there was understandable disillusionment with an institution which had allowed war to happen. Noel-Baker feared that 'the whole question of League policy might be adversely affected by irresolution if not wrangling in London. In early September 1942, however, F. P. Walters, seconded by the Foreign Office to its Research and Press Service and located 'for the duration' in Balliol College, Oxford, was able to report some progress. A committee had been set up by the Foreign Office to examine institutional possibilities much as the Phillimore Committee did two decades previously. They put pen to paper in workmanlike fashion, but their recommendations awaited scrutiny by a 'top-level' review.

A parallel enquiry in the months that followed was one looking at the practicability of reviving the Permanent Court of International Justice. William (later Sir William) Malkin, one of its members, and a former legal adviser to the Foreign Office, sent a copy of recommendations to Noel-Baker, who found it a splendid piece of argument and writing. 'I just have a general feeling', Noel-Baker confessed later, in February 1944, 'that after this war it will be "all or nothing" for western civilisation, and that unless we can make the general international organisation succeed, it will not matter much what we do about the Court'. Assuming the organisation did succeed, then, 'I believe that the closer the connection the Court has with it the better'.[8] It is noticeable in this and in other correspondence that the old League hands Noel-Baker, Walters, Zimmern, Butler, were as sure in the dire 1940's as they had been 20 years previously, that those who set out to frame a new charter must very carefully address themselves to defining such terms as 'aggression' and 'security'. This would be a formidable undertaking.[9]

A particular advantage would be gained from using the experience of trusted League staff. After the initial panic at Geneva in midsummer 1940 (when valuable records were hastily burned), Sean Lester, as custodian, supervised the evacuation of the League Treasury and the Refugee Department to London, movement of the I.L.O. to Montreal, and transfer of much of the Secretariat to Princeton, New Jersey. A budget, tiny in comparison with the Genevan one, was largely sustained by British and Commonwealth efforts despite their war burdens. Henceforth, whatever plans were being laid in London or Washington, the help of experienced League staff should be enlisted.

Not all creative thinking was plain sailing. It is interesting to return to the spring of 1941 when discussion was reverberating in many quarters. Two Oxford dons, A. D. Lindsay, Master of Balliol, and the classicist Gilbert Murray drew up for the Executive Committee of the League of Nations Union, a paper under the title *Statement of propositions on world settlement after the war*. Philip Noel-Baker, however, and with Lord Cecil's substantial agreement, disagreed with every paragraph. Explicit assumptions in the original draft were that a post-war world would see 'nations converted against aggression'. Germany and Italy, very likely, would be the exceptions. A League, virtually a non-political entity could be made to work, with the United Kingdom and the United States looking after political questions to do with armaments and war. These assumptions 'only have to be stated for their falsity and even absurdity to be seen', pointed out Noel-Baker. It was quite unrealistic to conceive of a world without potential aggressors for aggression as fact or threat was related to economic disparity, competitiveness, and uncertainties. For survival the smaller modern world must arrange for collaboration rather than division. By-passing the legitimate political concerns of the League just would not do. We had to take to heart the lesson of the successes and failures of the League over its 20 years of existence. In the light of such stern criticism, Lindsay could not forbear writing to Irene Noel-Baker, saying how depressed he felt when what he was trying to say was not understood by her husband.[10]

The 15-page pamphlet '*What kind of a League?*' circularised by Noel-Baker may be regarded as part-manifesto and part-rejoinder to head off what he considered would be inert ideas. His arguments encapsulate suggestion and admonition. If only League members had carried out their plain obligations, the disputes which occurred before and after Munich could have been dealt with. The institutions of the League – judicial, political, consultative, administrative – were not found wanting. They must be revived. Neutrality and retreat in the face of aggression on the part of Britain and France (what others referred to as 'appeasement'), undermined both the Covenant and other agreed accords: thus collective and positive determination was crucial. Noel-Baker went on to insist on a point with which he was to be much occupied over the succeeding three decades, namely, that unilateralism is inherently unstable. As far as possible, the basis of the post-war system must be universal, there must be no political side-stepping by the Great Powers. In terms habitually employed by Cecil and Noel-Baker this meant that 'Great Britain is the natural, if not the indispensable leader of the League' and a committed government backed by vigorous and informed public opinion would both save the national interest and international concord.[11] A combination of official sponsorship and of 'unofficial opinion' (for instance, the League of Nations Union and like-minded groups), he saw rather sweepingly as reinforcing the establishment of a successor to the League of Nations, for, as he had pointed out to his brother Alan Baker in October 1940, 'unless this war is being fought for an international organisation that will stop future wars, it is certainly not worth while at all'.[12] In fact, at that point, and in common with many others, he seems to have believed that the war might not last all that long and so thought had to be given to preliminary discussion of a successor to the League.

It is most unlikely that in the early 1940's, Philip Noel-Baker ever clearly visualised an international organisation, and its Secretary-General, having to face what one writer has described as 'cold war in a bipolar world, where the conflicting strategic and military desires of the two sides were disguised in an ideological garb . . .' where, all too often, political initiatives publicly aroused wrath from one side (or both) and their tenure and usefulness was undermined.[13] In this respect, Sir Eric Drummond, working rather less in the open than did his successors Trygve Lie and Dag Hammarskjöld, was able to retain more support for his position though he did not escape criticism. Noel-Baker was to reiterate on numerous occasions that the quieter processes of international negotiation being undramatic, rarely earn the attention and constructive concern of the world's press. Even so, the executive must be a leader. This very point of leadership was exercising the minds, shortly before the United Nations was instituted, of two League veterans, Philip Noel-Baker and Frank Walters. Writing from Oxford in some irritation, the latter had little time for the proposal of the major powers that the Secretary-General should serve a term of three years and be assisted by four deputies. A temporary posting such as this would attract mainly professional diplomatists and hardly favour the growth of *esprit de corps* in a loyal, strong secretariat. Would Noel-Baker explore the tabling of objections in the Commons and in the press? After some consultation Noel-Baker replied that the three year rule applied only to the Secretary-General, not to other members of the secretariat because 'they were afraid of picking a dud, to whom they might be tied for a long period, after he had proved his unsuitability'.[14] In retrospect, over the 40 years of the United Nations, Secretary-Generals have served for periods of moderate length and for always more than three years. In very different ways they have managed to outlast a good deal of criticism.[15] A contributory factor no doubt to this success is that the chief executive has been seen as a candidate from an 'uncommitted' nation. The first appointment attracted the attention of many well-known persons and, for instance, Hugh Dalton has recorded the eagerness of Anthony Eden to secure the post:

'Phil Noel-Baker had spoken to me <in February 1946> only the previous day about Eden's strenuous efforts to this end. Eden, he said, had seen Bevin about it, and had got Churchill to see both Bevin and Attlee about it. Eden had also arranged that a number of distinguished foreigners should canvas on his behalf. Phil told me that he, himself, had urged both on Bevin and on Attlee that apart from everything else, our party would never stand for Eden being the British nominee.'[16]

From the vantage point of a later, much more polarised world it is perhaps slightly unfair to brand as fanciful the idealism of those who upheld the League. In 1919 many would have shared the optimism of Noel-Baker that 'responsible representatives <in the League Assembly> (who) will be able to act without constant reference for instructions to their Foreign Office at home . . .', that they would develop 'a habit of cooperation that will facilitate agreed decisions . . .', that these delegates would be guided 'by instructed public opinion which will have the full merits of all disputes laid before it for judgement'.[17] The same advocate frequently lent to his argument the sentiments of Guiseppe Motta, an eminent Swiss delegate, that 'Coercion will be within its sphere of action, but it will rule above all by moral force', and that the League's universality should be construed 'not only <as> a postulate of pure reason, but, above all, <as> a postulate of practical reason'.[18] Twenty years and half a dozen crises later Noel-Baker, as we have seen from his appraisals close to 1939, tempered idealism with realism, and optimism with saddened caution. Moral force and publicity had appeared 'cleansing and clarifying and compelling' to the great originator Woodrow Wilson; a generation later they presented to would-be rejuvenators a need for strength. It was no use agreeing to live in peace unless that peace was to be defended. Noel-Baker and Gilbert Murray had concurred in that in 1939. Whichever way they looked, either backwards or forwards, the crucial problem remained how best to persuade states to accept pure-and-practical reason in political terms and so go on to effective action. As we shall see later in this chapter, there was an inclination among the Allies, as they scented a distant victory, to believe that their moral judgements based on reason (and based on force) would have a broadly acceptable sway. It had happened in 1919; it was expected again at the cessation of hostilities. Arming the Covenant may have been in Noel-Baker's mind when he returned to Robert Cecil proposals for a new Covenant in September 1943:

‘You ask me not to be too angry with <your> Draft. The boot is on the other leg. I hope you will not be “too angry” with my comments . . . we should, in fact make proposals more and not less ambitious than those of the old Covenant . . . we should make it quite plain to the public that we intend to eliminate the weaknesses of the past.’[19]

By common consent, a major inadequacy of the old League of Nations had been the failure of the American electorate, not only to support the concept of international conciliation but more pointedly to back President Wilson. Franklin D. Roosevelt, and Cordell Hull, America’s longest serving Secretary of State, were untiring in their efforts to give life to the seminal ideas of the Atlantic Charter of August 1941, the declaration of agreement between the charismatic leaders of Britain and the United States, as to the shaping of the post-war world. A ‘Declaration by United Nations’ was drafted by Cordell Hull, thus earning him acknowledgement by a grateful President as ‘father of the United Nations’.[20] Couched basically in terms cementing wartime alliance the document, signed in January 1942, looked towards a scenario less dictated by conventional and limiting alliances and the hypothetical balances of power. Custodial functions were implicit in the recording of a shattered world; a ‘United Nations Association’ would depend upon the watchfulness of ‘Four Policemen’, the United States, the United Kingdom, the U.S.S.R., and China, allied in war, henceforth to be united in peace – this was Roosevelt’s vision towards the end of 1942.[21] Winston Churchill, by all accounts, was less sure that this was the main concern. ‘Finish the war first’, had been the constant priority in Churchillian terms. Eden, his deputy and a politician with more diplomatic sensitiveness, had seen the new Association embarking on three main tasks, namely, to continue the ‘technical’ and specialised work of the old League, to seek to remedy the clear failures of the predecessor, and to incorporate as directly as possible the energies and visions of the United States. These suggestions reached Noel-Baker in the course of a conversation he had in 1942 with Smuts and Cecil.[22] Roosevelt by February 1945 had made up his mind where to put the new organisation. ‘Not Geneva. Geneva’s unlucky, has an unlucky record . . .’ And as to the question: ‘how do you deal with the Russians?’ Cordell Hull and Roosevelt were largely of one mind about Soviet intransigence for, as Hull put it, the Russians ‘should be educated, not surrendered to’. More specifically, and a month before he died, Roosevelt told Congress that the Dumbarton Oaks Conference had secured agreement over 90% of east-west security problems: the other 10% had been ‘ironed out at Yalta’.[23]

Retrospectively one may argue long and loud about whether the founders of the United Nations saw real consensus as either always desirable or always likely. Certainly in the fabric of wartime concordat there were visible strains, the vestiges of old suspicions and the budding of new ones. Unanimity regarding arms control, human rights, trusteeship of former colonies, the independence of certain European minorities was all too obviously imperilled. Noel-Baker was one, most clearly, who saw a future world organisation as having to work *with* 'realities' not in spite of them. Twenty years of Genevan mediation, or attempts at it, had revealed a body with supranational authority as a chimera. In more positive terms, one could wish to see such an organisation offering a static function as convenor of conference, and initiator of enquiry yet taking up a more dynamic role in encouragement of preventive and constructive action.[24]

Where Noel-Baker had worked untiringly in beleagured London in a campaign for replacing the League it is interesting to observe the efforts, largely discharged in Washington, of a devoted ally, Charles (later Sir Charles) Webster. He and Noel-Baker had much in common.[25] Both were Kings College men under the tutorship of Reddaway, Lowes Dickinson, and Pigou. Each had been awarded a Whewell Scholarship in International Law, each was a member of societies and reading parties which met to look at history critically and deductively, with a view to improving the coherence of international politics. Noel-Baker on graduating went to Ruskin College, Oxford as Vice-Principal leaving Webster to research as a Fellow at Kings in Cambridge. Their paths crossed again in the Paris of 1919 when Webster, an Intelligence Corps officer and Professor of Modern History at Liverpool *in absentia*, met Noel-Baker, recently demobilised from Quaker ambulance work. The former held a secretaryship in the Military Section of the British Delegation, the latter was concerned more with a political brief. Their common concerns ranged over arms control, verification of defence agreements, border questions, and the deployment of military task forces to aid refugees, the refugee relief work of Nansen. Webster returned to his Liverpool Chair to teach and write, keeping in close touch with his old League associates Zimmern, Temperley and Noel-Baker. When the first-named resigned from the Wilson Chair of International Politics at Aberystwyth in 1923, Webster followed and built a world-wide reputation for his department. After nine years he assumed the Professorship of International History at the London School of Economics, a companion chair to the one vacated there by Noel-Baker's taking up his first parliamentary seat of Coventry in 1929. Each of the professors saw travel and wide extra-mural lecturing as essential to authority and knowledge, and by the time war broke out in 1939 their joint collaboration, more ad hoc than continuous, was impressive.

In 1942, when Noel-Baker and others were initiating a campaign for institutional reconstruction, Webster was recruited by the Foreign Office to work on draft schemes for a successor to the League of Nations. The work that he undertook was done alongside F. P. Walters in a department located temporarily in collegiate Oxford. Webster's sense of the practicable allied with his historical knowledge, urged the essential need to have a preponderance of power to undergird faith: that was the only way to bring about 'a positive power arising out of moral conviction'. As more substance was built into drafts, Webster was brought into the newly-formed Economic and Reconstruction Department of the Foreign Office. There, in the second half of 1943 he assisted H. M. G. Jebb (now Lord Gladwyn), producing memoranda on post-war security (adopted as British proposals at the Dumbarton Oaks Conference in September 1944) and wrestling with the complexities of national voting procedure (much of which was later to be subsumed under the name of the 'veto'.) Gladwyn himself has described their task in these terms:

'together we worked on and revised the "Four Power Plan" which became the "United Nations Plan" and was submitted to the Jowitt Committee – whose actual influence on events had not been very noticeable – and it was eventually approved by this body, though never by Churchill. Anyhow, it then formed the basis of our actual proposals for a World Organisation, which were the result of a further interchange of views with the Americans . . .'[26]

During the winter of 1945-46 Webster was Special Adviser to his old comrade, Philip Noel-Baker, and in this capacity served as Alternate Delegate to the Preparatory Commission of the United Nations. Their shared thinking as to how to go about the remodelling of the League must have taken account of at least three great problems. First, and a question as taxing in the 1940's as it was in the 1920's, how would an organisation of states varying in their intentions and attitudes, work both to preserve status quo and to facilitate peaceful change? Secondly, in what ways might such an institution balance a recognition and understanding of separate sovereignties, with a generalised encouragement of international spirit? Following on from the second dilemma, how far might it be possible to strive for the dissemination of universalist ideals and at the same time acknowledge the 'realities' of movements towards alliance?

There are indications that questions such as those above were to preoccupy the joint discussions of Charles Webster, Robert Cecil and Philip Noel-Baker, for instance, in 1944-45 when there were already signs that the U.S.S.R. preferred a world organisation to deal mainly with threats to security. Webster tentatively advanced approaches to these problems which must have earned the endorsement of his colleagues. In the first place, principles to govern action must be outlined clearly. It would not be useful to define too rigidly the conditions in which that action should be undertaken. In this way there would be emphasis upon the collective 'force' of the League and its successor, something that would be insisted upon by the lawyer in Cecil. On the second point of sovereignty, it could be argued that separate State identities would collectively strengthen such an institution and not weaken it. This differentiates a legal principle from a political fact, and if that was important to a lawyer it was realistic to the historians, for whom Webster spoke in similar terms to Noel-Baker in acknowledging 'that the universal interest in peace, which is indivisible, could be served only by those with the resources to preserve it . . .' At this point one imagines Noel-Baker enlisting the distant appeals of Litvinov and Motta. Finally, the universalist ideals of collective security need not be nullified in real terms if a nation's right to self-defence were established. As has been said before, it is unlikely that the three observers would have appreciated at that time, how firm and divisive the East-West dichotomy was to become.[27]

Noel-Baker's great work for the United Nations was rooted in the work he did for its Preparatory Commission in the autumn of 1945, and in the indefatigable service he rendered a year later as United Kingdom representative at Lake Success. When, in 1945, he became Minister of State at the Foreign Office, the Foreign Secretary was his taskmaster. Ernest Bevin was intolerant of any 'Utopianist' streak in his country's foreign policy. Oratory and philosophical argument he mistrusted. He shouldered his way through the verbal elaborations of his advisers to establish a solution, without worrying too much about theoretical vindication. Intellectuals within his own party were treated with disdain. One commentator puts the Foreign Secretary's attitude in these words:

'Among the junior Ministers at the Foreign Office, the enthusiastic and devoted Philip Noel-Baker was classified as an intellectual and was treated pretty roughly . . . The Minister's political colleagues in the Foreign Office had very little influence on his policies.'[28]

Noel-Baker made no secret of his regard for and loyalty to Ernest Bevin. On the day the new ministerial appointments were announced he wrote to Cecil:

'I think we could not do better than have Bevin at the Foreign Office . . . I am going to talk to you on the telephone about what I want myself; in the meantime, I will not say more than that I think Bevin's nomination gives me the best chance, both getting it and of doing the job afterwards.'[29]

Cecil ought to write a congratulatory letter to Bevin, thanking him for his loyal support of the League in the past, and saying that 'his sincere devotion

(COURTESY: B.B.C. HULTON)

Pl. 12. Assisting at the U.N. Preparatory Commission, London, autumn 1945. Left: Gladwyn Jebb (Executive Secretary)

to the policy of collective security <as shown in his speech at Blackpool Labour Party Conference> was the greatest guarantee the world could have. After a week or so, another encouraging note was sent to Cecil:

'. . . things are beginning well . . . and I have every reason to be more than satisfied with the other Ministers with whom I am, of course, in closest contact. It is a great comfort to me having Hector McNeil here.'[30]

Noel-Baker's trust in his colleagues, however, may represent to some a characteristic measure of over-optimism. Philip also wrote to his other faithful correspondent, A. C. Pigou:

'I was told that the cabinet <sic> was to be small and assumed it was to be nine or ten, otherwise I might have fought on that point. But of course I go to the Cabinet for all my own subjects, and, on the whole, I think it may make an easier situation with my Great Number One as it is. The money is all right. £5,000. As for the privy councillorship, that is coming along very shortly, or I shall know the reason why . . .'[31]

There was no note of rancour in Noel-Baker's correspondence over the failure of the Prime Minister to give him a responsibility corresponding to that Eden had held, albeit only for six months, in 1935, namely, Minister without Portfolio for League of Nations Affairs, and to that of Viscount Cranborne (actually a Parliamentary Under-Secretary at the Foreign Office from August 1935 until February 1938).

About this time, Kenneth Younger was appointed Parliamentary Private Secretary to Noel-Baker. They had a good deal in common and it is interesting to read in Younger's diary a sympathetic, yet objective view of their relationship as the amanuensis followed his senior from Foreign Office to Air Ministry. Three weeks into his Foreign Office duties Younger was writing:

'26th August 1945: Noel-Baker is undoubtedly a charming person and I think he will gradually give me as much scope as a P.P.S. can expect . . . He is engaged in series of committees on World Transport, U.N.R.R.A., and the setting up of the first Assembly of the U.N. He flits about from one to another and is never still . . . I can see that when my duties begin in earnest, one of the most arduous will be to keep track of him.'[32]

A back-bencher who has gained a foothold in government office at 37, understandably feels there is no time to lose in scaling the heights. Secure footholds are not easily assured if it is difficult to keep tabs on an elusive chief, and Younger's slightly amused exasperation shows a month later:

'16th September. He is one of those who does not organise himself or his work, undertakes three mens' jobs and keeps his assistants in a perpetual whirl. He seems to have big ideas for me . . .'[33]

A week later came the thought:

'24th September. I doubt if N.-B. is really a Socialist at all. He is a liberal internationalist . . . needs to be constantly reminded of socialist fundamentals.'[34]

Thirty years previously Noel-Baker, as junior to Robert Cecil in the Foreign Office, had found the civil servants in that awesome institution neither particularly welcoming nor too ready to put themselves out to provide the basic necessities of room and desk. Earnestness, and more particularly, idealistic fervour, were soon characteristics in the tyro that were not remarked with warm approval. Younger encountered a similar lack of regard, made all the more insecure when he found himself inadequately briefed and rarely able to consult with his Minister:

'21st October. I never see N.-B. and he appears to have no need of me, except for interviewing occasional stray individuals who ask to see him but are unimportant. Even in the House I seem to have little or no function.'[35]

Things did improve as Noel-Baker shouldered work for the Preparatory Commission of the United Nations, and his assistant encountered piles of paper and meetings of committees. Were, though, this Minister's sights raised too high?

'26th May. P.J. is away again. My job for him scarcely exists, as he does very little parliamentary work and seems to have a negligible amount of influence upon or part in the formulation of foreign policy, except in so far as the U.N. is directly affected . . . It is important (for a politician) to keep track of domestic matters . . . and in touch with political realities . . . both Noel-Baker and Anthony Eden have suffered from inattention to this.'[36]

Not for the first or last time, was a P.P.S. discerning in his ministerial superior, both a shorfall in the information reaching the desk 'where the buck stops' and, in consequence, perhaps, a lack of objectivity. It might be in the Commons that the gaps showed through:

'4th January 1946. Noel-Baker replied skilfully <in a debate on Indonesia> and got away without loss of credit, but he really satisfied no-one . . . He is very good in most ways, but he has a fierce anti-Communist and anti-Soviet prejudice which may be very dangerous.'[37]

Younger may have exaggerated the extent and direction of prejudice here, but 12 months later he uneasily wonders whether his Minister is not somewhat blinkered. Noel-Baker has accepted an invitation and come to speak to Younger's constituents in Grimsby:

'January 1947. He is of course a good speaker, and he put it across alright, but the more sophisticated, including Philip, must have been disappointed. It was little more than a catalogue . . . I knew he had no time to prepare the speech, so I was not too hard on him in my mind, but I was shocked by the revelation of his ignorance. It was clear that during the last 18 months he had not even read the papers intelligently on anything but foreign policy.'[38]

Once Noel-Baker was established in an official capacity, he was able to commence work as a member of a United Nations Preparatory Commission in the autumn of 1945.[39] In the June of that year, 50 nations meeting in San Francisco established what was in effect a working party around an Executive Committee. Representatives of 14 states were given extensive terms of reference. There was a need to establish for the United Nations, rules of procedure, modalities of voting, the processes of convening assemblies and committees, the preparation of preliminary agendas. Beginning with measures for regularising the transfer of the League's functions and assets, 10 special committees examined in great detail the aims and structure of the new international organisation. H. M. G. Jebb, appointed Executive Secretary of the Preparatory Commission, recruited a very efficient secretariat. Chairmanship of the planning group located in Westminster's Church House, would rotate every two weeks between China's Wellington Koo (the first to preside), René Massigli of France, Britain's Noel-Baker, Andrei Gromyko from the U.S.S.R. and Edward Stettinius from the United States. If two months were successful then the full Preparatory Commission would meet over the period November-December to convene the First General Assembly for January 1946. London's Central Hall would be the venue for the historic conference. Tremendous work was done in a very short time by the commissioners. Four achievements are worth particular examination, namely, the issue of continuity with the League, the relationship of the Covenant to the Charter, the interlinking of Assembly and Security Council, and the mechanics of collective voting.

Continuity, with all that Geneva had stood for, was not unhesitatingly welcomed in some quarters. Many felt a fear of arousing latent hostilities or creating doubts as a consequence of the League's chequered history.[40] Much discussion revolved around the crucial question: in what ways would the United Nations take over the work of the League? Would League functions be transferred, and if so, would this entail a *de jure* survival of at least some parts of the League of Nations? Majority preference was for the new organisation to assume certain functions previously exercised at Geneva, so securing a *de facto* continuity. Noel-Baker urged the Commission to accept at least three requirements to facilitate the work of an international body. Essentially, the specialised agencies would continue to translate the basic principles of the Charter, as successor to the Covenant, in ways that must 'end the nonsensical and monstrous puerility of power politics'. Then, the structure of an organisation which embodied these agencies, should develop an elasticity not always apparent in the more rigid planning of two decades earlier. Lastly, to promote both coherence and flexibility, there must be a close liaison between headquarters and regional agencies. Over-centralisation would lead to muddle, not to prompt and appropriate action by agencies.[41]

A considerable amount of investigation was carried out into the feasibility of regenerating the new organisation in its old Genevan home. British and British Commonwealth delegates would rather have Geneva. The United States, particularly its eastern part, was the choice of the U.S.A., the U.S.S.R., Central and South American republics, China, Egypt and, standing alone in the English-speaking world, Australia. In Committees Number Eight and Number Ten both Noel-Baker and Massigli strongly urged the claims of a European headquarters for the U.N. Geneva would make it easier for the exercise of diplomatic privileges and immunities by personnel, more importantly, it was a place 'as non-political and as non-national', as they could find and this was a strictly practical suggestion which should attract ex-neutrals and ex-enemies. Moreover, Europe was the 'natural and inevitable communications centre of the world'. It is clear that in this matter Noel-Baker knew that the Preparatory Commission were not enpowered to make a decision – it was a resolution that they were called upon to table. He appealed to the allied nations of Europe in terms that seem rather more oratorical than conclusive. Europe was 'wounded' not sick: the strength of her cultural and historical identities belied obsolescence. Where had the lessons of earlier and of more recent history been learned most readily? In Europe. Could anyone believe that in Europe the old follies of indifference, cynicism, and national sectarianism would revive? A rehabilitated Europe would have much that was positive to offer.[42]

It seems unlikely that British arguments swayed James Byrnes, Secretary of State, and Edward Stettinius, his chief assistant in the U.S. State Department, to accept that an American locale for the U.N. might lock together the prestige of the U.S.A. and the nascent organisation in a rather undesirable way. Suggestions and canvassing from Whitehall yielded little fruit. Stettinius considered Ernest Bevin 'abrasive', Attlee and his colleagues 'worn thin' by the strain of war, and discussion with Noel-Baker 'frustrating and barren of accomplishment'. The last-named struck the American as 'limited by his preoccupation with the defunct League of Nations'.[43] For his part, Noel-Baker believed that the manoeuvring of Stettinius must have ensured the primacy of New York in the competition for the site of the United Nations headquarters. He felt, late in 1945, that he had to rebuke Hugh Dalton for not helping to get the 'squalid inside story' of the affair across to the Attlee Cabinet.[44] The battle for Geneva may have indicated, not for the first time, a lack of 'reality' in Philip Noel-Baker.

Anthony Eden, strolling at Chequers with Edward Stettinius, spoke for many when he remarked that 'he liked Noel-Baker personally and he was a very sincere man, but did not feel he was a practical person as he was a dreamer and not a doer . . .'[45] Andrei Gromyko, for the U.S.S.R., stood out against a return to Switzerland. Sensing that Washington was opting for California, a 'deflated' Noel-Baker found even the British Cabinet disposed to let the matter ride. They would, he felt, let the whole business simmer although 'simmering will mean congealing'.[46] A two-to-one majority disposed of the issue and by the end of December 1945 it was clear that the headquarters would be across the Atlantic. Charles Webster made plain in his diary his regard for the doughty campaign of his friend, even though as it reads today there may be a hint of rationalisation about it:

'But the final result justifies the action of the Minister of State. By his courageous stand he has justified us in the eyes of Europe. Moreover, by forcing the U.S. to show its hand and seek for the seat, he has produced more important political results. As Stevenson <Adlai Stevenson> confessed in his speech, the U.S. can no longer pretend that a special responsibility for the success of the U.N.O. does not lie upon her by the fact that she has the seat. She sought it . . .'[47]

There are indications that this approbation might have been acceptable to Noel-Baker only with hesitation. He had confided his fears to Edward Stettinius three weeks before the vital proposal was tabled. 'I am convinced', he said, 'that if we go to the United States it means that Russia will have a free hand in Europe, and her power politics will make it difficult for the rest of us . . .'[48] It is quite possible that these fears were based on deductions from conversations just as much as they may have been instinctive. Noel-Baker came to appreciate the hard-edged rationale of Gromyko from discussions and he became uneasily aware that the idealistic, sincere Stettinius frequently side-stepped issues, partly because in his eyes a vacuum must be filled quickly if emerging inter-Allied differences were not to fracture the fragile post-war accord.

The decision to build the U.N. headquarters in New York was acceded to by Noel-Baker. (In this connection, it is interesting to notice what happened when, towards the end of 1946, the Ukraine tried to reassert the claims of Europe as headquarters site. Although he must have felt some regard, mainly a sentimental one, for a German or Parisian locale, Noel-Baker resolutely opposed the motion as being out of order and as constituting a reversal of a former agreed decision. A majority rejection of seven to three confirmed him in his judgement.)[49] As Minister of State in 1945, Noel-Baker could do no other than proffer his government's acceptance of the decision about the headquarters. He contented himself by making one thing very clear to the Preparatory Commission. He declared that representatives of the Big Five should not feel so much at home in one of their territories as to pre-empt democratic discussion (as had often happened in Paris after Versailles). Stettinius acknowledged his colleague's apprehension – 'his experience with the League was that such a system <viz. of private meetings> did not work and that agreements among permanent members ahead of League Assembly meetings had provoked resentment among the others . . .'[50] Nor was Noel-Baker convinced by Gromyko's belief that small powers were grateful for such consensus among the greater states.

The second achievement of the Preparatory Commission was a careful examination of how a Charter of the United Nations might relate to the former provisions of the League of Nations Covenant. Such a scrutiny was regarded as a highly complicated undertaking and, in fact, Foreign Ministers of member states in their submissions depended very much on advisers. Gladwyn Jebb records how Ernest Bevin ('a very lovable man') wisely left the minutiae of Charter issues to the experts, even though he was not very fond of Labour intellectuals:

'even the saintly and well-disposed Phil Noel-Baker, who served him loyally and with great efficiency in the Foreign Office as Minister of State, and who, incidentally, had been largely responsible for the successful operation of the "Executive Committee".'[51]

The United Nations Charter was signed on 26th June 1945 and formally ratified later on 24th October. In regard to the Charter, one or two basic points might be stressed. Primarily, the full implementation of provisions on paper depended upon a fundamental agreement between the Super-Powers. In the first flush of peace there were common expectations that the League system of mutual guarantees, legal undertakings and some provision for sanctions could be discounted to some extent, in favour of a more flexible arrangement based on concerted cooperation among great powers. Initially, few can have realised how rapidly the Assembly would fracture into splinters of 'client states'. In the aftermath of the nuclear ending of six years of war, it was supposed that all states would be ready to go beyond the Charter and prohibit the threat or use of force, not just the 'resort to war'. Progressive enforcement of this readiness would have a weight that the Covenant never managed to secure. Was though, the Charter quite 'weighty' enough? Some two years later, it is interesting to record, Lord Cecil and Noel-Baker went to Downing Street and raised the possibility of devising a Convention to buttress the Charter. The notion was put elsewhere (in a memo) by Noel-Baker and in similar terms, namely, that 'the Convention will be to the Charter what the Protocol could have been to the Covenant'. Clem Attlee told his visitor that he was worried lest this device should modify the Charter. Possibly recalling the failure of governments to ratify the Protocol 15 years previously, he confessed his inability to see how such definition of intent would ensure sufficient ratification. He would have to consult his Foreign Secretary, Ernest Bevin. The matter seems to have ended there.[52] Noel-Baker must have returned to his perspective of 18 months before, when he had discounted suggestions for amending the Charter in favour of an insistence: 'let us try to work it first'. At that time he had publicly recognised the imperfections of the Organisation's procedures. A continuing scrutiny was inescapable. We must, he said, 'throw the searchlight of our collective wisdom on the recent working of the Security Council.'[53]

Prospects for peace seemed reasonably bright in 1946. Noel-Baker, in February that year, assured the House of Commons of Britain's determination, 'to use the institutes (sic) of the United Nations to kill power politics', and some months earlier Ernest Bevin had seen the U.N. as the first step towards world government.[54] Contra opinion ranged from fatalistic to cynical. One observer may have had Noel-Baker in mind when he put it succinctly, 'High-mindedness easily became no more than a simple-mindedness, which abhorred the uneasy compromises of politicians between the dictates of power and a deference to morality'.[55] An instance of Noel-Baker's moral stance may be seen in the proceedings of the Security Council of 17th November 1946 when, as Britain's spokesman, he refuted an allegation from Andrei Vishinsky of the U.S.S.R. that there were deep-laid designs to overthrow the Charter. Was it not Soviet intransigence that was short-circuiting agreement within the Security Council? Would not constitutional reform best be brought about through the customary processes of discussion where these were founded in mutual trust? On this occasion it is not clear how far the United Kingdom attitude went beyond censure and towards buoyant optimism.[56] Noel-Baker would certainly not have carried everyone with him some months earlier when he had declared that 'nationalism prevails in the chanceries of many countries, in the cottages of none'. Some critics would not have seen oratorical flourish as legitimating such a degree of confidence.[57]

A second point about the U.N. Charter is a weakness, evident in there being no centralised system for facilitating interpretation of the Charter. As in Geneva, so in New York, the Assembly can and does ask the International Court for advice on legal questions but there is a width of possible interpretation of Charter Articles which allows for loopholes, neglect, and possible evasion. As a principle, external interference within bounds subject to domestic jurisdiction has always been proscribed, yet it is the extent and the validity of those bounds that has frequently caused dispute.

A large amount of self-interest is to be seen and not many would demur from one observation that, 'there has been a tendency on the part of individual members to play down the domestic jurisdiction principle in those instances where they want United Nations action and to stress its importance and inviolability when it is in their interest to do so'.[58] Both Covenant and Charter fundamentally provide for a continuity of watchfulness, and appropriate action as Noel-Baker emphasised in Parliament in August 1945, echoing similar words of Clement Attlee:

'Collective security is not merely a promise to act when an emergency occurs, but it is active cooperation to prevent emergencies occurring. What, I think, is required is a continuous discussion of international affairs, not spasmodic action at times of crisis.'[59]

Finally, neither Covenant nor Charter expressly ruled out regional groupings. When Ernest Bevin began to move closer towards alliances after 1945, the majority of the Labour Party followed him. Where Winston Churchill and many in Washington had viewed alliance in 'grand' and 'special relationship' terms, others owning broader political adherence saw the regional association as a device for harmonising interests and obligations. What Roosevelt had termed a readiness to accept responsibilities and a preparedness to make sacrifices for it could be discharged within more finite parameters. The North Atlantic Treaty Organisation, which was to be created in 1949 would be a tribute to an ideal and a response to reality. Nevertheless, this area of contention was to become a virulent one between East and West and those who drew up the Charter were not able, as Zimmern sees it, to 'dovetail' doctrines easily nor could they cope with 'the adjustment of widely opposing and, in some cases, contending wills'.[60]

The interlinking of General Assembly and Security Council was approached with great care by the Preparatory Commission. The experience of 20 years of Geneva revealed the hazards of what Woodrow Wilson had seen as the approach to 'open agreement openly arrived at'. National individualism might be encouraged rather than discouraged. Meetings with carefully designed agendas, all too often degenerated into Harold Nicolson's 'exercises in forensic propaganda'.[61] Both the League and the U.N. were envisaged as operating at two distinct levels. A General Assembly was to be the main representative body of delegates from member countries. Six ancillary committees would deal particularly with political matters, social affairs, the economic and financial field, the budget, and trusteeship. Essentially, the Assembly would be the instrument for members to raise issues or refer important world problems to the appropriate agencies and executive branches of the U.N. So far as possible, economic and social questions were regarded as belonging to the purview of an Economic and Social Council, whose interdependent relationship to the General Assembly had to be safeguarded. For the purpose of survey and report, for initiating and developing programmes of action, a number of commissions such as one for human rights could be formed. The second body, at a higher level, the Security Council, had a different constitution and function for it was set up, in the eyes of the Preparatory Commission, 'in order to ensure prompt and effective action by the United Nations . . . <with> . . . primary responsibility for the maintenance of international peace and security'. Some two years previously, Noel-Baker had seen the 'ground floor' as illustrating and advancing the principle of 'universality', and the 'upper floor' as functional in that 'it would group only Nations ready for close and active cooperation, especially in the field of collective security'. The Assembly would have a deliberate not an executive role, Noel-Baker had told his former colleague, Frank Walters, roguishly adding 'You will see that my ideas are very *un*governmental, indeed gangsterish!' Width of representation in the lower tier and effectiveness in action in the upper tier would do something, he believed, to reduce the 'running sore of misunderstanding' so obvious in relations among states.[62] Clear responsibility for executing action was assigned to the appropriate agencies of the U.N. who would be expected upon request, to give an undertaking to assist the Security Council. At the time of its inception there was not clear agreement as to whether the Security Council should or could discharge a continuous or a spasmodic function. Three types of meeting were proposed: 'regular', 'periodic', and 'extraordinary', depending to a large extent upon whether a hypothetical 'danger to peace' was judged as something which necessitated scrutiny, monitoring, and intervention either in a low-level situation or a critical one. Meetings would be public, and held under a rotating chairmanship. Especially important to the Commissioners in 1945 was the formation of a Military Staffs Committee to bring together quickly and authoritatively a body of technically informed opinion.

It is clear from Noel-Baker's writings that those who were in at the creation of the U.N. predicted with confidence that the Charter would be a more definitive instrument than the Covenant had been. One important distinction between 1919 and 1945 was that the functions and powers of the two bodies were clarified. Separateness was incorporated into the structure and into procedures: the Security Council, for instance, would not refer a dispute 'back' or 'down' to the deliberative body, the Assembly. Again, the Charter was designed to make the Security Council responsible for deciding what enforcement measures needed to be used to maintain peace. In 1924 the League had attempted to meet this demand with its Protocol, but the enabling machinery had never come into force. Thirdly, at the outset, the U.N. was to have a more secure basis for decision, in that findings of the Security Council (often though not exclusively as a consequence of the Assembly referring an issue to it) would be more binding than were the recommendations of the former League. In respect of the last-named principle, two points were seen as important. Emphasis in resolving contentious matters must first of all be placed upon improvement of the relationships between states. In this sense, action should be stressing prevention not merely an enforcement of edict. Secondly, 'intervention' where it was believed necessary should not be given a narrow, technical interpretation. Processes of enquiry, recommendation, and agreed implementation of decision were to constitute intervention as a medium of conciliation rather than coercion.[63] The United Nations, then, basing its work on the Charter, would be engaged simultaneously in interpreting different provisions of the Charter and in building up a body of customary law, thus, the Charter would come to be eventually a framework, as it were, imposing certain limits and laying down a number of directives. Differences of interpretation would remain without doubt, nevertheless, 51 governments had demonstrated their faith in the U.N. by ratifying the accords by the end of 1945.

Despite impressive progress in theory and in practice, there remained issues to trouble the initiators of the U.N. In the seminal pronouncements of the Creighton Lecture in London in 1946, Sir Charles Webster had warned the Royal Institute of International Affairs (of which Philip Noel-Baker was a stout patron) about the need to reject, instinctively, 'the idea of forming a naked Great Power Alliance'.[64] Mixed feelings predominated around 1946. If it were so that the Moscow Declaration of 30th October 1943 and the Dumbarton Oaks Proposals of 9th October 1944 were seeking to remedy a weakness of the League of Nations days where unanimity was demanded before action was undertaken, then this seemed to discriminate against smaller nations. At least on paper, under the League system, the views of smaller states were given fair weight. Again, if the new Security Council was to be dealing almost entirely with security questions and, moreover, if its function was to be a continuous one (as the U.S.S.R. preferred) the arbiters of action were likely to be major powers. Webster and Noel-Baker seemed to discern such a possibility. There was, too, a double-edged doubt in the opinion of *The Times* of 12th October 1944, in considering that if the world organisation were to exist for security as such, rather than for justice as such, the paradox and the unsatisfactory nature of it would not be overlooked for long, especially by smaller member states. In Noel-Baker's view, we were failing to ensure that there would be agreement by all members to act together to forestall an aggressor. The worst part of the Dumbarton Oaks scheme, he had told a friend a week after its provisions were announced the preceding year 'is what they have done about Security. In my view it not only constitutes no advance, it is a serious retrogression from what we had in the Covenant . . .' Moreover, as he and others realised, it might be necessary to act against not only covert aggression, but against the more constant risk of 'camouflage war' (to use Liddell Hart's expression) where a state might employ infiltration and proxy-warfare rather than risk an all-out and multi-retributive contest. Yet, in the last resort, whatever safeguards might be devised on paper it was not 'machinery' which could save nations. 'It was not the law or the machinery which failed before. It was the resolution of the Governments when the crisis came.'[65]

Very clearly the relationship of Council to Assembly had continued to worry supporters of the evolving United Nations. It is interesting to juxtapose the remarks of Philip Noel-Baker addressing the General Council of the League of Nations Union in the spring of 1943, with minutes of an interview 10 months later when he and others met with Eden, the Foreign Secretary. On the former occasion Noel-Baker was careful to speak for a desirable balance of representativeness to ensure that the Assembly was not just a talking shop and the Council a clique. The moral authority of states would thus be clearly visible even if it meant a two-tier system, which some critics (he must have had Konni Zilliacus in mind) might fear was irreconcilable with the principle of sovereign equality of states. Such a structure would not institutionalise a supra-governmental body (which he and Lord Cecil termed 'quite impracticable'), on the other hand, a bicameral organisation ought to seek somehow to press not *national* views but *people's* views. The last distinction, a difficult and debateable one, was not elaborated further.[66] Anthony Eden, in his room in Whitehall was candid and optimistic. The Moscow Declaration of three months earlier was based on a record of private four-power discussions. Ministers had had 'to tread carefully' to accommodate the stern security-conscious views of the U.S.S.R. (which, though, had been 'most helpful') with the vague, overly more democratic feelings of the U.S.A. Eden, sensing the 'isolationist' tendencies across the Atlantic had felt disappointed at the poor progress made, though he intimated that the issue of adequate representation of greater and smaller powers could somehow be settled.[67]

Two very significant developments were to cast the inter-relationship of General Assembly and Security Council increasingly in a new light. First, the characteristics of the member-states had been marked by developing nationalism. Of the 50 states signing the Charter at San Francisco in June

1945, almost one in four were Asian or African States, most of them newly independent. This proportion, twice that of the League in 1919, skewed the focus of concern away from Europe. Even a poor and politically backward country now had a vote and, collectively, their influence, whether 'unaligned' or 'mediatory' or slanted towards a Great Power pole, was to be considerable. In several ways smaller nations began to use the General Assembly, primarily, for stating their own opinions and for exercising at least a verbal autonomy, secondly, for associating themselves with 'like-minded' states of comparable rank, and thirdly, as clients or supporters of a particular Great Power. As a consequence, the cutting edge of both General Assembly and Security Council became blunted somewhat by political and ideological considerations, firmer and more strident than those which marked progress in Geneva. Secondly, as a consequence of the considerations just mentioned, members sought to interpret at least one Article of the Charter with varying degrees of self-regard and Article 51 is an example of this, namely:

'Nothing in the present Charter shall impair the inherent right of individual or collective self-defence if an armed attack occurs against a member of the United Nations, until the Security Council has taken the measures necessary to maintain international peace and security . . .'

The safeguard of Article 51 was construed as legitimating defensive 'arrangements' which, in the case of N.A.T.O. and the Warsaw Pact, were to grow into umbrellas or blocs.

It was in respect of voting procedures that the Preparatory Commission found achievement hard won. (Argument, in fact, remains unabated.) If belonging to the U.N., as one American has termed it, is 'a system of societal responsibility from which there is no ethical escape' then should the principle of no nation being forced to 'vote in judgement on itself' be held to be sacrosanct? Especially, if it results, as in the Security Council, in a state which does not wish a matter to be debated, being able to 'veto' discussion? It is interesting that in November 1950, four years later, the 'Uniting for Peace' resolution aimed to get around a possible stalemate by proposing that the Assembly could meet within 24 hours, at the request of a majority or if any seven Council members, if it were so that a veto had prevented the Council from acting to meet a threat to peace. Andrei Vishinsky of the U.S.S.R., which had been absent when the vote was taken, was to denounce this as a 'crude violation of the Charter' and a 'usurpation of the Council's privileges'. Nevertheless, many had argued, Philip Noel-Baker and Gilbert Murray among them, that the illiberal potential of the veto and other procedures was no reason for not persisting with an improvement of the mechanism of the United Nations.[68] Somehow the early belief that Great

Powers were 'trustees in council' and not masters subordinating the Assembly was never borne out: the veto was used more than was ever expected. Reality ensured that the right to withdraw from voting, and, further, the right to use the veto, were eventually agreed. After all, with or without the threat or use of legal sanctions, an attempt to punish or coerce a super power would result almost certainly in world war. There was an attempt by the British delegation on 1st December 1946 to suggest *inter alia* restraint in using a veto by any state which considered a proposal did not go far enough its way. The grounds upon which a veto action was based should be explained and, usefully, subcommittees might attempt the resolution of difficulties before final voting. This plan did not progress very far.

Not surprisingly, major powers constantly identified those who differed from them as hostile. Where the West saw certain Soviet moves as expansionistic and inimical to U.N. principles, the delegates of the U.S.S.R. deplored in discussions, votes and vetoes what they took to be manipulation and a backing away from the requirements of the Charter. It was not they who had abused voting procedures, rather, their opponents had abandoned the principle of unanimity.[69]

Generally in debate the United Kingdom delegation showed a reluctance to take too sharp a profile. This may partly have been because the British Government, as a colonial power, needed to take account of the attitude of newly-independent countries. At all costs, confidence as well as caution must be shown and even if they had agreed with Field Marshal Jan Smuts in private as to the perennial difficulty of distinguishing who was one's enemy, British delegates were much more careful in public.[70]

By the end of December 1945 the Preparatory Commission had done its job. As we have seen, it had to its credit considerable achievements in respect of facilitating a continuity in aims and structure between League and U.N., in distinguishing and coordinating the functions of Assembly and Security Council, and in laying down voting procedures. Investigation and discussion were the precursors of decision. Two things were now necessary: to bid farewell to the League of Nations and, then, to welcome the new organisation. There had to be a final League Assembly before the succession passed over in the January of 1946, though it was not at all clear that there was perceptible agreement about this. Suspecting that there were moves afoot in the London of late 1945 to sink the League into oblivion, F. P. Walters later puts the record in resolute terms when he refers to the possibility that the League would have no final marking as an 'ungenerous proposal':

'Ernest Bevin and Noel-Baker at the Foreign Office insisted that the Assembly should meet in its own home at Geneva, where its rules and traditions could be respected and its last decisions taken in dignity and tranquility . . . a debt owed to history, to the past achievements of the League, to the memory of the men who had gathered there in other days.'[71]

Noel-Baker was to be among those who met in the Palais des Nations in Geneva on 8th April 1946. Cecil, invited by Attlee and Bevin to be a member of the final Genevan delegation and to make a valedictory speech, raised the assembly with his call for perpetuating the work of the League of Nations: 'The League is dead. Long live the United Nations!' Doubtless, Cecil had in mind the opinion of Winston Churchill, writing to him on Cecil's 80th birthday in September 1944:

'This war could easily have been prevented if the League of Nations had been used with courage and loyalty by the associated nations. Even in 1935 and 1936 there was a chance, by making an armed Grand Alliance under the aegis of the League, to hold in subjection the rising furies in Germany . . . We tried our best, and though the road has been one of tragedy and terror, the opportunity will surely be offered again to mankind . . .'[72]

Addressing the final Assembly of the League, Noel-Baker cast a glance backwards before looking forward:

'My government supports the League to the very end. We know now that we who stood for collective security were right, and that our opponents who ridiculed us were always catastrophically wrong. We know now that the World War began in Manchuria 15 years ago. We know now that, four years after, we could easily have stopped Mussolini if we had taken the sanctions that were obviously required – if we had closed the Suez Canal to the aggressor and stopped his oil. Geneva was the first Parliament of the World. Our work has not ended, it has only just begun. This time both the governments and peoples are resolved to win.'[73]

It must be said that while the majority of his audience acknowledged the need, as the President, Mr. Carl Hambro, reminded them, to turn disappointment into use in cementing the structure of a new world security, many others on both sides of the Atlantic were more pessimistic. There seemed to be so many areas of the world where enmity and strategic designs forestalled an equitable solution to problems. If it were recognised that Ernest Bevin's wish 'to go where the hell I like without anybody pulling me up with a passport', was more boisterous than realistic in its oratory, a declaration of Noel-Baker's fell rather short of realism. At the Labour Party's 1946 Bournemouth Conference he proclaimed that 'despite the difficulties of the international situation a stable and permanent peace would be achieved'. The audience had applauded vigorously; the platform seems to have revealed some quieter, thoughtful faces.[74]

As preparations for the official inauguration of the United Nations went ahead at the beginning of January 1946, the attention of the press and of the B.B.C. appears to have been comprehensive, objective and optimistic.

'Austerity London' worked hard to clean up Central Hall in war-damaged Westminster. It took two months to refurbish and to provide seating for two thousand delegates from all over the world. On 9th January H.M. King George VI inspected the undertaking. Noel-Baker explained the layout of the building and showed his royal visitor the arrangements for recording and for translation. The new blue and gold flag of the United Nations screened the organ loft. That evening, at St. James Palace, King and Government dined the representatives of 51 nations. Journalists flocked to Noel-Baker's press conference and one, at least, found him 'a suave conversationalist, and slightly breathless speaker: he champions open diplomacy and an absolutely free press . . .' Others were invited to the Foreign Office itself where, in a severe red-curtained room next door to Ernest Bevin, the Foreign Secretary, Noel-Baker worked tirelessly through a 15-hour day aided by six secretaries and four constantly-ringing telephones. The secretariat had, said *The Spectator*, 'a spirit of almost religious fervour and at the same time of a strongly practical objectivity'. Doubtless industry was egged on by the belief current then among Labour politicians, that popular endorsement was empowering a 'Great Experiment' both at home and abroad.[75]

Sadly, within six months of the founding of the United Nations the divisive strains of a polarised world were beginning to sound. In January 1946, for instance, the World Federation of Trade Unions had put in a bid for full representation in the General Assembly and on the Economic and Social Council. Philip Noel-Baker felt unable then to support the request for one factor was that of commonsense, namely, that admission of a non-governmental organisation could create an untenable precedent in that any privileges accorded the W.F.T.U. would also have to be granted other bodies. This position was interpreted by the Soviet Union as one of hostility towards workers' representation and the United Kingdom delegate had to refute this. A compromise was achieved in the acceptance of a United States resolution that the W.F.T.U. be permitted to cooperate in a consultative capacity. In Noel-Baker's opinion it would give the Federation the chance to form 'a great indirect power by the creation of informed opinion' rather than grant them (and very likely others) direct representation. It was not a question, after all, of denying legitimate recognition to 'bona fide' groups: 94 organisations were applying for approval and 700 had been circularised to see whether they might like to send observers to U.N. meetings.[76] More vigorously the U.S.S.R. objected to the presence of British Forces in Greece and in Indonesia. Ernest Bevin felt bound to reject the charge that these actions constituted a threat to world peace, even more that they were hostile to Greek 'progressive' elements.[77] Britain at the time was in the throes of adjustment to a new role and was in the process of losing an empire. A three-man mission had been despatched to Delhi in March 1946 to talk about transition to self-government in India. Mountbatten, last of the Viceroys, had a timetable for imperial relinquishment on the front of his desk. Egypt was already asking for revision of the 1936 Treaty which had imposed a condominium of power in the Sudan and garrisoning by British forces in Cairo and the Suez Canal Zone. Farther east, the report of an Anglo-American Committee of Enquiry into Palestine was expected to come from the printers with recommendations (from the Americans) as to heightened Jewish immigration and lessened occupation by Britain.

Institutional progress seemed clear to participants by March 1946. 'At London, in 37 days', claimed Senator Arthur Vandenberg, 'the United Nations turned a blueprint into a going concern, an ideal into a reality. On January 10th we had a "scrap of paper", in 37 days we gave it life.'[78] 'It has been', said Vandenberg (a man given to euphoria), 'a phenomenal success!' Equally obvious, though, were the shadows of Great Power manoeuvring. The celebrated 'Iron Curtain' speech which Winston Churchill delivered at Fulton, Missouri, on 4th March 1946 appeared to divide the old amity between East and West in rigid and fatalistic terms. Many delegates feared it was a mistake to make the U.S.S.R. even more suspicious and uncooperative. Would it never be possible to work for 'solidarity' in other ways? Stalin certainly branded the speech as dangerous and warlike, and few can have been surprised when in Paris two months later the Foreign Ministers of former allies failed to agree on draft peace treaties, the withdrawal of armed forces, and reparations from former enemies especially Italy.

The United Kingdom Delegation to the Second Assembly had to deal with a host of important and tangled issues. The evidence is plain in the great collection of telegrams, consultative papers, delegation reports, speech notes and memoranda that Noel-Baker, the Delegation leader has left behind him. Rehabilitation of Germany, the relationship of the Four Power Zones, the feeding and housing of millions of 'displaced persons' (or 'D.P.s' as they became known) raised stark questions for a United States, wanting to be generous, and for a Britain, scarcely recovered from six years of attrition and conflict. Differences over Balkan frontiers reflected the confusions of the Hapsburg succession after 1918 and the East-West divide of 1945. In addition to the realities of post-war recovery and jockeying for strategic advantage there were the less certain problems of neutralism and independence in India, south-east Asia, and the Middle East. The Delegation seems to have coped resourcefully enough, though there is an instance perhaps of the results of pressure in one laconic message from

Noel-Baker, staying at the Washington Embassy, to the Foreign Office: 'my telegram No. 6186, paragraph 2, for "Belgium" please read "Bulgaria"'. It is quite clear, on the other hand, that the Delegation sailed under very clear orders and were assisted by a numerous collection of expert advisers.[79] Generally, the Labour Government of Attlee seemed 'on top of the wave', their delegates at the U.N., Hartley Shawcross, Hector McNeil and Philip Noel-Baker making an excellent team, fortified by assurance they had of Whitehall's firm support. Gladwyn Jebb, the U.N.'s first Acting Secretary-General, returning to London to a Foreign Office Under Secretaryship, recorded his confidence about prospects for the Second Session of the U.N. commencing in October 1946 stressing that, 'Phil's passionate attachment to and knowledge of the U.N. added weight to the British cause, just as it had done in the 20's and 30's at Geneva . . .'[80]

Fortunately, the bluntness and energy of Ernest Bevin did not lead to his intervening over much in the day-to-day work of the U.K. Delegation. The predilections of 'the big man' were plain enough as he enunciated them. First, charge the U.N. with guardianship of peace. Second, secure the buttresses of alliance and 'understanding' so long as they do not lead to alienation (what Attlee termed 'exclusive friendships'). Third, stand fair and firm – 'we are ready', Bevin had said, 'to put the cards on the table – face upwards'. Policies framed in such terms required much sensitivity and discretion in his assistants. Noel-Baker had had to reassure Parliament that His Majesty's Government did not mean to have an 'unambitious foreign policy'. There would be an underlying unity of approach despite the common impression, as one observer aptly puts it, that Bevin was 'disposed to live on two planes, that of guileless sonority – as though the world would be all sweetness and light if only foreign statesmen were as sincere as himself – and the plane of tough defence of British interests'.[81] Within the Foreign Office and at the Palace of Westminster, Bevin's junior ministers had to communicate as tactfully as they could the reservations and enquiries of Party members to one whose 'instinctive reaction to opposition had always been to flatten it'. It was perhaps easier for Noel-Baker and others to attempt to reassure fellow-Members that Britain's support for the U.N. was distilled from a mixture (Bevin's) of reasoning, experience, self-reliance, and intuition.[82]

In a fairly definite fashion those, like Noel-Baker, who brought theoretical detachment to scrutiny of detail, had on the one hand to convince a square-jawed Secretary of State of feasibilities, and on the other hand to win over diplomats to broader views. They did not always succeed. An instance of this is to be found in the diary of Lord Killearn who had left his Cairo Embassy to attend a London conference on Palestine:

'Noel-Baker <now Minister of State> in the chair. Not so good as Bevin; feet rather off the ground on "international lines" . . . whilst I have nothing but the most emphatic admiration for our good Secretary of State, Ernest Bevin, one cannot help being somewhat apprehensive in regard to international enthusiasts such as Noel-Baker.'[83]

At such a conference junior ministers had to work all hours of the day to prepare briefs and arrange consultation for a Minister, an increasingly exhausted one, who was always a getter-of-things-done. Prompt attention to duty was peremptorily demanded of all juniors with at least the saving grace that if a course of methodical action was brought only to an inconclusive end, the ministerial verdict (and half-praise at that) would often be a gruff 'let them wait 20 years . . .' Even so, despite the persistence of the Secretary of State and the devoted doggedness of his staff the problems of Britain's involvement in an Arab-Jewish conflict, as they were spotlighted in New York, almost proved Bevin's undoing. Liberal and Jewish opinions on both sides of the Atlantic were soured and outraged. The philhellene Noel-Baker also felt troubled that the British Government had intervened in Greece. He and others had somehow to reconcile their own unease over unilateral foreign policies (or what looked like them) with a resolute need to defend the Government and their Party Executive from the attacks of left-wing critics.

As Secretary of State for Air, Noel-Baker returned to New York on the Queen Elizabeth in mid-October 1946. Kenneth Younger, accompanying him, found the old elusiveness becoming more obviously a barrier to communication and understanding:

'October 17th-21st. Philip is mostly working in his cabin, charming as ever and seems to lack the capacity for relaxation. People consequently don't get to know him. I myself, after a whole year, still feel him to be remote. I like everything about him – think he has a fine and generous mind, but there is some human quality lacking, some absence of personal warmth which may derive from his lack of fleshly vices and his puritanical background. The pathetic thing is that he obviously wants sympathy and support, but I find it very hard to give it to him.'[84]

A most important item on the agenda for Britain's representative was the question of how the proliferation of atomic energy might be regulated. Noel-Baker, for Britain, emphasised that His Majesty's Government regarded international control of atomic energy as the most important and urgent question before the Assembly. Member nations had got to open their frontiers and grant free access to whatever extent might be required for international inspection and monitoring. The 'atomic energy armaments race' was already in progress, but it was not too late to halt it. A motion of his that disarmament proposals for outlawing atomic warfare be placed on the

Assembly agenda was carried, notwithstanding that its origin as a move by the Soviet Union occasioned hesitancy in some quarters.

The previous year had seen the establishment of U.N.A.E.C., the United Nations Atomic Energy Commission. Inescapably, there was a need to agree on measures of control and this would mean consensus and sacrifice. Anthony Eden had put it rather well in the House of Commons on 23rd November 1945:

'For the life of me, I am still unable to see any final solution which will make the world safe for atomic power, save that we all abate our present ideas of sovereignty . . . we should make up our minds where we want to go.'[85]

Self-sacrifice on this scale was by no means evident among the Allies. There was great secrecy. Lord Bullock has revealed that only a select few in Whitehall were privy to discussion of atomic energy policy. In six years the Cabinet discussed the topic less than 10 times. An advisory committee, chaired by Sir John Anderson (later Lord Waverley) kept its cards close to its chest and Parliament was denied a debate. In such circumstances it was not easy for Britain's representatives in New York to appear either informed or particularly honest.

Noel-Baker's speech to the General Assembly was warmly applauded. Younger was pleased about this and not a little astonished, as others had been, by the preliminary nervousness of a practised and articulate speaker:

'October 21st-31st . . . I had not previously seen him during the preparation of a speech. I had heard that he got very strung up about it, and that is certainly the case. He shut himself up for a couple of days and was barely approachable. To my surprise it was almost worse when he had to do a 12 minute broadcast on the Labour Government . . . I am sure he got more worked up and spent more tears and sweat on it than I should have done, in spite of his 25 years of political experience. I must say it was again a good speech, though not enough to explain quite that degree of fuss.'[86]

In the event, the proposals before the Assembly generated more heat than light, and most of the resolutions that resulted were nodded through in general agreement rather than being subjected to methodical scrutiny for implementation.

Another indefinite situation came about in November 1946. The issue was whether member countries would be prepared to help compile a census of 'troop strengths', as it was termed, and thus clarify statistics about men under arms, reserve numbers, and temporary conscription. Noel-Baker's suggestion at New York was that the proposals for census (emanating from the U.S.S.R.) would be best considered if they were taken together with questions of general disarmament. The outcome of their discussion, he believed, might well determine 'whether mankind passes through atomic war into another dark age'. Information about military strengths must be verifiable 'on the spot'. The British Government had nothing to hide . . . We were ready on any conditions to verify the information we furnished 'on the spot'. Mr. Molotov, for the U.S.S.R., accepted this. How, though, was the enumeration of 'first-line strength' and of 'reserves' to be standardised? In what way was the 'readiness' of one-year and two-year conscripts to be assessed? Were all countries prepared to divulge the arithmetic of their mobilisation calculations? Was it possible to quantify the proportion of troops that particular armies stationed abroad as well as in their home country? Despite earnest attempts at resolution no agreement was to be reached. Many of those working in committee in New York must have recalled similar abortive discussions in Geneva a generation earlier.

From time to time, Noel-Baker came to feel anxious about the way in which Service advisers assumed the existence of an ideological divide – the Iron Curtain postulated by Winston Churchill in his speech at Fulton, Missouri in 1946. A result of this was a more obvious melding of an Atlantic alliance welcomed by Bevin, as Bullock puts it, – 'his bellow of joyous relief echoed all over Europe' – but thought of unhappily by those who forecast a growing militarisation of the compact. There had, in fact, been much discussion of alliances when the Labour Party broadsheets *Approach to Foreign Policy* and *Cards on the Table* appeared in early 1947. Significant in their titling, the first admitted that a collective structure to solve international problems might work only within a limited scope, the second favoured, as Bevin might have put it, placing cards upward on the table while employing a strategy that kept in mind less obvious options and reservations. Not only Bevin at this juncture appeared to be moving from the idealist standpoint of 'one world' to the down-to-earth viewpoint of 'one free world'.

In November 1946, Prime Minister Attlee decided that Noel-Baker should return to take more obvious charge of his Air Ministry department. This was, perhaps, not an unreasonable expectation though it must have disappointed the dedicated internationalist. Younger noted the recall with regret:

'It was very sad Philip having to leave <New York> especially as the one thing he really cares about began just before he left – disarmament. It has been much the biggest thing in the conference and has stolen the headlines for the past three weeks. It was encouraging to find that Bevin, who has been almost occupied in the Council of Foreign Ministers, asked that Philip might stay. But after one delay of about a week the P.M. said he must return to take charge of his ministry. From that angle it was right, but it was a shame his having to leave at that moment.'[87]

From the commencement of November 1946 the idealist in Noel-Baker was beginning to show exasperation, born of many toe-to-toe encounters at the U.N. A report to him of General Assembly proceedings of 30th October 1946 carried his pencilled footnote in these terms:

'I confess that Molotoff's (sic) speech, followed by the actions of the Soviet group in the committees of the Assembly, and in the General committee, alarms me considerably. There is an irresponsibility and an aggressive impudence of allegation and attack which we have never seen before . . . Broadly, the three Soviet delegations appear to be working to sabotage, if not to wreck, the Assembly. Perhaps I am over-interpreting what I have seen, and I should be grateful for the views and the experiences of those who have been sitting in the committees. I do not think that we should change our general attitude of courtesy and patience combined with firmness. I think the Soviet delegations are rapidly alienating the main body of the Assembly, and even the Czechs and the Poles, not to mention the French and Norwegians, are gravely exercised in their minds. But we should do well to consider if we should try to mobilise opinion for the defence of the Rules of Procedure and against the obstruction which seems to me to be the deliberate policy of three delegations.'[88]

Already some weeks earlier, the United Kingdom Delegation had been disturbed at the disputes between the United States spokesman on the Security Council and Mr. Maniulsky of the Ukraine Soviet Republic. There had been differences of opinion as to whether points about unrest in the Balkans represented matters of substance (and so legitimate Security Council business to be pursued further) or whether they were procedural (in which case it ought to go to a commission or sub-committee). Noel-Baker reported by telegram to Ernest Bevin thus:

'It seems to me that we were lately in danger of getting involved in an exchange of detailed and rather irrelevant arguments – and, in our lighter moments, of pleasantries, spiced occasionally by overt or covert insults – which tends to obscure the whole issue . . . No sooner have I answered a number of Mr. M.'s points than he dips into his bags for a few more, without I suspect, looking at them very carefully beforehand. When is this going to end?'[89]

Before he left Lake Success, Noel-Baker worked through disarmament proposals in the U.N.'s political committee with great effectiveness – 'did them brilliantly' according to Younger. The diarist goes on:

'Maniulsky in the chair was, of course, hopelessly biased – he and Molotov might have got away with almost anything if Philip had not been quite brilliant in keeping the committee on the rails. All the delegates and most of the press were more than complimentary after he had gone. He dashed straight from the committee to the airfield, feeling I think elated, but at the same time sick of having to leave the work only just begun.'[90]

The general demeanour of Noel-Baker did not escape attention by journalists during the debut of the new world organisation. This 'Practical

Internationalist' was assured and experienced. He spoke French, German, Greek, and Italian well: he was seasoned in cosmopolitan encounters. Intrigue he disclaimed; seriousness of purpose was his characteristic and he had clearly meant very earnestly the affirmation 'Politics to me are more a responsibility than a hobby'. The staunch advocate of global collaboration saw 'nothing inconsistent in the fact that his duties in London <he had recently become Secretary of State for Air> concern competition among the world's airlines, while his role in New York is to seek cooperation among the world's diplomats'. The American correspondent of *World Report* in November 1946, while acknowledging Noel-Baker's competence upon the world stage, was less sure that this was true of the domestic scene. 'Against him', it seemed, 'stands a lack of popular magnetism and, so say Labor politicians, lack of political color.' The conclusion is phrased, perhaps, in rather nebulous terms: 'Because his background and training make him concerned with problems of the present than with prospects of the future, Noel-Baker now is occupied with the U.N. and leaves to others speculation about Britain's Foreign Ministry."[91]

Autumn 1946 had, in fact, brought a change of scene for Noel-Baker. Attlee granted that Noel-Baker had served in the Foreign Office 'with great distinction . . .' but after consulting the Foreign Secretary it was decided that there should be a reshuffle in his department.[92] It is supposed, according to Ernest Bevin's biographer, Alan Bullock, that the former had conceded to party feeling when making first appointments, by agreeing 'to Attlee's choice of the high-minded and respected Philip Noel-Baker as Minister of State at the Foreign Office, where he had little, if any influence on policy and in October 1946 was replaced by the more congenial Hector McNeil'.[93] Clearly, Ernest Bevin felt easier working with the less intellectually sharp McNeil: they understood one another's minds. Noel-Baker was one of those always bringing schemes to the doorstep of Downing Street – like 'a hen laying eggs' Bevin had remarked. McNeil's debating skill would be an asset at the United Nations. What portfolio should Noel-Baker have? The Prime Minister proposed promotion to the rank of Secretary of State for Air as from 4th October 1946 and Bevin, with relief, assented. 'I agree with you about Noel-Baker. I think he will do well and his knowledge of my policy will be useful in shaping defence and he did well at War Transport.' Hector McNeil, Christopher Mayhew, and Patrick Gordon-Walker would provide Bevin with 'a good set up'. Kenneth Younger's diary has something to say about the change of scene for Noel-Baker:

'October 5th-12th. Philip's removal was due I think, not to any major policy disagreement, but to a general difference of approach as between him and Bevin, and a consequent reluctance on the part of Bevin to make full use of his advice. That being the fact, I daresay Attlee was quite justified in moving him, since Bevin is appallingly overworked and must have the team he wants. At the same time I cannot help fearing that our line at the U.N.O. will lose some of its international inspiration, and that we shall concentrate solely on driving a series of hard national bargains alongside the Americans.'[94]

Philip Noel-Baker, whether as a member of Preparatory Commission committees, or as a delegate at New York, or as speaker and writer on countless occasions has made no secret of his impatience and dissatisfaction with some of the activities of the United Nations. He has often described the U.N. as having no more teeth than the League, because its members do not have the understanding and the will to provide for collective and forceful programmes. Arbitration and intervention appear to be half-hearted on many occasions. Many important questions are settled elsewhere in Foreign Offices through compromise, barter, and threat. 'Peace', according to one U.N. official, 'as an operative purpose and as an operational programme has not yet found its proper place in the U.N. system, because the international system is not ready to undergo the transformations which such a move would require.' 'The peoples of the United Nations: We or They?' is still an unresolved question for many people.[95] Transforming attitudes and diverting prejudices is a legitimate function of the United Nations as it must be for the educative role of a back-up organisation, like the United Nations Association. Noel-Baker has rarely hesitated to address candidly those he has met in the Members Lounge of the U.N. Building, and those whose task it is to report upon the formal and informal business of the United Nations. In the very beginning days of the U.N., Noel-Baker urged journalists to accept two things. First, that an unequivocal approach was a sine qua non for progress. 'Paper conventions that no one applies will no longer do', he pointed out, 'and if we do not succeed together and get real results, we shall suffer, and suffer atrociously, in isolation.' Secondly, the 'fourth estate' had an onerous responsibility to present events and attitudes fairly. Had newspaper correspondents and the proprietors of the press given the U.N. 'a square deal'? Did they report what really mattered or did they disregard the big and vital events, to cast a searchlight on trivial incidents and report them as quarrels and disputes? What should be reported, already in the first year of the organisation's existence, was 'an astonishing measure of agreement'.[96]

On numerous occasions in Noel-Baker's experience, people had faced him with the question: 'United Nations – success or failure?' 'I feel', he once said in a broadcast response to that, 'as the Founders of the U.S. Constitution might have done in 1786. It will be years, they declared, even decades before we're sure we shall win . . .' It had struck him that the three maxims of Fridtjof Nansen, an indomitable explorer and organiser, were most appropriate:

'Never stop because you are afraid – you are never so likely to be wrong';
'Never keep a line of retreat – it is a wretched invention';
'The difficult is what takes a little time; the impossible is what takes a little longer.'[97]

For Noel-Baker, in the last few months of his life, change would come about if men and women everywhere could be made to see:

'that the vital interests of their nation are not in conflict with the vital interests of other nations. Just the opposite is true – the really vital interests of all nations are common interests, which they can only provide by common action in common institutions founded on common law.'[98]

Change, too, in a media-conscious age would be positive and public if, as Luard puts it, 'the character and direction of confidential discussions is influenced by knowledge of public encounter to come'.[99] First and last, one returns to Philip Noel-Baker's theory of the binding and generative force of public opinion – that concept which saw an international organisation as created by 'common interests' and kept together by 'common action'.

CHAPTER 8

Magnum Opus: *The Arms Race*, 1958

A REVIEWER OF NOEL-BAKER'S *The Private Manufacture of Armaments* in 1937 considered it 'clear, taut and elegant'.[1] Twenty years later, clarity and elegance are more obvious in a work acclaimed the world over, *The Arms Race*, which appeared in June 1958. The fruit of a lifetime of study was how *The Times* saw it – 'a dispassionate appraisal of the possibilities of international control of disarmament . . . The data was voluminous and its collation masterly, though not everyone accepted his thesis'. Another commentator believes it remains as 'a landmark of lonely eminence in the literature of the subject'.[2]

If the purpose of *The Arms Race* was to act as an exploratory medium, its construction was monumental and encyclopaedic. In addressing the world of the 1950's the author compiles a hugely detailed case, itemises, and differentiates cause and effect, motive, and method, as he had done throughout his public missionary years, conscious this time, that there is no looking back from the Nuclear Terror. Transforming the incantation into action is no longer a process over which we can theorise and delay. Saving our own necks and civilisation itself must now be the strongest and most direct of incentives. Nor will any nuclear 'exchange' be less than apocalyptic, without any Hague Convention or Esher-type Periods A and B. The work is built on immense lines. There are 8 Parts and 45 chapters. The starting point is a consideration of how the arms race has acquired its momentum. There follows in Parts 3 and 4 a broad-ranging survey of nuclear armaments, followed by an analysis of national and international attempts to regulate nuclear development and proliferation. Part 5 discusses the potency and threat of non-nuclear weapons. A following section which charts progress in practical schemes of conventional disarmament necessarily traverses ground much trodden in earlier years. Again, too, in the pages that follow, Part 7 points up the constant concern of its author with the possibility of disengagement and demilitarisation. The last word has to do with comprehensiveness, and the staging of control processes. Only gradual and realistic approaches will steer us clear of 'facile optimism' and 'facile pessimism'.

For Noel-Baker the greatest challenge of the Arms Race is the one that is internal to most of us: the 'self-induced hypnosis' of a defence posture against a predicated Threat. The ubiquitousness of a posture such as that, setting off a chain-response in the attitudes of everyone else, can only be met by a comprehensive and multilateral plan to decrease tension and reduce weaponry. Partial agreements are insufficient. Nothing short of final goals must be established from the start. Had there ever been a prospect of this coming about? In May 1955 there was a 'moment of hope', it seemed to Noel-Baker. Three years of work by a Disarmament Commission, set up by the United Nations, had framed a Six-point Programme for all-round arms reduction.

Nuclear weapons would be prohibited completely in coordinated stages. Conventional arms were to be reduced by progressively lowering permitted levels and ceilings. True, the programme was largely the work of a small committee of 'atomic powers'. Certainly, the progress of negotiating had been gravely hampered by Soviet obfuscation. After three months of wrangling, a gratified West saw the U.S.S.R. accepting the proposed objectives. Was the Nuclear Threat the impetus removing the log-jam? Did the vision of Apocalypse, a threat to everybody's future, dispel hypnosis and fatalism and bring accord dramatically nearer? The momentary feeling of hope must have been felt by the seasoned disarmament campaigners and by their younger followers. Yet the 'moment' passed. Noel-Baker sees the West backing away from the table after six months of prevarication. There is a return to the universal suspicions of the other side's evasion. Arms are being hoarded. Reduction represents weakness. Negotiation must proceed from 'strength' – *our* strength.

Today's arms race, hypnotic perhaps, spiralling, certainly, is in Noel-Baker's eyes a progression with a long history. Defence spending by the major nations trebled in the 30 years preceding 1913. Following the explosion of 1914-18, there ensued a period of restraint to be succeeded by a frantic eight-fold arming of a nervous Europe. Most nations, understandably, do not move much further than the defence, entirely legitimate, of their own territory. On occasion, it is clear, the smaller members of the herd will perceive a rogue elephant in their midst and arm themselves against the likelihood of aggression. Noel-Baker, however, sees the non-interventionist role of the United States before the 1939 war and the over-interventionist intentions of that nation after 1945 as destabilising factors. In the former instance, an 'isolationist' power was spending in

1939, only two-thirds of what Britain spent and one-fifth that of Nazi Germany. The number of men under arms in the U.S.A. was only 100,000 more than in the United Kingdom and 'far, far less' than in France, the U.S.S.R., Italy, Japan, and Germany. Would Europe have been a safer place if America had acted more resolutely to defend democracy for its founding fathers? The question is implicit in the writings of one who saw the potentially strong deserting the concept of the League. In the wake of 1945 there was a period of emerging anguish as a demobilised West, and a fearful 'neutralist' group of nations, watched the occurrence of coups in client states of the Eastern bloc and saw armed capability maintained. The arms race inevitably acquired a new momentum. It was a response that might be termed *reculer pour mieux sauter*.

That old imperative of rearmament – 'keeping the lead' – has acquired in the nuclear age, a new and sinister distinctiveness. Three modern changes strike chill in the writer of *The Arms Race*. Primarily, we are into an age of sophisticated strategy – the 'thunderbolt geometry' of modern belligerence.[3] Secondly, the peculiar nature of thermo-nuclear and chemical weapons, increases both their offensive power and their potential as agents of mass, and so indiscriminate, destruction. The function of such weapons within defensive systems is not at all easy to legitimise. Thirdly, the rate at which many of these devices become obsolete leads to colossal waste and a stimulated need to advance research and develop alternatives. Noel-Baker might have added two further developments which, even in the 50's and most obviously since then, fuel competition in armaments. Arms are traded or 'exchanged' between 'clients' who use them to prime a 'capability', located in a place which is strategically significant. Many of these locations are in under-developed territories; contest in such places may erupt into the 'proxy war'. In the second place, again in the 50's as later, sophisticated weapons are explicitly designed to lock into a *weapons system*. Thus, to offset coordination of militaristic intent, it is more than ever necessary to design schemes of general disarmament which defuse the interactive components in those systems. It is surprising that Noel-Baker does not place more emphasis on these two critical factors in *The Arms Race*, for he was constantly taking them into account in other places at that time.

In 1958, Noel-Baker was in a position to look back over his experience of the nuclear debate, as representative of His Majesty's Government at the United Nations in 1945 and 1946, and as participant in countless public discussions in print and on the platform and in conferences such as the annual one at Pugwash. There is no doubt that he had access to 'top-level expertise in the scientific and military field'. Part 2 of *The Arms Race* examines carefully the problems of atomic weaponry. The very production of what are increasingly referred to as 'nuclear devices' is escalatory in that the fision-fusion-fision process is common to both 'civil' and 'military' processes. Thus, non-military and military sectors are locked together and tend to be mutually reinforcing. It follows from this that one sector may 'shield' the other. Clandestine development and accumulation of fissile stocks are not difficult achievements. Further, destructive power is no longer straightforwardly related to size: the smallest elements may have immense power. 'Taming the bomb', to the writer of 1958, introduced fresh criteria on the moral plane in addition to the questions of the conventional disarmers. If now, some (nuclear) weapons were 'strategic', in a sense geo-political, and others 'tactical', then who was to take the decision about use? The politician? The general? Readers in 1958 were freshly aware of the distinction between 'clean' and 'dirty' thermo-nuclear devices. For them, Noel-Baker's query is 'are we moving out of the "purely military" uses of a weapon deployed to deal with a specific politico-military situation, into a "total response" situation where lasting effects of nuclear fall-out will result from that specific military resolve?' The first decision becomes the final decision. None of us, urges Noel-Baker, can escape the consequences of choice and decision. He quotes Henry Stimson's view in 1945 of the atomic bombing of Japan as 'this deliberate, premeditated destruction <being> our least abhorrent choice'.[4] More obviously and completely than a previous generation, we have to decide between use and restraint and between peace and oblivion. At this point in his discussion, Noel-Baker implies that we somehow lack the courage of our convictions: we are back to that state of 'self-induced hypnosis'. The appeal of Prime Minister Attlee in November 1945 for banishment of the nuclear arsenal is quoted without adding (a surprising omission), that at that time Attlee and his ministers were negotiating with the Americans for the development of a British bomb, and doing so without informing Parliament.[5]

Was it ever feasible that an international authority might lay the foundations of nuclear control? Already in December 1945, the three major atomic powers had persuaded the General Assembly of the United Nations to set up a commission with the twin aims of controlling nuclear energy and eliminating its belligerent use. Washington encouraged scientists like J. Robert Oppenheimer, and politicians such as David Lilienthal (who had cut his teeth on the great rural development schemes of F. D. Roosevelt in Tennessee) to press ambitious proposals through working party and committee. Total control was thought inescapable. A United States plan, called the Baruch Plan after its chairman, proposed an agency of international control, the International Atomic Development Authority, which would oversee the surveying, and mining of uranium, the siting of plants, reactor construction, and research and sale of nuclear products. This was Noel-Baker's long-hoped for generality of response from a fearful world. In day-to-day terms the work of the suggested supervisory authority would incorporate that function he had called for before 1939, in a word, an 'investigatory' one. 'Periodic inspection' of 'dangerous processes' would be continuous as a form of methodical and objective reporting. Only 'safe' activities would be permitted during the transition period when facilities would be demilitarised. Proposals such as these, involving not only international control but also working management, did not find favour in Moscow. Reiteration and some refinement of the case for management was largely met by a Soviet demand for tighter inspection and destruction of existing nuclear weapon stocks within three months. Noel-Baker sees the gulf widening as the East began to suspect an arrangement for 'interference' and the West to reject an intemperate attempt to cut out its nuclear superiority.

Sadly, Noel-Baker records the loss of hope as suspicion and vituperation inflamed discussion in New York. Soviet representatives voiced fear of financial and industrial monopoly by others and held that this conferred a dangerous feeling of superiority. Wasted in war, the U.S.S.R. desperately needed to restore its economy and would put up with no interference in its politico-economic autonomy. Recriminations were hurled across the Atlantic that American plans for committees, and monitoring schedules were nothing other than efforts at intrusions. If the Russians had been 'seriously interested in disarmament and peace', Noel-Baker believes, would they not have sought to amend the United Nations schemes through exploring guarantees rather than destroying the plans? Had we been too ambitious, too precipitate?[6] Did our arguments, and the consensus apparent behind them, appear to be a threat and impel the 'threatened' to take refuge in an 'anachronistic conception of sovereignty'?[7] There is no sounding here of a notion which may have occurred to an old League Hand, that the finality and malevolence of nuclear arms turns the accommodation of a Litvinov into the obduracy of a Vishinsky.

Part 3 of *The Arms Race* moves on to take a look at the possibilities of inspecting armaments more generally. Echoing some of the recommendations of the previous decade, there had been vigorous attempts by the British and French governments to do something about the stockpiling of materials. Proposals, tabled in May 1955, were accepted in all quarters in the interests of 'possible, prolonged, peaceful coexistence'.[8] Further detailed discussions, however, repeated the reservations of abortive pre-war conferences. On site scrutiny would rarely be totally effective. Duplicity and concealment were always possible.[9] More significantly than ever before, a specific group of powers – 'the nuclear club' – would want to retain the quite distinctive potential of a particular means of waging war, the thermo-nuclear device. Novel, too, in the 1950's, was realisation that inspection and proscription of any facet of the nuclear industry would very likely hamstring civil developments, to which any up-and-coming power would aspire.

Aside from technical considerations, as imponderable, it seems, in the mid-1950's as they had appeared two decades previously, certain political considerations are now stressed by Noel-Baker in *The Arms Race*. A writer who was more of a political analyst and historian would surely have mentioned these ideas earlier. He sees the Kremlin, half way through the century, shedding few tears over the demise of grand schemes for international ownership and management of nuclear resources. Russian nuclear development should be in Russian hands. Khruschev and his colleagues, looking westwards, may well have concluded, in view of what was happening in Hungary, Czechoslovakia, and Poland, that negotiated reduction of arms would be a better safeguard than reliance upon allies with secessionist tendencies. All sides would, in any case, have recognised that severe reductions in the nuclear armouries were not really likely, given that a ban on these weapons would have broken down the advantage of the West in that respect. Moreover, however genuinely dedicated to the cause of peace Eisenhower was in the White House, he had in his Cabinet some who held to a hard line of 'peace through <maintained> strength'.[10]

Part 4 returns to proposals for nuclear disarmament after a break in continuity of argument. The obligations of nuclear disarmament are seen as four-fold. We must neither manufacture nor test nor stock nor use these devices. Total control is only achieved through ensuring these interdependent obligations. Noel-Baker's concern here is more far-reaching than in earlier calls for disarmament. Control goes beyond mere inspection. The concept of 'freezing' production and stockpiling necessitates, as did the suggestion of ceilings on conventional arms, the readiness of all to subscribe to a collective imperative. The statutes of the International Atomic Energy Authority, even if they succeed in binding the public acceptance of states, can do little to prevent 'diversion' of stocks from civil to military use. An illicit siphoning off of three per cent of uranium stocks would pose grave hazards to security. Washington's plain reluctance to surrender its safeguard against clandestine procurement is termed by Noel-Baker a 'defeatist exordium'.[11]

A new arsenal of weapons requires testing. The very act of testing, in the case of nuclear arms, incorporates a hazardous degree of risk from 'fall-out' and this must surely call for prohibition. 'As with a ban on the *use* of nuclear weapons', Noel-Baker points out, 'the question is not *whether*, but *when*, the ban shall be imposed.'[12] The argument is now given another ratchet by being directed at those who, in 1958, espoused the call of 'Ban the Bomb'. Proclaimed as the essential step towards nuclear control it is an illusory strategy. Perhaps after all, he declares, it is Soviet propaganda. More likely to gain the approval of both sides, and ultimate acceptance would be some development similar to the one put to the United Nations on 19th April 1955 by Britain and France. Nuclear reductions could be made effective, they suggested, as soon as 75% of conventional arms had been eliminated. A graded reduction on these lines, Noel-Baker feels, would be a better way of working, particularly if some sort of control could bridge the 25% interval. The provision of safeguards is treated rather loosely. He wonders, for instance, whether sanctions applied by the I.A.E.A. against a state transgressing the code, would exercise even the effectiveness of a Security Council resolution. (The excluding function of the veto is to be borne in mind.) Holding (in trust) a stock of nuclear weapons (suggested by Jules Moch of France in 1955) may be a modern translation of the old suggestion of a central stockpile maintained by the League, but is it not an impractical idea in view of civilised man's abhorence of its indiscriminate finality? Clearly, 'a very broad and robust regulation of armaments' (the phrase is J. R. Oppenheimer's) would not give *absolute* security, and would depend upon nations accepting limitations of national sovereignty and practising a hitherto unusual degree of international cooperation.[13] The half-spoken fear of Noel-Baker here is that a combination of betrayal by 'the hawks' and the brake-effect of public ignorance and fatalism would disable present and future conferences as surely as had happened in the past.[14]

The arms race, while it hesitates to legitimise indiscriminate horror, inevitably normalises a good deal of research into means of mass destruction that depend upon chemical and biological elements. Noel-Baker, who had never forgotten the sight of gassed infantry in 1915, deplores the militaristic rivalry of laboratories before 1939. The fact that poison gas was not employed during the ensuing World War was not so much restraint imposed by the Geneva Protocol of 1925, as the result of War Office calculations of gain and loss. In hideous fashion, the 'effective' product of research is taken up into the war-wager's repertoire. Some weapons are resorted to as conventional media of attack (*less* often of defence) as was fire in the 1940's, though it had been strictly forbidden before 1939. There is, Noel-Baker points out, a moral imperative attached to the use of weapons which are regarded as morally repugnant. The Geneva Conference of 1932 made clear (sadly, without lasting effect) that curtailment of use, following on disclosure of existence would mean that states would renounce their right to retaliate in similar fashion against an aggressor who struck first. In 1958 there was already some discussion of the precept 'no first use', though this was to gather momentum in succeeding decades.

Noel-Baker recalls that during the 1920's and 1930's there were many earnest attempts to distinguish between offensive and defensive weapons. The Versailles Treaty of 1919 imposed *qualitative* limits in forbidding Germany and her former allies the possession of heavy artillery, tanks, and submarines. Robert Cecil and President Hoover had both proclaimed, in 1932, the need to reduce offensive strength by specific abolition, seeing this as retaining defensive capability and unimpaired security. Shape was given to proposals such as these in Britain's Draft Disarmament Convention the following March, but nothing more was heard of the move. In 1958, as the Missile Age is entered, the author of *The Arms Race* is less sure about the distinction. What is increasingly being defined as a 'scenario' is based on the theory (of hoary ancestry) that the best means of defence is attack, seen as the possession and continual acquisition of a 'capability'. Great improvements in accuracy, manoeuvrability, range, and means of launching have meant that a state's defensive 'posture' is made up of weapon-systems which other states will see as potentially hostile. Noel-Baker's point is that the very complexity of the systems leaves us with problems of identification and decision. (The tortuous vocabulary of the experts does not help.) How are we to decide which weapons are primarily 'defensive' and which might be used to make a 'first strike'? In what tactical circumstances, say, of overt threat or actual invasion, might certain first-line or reserve armaments be deployed? There seems in 1958, as there was for Noel-Baker 20 years earlier, no alternative to the total elimination of designated weapons, whether they are seen as 'defensive' or 'offensive' in nature. Unhappily he recognises that the arguments circle back to the 'realists' dictum that qualitative disarmament will be political emasculation if it depends upon removing the nuclear option a state possesses. This situation is paradoxical in at least two respects which are perhaps only implied here. The momentum of stock-building to enhance defensiveness, a process largely retaliatory, has contributed to phases of nuclear stalemate. While that state of balance might be considered to provide an opportunity for disengagement and reduction, it has highlighted the importance to some states of retaining an 'option' and a nuclear one at that. At least one observer regards, perhaps rather shortsightedly, the prime international problem in these circumstances as 'the enforcement of peace, and, not the curtailment of the means of waging war'.[15]

One or two arguments in *The Arms Race* were perhaps not particularly relevant to the nuclear age as it already was in 1958. The old plea for reduction of air forces was never likely to prove a popular recommendation, either in the days of rudimentary aviation or now that the modern state depended so much upon its use of the air. There is little concern nowadays that civil aircraft represent a force that might be converted to aggressive use. Again, how useful is it to suggest that modern navies may be scaled down on the lines suggested in the Versailles Treaty of 1919, or the Washington Naval Treaty of 1922, or the London Naval Treaty of eight years later? Today's naval forces are made up of a small number of units whose design and function is highly specialised. Moreover, however sleek or imposing the hull, it may be sent to the bottom in a matter of minutes if hit by a missile launched from land silo, aircraft or submarine. The residual fear that one bloc may have superiority in manpower is still there, with the added and very difficult point that man-unit or tank-unit superiority will have to be balanced (rather, compensated for) by retaining a defensive-offensive nuclear 'shield'. Noel-Baker recognises that this disparity (sometimes the statistics are disputed) constitutes a very difficult nut to crack.

Nevertheless, a number of the criteria employed by the disarmers pre-war are of equal validity today.[16] One should not discount the relevance of long-held proposals for reducing armed manpower. Committees still ponder the practicability of schemes, recognisable as of respectable vintage, for limiting conscription, reserves, and expenditure. Noel-Baker welcomes the fact that the United Nations recruits personnel who are then sent overseas as 'the Blue Berets' to maintain peace and to separate contestants. He deplores, of course, the failure to recruit a more substantial interventionist Police Force such as the League of Nations suggested on occasion.

There is still everything to be said for continued examination of a process of budgetary limitation. Noel-Baker reminds us that 'a sound, ingenious and workable scheme' was drawn up as far back as 1932 in the headquarters of the League. A crucial point then and now is that the 'straight cut' does not ensure equality of sacrifice. Simple comparisons of expenditure can be misleading. What has to be done is to devise a scheme for reconciling differences in accounting procedures and spending patterns so that Powers will recognise how the manipulation is done, consent to appropriate adjustment to offset, for instance, inflation and 'write-off' and, most important of all, agree to regular submission of accounts to an international, supervisory body. National funding of research and deployment ('the arms race in its most dangerous form') could be brought within bounds. In 1932 a League of Nations Technical Committee worked with representatives of 29 nations and, after meeting thrice a week for a year, was quite confident that 'audited' and 'preventive' supervision of spending was possible via unanimity and 'continuous observation'.[17]

The later pages of *The Arms Race* attest to the continued significance of geographical factors. There is still interest, Noel-Baker notes, in the possibility of demilitarising zones provided that (the point is implicit rather than explicit) disengagements are mutual. The draughtsmen of the League of Nations, redrawing particular boundaries, did not always manage to avoid leaving a vacuum which contenders subsequently sought to fill. In another sense, today's vacuum might be a nuclear-free area. Noel-Baker does not dwell much on something that might give a new meaning to the term '*cordon sanitaire*'. Equally there is a rather thin discussion of a concern, partly geographical, partly technical, namely, that of the foreign base. Dispersed military bases, while important strategically to the Great Power protectors of a state are, nevertheless, repugnant to many host communities. They are regarded by the client states as intrusions, increasing the host's vulnerability to onslaught by an enemy power. Not a great deal is said here about the possible demilitarisation of some bases – perhaps by way of 'trade-off' – and of an often-discussed notion, the internationalisation of others. Already, in 1958, technical innovations were superseding the facts of geography to some extent. Photographic reconnaisance had been refined over the years to give great accuracy and reliability. Satellites, rather than aircraft, would give a more comprehensive coverage with far less risk than the earlier methods, which essentially relied upon hazardous sampling. The more thorough the inspection, on the other hand, the less willingly nations appear to accept it. If it was once difficult, when tallies were submitted, to tell the liars from the statisticians, it is now usual to suspect the all-seeing inquisitive eye. Espionage is a constant fear. Noel-Baker, in discussing this in 1958, when techniques of observation were less sophisticated, insists that there was a certain degree of general readiness to accept long-range inspection. President Eisenhower, in the summer of 1955, had suggested an 'Open Skies' policy. The U.S.S.R., it is true, had at first demurred over aerial inspection, but they had gone on to announce their preparedness to establish an even closer type of observation, namely, the siting of ground control posts to monitor the likelihood of surprise attack. Naturally, if states were to use distance surveillance, with its operation through remote control and the interpretation of photographs, then there would be a premium on trust. The whole process must be multilateral. Evasion and subterfuge, at least on a large scale, are no longer possible. Can ways not be found of reaching agreement? Noel-Baker is optimistic as always:

'It is difficult to believe that if there were on both sides a genuine desire for armament reduction, agreement on an inspection system could not be secured!'[18]

Noel-Baker ends his account of the arms race on a note which is positive and not without hope. There is an acknowledgement of the paradox that states participating in an arms race, searching for greater individual security, do, in fact, lose much of that security. A wider acceptance of such a truth, and a firmer realisation that individual and common survival are linked more interdependently than ever, will do much to erode defeatism about practicable plans for disarmament.

The autumn of 1958 saw a wide public endorsement of *The Arms Race*. His restrained and reasoned warning 'of the wilderness which may be to come' was thought to signpost the need to work for understanding at top-level talks, and to recognise that negotiators' attitudes could change dramatically, as the Soviet position appeared to have done in May 1955.[19] Sincerity, a lucid explanation of political and technical complexities, passionate dedication, language free from emotionalism, were all acclaimed. 'Data had never been better collated' wrote *The Times,* believing that there was a convincing case for making a start on a two-stage plan for major reductions in conventional and nuclear arms stocks, followed by abolition of 'offensive' weapons. The system of inspection and control, devised in Vienna by the International Atomic Energy Authority would be a most useful precedent.[20] Few of his critics accused Noel-Baker of unrealistic campaigning. His case was too carefully marshalled and accurate in its detail for that. Careful readers might rub their eyes at the abolition proposals 'though once it would have seemed obvious' to readers of *The Times* and 'we should be puzzled to find an alternative'.[21]

A man such as Noel-Baker who, for 40 years, had devoted himself to peace and disarmament with remarkable pertinacity and integrity could not but err on the side of optimism in the opinion of his friend and colleague, Leonard Woolf. Even so, the whole thesis, prepared as it was 'with complete clarity and sobriety' was straight and compelling.[22]

For others, like Hugh Thomas (later Lord Thomas of Swinnerton), the thrust of Noel-Baker's case devastatingly exposed 'the ludicrous pretensions of the military planners' and the 'logical bankruptcy' of the great powers. Factual understanding which the book promoted would reveal the political negativeness, both of those who called for unilateral contracting-out of nuclear weapon politics and of those who espoused a 'deterrent' standpoint. Would not a vigorous and informed public opinion, supporting a realistic multilateral disarmament plan, benefit if the Labour Party should 'name Mr. Noel-Baker's volume a set-book for the coming summer, swing the Movement behind his ideas, and set them in the forefront of their general election programme and of their foreign policy when they are returned to power'?[23] There is, however, no evidence that

Noel-Baker shared Thomas' zeal, one year into the Macmillan administration and five years before that folded. Indeed, one might detect in the views of Noel-Baker at this time a hint, certainly, of tiredness, perhaps of disillusion. He had lost his wife in 1956 and had gone through a patch of ill-health and loneliness. Pinned to the manuscript of *The Arms Race* in his papers is a note, half-humorous, to Moira, his secretary: 'It gives me a feeling of despair, it is so little but perhaps you can keep it safely on the off-chance that I may finish it before 2000 A.D. Love, P.J.N.B.'[24]

His *magnum opus* is a memorial to Irene, his wife, for they had both shared a confidence that when the truth is fully stated it becomes an energising force if only complacency can be routed:

'The people, the men and women in the street, are, in their vast majority, indifferent, because their leaders, and the media, whose task it is to form opinion, leave them unalerted, sunk in deep dogmatic sleep.'[25]

Noel-Baker would have attributed to such as Pascal, the concept of public opinion as an agent of reinforcement. In the same breath he would have dismissed any observer's suggestion of despondency. In marshalling facts about armaments problems, and in outlining a prodigious number of possible moves for dealing 'robustly' with them, he had given the task his all as he told a friend:

'Four hours working in the morning, three to four hours walking in the hills in the afternoon, at an average altitude of 800 metres, and four to five hours writing in the evening. This was intensive work. Without my daily exercise on the hills, I could not possibly have maintained an average of eight to nine hours writing a day. When the work so required, I was able to do 11 or 12 hours without fatigue.'[26]

Every so often the handwritten drafts would be posted off to his old League colleague, Frank Walters, to Leonard Woolf, and to Prof. Pigou for their reading and advice.

Once published, editions of *The Arms Race* soon appeared also in Germany, Italy, Spain, and Japan, and throughout the English-speaking world. Generally, the press in many countries commended the book as an exceptionally comprehensive and well-organised work. Unemotionally written, such a compendium of fact and argument would be an invaluable aid to discussion, particularly in one assembly as a Member of Parliament in Britain declared:

'Its pink cover flared out from every corner of the House of Commons benches, since its publication coincided with the last major debate on disarmament . . . This is a book which transfers the onus from the visionaries to the realists.'[27]

More than one commentator in West Germany saw Noel-Baker's work as 'helpful'. His approach had avoided the abstractions and generalities that all too often resulted in *Legendenbildung* and *Euphemismus*, those responses employing myths and evasions to cloud unpalatable truths.[28] Elsewhere, authoritative command of fact in *The Arms Race* was acknowledged, yet its ideas were not accepted with enthusiasm. Pacifist opinion was unhappy with the proposition that the United Nations might accumulate a 'deterrent' stock of nuclear weapons to resist aggressors. Another view pressed with vigour was that of unilateralists who saw a disengagement, above all by Britain, as more likely to start 'the ball rolling' rather than the alternative of a slow and questionable advance towards multilateral objectives.[29]

There was perhaps more weight in the criticism of those who believed Noel-Baker too easily dismissed political factors in his writing. Was it really helpful, they asked, to give such slight prominence to those concessions among statesmen, which must precede agreement about the technicalities of arms reduction? More fundamentally, was there not credulousness and shallowness of perception in a writer who seemed to rely upon political settlements coinciding with agreements on disarmament?[30] Not for the first time the 'single-mindedness' and 'zeal' of Noel-Baker, was thought to under-estimate factors in a global situation which had to do with deep-seated rivalry and gladiatorial postures. Two aspects of this sort of criticism he always quickly rejected. First of all, he saw himself as unprepared to leave measures for bringing about disarmament solely to the initiatives of the two nuclear titans. All nations had a part to play in reducing the collective insecurity of the arms race. Secondly, he was never at a loss for words to refute the allegation that his arguments had more to do with 'the illusory security of the impossible' than with 'the insecurities and ambiguities of the possible'. With perhaps a streak of increasing frustration, his reply to a point such as this would be to aver that *The Arms Race* had everything to do with converting 'impossibilities' into 'possibilities'.[31]

Some critics of *The Arms Race* have dismissed it as an 'all or nothing' approach. 'Why not, indeed?', Noel-Baker might well have replied. In at least three respects he saw the process of disarmament as one working towards totality. These points he had stressed in *Disarmament*, 32 years earlier. The crux of a first, and last, approach is that *all* weapons need to be scrutinised and reduced. A balanced appreciation of the consequences of war is not 'diverted' by the nuclear threat, as one scientific reviewer put it, rather, one realises, once and for all, 'the unity of the problem'. Noel-Baker's field of view is a far-ranging, unified one.[32] As a consequence, all stages in the exercise of limitation need to be agreed and coordinated. Partial agreement as an end in itself can never suffice, but such decisions, as a means to an end (a total one), are desirable and possible. This last point appears in a letter Noel-Baker had written the year before to a member of the Society of Friends, in the United States, Gerald Bailey:

'Friends <Quakers> have no business to involve themselves in the diplomacy of disarmament by international agreement, unless they are prepared to recognise (as you folk at Quaker House presumably do) that the process inevitably involves compromises . . .'[33]

Finally, no agreement can be valid or last long unless all subscribe to it and rely upon it. Critics misunderstood Noel-Baker in 1958 (and continued to do so, particularly in Parliamentary debates) if they saw his stance as simplistic in requiring *all* to be achieved, otherwise, nothing had been gained. He did not dismiss the limited progress that seemed the only possible one – negotiated settlements were 'stations on the way' to something less remote and rather more tangible than Nirvana.[34] Equally, Noel-Baker would have had an answer to the critics who pointed out, that insisting on 100% compliance could still leave loopholes for those who might experiment or hoard *some* weapons, who would be tempted to evade *some* stages of inspection or prohibition, or who might be the eccentric and evil exceptions to an apparently reliable consensus. Chivalrous always towards his critics (even those who were derisory), the diverseness and unreliability of 'human nature', its character and its impulses, would have been granted. Scientists and humanists who called for 'a fresh attack on fundamental causes, nothing short of a new anthropology . . . some kind of medium or vehicle for the expression of scientific responsibility on an international scale' would have been listened to, and perhaps reminded of what pre-war, Einstein, Bergson, and Gilbert Murray had tried to achieve.[35] As always, there would be left with the commentator, the notion that nothing worthwhile and permanent is to be realised without the full and active resolution of an international arbitral body. Those who believe otherwise are the 'real romanticists'.

On 5th November 1959 it was announced in Oslo that the Nobel Committee had awarded Philip Noel-Baker the Nobel Peace Prize. The citation merely referred to the 'British politician and author of books on disarmament and the League of Nations', though there is little doubt that *The Arms Race*, that voluminous and masterly collection, had helped to seal the Prize, as *The Times* came to believe:

'He was the first Quaker to receive it since the Society of Friends had been collectively honoured in 1947. It was one of the worries of politics that hardly two hours after he had learned officially of the award, he was informed that he had lost his seat on the Labour Shadow Cabinet.

'Characteristically generous, Noel-Baker announced that the Nobel Prize money would be used for promoting the cause of disarmament through the United Nations Association (of which he was a pillar) and in other ways. At a dinner in his honour it was announced that he intended to travel round the world making speeches in the cause of peace. But he would have no traffic with unilateral disarmament and he became President of the Socialist campaign for Multilateral Disarmament.'[36]

In his introductory address at the Award Ceremony in Oslo, the Chairman of the Nobel Committee, Gunnar Jahn, presented his candidate as one who never abandoned hope of negotiated solution to political conflict. To selflessness and idealism were added the benevolence of the Quaker and the scholar's rigorous enquiry. Dealing with the retailers of shibboleths head-on had not made him intolerant or fanatical. For Noel-Baker the search for things other than palliatives must take the form of posing questions, and this was the approach he unhesitatingly adopted when he was Britain's representative at the U.N. and when he was campaigning publicly for a more peaceful world order. If Noel-Baker was the epitome of the reasoning, civilised man, his monumental work *The Arms Race* was an expression of faith that all nations must collaborate in workable measures to disarm the world. At the heart of the work for peace which the Nobel Prize was honouring was the premise that the sincerity of others could and should be tested.[37]

Noel-Baker's tall, lean figure and ascetic face commanded the attention of the Oslo audience in December 1959 because his acceptance speech was so unfeignedly modest. His honour had come about, he declared, because he had worked with Robert Cecil, Arthur Henderson, and Fridtjof Nansen. Their Herculean efforts for peace and for the League had been inspired by Nansen's resolute vision, symbolised by the name he had given his ship, *Fram,* 'Forward'. Their feverish attempts to get rid of war had met with little success, and, in general terms, had failed to bring about a more tranquil and united world although the institution of the League had pointed the way. Disappointment after disappointment had dogged the steps of those who had tried to apply the celebrated verdict of Earl Grey of Falloden – that the truest reading of history is 'the lesson that the present should be learning from the past'. Political conflicts within Cabinets, the 'solid principles of power politics', had prevailed to rob half a century of any other achievement than an escalating arms race.

'How could the Arms Race be ended?' asked the Nobel Prizeman. In great earnest he proposed an end to war, *all* war, not through regulation but, in words used by western governments in 1952:

> 'to prevent war, by making war inherently, as it is constitutionally under the Charter, impossible as a means of settling disputes between nations. To achieve this goal, all nations must cooperate to establish an open and substantially disarmed goal, in which armed forces and armaments will be reduced to such a point that no state will be in a state of armed preparedness to start a war.'[38]

Unless there was an 'iron resolution' to make 'general and complete disarmament' a unitary concept of supreme importance, Noel-Baker saw all partial steps as illusory. There are risks in testing the sincerity of others; the greatest risk is to do it half-heartedly or not at all. To succeed, a disarmament plan must make a step-by-step process clear from the very beginning and leave the steps open without scope for evasion. Reductions, budgetary limitation, measures of inspection and control will not be fashioned overnight – they might take six, eight, or ten years.

The technical measures towards agreed goals were not too difficult to specify. There must be lowered ceilings for manpower, reduction of 'conventional' arms, and unanimity as to the abolition of nuclear weaponry, the problems of clandestine accumulation of stocks by dishonest powers could best be met by contriving adequate safeguards and continuous inspection. Very clearly, the risks incurred in dissension and delay were 'incomparably less than the risk of allowing the arms race to go on' he believed.

Above all, his Oslo audience must see themselves within 'measurable distance of irreversible calamity'. There was a danger that people everywhere were being 'conditioned' to the acceptance of use of horrific weapons. Inescapably for Noel-Baker, public enlightenment and careful defining of objectives were indispensable for progress with disarmament.

Defeatism about the future was a crime. The danger was not in trying to do too much, but in trying to do too little. If politics was 'the art of the possible', then statesmanship was also the art, in Nansen's sense, of coping with the 'impossible'. Statesmanship of that kind was what was needed today. 'Our ship must be the *Fram*' he declared. 'There is no turning back!'

CHAPTER 9

Noel-Baker and Greece

THROUGHOUT MUCH OF WHAT PHILIP NOEL-BAKER said and wrote, there runs a deep vein of humanism. Greece was his spiritual home. Around the Ionian and Aegean Seas lay the fount of European civilisation, a land unparalleled in its achievements in thought and letters, architecture and athletics. It was a place of great beauty and of splendid panoramas. There was sterness there, too, in the aridity of plains and hills and in the tremendous courage of its people. Greece, even when cut off by distance or by war, could never lose its appeal. Mussolini's treacherous attack on Greece, Noel-Baker proclaimed in October 1940, might conquer the bodies of Greeks but never their minds or spirits. He attempted to take his listeners with him:

'I wish I could picture a Greek forest to you and make you smell the resin-scented perfume of the pines and of the thyme; see the Judas blossom and the cherry blossom and the hawthorn and the honeysuckle. I wish I could make you hear the people as they greet you when you pass; take you to their homes and let you see their hospitality, their courtesy, their laughter and their charm . . . I wish you could know Nico who was born a nomad in a wattle-hut, who learnt to read when he was 30, who came to be manager of a large estate, and who would talk philosophy or politics with any ambassador or king . . . I wish you could stand with me among the lilies in a garden that I know, or look down across the valley, with its winding river veiled by the golden leaves of ancient plane trees, shining against the autumn snow. I wish you could see a feast-day, with the village youths in *fustanellas*, snow-white kilted skirts, and the village maidens dancing very gay but very ancient dances in ritual circle to the sad, half-oriental music of the pipes and lute . . . even in the poorest village, the heritage of countless generations of civilisation can be seen . . .'[1]

It seems necessary here to make allowance for the speaker's generalisations and for a degree of romantic hyperbole. The ordinary Greek may hardly be aware of the Homeric past and scarcely be concerned to enthuse over it. A sense of shared 'heritage' is unlikely among a population which has seen a great deal of ethnic mixture over recent centuries. The patriotic broadcaster of the 1940's, the writer based largely in London, with the task of arousing an audience to help beleagured Greeks, may have painted the land of his second home in idealistic terms.

Greece seemed to represent the epitome of human striving, for greatness and, when pitted against natural and human obstacles, for life itself. Everywhere, he would remind his audience, in the 'thrilling beauty' of that country you came across the relics of Antiquity and saw against that backcloth the tough and sure-footed Greek of today 'thriving on hardship'. A previous generation had known bankruptcy, near-famine, and an invasion by refugees from Asia Minor. 'I shall never forget', Noel-Baker once related, 'seeing them camped in churches and in theatres, in the railway stations, on the quays of Salonika in the bitter winter wind.' A Quaker and a Philhellene, Noel-Baker often spoke of 'power of life', that stamina and faith which had borne along his own forebears in colonial North America, and which in similar fashion had enabled the peasants of Peleponesus to recreate a tolerant, prospering community after 1918. A great statesman, Eleutherios Venizelos, and one well-known among League of Nations workers in Geneva, had led them forward with the twin objectives of defending independence and cultivating friendship with neighbours. What an inspiring example to other democracies that was, thought Noel-Baker, at a time when the Greeks were being trodden underfoot by the armed forces of the Axis Powers.[2]

A return to Greece after lecturing in London or long hours among heaped League of Nations files in Geneva, accentuated a feeling of continuity between Antiquity and the present. Away from the problems and pressures of contemporary Europe one did not feel powerless and lonely, rather, there was the reassurance of restfulness and of still belonging to the world. To help others understand this kind of spiritual consanguinity Noel-Baker would on occasion tell a story:

'Three thousand years ago, on an island in the Aegean, there stood a city, Kerinthos. Its walls ran along the cliff, 300 feet above the sea. As Homer tells us, it sent two ships to help to bring Helen back from Troy. You can still see the walls of Kerinthos, if you go there today. In some places, four or even five courses of the great Homeric blocks remain. You can see the outline of its temple, of its market, of its gates, of its protecting fortress towers. Seated on a block of marble one summer evening, I found a shepherd boy. His flocks were browsing where ancient streets once ran; he was sitting, sometimes reading from a school book, sometimes watching the sunshine on the golden rocks and on the deep blue waves below, sometimes looking across them to where, just beyond his human vision, lay the site of Troy. Kerinthos is far from any village, and I asked him, "Aren't you lonely, here by yourself all day?" He looked wonderingly at me and answered, "How should I be lonely with the world stretched before my eyes?"'[3]

The particular corner of Greece to which Noel-Baker went for many years to recover his strength was the island of Euboea (Evvia), off the Attic coast, in the Aegean Sea. A journey eastwards from Athens of an hour or so brought the Noel-Baker Ford to Chalcis, capital of Euboea. Turning north, the car would wind through the forested sweeps of the island's mountainous backbone, where sinuous curves opened up tremendous views of pines and sea. Another hour or two and the village of Achmetaga would be reached, the lane leading past a huddle of low stone cottages to the wrought iron gates of the estate Irene Noel-Baker had inherited in 1919. The car would jolt across dusty cobbles into a courtyard surrounded on two sides by whitewashed walls of outhouses topped by a verandah railed in black wood. The provincial farm-villas of Ancient Rome must have looked like this. As boxes, trunks, and cases were unloaded, perhaps spilling some of Philip's books and papers, fan-tailed doves fluttered around the dull-red pantiles and a peacock stalked past flame-red oleanders. Into the house would go the procession of savant, his wife, his secretaries, and, usually, a young relative or two. Inquiring feet trod uneven boards to glance into rooms with tumbled dust-sheets. The Noel-Bakers were home, in a sense that a London square never gave them.

Today's Achmetaga is little changed. The sturdy white-walled house, more farm than mansion, has shutters of indigo blue closed to the shimmering heat of the courtyard. Around the front of the house, lawns and flower beds descend in various levels and shapes. Cypresses pierce a vast panorama of spurs and ridges, fold after blue-green fold, a huge and quite magnificent ampitheatre. A white statue stands at the head of a pool arrowing towards the distant hills. All is peace and scent, a haven in an ancient land. Noel-Baker's body and mind and spirit must have been utterly refreshed in such a place.

Edward Noel, founder of this Noel inheritance, arrived by a circuitous route in 1831. He was the grandson of Thomas Noel, second Viscount Wentworth, and was distantly related to Lady Byron who took an interest in him and his brothers after she parted from her poet-husband, Lord Byron. Edward was sent at the age of 16 to Fellenberg's model school at Hofwyl in Switzerland, where pupils were encouraged to learn from the environment and from their efforts at husbandry. Eventually, Edward Noel and Frederick Fellenberg, son of the Director, responded to the notion of Fellenberg himself that a school on the lines of Hofwyl might be established in Greece. This initiative had its roots in the Panhellenism of the time and in the knowledge that Capodistrias, President of a Greece now relieved of 400 years of Turkish rule, might be sympathetic. Lady Byron was quick to

(COURTESY: THE HON. FRANCIS NOEL-BAKER)

Pl. 13. The Noel-Baker house, Achmetaga, Greece

appreciate the worth of the enterprise. The young men had plenty of time, a sense of adventure, and perhaps they would learn more about the death of Byron at Missolonghi.

The two travellers reached the island of Negroponte (Euboea) then, as now, hardly an island since it was linked by a bridge to the Attic mainland of Greece. Accommodated in the town of Egribo (Chalcis), a place founded by the Venetians as a trading colony, they learned of a Greek scheme to encourage foreigners to invest in land and develop it through the more advanced farming methods of Western Europe. Their horses crossed low-lying malarial plains and gradually climbed into thickly-wooded uplands where sheep pastured.

Noel and Fellenberg found something to their liking in northern Euboea. A Turkish landlord sold them land named after a fomer owner, Achmet Aga, for 10,000 gold sovereigns. Lady Byron advanced money to help the purchase go through. Work commenced on the building of a comfortable *Konaki* (house) in an early Victorian style. The house, the dwellings of the servants, and a small chapel, in effect, the beginnings of an estate village, were all to be known as 'Achmetaga', the name the Noel domicile still bears. Later, adjoining acres in Drasi and much of Mount Candili were acquired for the estate. It was good land, with slopes that were reasonable to till, fresh running water, herds of deer, and the right kind of soil for the establishment of profitable forest described by a later descendant, Philip Noel-Baker's son, as:

'Aleppo Pine, Black Pine, Cephallonian Fir, Oak and Plane, with a mixed understory of Arbutus, Myrtle, wild Pistaccio, what we call "prickly Oak" and others, good for charcoal. Our forest was generally acknowledged to be the most beautiful and best-run in Greece.'[4]

In all, there was something like 10,700 acres of fir and pine in the Noel domain together with 50 acres of cropland.

All did not go well to begin with. Young Fellenberg preferred to try his hand at commerce in Athens and succumbed to a fever there in 1834. Edward, coping with bouts of malaria and dysentery, somehow managed to plant trees for building timber, olives and vines, with the help of a new recruit, an old school friend from Hofwyl, Charles Muller. A debt to Lady Byron was paid off after three years. Eventually, in 1895, the Muller family decided to sell their half-share in the estate and return to Switzerland.

Noel-Baker's wife, Irene Noel, took over the Achmetaga estate in the autumn of 1919 on the death of her father, Francis Edward (Frank) Noel. She had been married to Philip Baker for four years and their son, Francis, the present owner of the estate, was to be born one year later, in 1920. When husband and wife adopted the hyphenated name 'Noel-Baker' as their married surname in 1922 this sealed in the Greek connection. A woman of shrewd intelligence and one quick to size up practicability in affairs, Irene ran the estate through years of varying fortune. Land reform programmes in the early 1920's diminished the Noel holding by 3,000 acres and replanning after the Second World War was to expropriate further land. Constantly at her side was her 'bailiff', the first one Nico Cantas, a Vlach shepherd who taught himself to read and write after appointment, and then after Nico's death in 1935, his nephew, Arghyris Balatsos took over.

The investment of the Balkans by foreign troops severed the link between the Noel-Bakers and their Greek home in 1940. The travails of his adopted land urged Philip Noel-Baker to make a special plea in 1943 for the immediate resuscitation of Southern Europe the moment hostilities ended. Several million tons of food and a fleet of lorries had been assembled two years later by 47 nations and the pitiable villagers of Greece, suffering both from hunger and from internecine strife, were among the first to receive help.[5]

During the actual hostilities of the Second World War, the island of Euboea and the village of Prokopi where the estate of Achmetaga lay was not spared privation according to Francis Noel-Baker:

'. . . the village was occupied first by Austrians, resting from the invasion of Crete. They behaved in an exemplary fashion. Next came Italians who did not. They got drunk one night in 1943 and set fire to our house. Explosives in the small cellar blew up and there was nothing but four corners standing grimly among the charred ruins when we returned from London at Easter 1945 . . .'[6]

With the ending of war in Europe in June 1945, the Noel-Bakers were understandably most anxious to see what had happened to their Greek idyll. Philip thought about the idea carefully and in November put a case to the Foreign Office for Irene to go. The application was perhaps couched in somewhat exaggerated terms. Restarting timber exploitation would, it was stated, help revitalise the economy of a shattered country. The return of a family which had managed its own enterprise for over a century, must be a boost to the nation's moral confidence as the Greeks would see it. He added that as Chairman of the Conference on European Inland Transport he was asking the Prime Minister if he might accompany Irene en route to an inspection of railways and waterways in Italy and Greece.[7]

There were other letters to write and people to see. Herbert Morrison, the Home Secretary, was asked for exit permits. Contacts at the Air Ministry were approached about availability of flights to Athens. Might his son, Francis, then serving at Middle East Headquarters in Palestine be granted compassionate leave to accompany his mother? The strings pulled in the Middle East failed to respond, indeed, the tactics seem to have been rather counter-productive. Any suggestions of political influence in favour of one particular applicant for such leave created a sense of unfairness, was the regretted and implied rebuke of Edward Grigg, Minister Resident in the Middle East. More pointedly, Britain's envoy in Athens telegraphed the Foreign Office regarding Captain Francis Noel-Baker:

'I rely upon his family to see that as a British officer he refrains from dabbling in politics. We are still dealing with a very delicate situation.'[8]

The warning from Athens is corroborated by Hugh Dalton, writing in his diary after lunching in London with Irene:

'Francis is back from the U.S. and frightfully eager, quite naturally, to be in Greece, but Leeper (Sir Rex Leeper, Ambassador to Greece) has specially warned the Foreign Office against allowing this dangerous and subversive young man into the country.'[9]

Hugh Dalton's fondness for dealing in 'secrets' is well-known. If it suited him, he was ready to reveal a confidence with a knowing wink across the table and behind a glass. Talk of Irene's impending Greek visit need not exclude reference to Francis joining her and Dalton's opinion of its feasibility. As for Philip staying any time in Greece, Irene was in favour of it, yet at the same time she showed a tremulous anxiety about the consequences for her husband's political career. When she 'shrilled a good deal against Attlee' the old family friend offered reassurance. Dalton's own private view admitted of reservation it seems some weeks later (similar to that of 1943, mentioned above in a previous chapter), 'He (Noel-Baker) is a most charming person, though sometimes a little troublesome and over-pressing and subjective in his views.'[10]

A conjunction of Noel-Baker charm and persistence won the day on 12th February 1945. Irene, nervously facing her first flight, emplaned aboard an uncomfortable Dakota of R.A.F. Transport Command. Thirteen items of luggage were piled around her. The journey was tedious but she staved off air-sickness by beginning a diary in a cheap school exercise book. On arrival, there was compensation for a bumpy landing, in being motored to a hunting lodge near Caserta for lunch with the Commander-in-Chief, Field Marshal Alexander. There was talk of the mutual friendship of 'Alex' and Philip and, delightful surprise, a tin of caviare straight from the Yalta Conference appeared. Perhaps, the Allied C-in-C suggested, the Noel-Bakers, through their Quaker connections, could do something for the enfeebled *bambini* of Naples?

Dawn brought an issue of a five-day's supply of army rations and an early flight across the Adriatic. 'Heavenly to see', Irene wrote, 'those lovely golden, pink, blue and purple colours of the land and sea and mountains of

Greece once more.'[11] Her promptness and attention to detail made Irene push open the doors of offices in Athens, to discuss with field representatives of the Red Cross and U.N.R.R.A. how medical supplies might best be secured and space chartered in lorries and coastal craft. Eastwards she went by army lorry to descend stiffly in Chalcis (Halkida), capital of the island of Euboea, for dinner with the Black Watch, then garrisoning the island. A hot bath was particularly welcome when she was told that this could only be a once-weekly provision.

Not everything was ruined when Irene reached Achmetaga, although six or seven miles of the forest had been scorched by German troops firing incendiaries against local partisans. There was a wonderful reception on her arrival – flowers, weeping, kisses, laughter. Apart from the rejoicing she found the conflicts between Communist and non-Communist distressing. Yet, first aid must be given regardless of these affiliations. 'I promised them help', she wrote, '. . . seed, food, clothes, medical supplies – whatever their political implications.' As she expected, 'The peasants are much easier to deal with than the reactionary rich business people of Athens'.[12] When it was pointed out to her that the man she chose as building foreman was, in fact, the leading village Communist she represented this as an instance of her own magnanimity.

The first problem, and the most intractable, must be how to reactivate the mill and then how to clear and replant vineyard and olive grove. There was, thankfully, no shortage of willing help, indeed, she understood them to say '. . . we who have eaten your bread for so many years, surely we can work for nothing for a time and repay something of what we owe you'. The old Victorian home of the Noel-Bakers presented a deplorable sight:

'I went at once to see the house and wept bitterly over the devastation . . . everything needs repairing and building and painting. The peasants, some of them, have pulled down the pipes in the kitchen wall to make bullets out of the lead, and water was flowing out everywhere – the kitchen is now completely destroyed . . .'[13]

Ahead of Irene's seigneurial inspection a British military patrol had reconnoitred the area and pronounced it safe to visit. Local people cautiously venturing out from their homes had lived for several years on a diet of nuts, vegetables and occasional eggs. Their needs for sustenance could be met if a pair of gaunt oxen could be put to the task of a spring sowing of corn and if army mechanics were able to mend the delapidated tractors. Irene's courage almost deserted her in face of the uphill labour and she felt Philip ought to know of this, '. . . it really is heartbreaking to see nothing but emptiness and complete desolation, and I did want you then for comfort'.[14] A week later, Irene felt better, especially as she had been told that open-cast magnesite mines on the estate could soon be restored to profitable working if a supply of pit props could be procured from somewhere. More cheerful news was telegraphed to Philip:

'Most moving and successful visit to Achmetaga. Hope to return permanently Monday 12th. Well. Love.'[15]

Philip's reply reached Irene some weeks later via a much delayed British Forces Post. The terse message on wartime brown paper told his wife that he was extremely busy with ministerial duties (at the Ministry of War Transport) but he might be able to spare two weeks to be with her. He had every confidence in Irene's ability to rebuild the estate as he told his son, 'M. will be able to get things going at full speed both on the fields and in the forest'.[16] Meanwhile, Noel-Baker must seek the Prime Minister's permission for a Mediterranean visit. Churchill readily agreed, adding, 'I hope the estate will be revived'. Philip, reassured, now gave some of his mind to the domestic details of their Greek home and despatched from Whitehall a matter-of-fact telegram to Irene ahead of his arrival:

'Certainly get contractors for fire wood to handle maximum possible quantity this year also lime kilns. STOP. What about tractor? STOP. Received letter March 6th with diary. STOP. Very happy well love Philip Noel-Baker.'[17]

Some days before Noel-Baker boarded the aircraft for Greece, he received a further report from his wife. Clearly, with her sleeves purposefully rolled up, she was coping reasonably well with six different ministries in Athens. Coordination at the top was not surprisingly rather chaotic. Fortunately, the roads on Euboea were much better than elsewhere and she had managed to get things through to a number of famished villages. British Army trucks had taken in 500 tons of potato seed and over 200 garments for women and children. Further inland, though, there was great suffering. Philip's visit was brief. There was in his mind, as with his other Labour Party colleagues, doubt about the outcome of the General Election which would surely come about in early summer. He and Irene had lunched with Harold Macmillan in mid-April 1945 in Athens, and talk had moved from the situation in Greece to the shape of political developments in Britain. Macmillan's confidence in an eventual Conservative victory was clear and there was a touch of earnestness to the speculations. Macmillan later wrote of his guests:

'They are reformed characters now about E.L.A.S. [the Communist-led faction in Greece]; but we chaffed them a good deal. I expect they will lapse when the British elections come!'[18]

Irene's interest in British politics was inconsiderable and her husband felt he must return to the preparation for hustings as soon as possible. He was, though, glad that his stay had turned out 'a most unqualified success' and he would be able to report personally to Churchill on the situation in Greece.[19]

Noel-Baker's visits to Achmetaga during the next two years were short and infrequent. Irene, to a large extent, appreciated the burdens that her husband, now a Minister of State at the Foreign Office must carry, nevertheless, as in the years before the war, she wrote to him in a rather folorn manner of her loneliness. Fortunately, she was made of stern stuff in a practical sense and had the irreplaceable aid of a number of very capable Greek estate managers.

The Noel-Bakers had always seen themselves as an integral part of the Greek community, although their foreign patrimony was resented by the more radical Greeks. It seemed entirely legitimate to Philip and his wife to press for compensation in the same way as native-born Greeks sought relief for war damage. Originally, Irene had claimed in February 1945 £8,000 as going some way to meet the loss of animals, motor transport, and buildings. There had been wholesale requisitioning by the Greek Government to further their early Albanian campaign in 1940. Later much damage had been done during enemy occupation and the bitter house-to-house skirmishing of Communist partisans during 1943 and 1944. Nine years elapsed and definite restitution had still not been promised by Athens. It was, indeed, disheartening to Irene and Philip when a fresh attempt to expedite the affair, this time through the British Embassy in Athens, brought a reply that indicated there would be no help for the parlous economy of Achmetaga. Greece was poor and, so it was explained in tactful terms, even native Greeks were unlikely to receive significant redress.[20]

Philip Noel-Baker suffered a shattering blow on 7th February 1956 when Irene died from a sudden heart attack. After almost 40 years of marriage the wrench was nearly insupportable, although both partners had resigned themselves to long periods of separation from time to time. No longer a Minister, Noel-Baker was able to leave London and return to the place he loved so much, his spiritual home at Achmetaga. He had been unwell, moreover, for some time and had been taken into hospital from his cottage at Buttermere. Medical opinion (from a consultant surgeon offered by Anthony Eden) was that a long convalescence was needed. Staying some eight weeks on Euboea, Noel-Baker took upon himself some share in day-to-day estate management. He felt most alone in the evenings and at weekends. For the first time in his life he was able to compile a diary. In its pages are to be found the poignant remembrance of times past when he walked and climbed the neighbouring slopes. Stumbling along a steep-pitched rocky incline he would look down and recall picnics under the plane trees and the heady luxuriance of spring flowers in April. There would follow, in May, masses of lilac everywhere, roses, large yellow daises, and Irene's flowering creepers and bushes, now resplendant. May also brought the Feast of St. George when local people, decked in their finery, tumbled out of church after the service to roast lamb over charcoal in the open, and quaffed beer. It was easier to deal with grief there than amid the friendly but pressed condolences of crowded Athens, say, at the Hotel Xenias Melathron where the two had so often stayed in the old days.

The mule-driver, encountered one morning splashing his face at an ice-cold spring, was he who had captained formidable village footballers, grateful for the hard-baked pitch Irene had given over to them. Wherever he looked there was evidence of the thrift and energy of his late wife after the war:

'everything was derelict when she took it over – a jungle of brambles, "stinking walnut" trees and other useless and unsightly growth. She cleared it all and uncovered perhaps 10 acres; turned much of it into a lovely orchard through which she made a romantic little path down to the river from the house.'[21]

Out of charred ruin, buildings had been carefully planned by his wife 'to fit the landscape and look good'. Water channels were groped for in the underbush, dug out carefully, and soon the red soil was green with sprouting wheat and maize. Irene's own fingers had assisted at the tedious business of grafting new olive trees, the bailiff Arghyris constantly at her side. Perhaps, she had suggested, a hardier type of olive should be tried since the irrigation tank and the piping they had could reach only 150 or so trees. The village itself, as he walked through it again, bore witness to the concern of Irene and Philip Noel-Baker. Land covered with bramble, gorse, and heather and burnt in 1949 had been replanted. Fire had been put to the forest by Government forces seeking to eradicate E.L.A.S. guerillas, 'an act of vandalism' which Irene never forgave. Philip, approaching the huddle of houses by way of the tracks of the resin-gatherers, was satisfied with what was now a memorial to Irene's industry:

'The village is not everywhere as tidy as she would have wished. But Irene's inn, her resin stores and other farm buildings by the inn, her fences, gates and stiles, were always and still are in excellent order, and give the valley, to the passer-by, an appearance of being cared for, and cared for with a sense of its aesthetic value.'[22]

As for the football pitch where he, too, had so often enjoyed a vigorous game, he would now see to it that trees were hewn for a new set of goal posts. In the shade there would be erected a small pavilion, in memory of his wife, just as soon as the stony ground could be cleared.

Towards the end of his stay, Noel-Baker felt able to take part in a public occasion. Ten thousand pilgrims swarmed in for the Feast of St. John the Russian on 27th May. Food stalls serving coffee and sweet concoctions were set up in the lanes. Behind stalwart brass bandsmen there wound a procession headed by a black-robed and bearded Bishop, a psalmist, the local magistrate, and the lean slightly stooping figure of Philip Noel-Baker. Before 'Irene's inn' in the village square the procession halted, reverently lowered the wood and glass of St. John's funeral bier, and crowded in intently to listen to a homily by the Bishop. Theology was mixed with politics in the utterance. When the memory of two E.L.A.S. patriots, hanged by the British, was invoked there was no condemnation of their English guest who, it was remarked, had spoken up for *Enosis*, the union of Cyprus with Greece. It was, though, Noel-Baker wrote, a combination of episcopal oratory and exaggeration on the part of an Athenian journalist that described in a newspaper some days later the eminent Englishman as breaking down and weeping in contrition for British crimes.

Philip Noel-Baker was always immensely proud that his wife Irene was known so widely throughout Greece and with such affection. 'The door of every Ministry and every Government office was always open to her' he recorded in the diary:

'Every department with which she had to deal, her bank, her lawyer, recognised the estate as something more than a farm, a forest, and a piece of land, something different from other properties, something that was precious to Greece. This they had learnt because for many years they had dealt with her. The Customs officials at the frontier, the guards on the trains, all knew her name, and always passed her through with touching courtesy and respect. Very many ordinary people knew her work during the war, and very many officers in the army remember how she went regularly to Achmetaga all through the Communist seige of the village.'[23]

He had received, during his stay, fine expressions of gratitude for Irene's influence on Anglo-Hellenic friendship from the Queen, the Prime Minister, and the Foreign Minister. These were all people who had known Irene well and the King and Queen were godparents to Philip's grandchildren. One commendation that he knew his wife would have been most proud of was the remark, an unsolicited one, of the sergeant of the Royal Palace Guard. Himself a Euboean, he had admired Irene's fame in the province, adding that she was the best and kindest employer in the whole of Greece. Understandably, those Greeks who had little time for the imperiousness of Irene do not seem to have made it known to a sorrowing husband.

Irene Noel-Baker should have a memorial thought Philip in the year that followed her death. An architect, celebrated for his restoration work in the Agora of Athens, was designed to design a Credence Table for the Church of St. Paul in the capital. Commemoration inscriptions would be in Greek, Latin, and English. In Euboea, at Whitsuntide 1957, it was hoped that King Paul and Queen Frederika would unveil a dedicatory stone to be set in a wall of the school near Achmetaga, a school in which the Noel-Bakers had shown much interest.

(COURTESY: THE HON. FRANCIS NOEL-BAKER)

Pl. 14. The King and Queen of Greece visit Achmetaga, 1963. Francis Noel-Baker on left, Philip Noel-Baker on right

The family itself, eventually decided to mark Irene's life in a way which would make her concern for village welfare a continuing one. A welfare enterprise was set up in 1964, the North Euboean Foundation, supported by OXFAM, the Save the Children Fund, War on Want, and by the Greek shipowners of London. The work of the Foundation has been described by Philip's son, Francis:

'We built a little Health Centre at Achmetaga, in memory of my Mother, equipped it fully including X-ray Unit, and staffed it with successive British volunteer doctors. We established three Agricultural Extension Teams, each with a Land Rover, and set up Boys' and Girls' Clubs in most of the 39 villages in our District, with three government home economists in charge. There was also a British volunteer veterinary surgeon and his or her Greek counterpart, each with a Land Rover, instruments and drugs. We sent parties of young local schoolchildren to England for a month's good eating and a medical check-up. And with the help of Arghyri Balatsos, we sent 114 young men to seek their fortunes in Canada. Most of them did well, and sent for wives and relatives to join them . . .'[24]

Year after year, Philip Noel-Baker returned to the peace of Achmetaga. He would come for two or three weeks, at Easter or around Christmas and New Year. Irene would have been there for perhaps three or four months. The Achmetaga Visitors Book records a stream of friends who came to wander through a series of comfortable rooms or in the garden, where they might be given a job to do by Irene. Philip's invitation to a guest to accompany him on a walk was usually accepted with some reluctance, since to do so was to bring on breathlessness if not near-collapse from exhaustion in anybody else than the host. Philip himself would rise early, swim in a pool which was fed by piercingly cold water, work in his study, and then take himself out for what he termed his 'thinking walk'. This last escapade, occupying many miles and several hours, was relieved by a supply of fresh fruit and drinks hidden en route at strategic places by the vigilant bailiff, Balatsos. After dinner Philip's guests of his own ilk might climb to his cool, airy work place in the eastern part of the house.

The Noel-Bakers were less happy at Achmetaga in the last decade of Philip's life. There was a good deal of unrest in the village, now renamed Procopi, after 1974 over the possession by 'foreigners' of so much valuable forest land. It was Francis, the son of Philip, who took the brunt of opposition to the family's continued possession, and it was he who saw the furore locally as one orchestrated by radicals on the Left, with the government of Karamanlis in Athens unwilling to do anything other than indicate the likelihood of expropriation. Philip in London kept in close touch with legal and other developments. When he did come to Athens it was with disappointment and frustration that he found Government ministers unwilling to see him. He cannot have been unaware of the strength of feelings in a country struggling to get on its own feet after the trauma of war, and a land still rent by internal confusions and dispute. If for him Greece was still a wonderful place, for the Noel-Bakers at Achmetaga the world stretched before their eyes was a different and a challenging one. It was never Philip's doing that the Noel-Bakers in Greece acquired 'good friends' and 'good enemies.'[25]

CHAPTER 10

Disarmament: The Latter-day Stance

In the years after 1958 and his imposing analysis of *The Arms Race*, Noel-Baker appears more detached from the power-core of the Labour Party and from any seat of influence. Those on the Right of his party regarded him as a rather idealistic challenger both of traditional diplomacy, of customary alliance, and of rather unimaginative and stolid policy making in international affairs. Those on the Left were impatient with his insistence on collective agreement and security – they preferred the shorter-route, shorter-term approach of unilateralism. Bevin, Morrison, and Attlee were not pleased by his irreverential questioning. As Labour Party Chairman during the year 1946-47 Noel-Baker had faced both wings. That experience had perhaps chastened rather than encouraged him, tinging his attitudes with some frustration and sadness, though this was seldom amplified. The period that ensued was marked by clamour and disputation and by a campaigning that never lost sincerity and authority.

The post-war Labour Government was, in Kenneth Morgan's words, a 'gifted administration' with obvious competence, faith, and legislative vitality.[1] Noel-Baker, though, was not one of its 'prima donnas'. His vision, intensity, and skills were less evident publicly than those of many of his colleagues. Like them, though, he cannot have been unaware of dualism between elements in the constituencies and in the Trade Unions pushing for 'socialist advance' and the conservative gradualism that marked policy formulation in the Cabinet Room. He may have chafed somewhat at the limitations that loyalty to colleagues and associates imposes. Staunch campaigning on behalf of the United Nations might trigger suspicions on the Left of the Party. After all, Stafford Cripps had referred to the League of Nations, 10 years earlier, as an 'International Burglar's Union' and dismissed the idea of collective security. There were those who saw the infant world organisation as a body too much dominated by the interests and persuasiveness of the United States. These were fears commensurate with reservations held by the Right of the Party as to how far the U.N. might be permitted to interfere with (if not abrogate) the legitimate autonomy of a member state. On the other hand, if Noel-Baker followed too closely the line laid down by Ernest Bevin, he risked alienation among members of the Labour Party's Foreign Affairs Group, whose garrulousness and factionism irritated the Foreign Minister and aroused his contempt. The ship of state had to proceed with sails rather carefully trimmed, her officers anxiously scanning the horizon for rough seas, the while looking over their shoulders at a crew only too ready to growl in disaffection.

A man of vision with an instinctive preference for honesty of intent and for straight-dealing, Noel-Baker was severely tested in the 1950's as acrid debate raged in Labour Party circles. The issue was clear enough in its enunciation. Should Britain produce nuclear weapons and assist in their deployment? The case for and against these armaments was of course, formidable in its complexity. Campaigning with a slogan such as 'Ban the Bomb' did little other than pitch conjecture and dialogue in superficial and short-range terms. Labour's Left Wing, in which Aneurin Bevan, Ian Mikardo, and Barbara Castle were prominent, voiced its opposition to further development of nuclear weaponry. This put the National Executive of the Party into rather an awkward position for while a divisive thrust must be contained, there was among them the recollection that across the political spectrum, successive administrations had gone along with what they considered to be the 'political grain' in cultivating an independent deterrent, partly legitimating this in the context of strengthening Anglo-American relations.

Party leaders feared that if Britain renounced the manufacture of nuclear weapons then, logically, such a unilateral rejection would mean the end of a number of defensive alliances. Ironically, it was Bevan who was to voice this consequence at the Brighton Labour Party Conference in 1957. It was Noel-Baker's task, and he must have recognised the logic in it, to present a Labour Party policy that worked forwards from its nuclear armoury to develop a deterrent potential rather than a destructive one. Richard Crossman, tongue in cheek, saw the oddity of this. At Executive meetings:

'Only Philip Noel-Baker was left defending the Government and urging that we must prepare for a major nuclear war and for major conventional war in Europe at the same time. This is what pacifists finally came to in their old age!'[2]

(This imputation would have sorely displeased its target figure.) Hugh Dalton, too, recognised that for Noel-Baker, the position supporting the

Government's case in a defence debate was likely to be an onerous and unwelcome task. The debate went 'pretty well' he recorded in March 1953: 'Half a dozen pacifists abstain. Attlee opens, all right. Phil winds up, very nervously, very earnestly with that plaintive note in his voice which has become habitual, with *many*, too many notes. He has long gone past his climax. Rather pathetic, remembering his form of decades back.'[3]

Frequently, Noel-Baker had long discussions with Hugh Gaitskell, George Brown, Aneurin Bevan, and others, to explore ways of pressing the Government to seek high-level talks with other major powers and to advance along a path of multilateral disarmament. Those of the Centre and the Right, Noel-Baker among them, realised that it would be impossible to renege on commitments to the N.A.T.O. Alliance. It was the Labour Party, as Noel-Baker saw it, who had originally proposed and adopted N.A.T.O.: 'because it was the first true pooling of arms strength [sic] behind the democratic rule of law, because it was built on and subject to the Charter of the United Nations.'

Furthermore, he told the Scarborough Conference of 1954, N.A.T.O., as an alliance, could only be set in motion in reply to an aggressive violation of the Charter. Unilateral withdrawal from our responsibilities to maintain this degree of collective security would be reprehensible.[4] There was generally a strong rebuke for those at Conference and elsewhere, for those 'Crossmanites' (followers of R. H. Crossman) who expressed reluctance to make common cause with a capitalist United States and certain other European nations because it was 'unsocialist'. Sentiments such as these were, for Noel-Baker, 'false, unrealistic clichés, based on a purile and defeatist idea'.[5]

Naturally, in the minds of those who spoke and listened at Scarborough, there was the eminent objective of fostering unity in a party that was splintering dramatically on crucial issues. 'I do not know', Noel-Baker told Attlee, 'what kind of rows you may have in the National Executive on May 18th [1954], but I imagine there may be a struggle with no holds barred.' Aneurin Bevan had already resigned from the Shadow Cabinet, stoutly proclaiming that leaders of major powers should not be diverted from arms negotiations by any differences over the rearming of Germany, in itself, an unwise step. Within 12 months, in March 1955, the Parliamentary Labour Party (P.L.P.) withdrew the whip from Bevan, angered by his criticism of their tardiness to press for Four Power Talks. Labour once again, wrote *The Guardian*, is beginning its weary round of trying to discipline the undisciplined.[6]

In March 1955 the Labour Shadow Cabinet had already decided to place a resolution on the Commons Order Paper in the names of Attlee, Morrison, and Noel-Baker speaking for the Party, which would call upon the

Government to enter discussion on the H-Bomb with the United States and Soviet Governments. Aneurin Bevan was particularly pleased that the initiative seemed at last to by-pass lack of boldness in the Party leader. Interminable committee meetings followed, examining the detail that a wide band of the Party could accept, moving them on from any short-sighted preoccupation with mere banning of weapons, helping them shape attitudes towards the international disarmament discussions then proceeding at Geneva, and encouraging them 'to relate these in turn to the other opportunities for political settlement in Europe'.[7] Within a month there was every prospect of broad agreement on commending multilateral disarmament by stages, a course of action dear to the heart of Noel-Baker, but accepted only slowly by the Parliamentary Labour Party. As a first step, there must be an end to the testing of nuclear devices. In turn, an embargo must be placed upon production of such weapons. Consequently, existing stocks would need to be deployed under international supervision. To those who enquired (as they still do) whether disposing of the nuclear 'advantage' would not leave allies vulnerable to attack from conventional forces, it was stressed that at each stage of this disarmament process an appropriate reduction in non-nuclear forces must be undertaken.[8] Then as now, there was the countervailing opinion that non-nuclear (conventional) forces must be increased to work towards 'balance'. It certainly seemed to many as though 'the challenge of coexistence', as Hugh Gaitskell had termed it, could be taken up and accepted.[9] There had, though, to be agreement on a firmly-based policy 'Comrades, do not let us try to liquidate each other . . .' was the plaintive cry of Noel-Baker at the 1958 Conference.[10]

Things came to a head at the 1960 Labour Party Conference, the 'Battle of Scarborough'. Gaitskell and his Executive stood firm on support of N.A.T.O. Frank Cousins, leader of the largest Union (the T.G.W.U.), felt he had to proclaim 'socialist policies' by advancing a unilateralist approach. There was, as he saw it, force and reason on his side for, like Ernest Bevin, he had 'learned in the hedgerows' (and in innumerable smoky Trades Union committees). He worked on his audience instinctively and with flair. Despite Cousins stressing that he was concerned primarily with wider issues and shifts, the Right of the Party sensed the danger of dissension, and acted quickly if not to abort the threat at least to secure compromise.

Gaitskell, Leader in succession to Attlee, moved to defend himself and party in a remarkable fighting speech. Bevan, now, was no longer alive to stand by him. An impassioned plea was that a nuclear deterrent would protect the freedom of the British Isles. With the means to speak up for ourselves, as it were, we should be less enfoefed to the United States. His audience did not find the fighting argument convincing. In the ensuing debate there was perhaps less emphasis than in the years that followed on the suicidal factors of fall-out and long-term environmental devastation. It was the moral unacceptability of nuclear warfare that transfixed the hall. For Noel-Baker on the platform there was the agonising thought that reliance on an independent nuclear deterrent, ran counter to all that experience showed as conducive to the budding of world peace. Was the vociferous rationale of the 'realist' to overturn Labour's traditional support of collective security? Did more immediate endeavours for party unity and the distant, less tangible objectives of avoiding war depend now upon subscribing to a balance of terror? Instinctively, he must have recoiled at the concepts of deterrence and alliance that the prescription offered for they were as illusory as that older balance of 'forces' which Cecil and Noel-Baker had rejected over many years.

Deterrence as a concept was not one that Noel-Baker could dismiss. He had put it to the Labour Party on a number of occasions, that banning nuclear weapons unconditionally would make aggression more and, not less likely. While there might be general agreement among Labour colleagues that we should:

> 'uphold the Charter, make it certain that aggressors cannot win, and on that firm foundation get a true disarmament system with cast iron guarantees that atomic energy will be used for peaceful ends alone.'

for others, the requirement that holding the ring meant arming the margins with nuclear weapons was distasteful if not totally abhorrent.[11] Noel-Baker certainly considered his own standpoint consistent and saw his opponents lost 'in a strange tangle of contradictions'. He felt no shame in declaring to his constituents that in this and other non-pacifist aspects he was on the Right of his Party.[12]

The drama of Scarborough is still interesting a quarter of a century later. The Press of the day, or at least, certain sections of it, became greatly concerned with what they interpreted as a cleavage between 'radicals' and 'establishment'. Journalists flocked to the press conferences of a group, the Campaign for Democratic Socialism, hastily set up by George Brown and Bill Rodgers, to witness what they understood to be an exercise in 'damage limitation'. In doing this, they overlooked the nuances of Cousins' position and, indeed, that of Noel-Baker. These men were taken by issues wider than that of bridging sectarian differences. They believed they sensed moral and idealogical shifts outside the conference hall that were not often clearly expressed and were most certainly not demonstrated by the loud rumbles of block voting. Nobody, whether inclined towards unilateralism or multilateralism, could ignore the sustained fervour of those who marched upon Aldermaston or crowded into Trafalgar Square. It was wrong, moreover, in Noel-Baker's view, to dismiss such manifestations of public concern in polarised 'To' and 'For' the 'Bomb' terms. We had an international organisation founded to work for peace: we should work through it. Of course, the moral polemic must be heeded, Noel-Baker told Hugh Gaitskell, but the Party would respond most strongly to a Leader who in Parliament and country made a vigorous plea for multilateral disarmament. There was 'a tremendous public waiting for this'. Without a firm lead and a positive manifesto the Party would go on tearing itself to pieces.[13]

In the year prior to Scarborough and when the prospect of a clash in the conference hall evidently was anticipated, there was a degree of maneouvering by both Left and Right on the issue of unilateralism. Michael Foot, R. H. Crossman, Denis Healey and others, writing largely in the press, saw a helpful compromise in the shape of Britain joining a 'non-nuclear club'. European states and countries in the Third World would elect not to develop a nuclear potential. British membership would, of course, involve disengagement from nuclear alliances and a radical revision of weapons commitment. To the campaigner this would not be impossible, indeed, they derived encouragement from hearing their leader Hugh Gaitskell declare that in a world where 12 more nations might produce nuclear weapons within 10 years, there was no argument for not trying to frame proposals.

'Illusory' was Noel-Baker's verdict on the scheme. This was only 'a second best' attempt to demoralise the world. It would leave untouched other weapons of mass destruction, might even precipitate a surge in conventional arming. Weapons research would not be restrained. Was such a partial decoupling likely to induce nations to accept a situation of comparative inferiority? This kind of attempted 'control' he attacked elsewhere as 'a dangerous semantic aberration'.[14] Nothing, he insisted, must confuse or divert the move for general and complete disarmament. The agreement parallels the one he habitually employed against the unilateralists. He was to put it at the Scarborough Conference in these words:

'If we now let the world believe we have lost hope of general disarmament we shall deny the very forces on which our hopes for peace and socialism depend.'[15]

Twelve months later, in October 1961, battle was resumed at the Trades Union Congress in Brighton. Out of 658 motions on the agenda, 185 dealt with nuclear disarmament. The excitement among delegates was intense. George Brown, the Party's Deputy Leader, assiduously arranged an eve-of-conference demonstration and a number of 'fringe' activities to drum-up support for a leadership he saw as menaced by unilateral secession.

Noel-Baker felt he had to swing into line with the rest of the Party Executive as one observer saw it:

'Perhaps Brown's biggest catch was Philip Noel-Baker M.P., whose record of work for disarmament for over 40 years was second to none among Labour M.P.s.'[16]

The decision of Noel-Baker to align himself with the platform can not have been an easy one. Which supporter of extant institutions, covenants, and charters could do otherwise than secretly applaud the stern declaration of Frank Cousins, now with his back to the wall, that principle should not be sacrificed in the interests of uniting a party? The standard-bearing of Cousins, redoubtable at Scarborough, now became an inevitable fiasco in the storm of defence from the platform and submission by delegates. Noel-Baker must have concluded that the artifice of a Cousins, schooled as he said instinctively in the 'university of life', failed to ride over the protectionist and insular preferences of Party delegates and, behind them, the short-sighted and ill-informed Common Man. He had seen all too often the crushing defeat of a would-be attempt to declare and define a range of options. Yet, there was evidence that out of public confrontation there could come realisation. Nothing would ever be quite the same again. He would no doubt have agreed with one commentator who believed that the issue of the Bomb (and the issues visible behind it):

'had awakened the spirit of radical dissent throughout the Labour Movement as nothing else before or since. The challenge was not simply to the details of a particular defence policy but to a whole way of thinking, to a style of leadership as well as a concept of policy.'[17]

Meanwhile, in the same month, over at the Labour Party Conference in Blackpool, a three-to-one majority retrieved and endorsed the defence policy of Hugh Gaitskell.

Noel-Baker, henceforth, was to be seen as distanced from a unilateral approach which, to its adherents in C.N.D., was seen to be pragmatic, feasible, and morally superior to the suspected inconsistencies of the multilateral preference. As we shall see later in this chapter, he was to be misrepresented on occasion as belonging to the unilateralist lobby. An early instance of this is in a description of a House of Commons Question Time in 1962. Harold Wilson, questioning Edward Heath (then Lord Privy Seal):

'showed none of the knowledgeable irreverence of Philip Noel-Baker, the aged Nobel Prize winner, who asked that the C.I.A. stop supplying military equipment to the right-wing government of Laos . . . When he returned to question a week later, Wilson was again outflanked on the Left by Noel-Baker who had become a unilateralist radical in his old age and made Wilson seem like someone seeking the Foreign Office seal of approval.'[18]

The description is inaccurate on a further account: Noel-Baker was a surprisingly active and fit 'aged' man of 73. Another criticism of Noel-Baker is just as far off beam, when two years later in 1964, doubt was voiced as to whether Noel-Baker and others might persuade Harold Wilson, some months before his premiership, to adopt a narrower European policy should Labour come to power. This would be a most unlikely step for a veteran European and world citizen to take.[19] Much more of the real Noel-Baker was evident in remarks made on the opening day of the 1960 Scarborough Conference:

'The real choice, the only choice, before the Labour Party Conference is whether we shall try to get disarmament by the honourable, but desperate and, as I think defeatist method of unilateral action by Britain, or by the world agreement for which the Labour Party has stood for 40 years. To abandon the party's policy at such a time would be political suicide at home and a betrayal of the foreign socialist parties with whom we have always worked out the programme.'[20]

The conjunction of the adjectives 'honourable', and 'desperate', and 'defeatist' is a significant and accurate pointer to the direction of Noel-Baker's attitude to unilateralism. Our approach to disarmament must be multilateral he had reminded the House of Commons on 11th February 1960, and again in July 1960. Disarmament treaties had their risks and might even increase complacency rather than reduce it. The Labour Party must table a practicable programme of disarmament and seek international accord to this end. There should be a degree of freedom from dogma, an ability to see the other viewpoints, and to make some allowance for them.[21]

Labour's back benches contained no more insistent advocate of phased approach than Noel-Baker. His constituency recognised this when they conferred the Freedom of Derby upon him in 1960 for, as his proposer said:

'Mr. Noel-Baker's voice is as one crying in the wilderness, warning nations of the wrath to come but ever pointing to the flickering light on the horizon which directed the way to human happiness and peace.'[22]

The broad policy of the Labour Party set out in their publication of June 1959, *Disarmament and Nuclear War: The Next Step* had earned Noel-Baker's entire approval. There was envisaged an agreement, preferably under U.N. auspices, to be signed by all nations save the U.S.A. and the U.S.S.R., pledging no manufacture, testing, or possession of nuclear weapons. Hinging upon successful negotiation of this agreement constraining proliferation, Great Britain would then announce an end to manufacture and possession of its own weapons. The statement was not, in fact, debated in full conference since a General Election intervened in early October 1959. In the country at large there was anxiety about over-dependence, 'lackey status', in regard to the U.S.A. Labour Members were at odds over the leadership's call for support of a nuclear N.A.T.O., for this meant provision of bases. The Joint Statement of 1961, *Policy for Peace* appeared to be on these lines. Already, in 1960, the cancellation of the Blue Streak missile carrier was taken to signal the end of an independent and viable British deterrent. Would something like this reduce or increase Britain's autonomy and influence? For Noel-Baker, the controversy was not about Britain's declining status as a 'troubled giant'. His country still had a part to play – as a member of an international force for collective security. One commentator has seen the stance in these terms:

'Philip Noel-Baker, later to play a significant part in the socialist Campaign for Multilateral Disarmament, was the most dedicated champion of general and complete disarmament and considered that nuclear unilateralism must be considered in this context. He bluntly stated that "unilateral disarmament would mean surrendering Britain's influence in the world-wide struggle to demilitarise the world". Noel-Baker consistently opposed unilateralism from its birth in 1957 to its death in 1961 [?]. He represented a strand of socialist thinking on foreign policy which has its roots in a collectivist approach to world problems.

'He maintained that adequate collective security in the thirties would have saved the world from war and consequently he doubted the validity of unilateral declarations and enforcements.'[23]

There is every sign from the speech notes on tattered grey paper that Noel-Baker kept in his pocket that neutralism or schemes for partial disengagement earned the disapproval of a veteran peace worker. His own party must not drag their feet nor wrangle over expedients. More than one correspondent was assured that while he did not ask the unilateralist to change views a difference of opinion was regretted. His own reason for sticking to multilateralism (undoubtedly, not the only one) was that the Party could not win the country on an alternative. As for neutrality towards an aggressor and his victim, it would be both illegal under the U.N. Charter and immoral. It would not be politically tenable for 'no true Socialist can hold another view'. Meanwhile, there was urgent work to be done at Transport House where, he confided to J. E. Meade, the eminent economist, he had never been able 'to make H.G. [Hugh Gaitskell] take a real interest in disarmament . . .'[24] It was not long before committees were set up at Party Headquarters to examine specifically multilateral proposals and the role of the United Nations in relation to arms negotiations. Within the Palace of Westminster itself Noel-Baker was to be seen perusing and scribbling in the Commons Library, hurrying (with a hint of the old Olympic fleetness) to Lobby or Committee room. To the end, despite failing sight and hearing, he remained proud of an ability to remember faces and places and facts.

Twenty years later, in autumn 1980, the refuting of the label 'unilateralist' came upon an ageing Noel-Baker. The Labour Party

Conference was to be held in Blackpool. There were many draft resolutions calling for closure of United States bases in Britain and for unilateral disarmament to be implemented as soon as possible. It is significant that Noel-Baker chose to speak to two composite motions which had been endorsed by the National Executive and adopted unanimously by the Conference. The dangerous escalation of the arms race was deplored. He recalled that in 1978 the United Nations had convened a Special Session on Disarmament, the so-called 'S.S.D.I.' A World Disarmament Campaign had been proposed: governments had made serious pledges. Conference should urge the British Government to honour its intentions. It was appropriate that the Labour Movement should do its utmost to collaborate with workers of all nations in promoting multilateral disarmament. 'Negotiation and persuasion' could bring about the abandonment of intermediate range missiles, could work towards the establishment of a nuclear-free zone throughout Europe, and, above all, give meaning to the Final Act which concluded S.S.D.I. in 1978, a statement which incorporated a consensus about the urgency of multilateral arms reductions.

The old campaigner was much disconcerted when his copy of *The Guardian* at breakfast represented him as a proponent of a unilateralist policy which could sweep the country and sweep the world. A reply to this was hastily concocted. The words 'unilateralist policy' were the insertion of a journalist. Plainly, *multilateral* disarmament, for Noel-Baker, remained as 'general' as ever, that is to say, all arms, nuclear and conventional, must be involved, and all nations, in progressive stages, would be required to disarm and reallocate correspondingly the resources so released to the economic and social improvement of the developed and developing world. 'Your colleague calls me a "Pacifist"' was his indignant rebuttal. Never since 1919 and the formation of the League of Nations had Noel-Baker seen himself in that light. One who helped organise the Peace Ballot of 1934-35 and who had served in Churchill's wartime Coalition Government had been prepared to stand to arms in common cause. What really mattered was that readers of *The Guardian* should recognise a united Labour Party asserting the dangers of military escalation, supporting the World Disarmament Campaign, and, of course, grounding their belief in the Final Act of 1978. To any doubt whether the United Kingdom would have real influence to promote this policy, he retorted that no country (under, naturally, a Labour Government) which had demilitarised and transformed 'the greatest military Empire in history' was likely to be seen as ineffectual.[25]

Five days later, no newspaper column had set the matter to rights. Noel-Baker felt a 'sense of keen outrage'. Should he resort to action for libel?

Legal advice was sought, meanwhile, the Editor of *The Guardian* was again approached. Half a century of friendly relations with the paper was appreciated but nothing could excuse failure to correct 'grave misreport'. This omission had resulted in anxiety and expense (since the original letter had been sent poste-haste by taxi). Personal defamation was bad enough; more importantly, the World Disarmament Campaign he saw as 'grievously damaged'.[26] A similar misunderstanding occurred 12 months later in October 1981, also after a Labour Party Conference. This time the protest was not so anguished, merely, 'respectfully' uttered. He was unable to accept a caption-writer's phrase 'powerful *unilateralist* speech'. Nothing remotely unilateralist, he pointed out, was contained in his address. He respected the opinion of unilateralists, welcomed their support for world disarmament campaigns and, indeed, believed that many of them would strongly advocate multilateral processes. (In this respect, one feels, his benevolence may have clouded his discrimination somewhat.) Nevertheless, he went on:

'in 70 years I have never myself urged unilateral disarmament by Britain because it would not save us from extermination by the "fall-out" from a U.S.-Soviet nuclear war; and because I believe it would not be accepted by the British electorate.'[27]

Disarmament on more than one front was clearly in Noel-Baker's mind. Unanimity of approach to the problem could surely be reached, he concluded, if Britain were to press for firm *unilateral* rejection of a missile system such as the Trident and, also, of the neutron bomb and then to take the lead in urging *multilateral* world disarmament down to the levels pledged at the S.S.D.I. This step would be in line with the aspirations of the old League of Nations days, namely, that states retain only sufficient arms and forces to uphold international law and order.[28]

In the last 20 years of his life, to take a longer perspective, Noel-Baker had been at pains to stress what he regarded as the inadequacy of mere *control* of arms as an end in itself. It was of little use, so he had thought, in 1963 to try to tie down the lid on a vessel that continued to boil. Technical constraints were possible but as a 'safe' way of lessening a state of tension they were illusory. There is no safety in allowing states to continue 'edging for strength' in defensive or offensive postures. Essentially, general disarmament is a political procedure: the *political* constraints are the only ones that both generate and follow on from disarmament programmes. The Noel-Baker of the 1920's and 1930's had never thought that general and complete disarmament would be achieved by means of a single treaty. A gradual and staged approach was the best means to this end. Specific measures of reduction of course, constitute 'control'. It is not altogether easy to see the consistency of Noel-Baker's logic here, for if one pursues his analogy one can prevent over-boiling (a state of hostilities) by progressively lowering the heat and so the temperature. Manipulation of circumstance by agreement, that is to say, a mode of control, seems to be the only possible approach to general and complete attainment of a disarmament objective. The end justifies experimenting with means.

The possibility of achieving 'general and complete' disarmament through discrete stages had, after all, been examined very thoroughly by the 18 Nation Disarmament Committee after 1961. Their recommendations had envisaged a process in three stages of reduction, viz. of 30%, 35% and 35%. For Noel-Baker, consistently calling for a graduated approach, there are one or two riders to add. Firstly, a disadvantage of staging disarmament must be faced. Too many regard this arrangement as a weakening of one or other participant. This may be unavoidable but it is neither reassuring nor readily tolerated. Bargains must be struck. Geographical, political, economic considerations – the components of a nation's strength – need to be weighed. The multivariate factors involved in inspection, control, dismantling, and enumerated destruction of stocks call for the most serious, comprehensive handling. Moreover, as he had suggested at the beginning of the 60's, if the balances are not kept in trim, then factors which are improperly controlled and measures which are only partial may leave disarmament harnessed to military policies. The world was well aware of how states sought to redress a perceived disadvantage and, in turn, how often this would destabilise a sensitive state of affairs.[29]

A further consequence of phasing disarmament is the disarray it may cause to alliance.[30] The rival blocs of N.A.T.O. and of the Warsaw Pact have gone progressively nuclear. Noel-Baker does not often deal with the consequences of proposals for 'decoupling' or the removal of emplacements either side of a Curtain or a Wall.[31] The reader of much of his work over the years must feel that certain historical perspectives are inadequately viewed. The implications of stirring the muddied waters of political situations in Europe need more sustained examination.[32]

The Special Sessions which the United Nations eventually called together in 1978 and then in 1982 were staged to facilitate the widest possible examination of all modes of disarmament. On the first occasion, there congregated in New York 20 Presidents and Prime Ministers, 26 Vice-Presidents, 54 Foreign Ministers, and 100 ministers of senior Cabinet rank. Noel-Baker, mentally, was inextinguishable. Physically, he found it hard to cope with near-blindness, deafness, and 'useless legs'. Somehow, his never vanishing charm, patience, and consideration masked the frustrations over getting out and about. He never gave way to the resentment and public railings of elderly savants who feel themselves similarly pinioned.

Everything was attentively listened to. Orations at the speakers rostrum were 'sensationally good'. Four ways of working were the objectives of S.S.D.I., the goals for which Noel-Baker had so long been working for. Abolition of nuclear arsenals came first. Then a phased doing away with conventional weapons. General disarmament on this scale would release resources which could be calculated. Finally, the resources would be transferred to specific programmes for ending world poverty. There was nothing new in the outlining of these proposals save that the observer of so many conferences, commissions and reports saw here a splendid endorsement of aims and method in the Final Act Document, for him 'the greatest state paper in history'. Nevertheless, at the point where optimism meets realism Noel-Baker was not at all surprised that the recording of S.S.D.I. in the worlds press and, indeed, a good deal of informed discussion of the prospects of (and for) Apocalypse were veiled in a mist-like 'conspiracy of silence'.[33]

The Final Document of S.S.D.I., subscribed to by 149 states, had given a mandate to two bodies to carry out a comprehensive survey of arms reduction. The U.N. Committee on Disarmament was to bring 40 nations to Geneva; the U.N. Commission on Disarmament represented all member states of the United Nations and met in New York. Eight months before he died, Noel-Baker urged that the lesson of earlier surveys be taken to heart, namely, that all participants have to accept 'sacrifice' of power and prestige: nobody can stand apart from the scheme of disengagement and reduction.[34] Demilitarisation as an objective is far wider and deeper than any denuclearisation he frequently reminded an audience. The civilised nation can not indulge the temporary recourse of the chronic drunkard to 'just one more'. The continued possession of arms encourages experiments within the lethal armoury with new agents of destruction and with new weapons 'systems'. Again and again we are told that it is not the 'pacifist fanatics' who will make most progress in effecting arms reduction. Stern criticism, perhaps, but Noel-Baker gives always most room to the campaigner who renounces fatalism, complacency and ignorance. Problems have to be illumined realistically – 'it is better to light a candle than to curse the darkness,' he would say. It may have been in a moment of frustration that he told a Tokyo audience in 1981, 'so far I've mainly cursed the darkness'. Three-quarters of a century of public endeavour attest his capacity for clarifying and encouraging others.[35]

During the interim period between S.S.D.I. and its successor, scheduled for the summer of 1982, Noel-Baker set up regular consultation with a group of associates. They included the Premier of Sweden, Olof Palme, the Director of the Stockholm Institute of Peace Research,

Dr. Frank Barnaby, and a fellow Nobel laureate and Irish jurist, Sean MacBride. Their comments and recommendations as to the needs and direction of action for peace are set out in a publication which appeared in 1978 with the rather portentous title, *Disarm or Die: A Development Reader for the Leaders and Peoples of the World*. Hopes of eventual success are not pitched high. The long history of disarmament negotiations reveals, for one of its oldest living observers, the frequency of easy surrenders to hastily judged obstacles (they would not too easily have defeated Nansen), and a complacent satisfaction with temporary expedients.

An instance of a much earlier failure to reach an objective that Noel-Baker writes about in *Disarm or Die*, was the fate of President Truman's 'Six Principles' in 1952. In whole-hearted fashion those principles set out not to regulate hostilities but to make them inherently and constitutionally impossible. Western proposals for strictly delimited manpower ceilings were elaborated 18 months later in what became known as the 'Anglo-French Memorandum' of 1955. Discussion in less-public committees made tangible progress. Hopes reached a climax in the pronouncements of leaders from East and West. Hindrances to full agreement soon loomed up and methods permitting objective control and any form of intervention were seen as facilitating espionage. Schemes to reduce military power crumbled because they failed to preserve at least some advantage for participants. Fears of losing minimal power and prestige stymied the advance towards collective security and overall objectives became shorter-ranged and more hypothetical on account of lack of faith and impaired vision. Nations retreated behind contradictory pretensions; few ready to accept or even consider the risks of working for disarmament.[36]

It seems a pity that Noel-Baker, writing in *Disarm or Die*, did not consider rather more critically another set of principles that he frequently endorsed, namely, the Axioms for Disarmament established by McCloy and Zorin, respectively for the U.S.A. and the U.S.S.R., in 1961. The basic idea here was that disarmament would proceed given a trinity of essentials – balance, mutuality, and verifiability. Truman's principles equally depended upon round acceptance of these criteria. The problems, however, of deciding just what represents a state of balance are formidable. In which respects are elements in a hugely complicated weapons system really comparable? Restriction and limitation of particular weapons, as in S.A.L.T. I (1972), or setting ceilings on aggregate numbers, as in S.A.L.T. II (1979) which was never completely ratified, has struck at least one other observer, not as disarmament, but as *legitimised armament*.[37] How vital in these difficult calculations is a state's estimation of *level of vulnerability*, or *invulnerability?* We appear, here, to have returned to certain aspects of the disarmament process which Noel-Baker so often branded as illusory, *viz.* that 'balance' as a criterion is a temporary contrivance and a partial measure, unsettled and unsettling. Theoretical levels, he writes, are easily transgressed. Mutuality may be a fair concept to insist upon but not only the cynic will point out that if quantitative reductions are secured, the parties to agreement may still hanker after qualitative advantage. Verification procedures, the writer tells us, had made impressive strides in technical feasibility and reliability. All too often, though, the critical element of trust is completely missing. We could achieve much more progress, in Noel-Baker's opinion, if we worked out policies on the lines of a 'no first use' declaration by the West. Alternatively, we might agree to withdraw all nuclear arms such as intermediate range missiles from client states. A promising innovation would be *transarmament,* a clear shift from offensive to defensive armouries such as the smaller countries Yugoslavia, Sweden, and Switzerland have preferred. This could be represented to the population as a whole in positive and not negative terms, as a move from vulnerability to enhanced invulnerability. It is implied, in his words, that the plain man will appreciate that measures of this kind have to do with better value-for-money and with preserving some moral integrity in our attitude to defence.[38]

Predictably, in *Disarm or Die,* Noel-Baker returns to the theme of censuring measures of partial control which fall short of objectives they ought to pursue. Discussion such as S.A.L.T. I and the Vienna talks on Mutual and Balanced Force Reduction (wallowing in choppy waters since 1973) 'were never aimed at disarmament, but only at arms control'.[39] Partial control measures never get to grips with the illusions of deterrence and bluff. The objective of eliminating armouries is lost, paradoxically because we are too humane. The Hague Conferences of 1899 and 1907, graphic memories for the young Philip Baker, were diverted in their main conclusive thrust by motives which resulted only in the refinement and codification of the Laws of War. Today, he sees the classic objective of emptying the arsenals as superseded by attempts to restrain the acquisition of weapons. The 'denuclearising' of zones such as Antarctica, parts of Latin America, the Sea Bed and Outer Space while desirable in themselves scarcely begin to address the problem of dealing with the mounting crescendo of warlike enterprise elsewhere. Frank Barnaby, of the Stockholm Institute, agrees with Noel-Baker's assessment. Is tinkering on the periphery likely to bring much significant pacification in the near future? Are 'piecemeal measures' ever able to contain the obvious pace of qualitative improvement and strategic emplacement?[40]

When it did reconvene, in June 1982, the U.N. Special Session II confronted, in the challenging statement of the Secretary General, Javier Perez de Cuellar, 'a very real possibility of the Apocalypse', and, since it had met last, 'a sorry record of failure'. Over a good many months in the earlier part of 1982 there had been an expectation that a Comprehensive Programme of Disarmament would be worked through at the Special Session and, thereafter, submitted for approval and implementation. This would be the culmination of four years of work in committee.

Perhaps more emphatically than for many years, public opinion in many parts of the globe was responding to an elaborate programme of information, encouragement, and mobilisation. In the words of Jan Martensen, Assistant U.N. Secretary General, much of the debate on nuclear and other issues was being moved out of the 'glasshouse' (the U.N. Building) and into the streets – where it belonged. Realising that attempts would be made by governments to turn the Comprehensive Programme into a scheme for partial measures, a number of people in Britain reconstructed the World Disarmament Campaign, (flagging somewhat since S.S.D.I.) this time with a United Kingdom section. They would work alongside similarly-minded groups elsewhere in the world. Lords (Fenner) Brockway and Noel-Baker (also now a Life Peer) were co-Chairmen. Brigadier Michael Harbottle, former Chief of Staff to the U.N. Peace Keeping Force in Cyprus, was its General Secretary. Ideas about structure were carefully thought out although Noel-Baker attributed their origin to the coincidence of the Chairmens' birthday parties on a November day in Cheltenham the previous year. Lord Brockway had asked his friend, 'How about us starting a World Disarmament Campaign together?' Noel-Baker replied, 'Fenner, you're my senior (by one year), I must do as you say'. They went on to define and elaborate strategy and methods at a crowded meeting in Westminster's Grand Committee Room.[41] Special efforts went into liaison with press and radio to try to ensure extensive coverage of the Special Session and the Comprehensive Programme.[42] Some 650 support groups, representing churches, professional and educational groups, and Trade Unions made it their responsibility to tramp British streets eliciting signatures for their country's section of a world-wide petition. Governments would be urged to secure the successful attainment of the Comprehensive Programme and the petition would be handed to the Prime Minister and to the Secretary General of the United Nations.

International contacts in person were struck. In early August 1981, the two Nobel Prizewinners, Philip Noel-Baker and Sean MacBride had had talks with an all-party Disarmament Group comprising half the members of the Japanese Diet. Visits were paid to Hiroshima and Nagasaki. It was in

(COURTESY: THE HON. FRANCIS NOEL-BAKER)

Pl. 15. With Mr. Sadao Nakabayashi of Japan at the United Nations, June 1982

Hiroshima, on the 36th anniversary of atomic bombing that Noel-Baker, according to his own record, nearly lost his composure only to regain it. How utterly sad it was, he said, to condemn the United States who were carrying out a nuclear test on Hiroshima Day. His great-great grandfather had fought at George Washington's side in 1776. Fifteen thousand Japanese crowded into an enormous gymnasium in scorching heat, hung on to the appeal of the frail Englishman, vibrant in voice yet as frail as the two sticks on which he leaned. His words were sharp and brief:

'We have four minutes: let's make the headlines in the Press. Let's say, all of us together, the loudest "No", the mightiest "No" ever heard in the world. Let's say, "No More Hiroshimas! No More Wars!"'

Afterwards, he wrote that 15,000 voices shouted 'No' as they had never shouted before. 'I thought the roof would fall about our heads.' They made the headlines. 'Our "No" appeared on the front page of every paper in Japan.'[43] In Tokyo, a Buddhist divine and Noel-Baker, both nonagenarians in wheelchairs, had led a peace march in pouring rain under an estimated 10,000 umbrellas. On to Moscow went Noel-Baker to satisfy himself about the commitment and objectivity of the Soviet Peace Committee. Not all his associates were as reassured as he was. As expected, the sincerity and long experience of the celebrated Quaker gained much esteem from Soviet journalists, impressed by a man who could reply, 'Litvinov? Ah, yes, I knew him well!' Neither heat nor cold ever upset Noel-Baker even at an advanced age. Anxiety, however, was often expressed by members of his entourage. For many years overcoat, hat, gloves, and umbrella were scorned by the object of their solicitude. In his 91st summer, apart from Japan, Noel-Baker paid visits, connected with disarmament, twice to Canada, thrice to France, once to Spain. A sports conference in West Germany was delighted to have a celebrated Olympist come among them. His actual birthday that year was spent on the pavement slabs outside St. Margaret's, Westminster, as a participant in a vigil for the World ¨isarmament Campaign.

In the eyes of those who sat through the Special Session of 1982, Noel-Baker among them, there was movement on two planes, the governmental and the non-governmental. Speaker after speaker, wearing a government accreditation in the lapel, mounted the podium. For many, this sounded like peroration rather than practicality. A rather grotesque 'shopping list' of essentials for survival was intoned, without the more powerful states, at least, committing themselves within specific parameters. There was impressive if not rather indeterminate consideration of problems such as 'freezing' weapons and budgets, verification procedures, zones of détente, bans on testing and proliferation, redeployment of resources, and

(COURTESY: THE HON. FRANCIS NOEL-BAKER)

Pl. 16. Addressing the United Nations Special Session on Disarmament, June 1982

'confidence building'. A thought that occurred to Noel-Baker and numerous others present was that all too many members were prepared to dance an elegant quadrille in the fatalistic belief that the initiators of policies must be not 'We the peoples', the ascribed signatories to the final documents, but the executives of Great Powers, located in Washington and Moscow. On the second level of activity there was more plain speaking, more sincerity, and more visible action. 'Non-governmental Organisations', or 'N.G.O.s', sent several thousand representatives to midsummer New York. A mass march and rally on 12th June 1982 was estimated to have poured one million people down 42nd Street and into Central Park. From four continents a huge crowd of concerned individuals walked, danced, or rode in wheelchairs to make up a colourful, good-natured day. Concern was articulated in waiting upon Session delegates, in debate at 'fringe meetings', in manning bookstalls. Noel-Baker was an assiduous worker in these modes. In Lord Brockway's words:

'He overdid it, never refusing an invitation to speak . . . or to address the throngs of demonstrators, as well as the U.N. itself. He was nearly blind, unable to walk without help, yet his faith poured forth, in torrential words whenever he spoke.'[44]

The intensity, loquacity, and astounding, unassisted memory of the frail, gaunt Englishman marked him out as a quarry for delegates and visitors. It was never easy for his companions to 'protect' him and relieve the strain. On one occasion, the press of admirers and questioners almost suffocated Noel-Baker, who was then manoeuvred with great difficulty into a lift. The veteran, it seems, remained calm. Faith in the power of public will was never failing in the case of Noel-Baker. In June 1958, in an onthrust of optimism on this score, he had written to the Quaker, Sydney Bailey:

'Lenin used to say that 60,000 Communists could easily conquer and keep control of Russia. Forty years of history have proved that he was right. Sixty thousand Friends could disarm the world if they gave their minds to it.'[45]

It was a picturesque but hardly sound analogy.

Noel-Baker may have been regarded as a right flank member of the Labour Party but he retained to the end, in writing and in speaking, a tolerance that spanned most of the political spectrum. A criterion for his preparedness to accept the position of others was their recorded attitude towards work for peace and disarmament. In mid-October 1980, for instance, his predilections had surfaced in Blackpool when Labour's Annual Conference had to elect a new leader following the retirement of James Callaghan. On the whole, the Conference had been a good one. Constitutional changes providing for an electoral college and for the mandatory reselection of M.P.s were for the better. Party horizons linking disarmament and development were now clearer than hitherto, a point of much relief to a great campaigner on their behalf. Callaghan, on the other hand, ought to reconsider what was sensed as his intention to retire: he should continue as leader. Noel-Baker told Alec Kitson, the Chairman of the Party that he was writing to Callaghan:

'. . . to urge on him, not only that he can hold the Party together better than anybody else but also that he should lead the other nations in the U.N. in drawing up a world treaty by which the promises of 1978 [at the U.N. Special Session when he accompanied Callaghan, then Premier] on armaments and world poverty can be carried into effect. If he would make this and unemployment the great issues of the day he could, I am sure, win the next election and make for himself a place in history which future generations will remember with deep gratitude.'[46]

On the same occasion at the Conference, Noel-Baker showed he had not lost his political initiative when he put his reservations as to the leadership contest to the Deputy Leader, Michael Foot. It would be a 'disaster' if either Denis Healey or Peter Shore were to get the leading nomination. On another tack, he had approached Tony Benn, whose candidature had been withdrawn to show his dissatisfaction over the lack of constitutional change. Here was the man to aspire to Foreign Secretaryship, not to Party Leader:

'He [Benn] is very sound on the United Nations and armaments, he has the guts to persuade or override the Foreign Office bureaucrats – they can be persuaded; I had to work hard with them when I was in the Office but they never gave me much trouble. In the end they always "went along" – and Tony is a very good speaker which is of immense importance in the United Nations. I think he would be prepared to give as many weeks in New York as were useful – two or three days by Presidents or Prime Ministers [e.g. you] are of real importance. But as a rule, Foreign Ministers must stay a good deal longer if they are to get any significant result . . .'[47]

Two ballots were, in fact, needed to give Foot the leadership on 10th November; his nearest rival, Denis Healey, 10 votes lower, was returned unopposed as Deputy Leader. Noel-Baker wrote to Foot congratulating him on his electoral victory and adding:

'I remain dismayed that 129 people should have voted for Denis [Healey]. I am sure you will win them over, and even Denis seems to be talking much more sensibly about disarmament than he has ever done before, but, alas, his record is bad.'

A talk with Healey and one or two of his close advisers would be the next step for Noel-Baker.[48]

Eighteen months before he died, Noel-Baker was envisaging a chance for the Labour Party to reassert the primacy of disarmament issues and, particularly, to move to confront a recent charge from the Prime Minister, Margaret Thatcher, that the Party was wedded to the unilateralist standpoint. Earnestly, he wrote to Michael Foot:

'My idea is that a group of Labour Party experts should prepare a draft treaty of world disarmament which shall be general and complete carried out in stages. To the treaty should be added schedule[s], showing the actual reduction of manpower, weapons and equipment, and military budgets, which would be made by the principle [sic] military powers at the end of each stage. If you launched such a treaty with appropriate publicity, it would gain attention throughout the world.

'May I have a chance of talking with you about this idea and how it could be carried out in an early future.'[49]

Some months later, Noel-Baker felt the need to send the Party Leader a reminder which ended:

'I shall write separately about my proposal that the Party should publish a model draft treaty of world disarmament. I will try to get some help before I put it to you again. It could be a winner.'[50]

For whatever reason the 'favourite' never left the stable.

If Noel-Baker's tolerance extended over both wings of the Party to which he was deeply loyal, his criticisms were stern of those who had broken away from the Labour ranks at the beginning of 1981, those who were popularly and perjoratively cast as 'the Gang of Four'. He wrote in a letter to Ron Hayward, General Secretary, at Walworth Road:

'I am outraged by the effrontery of the gang of traitors in using the words "Social Democrats" to describe themselves – quite unlike the S.D. Parties in Germany, Sweden, Norway etc. Ought not these European parties to support M. Foot's magnificent stand on World Disarmament and Third World Hunger? Think over the idea.'[51]

Apart from disloyalty to one's party affiliation (something which gravely distressed this constant man), solidarity was a *sine qua non* for a party facing a 'difficult' electorate in a divided world. A sad point in this connection is that the aged peer felt unable to make a financial contribution to the Party's 'Solidarity Campaign'. He was, he told the Party's Treasurer 'heavily overdrawn and in debt'.[52]

Some of Noel-Baker's last thoughts were to do with the basic premises which ought to illumine world counsels and advance international order. First, that 'defence' as a legitimate response to aggressive posturing must be non-provocative, non-nuclear, and set within the context of a comprehensive strategy, not for contest, but for disarmament and world security. It would be indefensible to seek to defend moral values by any other means.[53] Second, the interdependence of the arms race and world poverty. 'From warfare to welfare – an idea whose time has come' was his message, in mid-1981, to a meeting commemorating the 25th anniversary of the Bertrand Russell-Albert Einstein manifesto against nuclear arms. Quoting the declaration of President Eisenhower that 'every warship, every airplane, every gun is a theft from those who hunger and are not fed' he went on to reallocate the immense sums spent by the world on arms each year. The 'savage, shaming, stabbing facts of world poverty' could be transformed by a budgetary process, essentially 'easy and exciting' which invests £40,000 million a year in sectors such as agricultural improvement, better shelter, public health, education, and urban renewal.[54] 'I am, my Noble Lords, no pacifist fanatic', he had said on one occasion when the Upper Chamber was debating the economic consequences of the arms race, 'but the statistics stand like tombstones.'[55]

The links between disarmament and world development received much scrutiny at meetings convened by the United Nations but never more intensively and productively than in the working groups of the Pugwash Movement in which Noel-Baker was a whole-hearted and frequent participant. The Movement began in 1956 as a manifesto signed by Bertrand Russell, Albert Einstein, Frederic Joliot and others, calling upon scientists from East and West to meet, inform each other, and attempt to influence their political rulers to keep peace in a nuclear-threatened world. 'We appeal', the manifesto put it, 'as human beings to human beings – remember your humanity and forget the rest.' Meeting first in Pugwash, Nova Scotia, representatives of more than 30 nations have come together annually in various places. After 22 of these brain-storming sessions a reviewer put the formula for their effectiveness in terms which must have meant everything to Noel-Baker:

'we recognise as valid limits only those of our effectiveness . . . We bar no holds in our discussions, and we do not accept previous failure as an excuse for quitting.'[56]

Noel-Baker attended 15 Pugwash seminars, read a paper at most of them, and was an active member of the British delegation's executive. Fellow-members at Moscow in 1960 had readily agreed with him that disarmament followed readily only from the basic proposition that war was anachronistic and must be abolished. The scientists conceded that acceptance even of this concept would pave the way for political 'will' and facilitate technical examination of disarmament measures. Meeting the following year in Vermont, the Pugwash group once more emphasised with Noel-Baker the needs of trust and an absence of hostility among those who would negotiate over the proliferation and clandestine accumulation of weapons. In the years that followed, in England, Czechoslovakia, and Yugoslavia, Noel-Baker returned to the convoluted distinction between what might be termed 'offensive' weapons or 'defensive' weapons and found, to his chagrin, but not to the surprise of the other discussants, that little progress had been made over three decades in differentiation as a prelude to control if not abolition. Moreover, by 1964, there was the suggestion of a 'freeze' of strategic nuclear weapons – the era of 'delivery systems' had arrived. A proposal of Noel-Baker that year was 'realistic' in its framing and ought to have appealed to a wide spectrum of opinion on both sides of the Atlantic, namely, that:

'if within two years no Disarmament Treaty had been signed, any Party to the Freeze might reclaim freedom.'[57]

The assembled scientists lost no time in looking carefully at yet another problem in distinction. This time, in the nuclear age, it was the relationship between 'tactical' and 'strategic' scenarios and armouries. Among others, Noel-Baker expressed dismay that the possibilities of disarmament were hampered by geopolitical considerations, foremost among them the fear that a country which reduced its nuclear weaponry then felt menaced by the superiority in conventional forces of others. Thus, however willing a government might otherwise be to initiate arms reduction, strategic factors and the fear of additional 'vulnerability' precluded action.

Twenty-five years of earnest debate and careful recording convinced the 'Pugwashites' that their counsel had not been lost on world statesmen. They believed that their expert advocacy had been instrumental in bringing about a 'partial' test-ban treaty and a non-proliferation accord.[58] At his last appearance at the seminars, in Canada in 1981, Noel-Baker made his opinion plain as to their importance. Speaking 'with diffidence and in poor physical condition, for which I apologise', he saw their mission as 'churning out the facts – the truth – about armaments and war'. They must build up a corps of experts who could answer the bureaucrats and militarists, and defeat them on their own ground. They must give the non-governmental organisations (N.G.O.'s), 'that great popular force of world opinion', the authoritative information they required 'to fuel their campaign . . .' Stopping war was possible and was something they could all bend their energies to. It was an idea, he said, 'of immense dynamic power'.[59]

CHAPTER 11

Champion of Collective Security through the U.N. 1949-1982

THE CONCEPT OF COLLECTIVE SECURITY WAS ONE always close to the heart of Philip Noel-Baker.[1] It was never an easy concept to define. The notion of states, members of an international organisation, resolutely acting together to deter aggressors and to build a more peaceful world was certainly in the minds of the idealists who had framed the League of Nations Covenant in 1918. In the first flush of enthusiasm for the League, born of war-weariness and a concern to manifest common humanity, nations were envisaged as 'united' on a moral plane. A generation later, as the world attempted recovery from a second world war, the enthusiasts – Cecil, Noel-Baker, Angell, Gilbert Murray – were scrutinising the concept more keenly. Were we acclaiming the existence of a world forum when all we had was a set of rules, broken as often as they were found inconvenient? Could any degree of collective security be attained in a world divided between a polarised East and West and their client states? The stalemate that resulted from confrontational postures among nations seemed to have little to do with any sense of general security, based as this must be on reassurance and predictability. The 'open diplomacy' of Wilson's days appeared more than ever to be 'frozen diplomacy' where 'open covenants . . . privately arrived' at were preferred.[2] Today's world in their estimation was coming to rely upon evasion and ambiguity, the politics not of responsibility but of excuse.

Noel-Baker was a Quaker as well as a seasoned politician. He took in his stride the criticisms of collective action that were most often voiced, namely, that a theoretical code does not logically address the solution of a political problem – the retort of the 'militarists', or that a collective resort to force (and readiness to use it) is immoral – the attitude of the 'pacifists'. His rejoinder to points such as these was that 'law' must be endowed with 'power'.[3] The 'fighting Quaker' in Noel-Baker dealt resolutely (often in press columns) with the charge that an international organisation too often adopted a legalistic approach in a pietistic tradition.[4] Clarity in perception and tolerance in judgement he would stress were essential if security were to be promoted among those who live in a confused world. Attitudes such as these were, for Noel-Baker, not only the hallmarks of Quaker and realist: they were indispensable to civilised living in its dependence upon the rule of law and the sanctity of human rights. Only if an international watchdog were empowered to work for these ends was security possible to any extent. An affirmation on these lines illumined one of his very last public statements in June 1982. 'Blind, deaf, and as you see, a cripple' he commended to a New York audience the standpoint of Franklin D. Roosevelt. The feeling of security depended upon affirming and ensuring essential human freedoms. We and our leaders must come to rely upon understanding, tolerance, and iron willpower. Nothing was ever 'out of reach' he declared.[5] Always for Noel-Baker, the faith of the Quaker sustained clear views and a sense of progression by stages. He put security in these terms in *The Arms Race* in 1958:

'Lasting peace and justice will only come from the gradual cumulative interaction of many policies and great reform: a conscious persistent effort to strengthen the deliberative institution of the U.N. . . .'[6]

In seeking ardently and consistently for the realisation of collective security Noel-Baker might be thought an 'impossible' idealist. A fellow-campaigner for the international cause, and a former Under-Secretary General of the U.N., Sir Brian Urquhart, thinks that this was never so:

'To say that Philip Noel-Baker was a determined idealist would be much too easy a description. Certainly, it is true, that to a far greater extent than anyone in my experience, he preserved undiluted into old age the driving enthusiasm of youth. The world disasters through which he had lived only served to strengthen and temper his enthusiasm. But in Philip's writings on disarmament and world affairs one finds, mingled with dauntless idealism, a fearless grasp of inexorable truths about international politics and events – truths which most politicians much prefer not to face. In fact, it is precisely this tendancy [sic] among most politicians which renders international organisations like the United Nations, after an enthusiastic start, so difficult to make effective in the long run.'[7]

Increasingly in Noel-Baker's later days there was a touch of pragmatism in his idealism. This shows particularly in two respects. First, the written codes of precept and practice drawn up by the United Nations should be allowed to stand without frequent modification. His ministerial observation to the first Plenary Session of the U.N. in 1946 revealed both impatience and well-honed experience:

'Let me say at once that my Government do not think it wise to attempt, at this first Assembly, to amend our Charter. Whatever changes we would like to see, surely we agree that this course must be premature. We must try, first, to work the Charter, if only to discover by experience what is really wrong. But if it is not useful to discuss amendments it is useful to discuss why there is already such widespread anxiety about the Council [Security Council], why already there are such insistent demands that amendments shall be made.'[8]

Security must be worked for, built steadily and empirically, worked for by the rule and not according to hunch or preference. Secondly, a more secure world is not more ordered merely because the people in it are better informed. It is the juxtaposition of 'governmental and public opinion' that will exert leverage and rectify imbalance. In 1925 he had pointed out that a government's decision without intelligent popular support would never be sufficient in itself. 'Nothing could be more unfortunate than that the British Government should accept the Protocol, if the British people did not fully comprehend the obligations that were thus assumed.'[9] An informed electorate, in his view, enables a government to work for greater security through the ordinances which substitute open agreement for covert machinations. Thus, on one occasion he had assured Parliament:

'We are determined to use the institutions of the United Nations to kill power politics in order that, by the methods of democracy the will of the peoples shall prevail.'[10]

Sadly, for one who had watched the League and the U.N. at work, the United Nations was becoming a tool with only limited possibilities of going beyond organisational intervention to achieve permanent success. President Wilson's 'witness box of the world' is more often a podium than a powerhouse. Governments perform rituals but do not necessarily learn much about the possibilities and limitations of security promotion: they have not learned to integrate what Noel-Baker's colleague Hugh Dalton once termed 'Force and Fairness' in international relations.[11]

In regard to the furtherance of general world security through responsible collective action Noel-Baker kept in view the precept of his admired Nansen: 'the impossible takes a little longer'.[12] Dogged imperturbability must have been tested severely as one power or another broached the obligations of U.N. membership and resorted to unilateral action. Crises flared in Korea in 1950, in the Congo in 1960, in Cyprus, the Middle East, Vietnam, over the Suez Canal, and over the Falkland Islands in 1982. Each of these was taken in hand by the Security Council as a threat to peace. World-wide there was great anxiety and debate. Within Britain itself, during those 43 years Noel-Baker remained in the forefront, in Parliament and elsewhere as an indefatigable champion of the U.N.

The Korean conflict posed stern questions to upholders of the U.N. role as peacekeeper. A powerful force of North Koreans had crossed the frontier of the 38th Parallel into South Korea on 25th June 1950 and this represented a clear case of aggression. There was now a firm obligation on the part of members of the U.N. to act promptly, decisively, and collectively. In what respects, though, would it be morally right and politically feasible to enforce peace? Sixteen states, among them the United Kingdom, responded to the condemnatory resolution of the Security Council and supported the establishment of an expeditionary force under the veteran General Douglas MacArthur of the United States, which was the main contributor to the force. It so happened that the U.S.S.R. was boycotting the Council in protest against the inadequate representation of China, whose delegate was from the minority element on the island of Formosa (Taiwan) and, thus, no Russian veto was tabled. Ironically, the successful movement northwards of the U.N. Force raised more political problems in that there was every prospect that China would go beyond expressions of umbrage to full-scale military response. In the United States, voices on Capitol Hill looking to the unification and rehabilitation of a shattered South Korea were nearly drowned by a hawkish clamour to get to grips with 'Red China'. In that case, which way would Moscow move?

Noel-Baker had no hesitation in supporting with his Labour Government colleagues British participation in collective military action. 'Naked aggression' had to be checked. Had the United Nations failed to act promptly in this testing situation it would have been discredited. Nor could the operation have been mounted without the substantial military commitment of the United States. There was perhaps a risk that military commanders might be given too much authority and go beyond the cautious remit of the Security Council. Although, of course, field operations could not be directed by committee there was a vital need to coordinate Korean strategies in the light of an overall need to act as a peace-keeping force and, above all, to make sure that communications between the U.N. Force and New York were straightforward.

It would be intolerable, Noel-Baker told one audience a month after the Korean invasion, if members of the U.N., outwardly committed to stopping an aggressor and bringing about a negotiated peace, were to rely on secret dealings between themselves and on plans that were influenced by ideological persuasion.[13]

At the United Nations the exploration of proposals for a cease fire dragged on over 12 months. Much of the debate seemed occupied with apportioning blame. This was something that worried supporters of the U.N. like Noel-Baker. Undoubtedly, in this case, collective intervention was dealing with aggression. It seemed quite futile, in the eyes of Noel-Baker, to divert attention from the main peace-making task by spending time on the 'lie' that the South Koreans did all the provoking and that the United States wanted a fight.[14] There was every indication, so he believed, that the action of the North Koreans had been planned over a long period and that as a measure of *Geopolitik* it had received the quiet approval of the U.S.S.R. Even so, we had now to concentrate on securing a peaceful end to conflict.[15]

Proposals for a Korean ceasefire, originally tabled by the U.S.S.R., came up against three difficulties in June 1952. Communist China had become a party to the Korean dispute. Their forces were now fighting alongside those of North Korea after MacArthur's force had crossed the 38th Parallel. China demanded that all foreign troops leave Korea. A second demand was that the 38th Parallel should be the frontier between North and South Korea as it had been earlier, and not the battle line reached to its north. Finally, there was a Communist insistence on a repatriation of 171,000 Korean prisoners of war, without any discrimination, although 50,000 of them were understood to be unwilling to return. Noel-Baker felt strongly that some concessions must be made towards the China of Mao Tse-tung. The U.N. must work with Peking and not with Formosa. His Majesty's Government, when Labour was in office, and he himself had been a member of that administration, had recognised Mao's China not because there was a feeling of personal obligation but because the Chinese leader was in effective control. That was the right solution under international law. The United Nations Force must withdraw he told Attlee, now Leader of the Opposition. Any threat of bombing or blockade of China would lessen the chances of armistice, extend the war, and by 'striking hard' injure civilians. Firmer British pressure must be brought to bear upon the United States to restrain MacArthur from advancing beyond the 38th Parallel and so transforming the U.N. operation into something much more dangerous than a 'police' action of intervention.[16]

Exchange of prisoners took 18 months to effect. The South Korean leader, Syngman Rhee, very much an authoritarian, at first opposed the handing over of unwilling soldiers even to a neutral commission. In defiance of U.N. negotiators he released 27,000 anti-Communist servicemen captured from North Korea. Noel-Baker complained again to Attlee about the truculence of Rhee as something likely to abort the whole process of exchanging captives. 'He (Rhee) ought not to do it and ought to be stopped,' he repeated. Neutral assistance with repatriation would expedite the affair. Double dealing by South Korea, just as surely as hostility towards the Chinese, would put the brake on the work for a peaceful solution.[17]

The eventual settlement in Korea did not allay questions and anxieties in many quarters. Indecision and stalemate in New York 'froze' relations between the Great Powers. Disputes reverberated between Washington and London and between Commonwealth capitals. An opportunity came to Noel-Baker in 1953 to state the case for collective security in the plainest terms. He succeeded in persuading the Labour Party Conference meeting at Margate, that the mounting of an impressive multi-national action in Korea by way of intervention, was clumsy in some respects, certainly, but effective in limiting the sea of conflict. An enterprise, regional in extent, had prevented the escalation of a major world war. Something had been done to demonstrate that the United Nations could face up to an explicit challenge and, unlike the League of Nations, could resolve a conflict in practical terms. His words to the Party then grew stronger and sterner. Collective security would never be achieved if we waited for a millenium. Faith, hope, and charity, meanwhile, would help us along the way if we stood by principles of international solidarity. These never died or withered he declared: they were there to be incorporated in dealings with other nations despite political differences. Mere gestures of goodwill could never by themselves pacify a world.[18]

A second attempt to employ collective action was centred on the former Belgian colony in Central Africa, the Congo (now Zaire). In 1959 the imperial power had announced a programme to lead to independence over five years. The pace of reform failed to appeal to nationalists led by Patrice Lumumba who boycotted elections and compelled a reluctant Belgium to grant independence in 1960, rather than four years later. Lumumba emerged as Prime Minister of the first independent government. Belgian officials on service in the country were represented as puppets, white civilians harassed, and the army led by Belgian officers, seethed on the verge of mutiny. An outside world now began to take interest in the deteriorating situation. Washington expressed fears that Lumumba's government would be so fragile by the mid-60's that it must be drawn inevitably towards Moscow. Flying in Belgian troops to maintain order was seen by Noel-Baker and many others in Britain not so much as a legitimate protection of Belgian nationals, but as a move to restore colonial power and as such likely to rupture opinion in some sensitive quarters of the Commonwealth. Moreover, the reported intention of Brussels to support a breakaway from a Congo federation by the Province of Katanga would inflame African nationalism and shift valuable mineral resources towards South Africa, a state fast accumulating obloquy. There seemed no alternative to contain a 'threat to peace' other than requiring the Security Council to authorise a peace-keeping operation to stabilise the collapse, prevent civil war spreading centrifugally, and to maintain human rights among a population now menaced by mercenary terrorists.

Lumumba had proclaimed himself a 'positive neutralist' at first, but his strident calls for action made him the target of much criticism from Western countries and from Cape Town. Demands for aid went from his headquarters to Moscow. The moderate President of the Congolese Republic, Joseph Kasavubu, dismissed Lumumba in September 1960 and though the legality of this action was contested, Lumumba's subsequent death at the hands of his Katangan captors in February 1961 raised him to the status of a martyr. Pan-African sentiment condemned the separation of Katanga and promised the development of a more plainly Socialist Congo.

Dag Hammarskjöld, the Secretary General of the United Nations, stood resolute in an attempt to promote peace in Central Africa through U.N. intervention. The despatch of an expeditionary force in 1960 incurred Soviet displeasure as had happened over Korea a decade previously. In London, Harold Macmillan, the Prime Minister, prompted by questions, from Noel-Baker and others, was at pains to stress that the U.N. operation in the field was to create conditions for subsequent negotiations. Noel-Baker remained optimistic that the Congo operation would vindicate the interventionist role of the U.N. The 'realism' of this body showed the resourcefulness and dedication of its members, he believed, and in no way pointed to ineffectualness.[19]

The situation in Katanga caused Noel-Baker a good deal of unease. It seemed to him that mining interests in the Province, in which British and Southern Rhodesian concerns had a stake, should pay their tax liability of £40 million to the legitimate Congo government and not to the secessionist regime. The Union Minière, he considered, was clearly sabotaging the attempts of the U.N. to bring about a speedy settlement. Collective security could be nurtured in this part of Africa if commercial interests were prevented from exercising partisan influence. Furthermore, if the U.N. had to resort to sanctions to rectify a collapsing situation among contenders for power in Central Africa, then again, the private entrepreneur must be denied interference in collectively agreed action. Noel-Baker made this point emphatically in letters to the press, to the Secretary General, and to his party leader, Harold Wilson. To the last-named he wrote of the Katanga issue:

'I hope we can make a big thing of this at the Labour Party Conference. It is really intolerable that a big financial concern . . . should frustrate one of the most crucially important operations the U.N. has ever undertaken.'[20]

The Congo Operation had demonstrated the readiness of the United Nations to 'act for peace'. Unfortunately, there had been a lack of faith and resolve in some of its members to stand by the principles of the Charter.

A third instance of a conflict situation which developed away from legitimate United Nations intervention and mediation into an exercise in sponsorship was the war in Vietnam. Its origins lay in the divisions of South-east Asia as the peace of 1945 brought retreat of an occupying power, Japan, and progressive dismemberment of the former imperial territories of France, Netherlands, and Britain. France felt unable to accept a Communist guerilla leader, Ho Chi Minh, as head of a *bona fide* state, when French power was inexorably prised out of Indo-China (soon to be renamed Vietnam) unless the new state were included within the French Union. A confused situation appeared to clear briefly as the French, feeling militarily and politically vanquished, began to withdraw. The vacuum was filled in the southern non-Communist bastion of Saigon when Ngo Dinh Diem became an authoritarian President after 1954. Two Vietnams soon began to emerge, the one non-Communist in the south, supplied with U.S. arms and military advisors, the other in the north where fanatical followers of Ho Chi Minh, known as the Vietcong, began a deliberate campaign of ruthless incursion into settled areas. The assassination of Diem in 1963 might have provided an occasion for intervention by the United Nations but the chance was lost amid hardening attitudes. When an American naval vessel was reportedly fired upon the United States retaliated by bombing North Vietnam.

Noel-Baker now felt the pangs of inevitability that he had so often encountered before. He had circled the globe in 1962, visiting Canada, the U.S.A., Moscow and Central Siberia, Peking, Hong Kong, and Tokyo. He had encountered rising anxiety about the situation in Asia and dangerous complacency, too. 'Lazy defeatism and supine indifference are now the greatest danger . . .' he told a Japanese audience. Nevertheless, he rejoiced at the 'strong moral purpose and deep desire for peace' evident in conversation with the Emperor of Japan, with members of the legislature, and with journalists. Scarred by war and concerned every day about wider Asian security and prosperity, Japan would associate itself gladly with any British and Commonwealth initiative to bring the Vietnamese war to a speedy end.[21] By the summer of 1965 it seemed clear, as R. H. Crossman put it in his diary, that 'the President (Johnson) was now irrevocably and firmly committed to fighting the Vietnam War to a finish'.[22] The United States was fielding over 188,000 troops in the paddy fields and jungles. A letter to *The Times* from Noel-Baker lamented the way in which the American President seemed influenced by military advisers and the C.I.A. If the United States intended to keep Vietnam divided on ideological grounds, it would kindle animosity around the world and further reduce confidence in the ability of the United Nations to restrain one of its members.[23] American military participation continued to grow in 1966 with the doubling of the field force, despatch of a naval armada, and further aerial bombing raids. The Vietnamese war, Noel-Baker believed, was proving to be one of the most dangerous blows at the rule of law in international affairs. Originally, Washington, in the spirit and letter of Genevan agreements reached between the Great Powers in 1954, had undertaken to refrain from use of force and to make sure that free elections were held, supervised by the United Nations.[24]

In the House of Commons in July 1966 Noel-Baker made very plain his attitude to Vietnam in a response to a call by Edward Heath, Leader of the Opposition, for stronger endorsement of American action. Labour should have been in government two years earlier in order to affirm that the only solution Britain could support was a political one. War was reducing a pitiable country to an ugly desert. It was with regret that he felt unable to accept the American version of events as to the *causus belli,* namely, that northern forces centred on Hanoi had trespassed across the frontiers. Was it not rather that the Vietcong had revolted in 1960 because the tyrannical Diem had repudiated an international provision for free elections? Further, Diem had not honoured the amnesty promised those who had fought against the French. Objective witnesses sympathised with Hanoi's resentment. Emphatically, Noel-Baker cited the opinion of lawyers in the United States that the Asian conflict was a civil war. Intervention by any one foreign power could not be justified, indeed, it violated the U.N. Charter and accords reached in Geneva. Most certainly, what the U.S. Air Force termed 'interdictory strikes' incurred a grave risk of intensifying the conflict. Such measures had a military finality about them which would render negotiated compromise increasingly unlikely. He concluded by saying that he had confidential information that Hanoi might have come to the negotiating table had a five week bombing pause been extended.[25]

How might the horrendous war in Vietnam be ended? Noel-Baker worked out a plan in early September 1966 and showed it to the Foreign Secretary, George Brown. Previously, the main lines had been discussed with U. Thant, Secretary General of the United Nations. To begin with, a resolution must be put to the General Assembly in similar style to that which had brought peace to Korea in 1953. An open conference, perhaps in Geneva, should follow. General principles must provide for cessation of aerial bombardment, for a halt to the military build-up on both sides, and for a ceasefire. To follow disengagement, an amnesty and free elections must be proclaimed. A peace-keeping force would neutralise the front; a rehabilitation programme must resuscitate folorn civilians.[26]

Sensing that it might be necessary to buttress George Brown's resolve, Noel-Baker resorted to twin stratagems. Letters to Brown assured him that there was a chance to make 'a really effective impact' in New York. President Johnson, his popular support halved in 18 months, would surely listen. Speeches at the U.N. General Assembly (notes were enclosed) attested to a remarkable degree of agreement that the conflict must stop because it was wrong and it was fruitless.[27] At about the same time, Noel-Baker swung a public spotlight on to his colleague as they faced the Labour Party Conference at Brighton. Vietnam and the United States intervention were destroying the very fabric of international law and tearing the heart out of the Charter. The legacy of hate must end. Britain should take the lead in New York the next week with Brown as advocate. 'I believe', he went on, '100 nations will rally to his call.'[28]

There had been no real progress in achieving peace in Vietnam when the United Nations Session of 1966 ended. Restiveness was apparent in many European countries; in the United States recrimination and protest were gathering speed. In the spring of 1967, Noel-Baker, home from extensive tours, lost no time in commending the efforts of Paul-Henri Spaak, veteran European statesman, and of George Brown to rally support among allies for, a major collective effort to mediate. Better leadership was needed Noel-Baker thought, for he had asked, 'Are there no statesmen in the world who are able and willing to undertake together an act of this kind?' Who was there to convince Hanoi (he might have added, also, their radical sympathisers) that a just solution could be achieved?[29] Noel-Baker's fundamental magnanimity led him to tell the House of Commons of his conviction that both sides in Vietnam saw themselves as fighting for a just and noble cause. It only exacerbated the situation when the United States insisted on treating Vietnam as two nations. They were one entity. Security and international concord, either regionally or globally, could never be furthered if we persisted in falling back upon ideological distinctions. 'There is still time', Noel-Baker urged, 'The Foreign Secretary could still do it now . . . let him act before it is too late.'[30]

Noel-Baker retained an eager interest in the pursuit of peace for Vietnam although the achieving of that peace was not to come about until an anguished public opinion in the United States forced President Nixon to abort the enterprise and bring the troops home. The march of events by-passed controversies over the legality or otherwise of continued intervention by a Power whose first objective had been to contain the struggle. Reasoning in print and on the platform by Noel-Baker began to sound rather strained to observers who, while they had reservations about the motives and actions of successive United States administrations, lamented the inability of the United Nations to exercise a mediating role. Noel-Baker's view that customary international law could be 'supplemented, and if necessary, overridden by the Charter of the United Nations' must have had a mixed reception in many quarters, particularly among some North American lawyers. The opinion would have been put that while the Security Council had authority and responsibility in conflict resolution only, the prompt application of force by one of its members would remedy the situation. Noel-Baker retorted that this measure failed both in practice and in law. Nobody had had sufficient courage and faith to solve the problem of Vietnam. And 'what doors to international anarchy are opened by such a case as this?' he asked.[31]

If the Korean operation can be said to have brought about a successful intervention and resolution on the part of the United Nations, and the Vietnam War to have ended in futility and disunion, the Cyprus Problem of the mid-1950's, which was to fester for 20 years, did something to substantiate the peace-keeping role of the U.N. The Noel-Bakers, father and son, were to be closely and personally concerned with the disputed fortunes of that island.

When Philip Noel-Baker was Minister of State at the Foreign Office in 1945 he and a number of colleagues were in favour of giving Cyprus over to Archbishop Damascenos, then Regent of Greece. Union with Greece was termed *Enosis*. The island had affirmed the Greek tradition since classical times and had a Greek majority of 80% of its half million inhabitants. In the event of *Enosis*, however, it was generally believed that the Turkish Cypriot minority would increasingly become more vocal and be unlikely to reconcile themselves to a transfer from British colonial sovereignty to the uncertain tolerance of Athenian politicians. The Cyprus Problem was not just an ethnic division which might have been submitted to the International Court of Justice. Britain's War Office regarded Cyprus as a base for asserting British influence in the Levant and for protecting oil supplies and traffic bound for the Suez Canal. Britain's Foreign Office was anxious not to offend Ankara for Turkey was a keystone of the N.A.T.O. arch extending into the eastern Mediterranean. It is very likely that Whitehall prevaricated in the view that nothing definite would emerge from a situation where the two ethnic groups on the island and the parent mainland governments could never agree. Within 10 years the divisions seemed to be irreconcilable. The loyalties of Greek Cypriots crystallised around the dignified, strong figure of Archbishop Makarios and, to a more radical and secretive extent, around the fierce militarism of Colonel George Grivas and his band of E.O.K.A. militia. If Britain had enlisted the help of the United Nations in solving the problem of Cyprus feelings would have been less bitter. There was no formal approach to New York in the hope of settlement. Unfortunately, no progress came out of exhaustive discussions between contending parties and London showed its frustration by exiling the Archbishop to the Seychelles. Makarios, a political as well as a religious leader, was branded as unreasonable and Grivas was marked down as a 'terrorist'.

Philip Noel-Baker's involvement with Cyprus was close. His son, Francis, also a Labour M.P., had been invited by Whitehall to use his own good offices and first-hand knowledge as mediator between Britain and the interested parties in Cyprus and Greece.[32] Philip had enormous experience of problems arising out of political differences, was an adequate Greek speaker, and had contacts everywhere, none closer than Sir Charles Peake, the Ambassador in Athens. He made it his business to watch developments as they oscillated between Cyprus, London, New York, Athens, and Ankara. Was the problem to get out of hand as a consequence of politico-military disagreement, or was there a chance of international mediation as he always hoped there must be?

Cyprus should go to Greece, Noel-Baker told Charles Peake in March 1954. One must be careful how this was put to people since he had not had much success in persuading Labour Party colleagues. Peake, in his reply, saw attitudes growing more liberal when Winston Churchill left the Premiership and the more conciliatory Anthony Eden succeeded (as he did 12 months later). Meanwhile, Peake, having in mind Churchillian lack of tact, had advised London to avoid at all costs dragging the Greek Royal Family into the *Enosis* issue. Nor was it of any use, he had told the Government, feeling offended because the Greeks proposed to take the Cyprus Problem to the United Nations. Noel-Baker and Peake both agreed that this was the only sane approach.[33] Peake's warning was, in fact, timely. King Paul of Greece, Peake told Noel-Baker, was wondering whether his Prime Minister, Field Marshal Papagos, might be persuaded by Peake to take Cyprus off the U.N. agenda. If news of this leaked out it would embarass London and Athens.[34]

The Labour Party Conference in September 1954 gave Noel-Baker a useful platform. He would, however, have to interrupt his enjoyable work on *The Arms Race* and endure the long afternoons of conference oratory – 'that I shall not enjoy', he confided to Peake, 'indeed, I dislike it heartily'. Nonetheless he steered through an Emergency Resolution from the Executive deploring the Tory policy over Cyprus which, so he declared, showed reluctance to concede self-determination to the island. This position was one of contempt for U.N. principles. His audience agreed. Scarborough had helped to encourage clearer thought about the concept of *Enosis* Noel-Baker told Peake. The Left had been discomforted in their attacks on the Greek Government. 'I think', he added, 'Aneurin Bevan has finally committed political suicide.' However, Tom Driberg, also prominent on the Left flank of the Party had heeded Executive 'instructions' and had denounced with gusto the British Government's stand and had called for frank discussions with the islanders about full self-determination.[35]

A greater degree of discretion would have pleased Peake more. 'If the Greeks lose face on this question, they will only become more difficult to deal with,' he wrote. Britain should be grateful to Greece for being one of the few lands to side with her in 1940. An old, free country should be able to acknowledge the intensity and conviction of those who were searching for new autonomy. Why, though, were negotiations not sounded out quietly before being conducted in the public glare of New York? Inevitably, the atmosphere would become slowly more poisonous.[36] There was little sign of Britain's attitude to Cyprus becoming clearer. Even the Chief of the Imperial General Staff, Field Marshal Montgomery, was reported as telling Peake in October 1954 that 'he thought nothing of the strategical argument about Cyprus and said that it was fundamentally unsound to plant a G.H.Q. on an island'. Some time later, the Athens Embassy received a Foreign Office telegram saying that as long as press and radio attacks continued against the United Kingdom, no Minister or senior official was to go to Athens in any circumstances whatever. This seemed to Noel-Baker a counter-productive move.[37] It certainly had not helped when the Colonial Secretary, Alan Lennox-Boyd, went out of his way to brand *Enosis* as Communist. Peake was not happy, either, about the Noel-Baker position in public. He understood that Irene and Francis Noel-Baker wanted Philip to make a public declaration in favour of *Enosis*. Union with Greece, however, was a solution responsible Cypriots like Makarios were beginning to move away from.

A letter from Philip now seemed to show rather more consideration for the Prime Minister's position:

'Anthony made an admirable speech, except for that Cyprus passage, which was as bad-tempered and pointless as his speeches in New York and when he came back. He has a blind spot there!'[38]

Meanwhile, when the General Assembly of the United Nations reopened its Session in September 1955, Britain's Foreign Minister, Selwyn Lloyd, took a predictably defensive stand. Greece, he declared, was asking the United Nations to interfere in the domestic affairs of a foreign power so as to effect a territorial change favourable to herself. Such a move would open the flood-gates to claim and counter-claim. The Labour Front Bench at Westminster could not accept such generalities when Lloyd later reported to them. Noel-Baker was their most lucid spokesman. It was necessary, he averred, to end colonial rule in the Mediterranean as elsewhere and to affirm once more the ideal of self-determination as Article 1(2) of the U.N. Charter did. Strategic considerations advanced in justification of the British Government's stance failed to impress him. If Greece went Communist would it really menace Turkey? That country, after all, had common frontiers with the U.S.S.R. and Bulgaria. Was not the whole situation even resolvable within the context of N.A.T.O. since Greece and Turkey and Britain were all members, that is, if the parameters of an alliance were to be preferred to the wider bounds of international security? Short-sightedness and obduracy in London had hardened the hearts of Cypriots but it had not turned them into 'terrorists'. Were we giving way to the retort of Colonel Blimp, 'Gad, Sir, we can't negotiate with that feller Makarios. He's on the other side!' Fundamentally, this was not a confrontation between states: it was a question of human rights. Noel-Baker concluded by quoting Venizelos, the Greek champion of the League of Nations, who in 1931 had recognised the essence of ethnic differences in the Cyprus of those days when he had said:

'There is no Cyprus question between the Government of the United Kingdom and the Government of Greece. The Cypriot question exists between the British Government and the people of Cyprus.'[39]

In the autumn of 1956 Members of Parliament expressed anxieties about the deteriorating state of the Middle East. On 14th September Noel-Baker spoke for the first time after 12 months of indifferent health and the loss of his wife seven months previously. He was now clearly in favour of self-government for the two communities. There had been an offer to them in 1948 but it had been made rather faint-heartedly. The Turkish and Greek factions had nothing to fear provided they dispensed with force. United Kingdom policies were too inflexible. To his political contacts in Athens, he said, it seemed as though some sort of surrender was being demanded. There was no likelihood of the island being dominated by a Communist majority. The chance for the islanders and for Britain must be seized before it was too late. First, a truce was necessary (as we had discovered in Ireland in 1921). The banished Makarios should be allowed to return from the Seychelles to spearhead a movement for responsible autonomy and collaboration. The Colonial Secretary, in reply, expressed delight in seeing the Right Honourable Gentleman returning to his old powers, yet it must be stressed that British sovereignty over Cyprus, in the present state of the world's history, was absolutely indispensable 'if we were to discharge our proper responsibilities'. He and several other Members went on to reject Noel-Baker's suggestion that opportunities had already been lost and that we had knuckled down to any form of surrender. The member for Derby was recognisably sincere but wholly unrealistic.[40]

The tide turned more favourably in Cyprus in early 1959 when Greece and Turkey met in Zürich and reached a settlement which Britain approved. Two bases were assigned to the United Kingdom. Partition was rejected, indeed, the sponsoring powers guaranteed the security and independence of a new republic. General elections confirmed the existence of the new state on 16th August 1960 and Commonwealth membership was granted in March 1961.

Violence continued to pulsate until after the Cypriot flag was hoisted. There was little confidence generally that the new President, Makarios, would be able to hold the crumbling community together. A peace force representing seven nations (the U.N.F.I.C.Y.P.) was despatched to Nicosia in March 1964 and for more than 10 years held the ring. In every sense they stabilised the situation. On the other hand, while they kept the peace by separating contestants, they were not able to make the peace by handling and ameliorating underlying problems. Noel-Baker wondered from time to time whether this type of operation tranquilised or anaesthetised the situation and in this way tended to reduce the pressure to find a solution.

The whole peace of the Eastern Mediterranean was shattered in mid-July 1974 when an *Enosis* faction from mainland Greece attempted to assassinate the Archbishop and proclaim a coup. A puppet government was set up by an arch-terrorist, Nicos Sampson. Makarios was extracted under the noses of Greek armoured vehicles and flown out to London and on to the United Nations to protest. Unhappily, Ankara saw an opportunity to interfere and launched a successful invasion. Neither London nor Washington did anything that was either positive or long lasting to heal the anguish and dispute on the island. Turk and Greek were to face each other across a 'Green Line' with only spasmodic and fruitless intervention by anyone else. It was a great opportunity hopelessly lost in the eyes of Philip Noel-Baker who wrote:

'The Sampson coup as well as the Turkish invasion was a violation of the N.A.T.O. Pact Article One by the Greek Colonels; a violation of the Charter of the U.N. and it was a British obligation under those two treaties as well as in our capacity as a guarantor of the 1960 Constitution to oust Sampson . . .'[41]

Britain, with the advantage of an overwhelmingly strong military capability, could have stood by its international obligations and rebuffed the coup. Whitehall could not bring itself to employ force or any other form of sanction and so Turkish aggression seemed condoned. Noel-Baker believed that this was because Britain supported what were to him the

Machievelian power-politics of Kissinger, the United States Secretary of State. His condemnation ended on a severe note:

'A marvellous opportunity of assuring the independence of Cyprus, of strengthening communal peace there and of reasserting the sanctity of the U.N. Charter was lost – and lost for nothing – there was no real danger that a single British life need have been forfeited in Cyprus.'[42]

In fact, as Noel-Baker ought to have recognised, it was the Cyprus National Guard who both appointed and subsequently, 10 days later, dismissed Sampson. Intercommunal talks began though they met with deadlock even when Makarios returned triumphantly to the presidency by the end of 1974. Military confrontation subsided owing very much to United Nations intervention but the political conflict remained severe across an ethnic divide.

Another situation in which Noel-Baker played a prominent part was the clash between Britain and nationalist Egypt in autumn 1956, the so-called 'Suez Crisis'. It was a complicated business with misjudgement on all sides. If the Foreign Office in London placed strategic reliance upon Iraq and Iran as foils to Egyptian emergence as a significant Middle East power this could only embitter Gamel Abdul Nasser, Egypt's new and ambitious President. Standing by France because Cairo sent arms to rebels in Algeria was likely to stir feelings from Tunis to Aleppo. Britain would lose economically and politically if the Egyptians interfered with the traditional passage of merchant vessels through Suez. There was, in the wake of the sentiments of war, an over-reliance on the extent to which Eisenhower's United States administration would support London. Unhappily, the government of Anthony Eden fell into the position of seeing no other option than that of defiance or humiliation. They appear to have thought themselves into a corner where tackling the man of the moment, Nasser, would remove a blockage and in some way salve Britain's besmirched reputation. No Lion could afford to be considered mangy and clawless. A decision to use force split an already divided nation and incurred displeasure in the United States and within the Commonwealth. Precipitous action crippled the health and reputation of Eden, an ironical end to one who in former days had so stoutly supported restraint and international agreement.

A generation later, some commentators, among them Noel-Baker, were censuring not so much a neo-imperialist relapse by Her Majesty's Government as a period of disinclination to measure up to responsibilities. Failure to understand the Egyptians and uncertainty as to the nature of United States policies towards the vacuum in the Arab world resulted in an unwise withdrawal of financial aid for the Aswan Dam Project. Nasser retaliated on 26th July 1956 by proposing to nationalise the Suez Canal and to devote its annual revenue to building the Dam. Initially, at Westminster, party support for Government action was bi-partisan with Hugh Gaitskell, the Labour leader, approving vigorous reaction to a repetition of totalitarian threat, a consideration much in the mind of Anthony Eden who had resigned in 1938 after the surrender of Munich.

Israel's attitude to the charismatic chauvinist, Nasser, was one of irritation and irridentist raiding in the Gaza Strip, mixed with deep fear at the prospect of Arab encirclement from Egypt, Syria, Jordan, and Iraq. Eight years only of independence had made David Ben-Gurion, the septuagenarian Premier of Israel, determined to enlist France, a veteran colonial power, against an Egypt being armed by the U.S.S.R. and Czechoslovakia. Israel, the United Kingdom, and France would be equal partners in responding not so much to aggression as to 'threat'.

Earlier in the summer Noel-Baker had expressed his anxiety in a letter to *The Economist*. There must be some way of reconciling the legitimate interests of nations trading through the Suez Canal with the fervent aspirations of nationalist Egypt. No conflict of interest could be settled by putting a foot in the door as *The Times* had warned. We must look very carefully at the tangled politics of the situation rather than hope to impose a solution. Nor should we fall back, on times which were seen misleadingly as analagous like that of the dictators' challenge to democracy in the late 1930's and which might be considered as providing a precedent for unilateralist action. Why did the Prime Minister give such low-key prominence to the helpfulness of the United Nations? Was he fearful that the moral judgement of the world might go against the United Kingdom?[43]

London and Paris established a joint military planning committee in August 1956. Reservists were called up by proclamation. Telegrams and letters from the White House attempted to pour oil on the angry waters. When Parliament eventually reconvened, Noel-Baker tabled a number of questions about legal aspects of the Suez conflict. If Nasser's nationalisation of the Canal was illegal should the issue not have been referred to the International Court of Justice? Was the illegality so heinous, he speculated, because it followed upon a lack of consultation and was in some sense, a consequence of our own short-sightedness? Were we reacting over-hastily to the threat of a forced take-over? Military action contemplated by Whitehall was an emotive response to a strident challenge and there could have been an alternative, more rational response. In any case, would there never be a prospect of fairer international control of the Canal replacing the monopoly enjoyed since 1888 by the Suez Canal Company?

Her Majesty's Government, in Noel-Baker's opinion, had never waited long enough for the parties to the dispute – Egypt, Britain, and France – to work out agreed means of seeking a negotiated solution. Article 33 of the U.N. Charter provided for this. Why was it, particularly, that Britain backed France in preferring the term 'situation' to 'dispute' when the matter was referred to the Security Council? If this stratagem were employed so that the two parties involved in the issue, namely, Britain and France, could both use a veto in the Council's deliberations then this would be inconsistent with the spirit and letter of the Charter. There must be some reason why France and the United Kingdom had been unable to associate themselves, so the Prime Minister had put it, with a U.N. resolution condemning Israel as aggressor. Noel-Baker wondered whether they had already decided that Egypt could not be 'innocent'. His long experience of international mediation convinced him that nine of the 11 Security Council members would emphatically uphold settlement of a dispute by peaceful means. In that event, no unilateral action by a member could ever uphold justice. In all respects his country's government was tragically, dishonestly, and irresponsibly challenging the whole system of the United Nations. Members opposite, he declared, might laugh at the United Nations but the country would listen to that and take note. Having castigated the grotesque mishandling of the Suez Affair in a long and passionate speech, Noel-Baker concluded that in many years of Parliamentary life he had never heard anything 'so perfunctory, so shallow, so irrelevant to the great issues we face'.[44] The United Nations was now the only hope of pulling out of the mess.

At the beginning of October 1956, at the Blackpool Conference of the Labour Party, there was only slight support for Eden's resolve. The Left increasingly prevailed and steered Members reconvening at Westminster into worried enquiry at first and then vociferous opposition. An Israeli invasion of Egypt on 29th October was responded to by an Anglo-French ultimatum ordering both sides to withdraw, failing which, their interventionist force would protect the Canal. Observers in many quarters suspected that the ultimatum was a pretext to impose a military solution and, indeed, a manoeuvre to overthrow a dangerous leader of Arab nationalism. United Nations resolutions proscribing resort to arms failed to prevent further Israeli advance and the mounting of an air-and-sea assault against Port Said by Britain and France.

In the noisy parliamentary debates that accompanied the despatch of an assault force to Suez the Government's case rested on two principal assertions, first, that the U.N. could not have intervened in time decisively, and, second, that Britain had moved not to stop Egypt but to prevent the escalation of a Middle Eastern war. Eden's strained appeal as 'a man of peace' did not go down well with parliamentary or national audiences. He was able to do little to contest the contemptuous charges of the Opposition that his decision to fight was not supported by most of the Commonwealth and that it repudiated the principles of amicable conciliation proposed by the United Nations. The turbulent hostility in the Commons Chamber on 31st October flaying 'a gang of murderers and disastrous folly' reminded one journalist of 'a hotly contested football match'. There was, wrote *The Manchester Guardian* the same day a duel between Eden and Noel-Baker, 'the latter pale and passionate about the failure to consult the United States Government before the ultimatum'.[45] Opposition benches exploded in anger when their occupants came to believe that the Prime Minister was evading direct enquiry. Even on the Government benches there was considerable unease, even disgust. In a world which had undertaken to respect the U.N. Charter, here was a government, in the eyes of one of its members, Anthony Nutting, reverting to 19th-century methods to settle a dispute and, in so doing, finding a '20th-century pretext for so doing'.[46] Moreover, the pretext appeared transparent. Noel-Baker wound up for the Opposition and Eden replied lamely to it. 'It would be hard to find in the annals of Parliament', Nutting concluded, 'a more disengenuous pronouncement by a Minister of the Crown.'[47] There followed a number of resignations from junior Ministers, including Nutting, and from the Foreign Office.

Suez issues roused the Commons once more on 1st November 1956. The Prime Minister believed that since the U.N. was 'not yet the international equivalent of our own legal system and the rule of law' it was best to act decisively. Again, R. A. Butler, Leader of the House, stressed that there had been no time to wait for U.N. action to restore law and order. There is no doubt that Noel-Baker was appalled by these arguments from across the floor of the House: the logic and the conclusions strained from it appeared to him fatally flawed. A vote of censure would be the inevitable outcome of the controversy. Against shouts of 'Law not War' from demonstrators outside the Chamber, and clearly audible in the corridors, a Government amendment sought approval of 'prompt action' to safeguard what were termed vital international and national interests. Equivocation such as this stirred the anger of the Opposition and misgivings even on the Government benches. Noel-Baker lost no time in challenging Eden's apparent brushing-aside of a resolution from New York calling for a cease-fire. This was no recommendation, he pointed out, it was a binding decision. Above all, the country now had an opportunity to settle 'with honour' and there was a chance to help the United Nations 'acquire teeth and give us a real police force in the world'. This would both help ourselves and establish collective action in a way the League of Nations had been unable to do. He went on to reflect that Eden's declaration about being the same man now as the one who had always worked for peace seemed a strange way to persuade people you wanted peace. To the Prime Minister's statement that when a fire was seen the first question was not how it started but how to put it out, Noel-Baker added, 'We have poured on petrol.'[48]

Conciliation procedures were pressed again by Noel-Baker in mid-November. He wondered why fellow-Members had been told so little about the efforts of Dag Hammarskjöld, the Secretary-General, to intercede with Nasser. President Eisenhower had described the use of force to settle an argument as unacceptable and irreconcilable with the principles and practice of the U.N. and he had offered his help. Our political and moral standing would be lost inevitably if our actions were devious. In Noel-Baker's experience of almost 40 years of international peacemaking, no country gained by sidestepping or private dealing. Ministerial experience as Secretary of State for Commonwealth Relations had convinced him that, (as he put it in a heavy-sounding phrase), there was no other way than 'the constitutional convention of mutual consultation'.[49]

The United Nations, as a matter of fact, did intervene to cool the Suez Crisis. A United Nations Emergency Force of 6,000 men from 10 'uncommitted' countries separated the combatants and supervised withdrawal. A salvage operation cleared the Canal of blockships six weeks faster than expected. This was, perhaps, an escape route for London in practical terms, but more importantly, the ending of the Suez episode seemed to demonstrate the effectiveness of international goodwill and common sense leading to action to dampen down the glowing embers of zonal discord. In the light of this success, hopes were dramatically shattered for the optimists of the 1950's as armoured columns moved into Budapest from the U.S.S.R. to crush an insurrection. It seemed a repetition of the intolerance that had martyred Prague in 1948. To those who believed that the Suez Adventure might have encouraged this illicit aggression in eastern Europe the reply of the majority appears to have been, 'and what could we have done about it, anyway?' The realities of East-West juxtaposition in Europe put the brake on anything other than verbal protest. Noel-Baker and others noted with wry concern that neither the U.N., institutionalising world opinion, nor the politico-military entity of N.A.T.O. had been able to make a concerted response to the incursion against Hungary. An agitated House of Commons was left in no doubt by Noel-Baker that there was disgrace in Britain, being so taken with its 'squalid' quarrel in the Middle East that it had no time for the plight of Hungary. No government could be more devious than one which invited the Security Council to denounce Russian aggression on 28th October and two days later exercised a veto on discussion of the situation in Egypt. He believed, too, that the country had been blind to the significance of Soviet admission of 'downright mistakes' in dealing with other states. There was possible dissension within the Kremlin. His plea that there might have been a chance to reconsider notions of collective security in Europe between East and West was not taken up with much warmth by Members present. Harold MacMillan, Chancellor of the Exchequer, put it to the House that linking Eastern Europe and the Middle East was 'disingenuous and over-simplified'. When he went on to add that 'greater risks would have followed our inaction (in the Middle East)' both Noel-Bakers, father and son, seem to have been well aware that this could have been used also by the U.S.S.R. in extenuation of a pre-emptive advance against a putative threat from outside.[50]

The fiasco of Suez was to reverberate down the years. Suspicions of perfidy, intolerance, and secret collusion arose in the aftermath of actions as Noel-Baker voiced at Westminster in December 1956:

'Let me just say this to the Foreign Secretary. The world will read the careful, studied phrases which he used yesterday afternoon, and it will draw the clear conclusion that the charge is true; that the Government knew, before October 29th, that the Israeli attack on Egypt would be made, and that they laid their own plans with that in view.'[51]

The veteran internationalist pursued his investigations in succeeding years in correspondence with Anthony Nutting and with Sir Walter Monckton, the former Defence Minister. No conventions precluded enquiry into this 'sordid episode' he assured Nutting.[52]

Henceforth, the standing of Noel-Baker within his own party as champion of the U.N. became increasingly less marked. Nevertheless, in February 1963 he was given responsibility in the Shadow Cabinet for United Nations and Disarmament Affairs. This was seen by Anthony Benn in rather inflated terms as:

'a guarantee of Labour's intention to take the U.N. seriously and work through it for disarmament and cooperation. How brilliantly imaginative to put you in charge!'[53]

Eighteen months later, in October 1964, as an earlier chapter has related, Noel-Baker's name was missing from the roll of Harold Wilson's new government. There may have been, perhaps, a hint of rationalisation if not of realism, in Noel-Baker's declaring to his son, Francis, a year later, that he must turn down Wilson's offer to make him leader of a parliamentary team to evaluate the present standing of the United Nations. He felt he would not be able to persuade the team of his views on improvements to the Organisation: the position would silence and inhibit him.[54] This viewpoint appears unusual and rather unconvincing in one who generally did not lack self-confidence in utterance.

In the last few months of his life, Noel-Baker had to wrestle in public with another stern challenge to the U.N. The issue exploded at the beginning of April 1982 after burning for some 20 years when Argentina laid claim to the Falkland Islands (Las Malvinas), a British dependency in the South Atlantic. A junta in Buenos Aires, led by an uncompromising General Galtieri, came to the end of its patience and occupied the whaling station of South Georgia. The government of Mrs. Margaret Thatcher in London saw this as a challenge to British dominion and to the islanders' right to 'self-determination' and hastily assembled a case for discussion by the Security Council. Meanwhile, a task force was collected together as a punitive expedition and took up stations for an 8,000 mile voyage. Intensive discussions followed in New York and were also conducted by General Alexander Haig, the United States Secretary of State, who attempted, as a 'fair broker', to use his country's good offices and who commuted intensively between New York, London, and Buenos Aires. Towards the end of April the situation was deteriorating rapidly. The United States, a founder-member of the Security Council, seemed, however, to be throwing its hands up in despair in declaring that although aggression could not be condoned they would stand aside from the conflict. Britain's Prime Minister revealed to her critics impatience and scepticism and, inevitably, British landings in the Falklands followed.

One of Noel-Baker's oldest friends, Gordon Evans, has described how the eminent peace worker took the news about hostilities in the Falklands. Noel-Baker had spent a long day in Geneva and then flown in for the Annual Council of the United Nations Association in Oxford. Awakened at 6.0 a.m. by Gordon Evans, Noel-Baker realised also that Parliament had been recalled and that he must take his place in the House of Lords. He went into breakfast in a wheelchair, took part in the morning session of the Council, and begged a lift to London from a Council member. At Westminster he spoke in the Lords Emergency Debate, and persuaded a fellow-Peer (and retired Archbishop of Canterbury) to drive him back to Oxford to deliver a report on the debate. 'Blind, deaf and lame, such was his spirit and sense of responsibility,' adds Gordon Evans. As one man, representatives of 300 branches of the United Nations Association rose in the Oxford Examination Schools and cheered the venerable Peer.[55]

What could one do at the age of 93 apart from button-holing people where possible and, certainly, writing to newspapers? After talking things over with Lord Carrington, the Foreign Secretary, and others, he wrote to the Prime Minister. Criticism of Prime Minister and Foreign Secretary by 'the trigger-happy Members of the House of Commons' was bitterly resented. 'I think,' he added, 'you have both acted very firmly and very wisely and the criticisms were wholly unjustified and mischievous.' Surely Carrington's offer to resign had not been accepted? After 60 years of international affairs he was convinced that the U.N. would intervene successfully. 'The Junta's aggression must be defeated,' there was no doubt about that. 'I believe Peter Carrington could get the U.N. to do this without bloodshed, which would be so dangerous to the Islanders.' A prompt acknowledgement from Downing Street confirmed that the Foreign Secretary had indeed resigned and also that the return of the Islands to British Administration had to be achieved.[56]

Two weeks later Philip Noel-Baker was registering doubts and unease as were certain sections of the press and a broad section of public opinion. A letter to *The Financial Times* he sent revealed rather interestingly in its phrasing a streak of old conservatism, possibly, in Galtieri's move being seen as 'an impudent and immoral insult to our national pride'. However, his ever-optimistic searching for peace castigated military reconquest as 'short-sighted and dangerous'. Were we relapsing, he asked *Daily Telegraph* readers, into 'the old diplomacy'?[57] Haig's commuting to Buenos Aires went outside the U.N. and seemed a useless ploy he assured one of his correspondents. The Secretary of State 'ought not to have touched with a barge-pole the rediculous "proposals" which the Argentinians were impudent enough to put to him.'[58]

Noel-Baker rose in the Lords on the afternoon of 30th April 1982 though he was feeling the effects of a tiring visit to Italy. Of course, a flagrant violation of the Charter by the Junta was inexcusable. There had been a 10 to one condemnation of the Argentinian assault in New York and Britain was in an 'immensely strong moral and legal position'. A joint Anglo-American approach demanding total withdrawal and resorting, if need be, to diplomatic and trade sanctions 'would have brought home to the civilised world the true nature of the crime' and might well have brought about the collapse of the Junta. If all this had failed, then, he emphasised, under the Charter, we would have been entitled to rely upon the military support of other member states. A collective response would have been feasible and acceptable. Lack of patience, feebleness of belief, and 'war fever' had destroyed the moral basis of our case.[59] There was now no respect for an incautious Prime Minister and for the lack of courage among her advisers.

Forty-three years of championing the United Nations had not seen the death of power politics as Noel-Baker had hoped. There had been failures 'to work the Charter', to use fully the potential of an international organisation to bring about reconciliation and a safer world in the Congo, in Vietnam, and in the Falklands. To the very end, this man nine decades old, was intoning a litany of hope, not ritualistically, but in a spirit of pragmatism, the hope that by ordered reason and will, people everywhere might underpin an international body founded to work for security and peace. He appeared undismayed by cynics and opponents, gently discounting their charge that his head remained in the clouds. 'Whatever,' he would ask, 'do you consider to be the alternative to conciliation?'[60]

The dynanism of Philip Noel-Baker faded quickly and quietly in the autumn of 1982. Physically, he was utterly exhausted, mentally, he retained an astonishing clarity and resilience. In public utterance there had never been room for self-pity and despair. For something like 75 years he had stood firmly and confidently and modestly in the public eye. Now, at home at 12 South Eaton Place, he left his books, his desk, and his favourite chair, that of Lord Robert Cecil, and went simply to bed. A colleague of very many years, Lord Fenner Brockway, equally indefatigable, writes of the last meeting of mind and spirit:

'I was with him the evening before he died and in faint whispers he told me of his confidence that within 10 years the world peace movement would become so strong that it would compel all governments to disarm. The nurses lifted the sheets to enable him to shake my hand.'[61]

Blind, deaf and lame at the end, Noel-Baker still had the power 'to attract and inspire intelligent and idealistic people, especially young people', everywhere he went writes one of his most faithful friends, who goes on:

'An aged man is but a paltry thing
A tattered coat upon a stick, unless
Soul clap its wings and sing, and louder sing
For every tatter in its mortal dress.'

For this companion as for a host of others, 'Philip's song of world disarmament and world cooperation for world development, the wave of the future, was never louder than on the day he died.'[62]

(COURTESY: THE HON. FRANCIS NOEL-BAKER)

Pl. 17. A disarmament campaigner still at 90

CHAPTER 12

Epilogue

PRECEDING CHAPTERS HAVE ATTEMPTED TO DESCRIBE the career of a very remarkable man and the main events in his life from cradle to grave. Inevitably, when faced by a mountain of material the biographer has to be selective and analytical. Appraisal, and judgement of a sort, accompanies documentation. The questions of critics must be faced. What does the name of Philip Noel-Baker mean to men and women in the 1980's? Which of his achievements will ensure him a place in international chronicles? What can be learnt from the passionate approach of one man over almost 80 public years to the task of promoting a more peaceful world, a world which today seems more distant than ever? A brief reconsideration of the areas where the lights of this Renaissance Man shone so brightly may help resolve some of the issues.

Many of the characteristics of Philip Noel-Baker's personality had been bred in the bone of his Quaker family. Simplicity, even frugality in style of living, was accompanied by compassion for others whose needs were clear. Allegiance to the Society of Friends had taught him that direct enquiry, tolerance, and modest approaches to a problem, 'learning from where the light shone', as he put it, generally brought in their train clarification and conciliation. Philip, the son, and Allen, the father, had believed in communication across social and geographical frontiers. Their family tradition had no time for 'futile fatalism' or 'facile pessimism', as Philip later termed it. 'I was born,' he once said, 'a congenital disarmer.' It is no accident that Noel-Baker, brought up 'straight' but not altogether 'straitlaced', developed as one who could not resist a challenge, whether in the athletic stadium, the political environs of Westminster and Whitehall, or in the public arena as campaigner. Sometimes, and perhaps with tongue in cheek, more than one critic described this public figure as never 'dispassionate' about anything. Noel-Baker would rise to the charge and enlist in level terms a legion of facts to show that what might be codified by common agreement in Covenant or Charter was really an enabling instrument, born of reason and practicality. He had always been, he affirmed, a midwife rather than a mystic. The period of gestation was, of course, a long one.

Noel-Baker always adopted a pragmatic way of working with institutions representing many countries. As an international civil servant in Geneva, behind a desk in the League of Nations Secretariat, his methods of translating recommendations into practice seem to have owed more to the workshop rather than to obstetrics. Bringing into being 'the living entity' of Wilson and Smuts required the design and construction of 'minimum machinery'. The Covenant of the League, the rules governing mandated territories, the Protocol, these were to be 'forged' and 'shaped'. His work alongside Nansen in the 1920's, when they had done their best to resuscitate refugees in Asia Minor, had shown him that to work for a more secure world you needed faith, energy, and a down-to-earth approach. Both in the field and in Geneva nothing should be left to chance. Due allowance was to be made for the pretensions and prejudices of others, meanwhile, ever ready to accept risks one held close to a set of carefully thought out measures. What seemed impossible to observers might take a little longer to secure. Noel-Baker acquired a feeling for the priorities that must never be blunted by tortuous discussion in conference chambers nor hidden by opaque phrasing in memoranda. This clear insight, modestly held, inspired many of his associates over the years. Service with the League taught him to 'look outwards' and to 'live forwards'. Generally, (though with some lapses in print) he came to believe in organic processes rather than in climactic agreement. Facts were there to be searched for, corroborated in detail, sometimes repetitively so as the books on his shelves and the footnotes in his writing showed. 'Fleet and fluent' in delivery and research he assiduously developed a network of contacts across Europe and the Americas.

When in 1924 he moved away from Geneva to accept a chair at the London School of Economics this inevitably projected him out of the optimism of the League-in-being into a world of wider doubt, speculation, and some disbelief. Inevitably, he became provocateur as well as protagonist. Five years was hardly time for a professor to acquire distinction, even so, the foundations for a large department of International Relations were laid during his tenure. His writing appeared to some critics to be stronger on the side of advocacy than of objective criticism and his mode in general was not that of the rigorous academic.[1] Resigning in 1929 to take up a parliamentary seat he lost no time in squaring up to the issues raised as Europe failed to settle into tranquility. How were governments to be induced to move beyond timidity and self-preoccupation to accept that a community of interests would be safer than the customary balances of power? Approaching questions such as these he was modest in constantly acknowledging the influence of Smuts, Wilson, Angell, Cecil, Leonard Woolf, Nansen, and Arthur Henderson. These ghosts, though, did not haunt him. They were the progenitors of a feeling that men of his thinking shared, namely, that there was an advance to be made at a time when the cry of 'no more war' was readily heard.

As the 1930's brought challenge to the ideals for which Noel-Baker stood, one can perhaps identify three phases in the responses which he and his associates adopted. At the outset of the decade there was an optimism still that vigilance and activity might persuade governments to accept some measure of arms control. The main thrust in regard to armaments was two-fold. Complexities of production and deployment had to be surveyed factually and comprehensively in print. Using this information, the peace campaigners went on to propose that governments reach accord on the processes of inspection and reduction. There were precedents for this in the military and naval agreements reached at Versailles, in London and in Washington. Drastic solutions would not be out of reach, particularly if public opinion were jerked out of its 'defeatist certitude'. Yet, the initial confidence of Noel-Baker, impressive in oratory, already went aground in shallows. One might wonder whether 'disarmers', as they were known, ever really came to terms with the fact that arms control was more often seen by states as temporarily (and conveniently) lowering thresholds in weaponry rather than securing effective abolition. It followed that agreed maxima tended to become permitted minima. Was it realistic to devalue the usefulness of conventional negotiations by saying that these must always be supplanted by public discussion between a plethora of 'parties', some more and some less interested in what disarmament might mean for allies and possible foes? It seems a pity, moreover, that the men of hope did not elaborate more usefully and to a wider public the difficulties of ever establishing a benchmark such as a 'status quo'.

The second phase was one of dismay that solutions envisaged as being achievable were being disregarded or opposed. Noel-Baker's own government already in 1922 had become 'platitudinous' and 'tame' in his view. Militaristic 'hawks' were putting the 'doves' and the men of reason to flight. Backing away from the 'vibrant hopes' offered by the League the politicians had disclaimed obligations and rendered the earlier years of hope 'a mocking memory'. When the Disarmament Conference of 1931 had been aborted Noel-Baker did not give up hope. The flag he would nail to the mast of the League would be a tattered one but it would fly proudly. Sure that 'mere protest leads nowhere', his 'constructive protest' would take its customary shape of public argument and private persuasion. Most of Europe was travelled in this guise. On occasion, his wealth of native optimism led him to read omens that were far from propitious. He was frequently prone to assert that 'if only' certain politicians or events had been otherwise, things would have turned out very differently. He was undoubtedly right in declaring that the actions of the League should be preventive rather than penal. He failed, however, to convince many observers that allegiance to League of Nations membership would somehow inspire its members to recognise an individual obligation to adopt common policies. Notably, in regard to the case for applying sanctions to belligerent Japan in 1931 or Italy in 1935, he appeared to many to be over-theoretical and far too sanguine.

The third phase, between 1936 and 1939, was, almost literally, a time for girding on armour. There was now less theory in Noel-Baker's approach. Governments must 'mean business' if they were to save international law, breeched by Franco Spain, Italy, and Nazi Germany. 'Safety First', the Baldwinian concept, was illusory: risks must be accepted. His platform stance was a firm one. The basic problem was how to organise a forceful response to aggression, to meet its ramifications 'four-square' and, in so doing, to put 'power' into collective security. How could we affirm and reaffirm a menaced democracy if we failed to support marshalling of resources in its defence? Intended as a legal and revitalising approach to a darkening Europe the message of Noel-Baker brought assent across political benches, as he intended it should, but it encountered alienation and opposition from the Left of his own party. Nor did the robust direction of the 'Arms and the Covenant' persuasion appeal to pacifist elements in the International Peace Campaign and the League of Nations Union. There is always the possibility that rhetoric clouds judgement and while Noel-Baker did not retreat from the resoluteness of arming international law when its consequences were pointed out to him by Lansbury, Cripps and others, he continued to maintain rather heatedly that Public Opinion might have saved a drifting League of Nations.

Membership of Churchill's wartime coalition did not prevent Noel-Baker from spending time discussing revival of a phoenix and the shape of the successor to the discredited League of Nations. As a core to the rationale there was a return to the notion of 'working' an international institution. A code or charter would delineate and authorise action but this must be on-going and not spasmodic with two main aims in view, first, that prevention is the most desirable solution and, secondly, that intervention, where deemed necessary, should be a means of conciliation rather than of coercion. Noel-Baker rendered steadfast service in 1944 and 1945 as a member of the United Nations Preparatory Commission and then as a Minister of State representing the United Kingdom at the U.N. In some respects he may have clung too much to the idea of continuity with Geneva, though there is evidence that he moved fairly swiftly to understand if not quite to accept that the East-West divide was more entrenched and fortified than it ever had been in the days before 1945. The fact that his universalist inclinations had so little influence on Ernest Bevin's foreign policies may be due, it is arguable, not so much to Noel-Baker's lack of realism as to a degree of poor faith and over-apprehension in Whitehall.

Things never quite reached apogee in Noel-Baker's political career. 'The reason perhaps is that he took politics very seriously,' writes Lord Thomas of Swynnerton, who worked closely with him in the 1950's. He did not possess:

'that combination of familiarity with ideas and a certain disrespect for them which, as Sir Percy Craddock once wrote, makes for victory in the political game in Britain . . . Preoccupation with issues, not tactics, probably was the determining reason for his relative political failure as it was with another of his heroes, Lord Robert Cecil.'[2]

We are back to his colleagues' earlier reservations about the soundness of Noel-Baker's judgement. There was, too, always a measure of diffidence which does not usually make for advancement at Westminster, something which Nansen is reported to have noticed in another context when he declared, 'I never knew anyone like Philip for being willing to do the work and let someone (else) get the credit'.[3] It is not easy for the ascetic intellectual to be readily accepted as one with an intuitive grasp of what may be politically expedient. His sympathy and support may too easily be enlisted by those who plead with great earnestness. 'Phil never really believes that God can possibly be on the side of big battalions,' one of his friends is quoted as saying. 'At heart he really prefers lost causes and small countries.'[4]

A coda to an immense concerted effort for peace lasted 25 years or so for Noel-Baker. Dislodged partly by age and partly by ideological considerations, from the power bases of the Labour Party, the veteran remained the prophet and did so without dishonour. He returned in print to survey and recommendation. For his mammoth volume *The Arms Race* he received a Nobel accolade in 1959 and popular applause wherever he travelled. It is sad that his proscriptions were so widely misunderstood. An insistence on 'generality' in disarmament, that is, that all weapons must be included, that all stages in disengagement must be coordinated, that all nations must subscribe to the process, earned him the label of 'impossible idealist' from those of Centre and Right. He did not find it easy in the hardest years of the Cold War, to refute the imputation of 'all or nothing', which struck him as quite incorrect, and to affirm that common interests and common survival must demand consensus in plan and action and that 'general and complete disarmament' could only be secured effectively through graduated first steps. The rider, and it was a large one, that universality in action precluded 'unilateralist' moves was, in fact, a consistent emphasis of his, but it brought opposition from the Left of his party, from the C.N.D., and from numerous pacifist groups. His conclusion that such steps would involve Britain's disengaging from alliance seemed sensible to some but inadmissable to many. There were those who never forgave him for what appeared to be equivocation about such matters when he had been Labour Party Chairman in 1946-47.

From time to time critics pointed to Noel-Baker's lack of clarity in distinguishing 'offensive' strategies from 'defensive' ones. An instance of this was the attitude, in his final years, to the maintenance of Western deterrence. It seemed reasonable to propose that the N.A.T.O. Alliance represented a pooling of strength behind international law and the U.N. Charter, and that this empowering could only be set in motion in response to a demonstrated violation of the Charter. After all, this interpretation of the possibilities and obligations of collective security was in accord with those who sought to put their shoulders behind the League of Nations after 1919. For Noel-Baker, already in 1960, it followed that any move to 'decouple' from a collective defensive association by way of unilateral disengagement or membership of a non-nuclear club would be 'desperate and, as I think, defeatist'. To numerous commentators this became an increasingly untenable position. How could deterrence be other than an inherently 'destructive' mechanism and, thus, something that could not be morally justified? Such a posture in their eyes conferred an air of legitimacy upon the process of arms procurement and deployment. Many workers for peace affirmed that they could never stand, as this man seemed to do, upon a basis which required the maintenance of arms, a 'capability', which was in essence an 'offensive' potential. At the heart of the matter of disarmament there was for Noel-Baker a sad irony in that the conflicting standpoints of 'multilateralist' and 'unilateralist' clouded and distorted the pathways to that general objective of graduated arms control and disarmament where rival preferences and political issues claimed more attention than technical feasibilities. Meanwhile, as he had foreseen in 1959, the arms race ground on inexorably.

Noel-Baker's standpoint in regard to unilateral action seems firmer when he was discussing the concept of collective security. For a state to have recourse to independent and, by definition, irresponsible action was to jeopardise the delicate balances that represent reassurance and freedom from fear among nations. In addition to political reality the equally sensitive structures of international law were imperilled in fact as in theory. Thus, the trangressions across frontiers which flared into the crises of Korea, Vietnam, Cyprus, Indo-China, Suez, and the Falkland Islands between 1950 and 1982 were condemned by Noel-Baker as situations which should have been resolvable through arbitration and possible intervention much more quickly and finally than was the case. International action had, of course, done something by way of judgement and intervention to settle issues in Korea, Cyprus, the Congo, Suez. Noel-Baker was not the only commentator of his time who perhaps failed to allow adequately for the wealth of political, economic, and historical variables that explained why solution was so slowly realised beyond a long, wavering period of stalemate.

There was always respect for another point of view (provided it passed the tests of logic and conviction) implicit, perhaps, in a fragment from Noel-Baker's repertoire of platform jokes (and kept in a special file) where one American general said to another, 'As I see it, our commitment to the peace process is only credible if our commitment to the war process is credible'. In the end, his own taut seriousness would either reduce the opposition to respectful assent or lead to their leaving the field not knowing how to reply. Noel-Baker was unfailingly generous towards those whose fatalism or complacency would have outraged others. They could at least write letters for the most potent weapon in the search for peace was the postage stamp.

Frustration clouded the last years though not overwhelmingly so. The great sportsman who swam at 90 (with assistance), and played a fair game of tennis in Battersea and Hurlingham in his early 80's reared up against advancing immobility, disdaining when he could, the elevator and the proffered arm (unless it were in the close company of an attractive young lady). Arthritic fingers were exercised each morning followed by as many 'press-ups' as the elderly peer could stand. Mind and memory remained astonishingly fresh, articulating clearly his remorse, fear, and shame at the nature and pace of the arms race but ever holding out hope.[5] Optimistic and forward looking in the main, he never really aged in attitude. The future and the present were in the hands of 'the budding time of youth', and in a sense, if we remained optimistic, we were all young and powerful.[6]

Two years before his death and in the wake of four or five surgical operations he exhibited a sense of proportion remarkably free from rancour or cynicism:

'It is marvellous and in some ways terrible to be 91. But people are so kind to me – even strangers in the train – that the compensations outweigh the handicaps and I enjoy my strange existence.'[7]

(COURTESY: DR. DON ANTHONY)

Pl. 18. Receiving an honorary degree at Loughborough University, 1976

(COURTESY: THE HON. FRANCIS NOEL-BAKER)

Pl. 19. Receiving a papal knighthood – the only Quaker ever to do so, 1977. Cardinal Hume

There was, of course, so much still left to do. He could never reconcile himself to the cliché that it was the journey, not the arrival, that mattered. In spite of what seemed to be the short-sightedness of others, he was sure, in the spirit of Robert Cecil, that *'le jour viendra'*.[8]

Noel-Baker's achievements, whether as international civil servant, sportsman, orator, writer, parliamentarian, peace campaigner, are plain to see. In sum, they constitute a formidable array of objectives consistently and convincingly approached and surmounted. Today's generation, while they do not have his name on their lips, can hardly fail to be impressed by the magnitude and width of this man's successes. The crucial question, though, is a didactic one. What may we learn from the life of Philip Noel-Baker? Every reader must draw his own conclusions but the biographer has a claim to advance objectively, and it is that from the life and thoughts of one of the most outstanding and knowledgeable workers for a better world, based on the rule of law, several things stand out as guidelines for those who would be active now and in the future. The evidence is in the thousand-fold boxes of his papers in Cambridge. Primarily, the effective campaigner is a 'dedicated mole', a meticulous collector of information. Those who disagree, who dismiss the prophet as visionary, are not able to refute his facts. Again, the worker for amity and law in the world must base understanding and suggestion upon empathy and practical experience – theoretical detachment is never enough. Above all, the vein of faith, hope, and confidence must be quarried deeply. Who but an incorrigible optimist could say of successive generations decimated by world war, 'I still find it hard to think that they died in vain'?[9] The optimism was rooted in a triad of beliefs, namely, that men everywhere, regardless of ethnic and political differences, are capable of uniting to save their planet from destruction. That being so, world problems can be settled by united decision and action. Crucial to the success and continuity of international 'programming for peace' is the buttress of informed public opinion. Philip Noel-Baker was one of those men of our times who stood most pertinaceously for ideals such as these. For him, regardless of opposition, misunderstanding, and even contempt, a more peaceful world was always worth fighting for.

Notes

Chapter 1 *(pages 1-30)*

The Cradle and the Crucible

[1] Baker and Baker, 1927: 8.
[2] Cf. Muir, 1968: passim.
[3] Alexander, 1982: 1467-1468.
[4] Baker and Baker, 1927: 97.
[5] 15 H.C. Debs, 16th March 1910, cols. 398-403; N.B.K.R. 4X/25.
[6] Was Baker entirely deceived? There seems little indication of the Kaiser's honesty of intent in view of the advice of his Cabinet and the relentless momentum of naval rearmament. Edward VII appears also to have been dismissive of the 1907 Conference. Cf. Balfour, 1960: 215-216, 277-279.
[7] Baker and Baker, 1927: 151.
[8] Baker and Baker, 1927: 252.
[9] N.B.K.R. 9/148 Philip Baker to Josie Baker, 19th November 1905.
[10] N.B.K.R. 7/66 Excerpts from autobiographical article for an Italian publisher, 1969.
[11] Skidelsky, 1983: 111.
[12] Noel-Baker, P., Founders Day Speech, King's College, Cambridge, 5th December 1946. Cf. Dalton, 1953: 41, 57.
[13] Pimlott, 1985: 42.
[14] A close friend of Philip recalls that in the last few weeks of life Noel-Baker enjoyed hearing extracts from Basileon read to him by his grand-daughter and others. Letter from David Hubback to Patrick Wilkinson, 12th October 1982, in possession D. J. Whittaker.
[15] Tennyson, 1974: 358, 241, 200, 224.
[16] N.B.K.R. 8/46 Noel-Baker, P., Founders Day Speech, King's College, Cambridge, 5th December 1981.
[17] Pimlott, 1985: 63. Pigou (together with Lord Robert Cecil) eventually became godfather to Philip's son, Francis.
[18] N.B.K.R. 9/146 Philip Baker to his parents, 6th February 1910; N.B.K.R. 9/47/2 Press report, undated, but February 1910.
[19] N.B.K.R. 4X/119 *Cambridge Review*, February 1912. The influence of Thucidides Book II was also thought visible. Cf. Alexander, 1982: 1467.
[20] N.B.K.R. 9/57/6 cutting from *Granta*, May 1912.

[21] Alex Nelson quoted by Dr. Don Anthony, personal communication.

[22] Tennyson, 1974: 254.

[23] Sir Roger Bannister's address at Memorial Service, St. Martin-in-the-Fields, 25th November 1982. Interview with Sir Roger Bannister, 1985.

[24] *Granta,* 23rd November 1912, 'Olympiads and the noble English press' by 'P.J.B.', pp. 87-89.

[25] Nakabayashi (Japan) and P. Noel-Baker interview, 13th June 1982. Transcript in possession of D. J. Whittaker. Cf. also Strode-Jackson obituary in *The Times,* 17th November 1972.

[26] N.B.K.R. 7/66 See note 10 above.

[27] Note in *The World,* 13th June 1912.

[28] Report in the *British Friend,* vol. XXI, 1912, 308-309.

[29] Quoted in Bartlett, 1944: 27.

[30] N.B.K.R. 9/47/5 P. Baker to Josie Baker, 28th June 1913.

[31] *Bootham School Magazine,* vol. IV, 1912-14, 435.

[32] N.B.K.R. 8/46 P. Noel-Baker, Founders Day Speech, 5th December 1981.

[33] N.B.K.R. 9/146/4 clipping from the *Daily News and Leader,* 4th August 1914.

[34] In *The Friend* of 21st August 1914, Philip Baker writes of his willingness to supply details of the Unit to those contemplating joining it. Allen's three sons were all F.A.U. members. See also Greenwood, 1975, vol. I; chapters XI, X.

[35] Rolph, 1973: 53. Friends House Library, London has a collection of papers mainly in the style of a magazine relating to the overseas work of the Unit. (Disbanded after World War I the Unit reformed in 1939 and saw service again on similar lines for a time.)

[36] N.B.K.R. (uncatalogued) A. Campbell to P. J. Baker, 6th May 1915.

[37] N.B.K.R. 9/92 Sir George Newman to P. J. Baker, 6th May 1915.

[38] N.B.K.R. 7/44/3 has a collection of letters and memorabilia. Cf. N.B.K.R. 7/44/2 for an account of the first gas attack in April 1915.

[39] Cf. memos in N.B.K.R. 9/92. Norman Angell, visiting Noel-Baker at Dunkirk in autumn 1914, was shocked by the incompetence of the R.A.M.C. Cf. Angell 1951: 101.

[40] N.B.K.R. 7/44/7 memo by Noel-Baker. Cf. N.B.K.R. 9/46/6 P. J. Baker and Josie Baker correspondence.

[41] N.B.K.R. 7/44/7; Pimlott, 1985: 96, refers to Dalton's visit.

[42] *F.A.U. Monthly Magazine,* January 1916, 'From Austria', pp. 16-17.

[43] See Chapter 9 below.

[44] N.B.K.R. 9/146/2 Philip Baker to Josephine Baker, 7th March 1915.

[45] Cf. N.B.K.R. uncatalogued letters, 1915. See also Bell, 1982, vol. II, and Poole, R., 1978 for accounts of Virginia's state of imbalance. She may have reached the edge of despair when she heard about Irene. The evidence is anecdotal. For further meetings between the Woolfs and the <Noel-> Bakers see later in this chapter.

[46] N.B.K.R. 7/44/3 reminiscence about appointment to the Foreign Office.

[47] N.B.K.R. 8/46 notes for Noel-Baker's Founders Day Speech at King's College, Cambridge, 5th December 1981. The scroll, in a side chapel, bears 210 names from the war.

[48] Bell, 1982, vol. II: 25-26.
[49] Bell, 1982, vol. II: 319. The by-election was at Handsworth near Birmingham. Noel-Baker failed to win the seat.
[50] N.B.K.R. uncatalogued letters, Irene to Philip Baker, 13th June 1921.
[51] N.B.K.R. uncatalogued letters, Irene to Philip Baker, 16th March 1922. Miss Rachel Crowdy (1884-1964) was created Dame in 1919 as a mark of esteem for her League of Nations work on social and humanitarian questions.
[52] N.B.K.R. uncatalogued letters, Irene to Philip Baker, 21st September 1922.
[53] N.B.K.R. uncatalogued letters, Irene to Philip Baker, 3rd August 1923.
[54] N.B.K.R. uncatalogued letters, Irene to Philip Baker, 20th and 22nd April 1924.
[55] Terms quoted in *The Friend*, 1924, p. 500.
[56] Bell, 1982, vol. III, 27-28. Desmond MacCarthy (1877-1952), the literary and dramatic critic, had earlier been attracted to Irene. The Molly referred to was his wife.
[57] Bell, 1982, vol. III, 28-29.
[58] Bell, 1982, vol. III, 81.
[59] Bell, 1982, vol. III, 69.
[60] Bell, 1982, vol. III, 70.
[61] N.B.K.R. uncatalogued letters, Irene to Philip Noel-Baker, 26th January 1930 and 21st July 1926.
[62] Nakabayashi transcript. See note 25 above.
[63] Noel-Baker, P., *History of the Achilles Club*, n.d., pp. 24-26.
[64] Interview with Sir Roger Bannister, 1985. The question was posed by Sir Roger at the Noel-Baker Memorial Service, 25th November 1982. Cf. Baker, P. J., 1920.
[65] N.B.K.R. 6/14 P. Noel-Baker to D. G. A. Lowe, 19th August 1928. Cf. leader in the *Manchester Guardian*, 25th August 1928. An example of Noel-Baker's extolling the fraternity of international sport is to be found in N.B.K.R. 6/22 in an article on the Olympic Games written for *Empire Review*, May 1924.

Chapter 2 *(pages 31-77)*

A Time for Hope 1919-1930

[1] Cecil, R., 1941: 105. Cf. N.B.K.R. 4X/28 P. Baker to L. F. Oppenheim, 28th December 1918. Eyre Crowe to R. Cecil, memo 'Organisation' of 17th December 1918. Crowe seems to have preferred Baker to stay in Whitehall.
[2] Hankey, 1963: 11.
[3] Headlam-Morley, 1972: 2, 9. Cf. N.B.K.R. 4X/32 for Noel-Baker's memos, correspondence, drafts. See also N.B.K.R. 4X/34 and 4X/35.
[4] Headlam-Morley, 1972: 121. Cf. N.B.K.R. 4/35 memo by P. Baker, 19th May 1919.
[5] Hankey, 1963: 104.
[6] Noel-Baker, 1979: 16, 21. Although they appeared to part in mutual contempt there seems to be an element of latter-day rationalisation here. In fact, Noel-Baker replied politely enough to Hankey, expressing his gratitude for the

offer but declining because he preferred a League opportunity and, in any case, he did not see himself as a good enough economist. 'I hope you will not think me an obstinate or foolish young man', he went on, hoping for a chance of appointment to the Cabinet Secretariat and perhaps for some specialist work with the League of Nations. N.B.K.R. 9/38 P. Baker to Maurice Hankey, 20th August 1919. (Hankey's attitude to disarmament as Noel-Baker interpreted it, will be further considered in Chapter 3 below.) Cf. Carlton, 1970: 29.

[7] Lloyd-George, 1939: 2, 1490.

[8] Swartz, 1971: 25.

[9] Lloyd-George, 1939: 1, 38.

[10] Cf. Lloyd-George, 1939: 1, 124-127.

[11] Lloyd-George, 1939: 1, 152-153.

[12] Bartlett, 1944: 117.

[13] Bartlett, 1944: 126, 208.

[14] Binkley, 1929: 612.

[15] Woolf, 1964: 185.

[16] P.R.O. F.O. Min. 371/3081, no. 87527, of 28th April 1917.

[17] Wilson, Duncan MS., 1985: 137, quoting Woolf.

[18] Rothwell, 1971: 213n.

[19] Noel-Baker, P., in a tribute to Woolf in *The Times*, 21st August 1969.

[20] Smuts, 1918.

[21] Lloyd-George, 1939: 414.

[22] Quoted Robbins, 1983: 117.

[23] Winkler, 1948: 12.

[24] Robbins, 1983: 117ff.

[25] Beloff, 1969: 332-333.

[26] Temperley, 1920, vi, 461.

[27] Dubin, 1983: 469-470.

[28] Noel-Baker, 1926: 50. Cf. P.R.O. F800/249, fol. 81-82, dated 20th December 1918, for Noel-Baker's memos as a member of Cecil's Section. Cf. Raymond, 1960. In N.B.K.R. 4X/28 there is a collection of memoranda on legal issues. Some of the points raised, particularly by Cecil, are discussed again (in 1927) in N.B.K.R. 9/89.

[29] Walters, 1952: 40. Hankey's opinion is recorded in Egerton, 1978: 178.

[30] N.B.K.R. 4X/27 contains a memo from Baker to the Secretary-General, dated 13th September 1919, detailing the advantages of the League dealing publicly and more impartially with the general execution of the Versailles Treaty than would 'an alliance of victors'. N.B.K.R. 4/478 'Note on possible modification of the Covenant', summer (?) 1922.

[31] Cf. N.B.K.R. 4/478 for memos, probably all by Noel-Baker, on the aims and structure of the League, dated between 1919 and 1924. Whitehall opinion leaned towards keeping the British Delegation absolutely separate from any British subject appointed to head the Secretariat. Memo by Eyre Crowe dated 10th June 1919, in F.O. 608/242, fol. 204-206.

[32] N.B.K.R. 4X/37 'Note of present position with regard to mandates', written by Baker, dated 23rd June 1920, with a note that copies had been sent to Whitehall. Cecil Papers F.O. 608, contains an interesting record of a meeting Cecil convened in the Hotel Astoria, Paris, on 31st January 1919. Noel-Baker was among League officials invited to consider how the ex-German colonies might be best placed under mandate. Two years previously, Noel-Baker had been aware of criticism from the Labour Party in England and from American visitors to the League's Genevan headquarters. The note is detailed and carefully drawn up. Cf. Noel-Baker, 1926b: chapter VII.

[33] Roskill, 1972: 193.

[34] N.B.K.R. 4/463 P. Baker to R. Cecil, 3rd May 1921. N.B.K.R. 4X/25 where certain anxieties about his own ability to deal with 'difficult technical questions' are revealed in correspondence with Alec Lindsay of the Secretariat, 18th October 1923.

[35] N.B.K.R. (uncatalogued) Irene to Philip Baker, 5th May 1921.

[36] N.B.K.R. 8/71/4 broadcast by Noel-Baker, *The Listener*, 16th October 1935. Cf. Hoyer.

[37] N.B.K.R. 4/609 correspondence between Nansen and Baker, 16th and 22nd August 1921. Cf. also Noel-Baker, 1926b for discussion of collaboration with Nansen. See also Greenwood, 1975, vol. I, chapter XIII.

[38] N.B.K.R. 4/611 memo by Baker for Secretary-General, 'Russian famine – possible action by the League of Nations', dated 19th August 1921.

[39] N.B.K.R. 4/611 Humphrey Sumner to P. Baker, (?) August 1921.

[40] N.B.K.R. 4/611 P. Baker to A. Henderson, 10th October 1921. Cf. N.B.K.R. 4/472.

[41] N.B.K.R. 4/611 F. Nansen to P. Baker, 19th August 1921.

[42] N.B.K.R. 4/625 Noel-Baker's notes for a broadcast to the U.S.A., later given October 1923.

[43] Cf. note 42.

[44] Quoted Sörensen, 1932: 281.

[45] Quoted Stewart, 1986. Cf. N.B.K.R. 4/471 where there are notes for an address by Nansen in Coventry, November 1926, when he spoke about the relief operation in similar terms.

[46] N.B.K.R. 4/471 P. Noel-Baker to Bevil Rudd, 30th October 1922.

[47] N.B.K.R. 9/57/1 F. Nansen to P. Noel-Baker, 10th October 1927.

[48] N.B.K.R. 8/71/4 Testimonial from Nansen in 1924 to support Noel-Baker's application for an L.S.E. chair. He concluded, 'I would therefore congratulate the University which could have the privilege of his teaching . . .'

[49] N.B.K.R. 4X/25 F. Nansen to P. Noel-Baker, 16th June 1927.

[50] N.B.K.R. 5/67/1 Noel-Baker expressed dissatisfaction with Parmoor's tactics in a letter to C. R. Buxton, 7th July 1926. Cf. N.B.K.R. 7/44 and Walters 1969 ed.: 52, 271, for discussion of loopholes in the Covenant.

[51] N.B.K.R. uncatalogued, Irene to Philip Noel-Baker, 24th April 1924.

[52] Cecil, 1949: 239.

[53] *Idem.*

[54] See later in this chapter for an account of Noel-Baker's contribution to the Protocol.
[55] N.B.K.R. 7/44 undated memo by P. Noel-Baker, clearly late 1924.
[56] Richardson, 1986: 163.
[57] N.B.K.R. 9/92 R. Cecil to P. Baker, 21st July 1920.
[58] Quoted Miller, 1928, i, 162.
[59] Noel-Baker, 1926: 50. Cf. Raymond, 1960.
[60] Raffo, 1967: 326ff and Raffo, 1974: 186-196.
[61] Cecil Papers 51121, fol. 30-40, typed memo, presumably by Cecil, dated Berlin, 5th July 1924. Cf. Walters, 1969 ed.: 223-227.
[62] N.B.K.R. 4X/163 P. Noel-Baker to Bertram Pickard, Society of Friends, 1st April 1924.
[63] G.M.P., P. Noel-Baker to Gilbert Murray, memo, November 1924.
[64] Noel-Baker, 1924.
[65] Noel-Baker, 1924a.
[66] Cf. Zimmern, 1936: 358. Something of the thinking that lay behind Whitehall reluctance to incur the further obligations of 'guaranteed' mutual security may be discerned in a long Foreign Office memo of 10th January 1926 (C. 797/1/18) reproduced in Medlicott et al, 1966: 1-17.
[67] Cf. Mosley, 1968: 248-249. See also the opinion of Martin, Kingsley, 1969 ed.: 70-71.
[68] N.B.K.R. (uncatalogued) Irene to Philip Baker, 28th March 1921.
[69] Noel-Baker, P. in obituary of Lord Robert Cecil in *Dictionary of National Biography,* 1951-60: 201. Cf. Chapter 3 below for a description of the Peace Ballot.
[70] Noel-Baker, 1926: 55.
[71] Walters, 1969 ed.: 162.
[72] N.B.K.R. 9/89 R. Cecil to P. Noel-Baker, 17th November 1925.
[73] N.B.K.R. (uncatalogued) Irene to Philip Noel-Baker, 9th December 1923.
[74] Cf. N.B.K.R. 4/479 for Noel-Baker's stout defence of the Covenant in off-print for article for Münch, 1923: vol. 2. Cf. 118 H.C. Debs 5s, cols. 992-993, 21st July 1919.
[75] Bartlett, 1944: 200.
[76] Walters, 1969 ed.: 387.
[77] Noel-Baker, 1925: 34.
[78] Cf. the work of Noel-Baker on the categorising of disputes mentioned previously in this chapter.
[79] F.O. Papers, F.O. 608/243, fol. 9, P. Baker memo, 31st January 1919.
[80] Noel-Baker, 1925: 175.
[81] Noel-Baker, 1925: 109-112. Cf. Walters, 1969 ed.: 269ff.
[82] Noel-Baker, 1925: 139.
[83] Noel-Baker, 1925: 161.
[84] Noel-Baker, 1925: 133. Cf. Parmoor, 1936: 236.
[85] Zimmern, 1936: 359-365.
[86] 185 H.C. Debs 5s, col. 1561.

87 Zimmern, 1936: 349.
88 Noel-Baker, 1925: 176.
89 Cf. Cecil, 1941: 77.
90 Walters, 1969 ed.: 276. Cf. Northedge, F. S. quoted Berridge and Jennings, 1985: 3.
91 N.B.K.R. 4X/25 P. Noel-Baker to Edvard Benes, 8th October 1924.
92 N.B.K.R. 4/486, off-print of Noel-Baker, 1926a.
93 Cecil Papers 51106, R. Cecil to P. Noel-Baker, 14th February 1926.
94 G.M.P. 197, P. Noel-Baker to Gilbert Murray, 9th February 1926.
95 N.B.K.R. 9/89 R. Cecil to P. Noel-Baker, 9th May 1930. There is a copy in the Cecil Papers 51107, fol. 86.
96 Cecil Papers 51106, fol. 36-43, P. Noel-Baker memo to Eric Drummond: 'The failure of the League and its causes'. Undated, presumably 1922.
97 118 H.C. Debs 5s, cols. 992-993, 21st July 1919.
98 Henig, 1973: 15.
99 Dilks, 1971: 365.
100 G.M.P. 192, P. Noel-Baker to Gilbert Murray, 2nd October 1923.
101 G.M.P. 202, fol. 16-17, P. Noel-Baker to Gilbert Murray, 21st September 1927.
102 Cf. G.M.P. 213, 214, 215, 217. For a discussion *inter alia* of Murray's changing views on sanctions see Thorne, 1972: 382ff, 106-107.
103 Wilson, 1985, MS. chapter XXII, 3. Cf. also N.B.K.R. 9/89.
104 Lord Parmoor was Lord President of the Council in the short-lived 1924 administration of Ramsay MacDonald who held the portfolios of Premier and Foreign Secretary. When Labour came back in 1929 for two years under MacDonald, Parmoor remained Lord President and Arthur Henderson went to the Foreign Office. Noel-Baker, a professor at L.S.E. in 1924, took a parliamentary seat for Coventry in 1929, losing it two years later. In 1931 Labour fell away drastically and MacDonald formed a coalition, the National Government, which was to last six years.
105 Dalton, 1953: 214, 219. The diary entry was for 6th June 1929. Henderson's recruitment of Noel-Baker is referred to in Gladwyn, 1972: 39, 43.
106 Connell, 1958: 98.
107 G.M.P. 210, fol. 15-16, P. Noel-Baker to Gilbert Murray, undated, but 1927. The Covenant 'gaps' refers to the remote possibility that a member state might resort to war after waiting in vain for the three statutory months the Council was given to resolve a dispute. In today's parlance the 'gap' might be termed one of 'credibility'. In N.B.K.R. 5/67/1 in a letter to C. R. Buxton, dated 12th July 1926, Noel-Baker wondered whether Parmoor and the Government should not be pressing much harder at Geneva for fuller recognition of the arbitral device and for its help in sealing gaps in Covenant provisions.
108 Angell's *The Great Illusion,* 1910, was followed by *The Fruits of Victory,* 1921. When the latter was republished in 1972, Noel-Baker after 50 years must have seen it as a restatement of a very relevant thesis. The title, of course, was purposefully ironic and the book sketched the continuing dilemmas of a

floundering Europe. See Angell, 1951: 324 for Noel-Baker's response to the knighthood; pp. 298-300 for the Pound-Belloc incidents. Cf. Bisceglia, 1972: 263-273.

[109] Quoted Bisceglia, 1982: xi.

[110] Quoted Bisceglia, 1982: xii.

[111] Bisceglia, 1982; Birn, 1981; Ceadel, 1980, discuss these issues.

[112] N.B.K.R. 4X/98 P. Noel-Baker to Robert Fraser, 20th November 1930.

[113] N.B.K.R. 4X/98 R. Cecil to P. Noel-Baker, 29th November 1930.

[114] N.B.K.R. 4X/98 P. Noel-Baker to K. Zilliacus, 3rd December 1930.

[115] Noel-Baker, 1928 ed.: viii.

[116] Smuts, 1952: 301, address, Sheffield University, October 1931.

Chapter 3 *(pages 78-98)*

The Control of Arms: Pre-war Views 1926-1936

[1] Madariaga, 1929: 305.

[2] Noel-Baker, 1926: vii.

[3] See Richardson, 1986: 110-139, for a comprehensive account of Cecil's work with the sub-committee.

[4] Cf. the German views as expressed by Otto Hoetzch, *International Affairs*, vol. II, 1932: 51.

[5] Cf. Noel-Baker, 1934a: 3-25.

[6] Cf. Bretton, H. L., 1953: 138-156; *Documents on British Foreign Policy*, Second Series, vol. 4, no. 92. Cf. Richardson, 1969: 12ff.

[7] Madariaga, 1974: 275.

[8] Noel-Baker, 1926: 36.

[9] *Idem*, 49.

[10] Cecil, 1941: 152. See also 151-153, 139-140. Ramsay MacDonald's Government repudiated the Treaty ostensibly on account of reluctance to take on increased commitments across the Channel. They doubted, moreover, the effectiveness of League intervention where aggression had been identified.

[11] Noel-Baker's comments in a discussion following a talk on disarmament by General Sir Frederick Maurice are given in *International Affairs*, vol. 5, 1926: 130.

[12] Madariaga, 1929: *passim*.

[13] Renamed the Treaty of Mutual Alliance, the measure failed to be adopted in 1924; the Protocol also failed in 1925. Cf. Walters, 1952 ed.: 223-227, 284-288.

[14] Cf. the account by Hilton Young, 1926: 368-383.

[15] These points are dealt with comprehensively in Richardson, 1986: 150ff. Cf. also the correspondence in *Cecil Papers*, Add MSS. 5106, between Noel-Baker and Cecil in January and February 1927.

[16] Noel-Baker, 1926: 86.

[17] The stipulations of Versailles may be interesting to the modern reader more aware of fast action at sea. Four classes only were allowed: 6 battleships, 6

light cruisers, 12 destroyers, 12 torpedo boats. The capital ships were relatively light and, in fact, restricted to a 10,000 ton maximum displacement. No submarines or aircraft were allowed. Cf. Noel-Baker, 1926: 177-178.

18 Noel-Baker, 1926: 246.

19 *Idem*, 257.

20 M. Paul Boncour had stressed the difficulties in a League Council committee in December 1925. Cf. Noel-Baker, 1926: 259. (In today's disarmament debates the 'hegemony' principle has diverged to range over 'nuclear' and 'non-nuclear' capabilities. The issue of 'nuclear proliferation' emphasises the desirability of general disarmament in an urgent way that earlier disarmers could never have foreseen.)

21 Noel-Baker, 1926: 262-274.

22 *Idem*, 265.

23 *Idem*, 272.

24 Eight years later, Noel-Baker was advocating a disbanding of national air forces in favour of the establishment of some sort of international air force. See later in this chapter.

25 Noel-Baker, 1926: 289.

26 Noel-Baker, 1926: 301.

27 Noel-Baker, 1926: 315, 128.

28 Madariaga, 1929: 182.

29 Malcolm, Neil, 1926, *International Affairs*, vol. 5, 1926: 160-161.

30 *Idem*, 161.

31 Noel-Baker, 1934, *International Affairs*, vol. 13, 1934: 3-25.

32 Noel-Baker, 1934: 19.

33 *Idem*, 21ff.

34 Cf. N.B.K.R. 5/96 – speech notes for a British Commonwealth League lunch in York.

35 Holtby, Winifred, in *Challenge to Death*, 136-137.

36 Noel-Baker, in *Challenge to Death*, 189.

37 *The Aeroplane*, 4th July 1934, 13.

38 Noel-Baker, in *Challenge to Death*, 225.

39 *Idem*, 239.

40 J. B. Priestley in *Challenge to Death*, 307-308.

41 N.B.K.R. 9/88 Irene Noel-Baker to Konni Zilliacus, 1st July 1935.

42 *Royal Commission on Armaments*, 1935, Report, para 7, 258-259. Oral evidence of 30th October 1935.

43 N.B.K.R. 7/64 Memo of oral evidence to Royal Commission on Armaments.

44 *Idem*. Cf. the case as presented by Carnegie, D., 1931.

45 Noel-Baker, 1972 ed.: 84.

46 *Idem*, 81.

47 Cf. the case put forward by Harold MacMillan in *The Next Five Years*, 1935, mentioned in Chapter 3 above.

48 In 1972 a second edition of the first volume appeared with this reference to the abortive second volume – 'after the betrayal of democracy and peace at Munich . . . there seemed no point in trying to finish and print it'. Cf. Noel-Baker, 1972 ed.: xxii.

[49] N.B.K.R. 5/96 Notes of speech on disarmament to Royal Naval College, Greenwich, 29th May 1936. His 'pleasing sub-title', he joked, was 'why you should lose your job'. His remarks went on to take up the positive consequences of arms control policies.

Chapter 4 *(pages 99-138)*

A Time of Challenge 1931-1936

[1] Smuts, 1952: 300.
[2] Noel-Baker, 1979: xiii.
[3] Noel-Baker, 1926: 328.
[4] Both Dalton and Noel-Baker had lost their parliamentary seats in 1931. Both were influential spokesmen for the Opposition on foreign affairs. Noel-Baker's short tenure as P.P.S. to Foreign Secretary Henderson was, of course, terminated and he had to wait five more years before returning to the Commons. Pimlott, 1985, chapters XIII and XIV contains interesting glimpses of Dalton's approach to disarmament and international relations. In Dalton, 1953: 258, there is a brief reference to Henderson's efforts at the Conference.
[5] Noel-Baker, 1979: 70.
[6] Scott, 1973: 265.
[7] Walters, 1969: 509.
[8] The Optional Clause, mentioned in Chapter 2, was a rather complicated provision designed to facilitate the arbitral role of the Permanent Court of International Justice. Zimmern, 1936: 347, summarises it thus: 'The devotees of compulsory arbitration had to content themselves with the so-called "optional clause" under which states might voluntarily accept the jurisdiction of the Court for disputes of a legal character, with any reservations which they might wish to attach to their signature'. Cf. Walters, 1969: 125-126.
[9] Scott, 1973: 271.
[10] Scott, 1973: 269.
[11] Scott, 1973: 515. Richardson, 1969, has a detailed discussion of 'the German Problem'. Cf. also Richardson, 1987: 14ff.
[12] N.B.K.R. 9/91 Philip to Irene Noel-Baker, 21st April 1932.
[13] N.B.K.R. 9/91 Philip to Irene Noel-Baker, 30th April 1932.
[14] N.B.K.R. 5/147 P. Noel-Baker memo of 6th November 1933. Cf. also Richardson, 1969: 126-128, 205-207.
[15] Formed originally through Benes' concern to forestall resumption of power by the Hapsburgs the Entente was composed of Yugoslavia, Czechoslovakia, and Rumania. By 1938 this preventive alliance had crumbled not having dissipated fears of blocs to the east and west of it.
[16] The quotation is from Slocombe, 1938: 235.
[17] Walters, 1969: 554.

[18] Quoted in Scott, 1973: 294. In 1934 Baldwin was Lord President of the Council. He took over as Prime Minister from Ramsay MacDonald on 7th June 1935. Sir John Simon was Foreign Secretary until 7th June 1935.

[19] Zimmern, 1936: 408.

[20] Quoted in Scott, 1973: 289.

[21] Correspondence in N.B.K.R. 4X/98 indicates mixed feelings in both Henderson and Noel-Baker, understandable against the background of former high hopes and a fast-crumbling conference.

[22] Konni Zilliacus was then a member of the information section of the League of Nations Secretariat in Geneva. N.B.K.R. 4X/98 K. Zilliacus to P. Noel-Baker, 20th July 1932. An acid element in the judgements of Zilliacus was not uncommon.

[23] Quoted in Scott, 1973: 287.

[24] N.B.K.R. 5/147 P. Noel-Baker to K. Zilliacus, 23rd November 1933.

[25] N.B.K.R. 5/148 P. Noel-Baker to Kingsley Martin, 28th March 1935.

[26] N.B.K.R. uncatalogued, Irene to Philip Noel-Baker, 22nd June 1933 and 23rd June 1933. Given the tension of the summer of 1933 and the very obvious dilemmas of Philip (and of Henderson), his wife's advice seems neither very understanding nor does it read consistently. There seems to be no extant reply from Philip to these earnest pieces of advice. Virginia Woolf had noticed Philip's despondency. In October 1933 she commented, rather mysteriously and as sharply as ever, on the tenseness in his countenance and disposition – 'Phil does not truckle to the arts for which I like him. I always think about his teeth being filed'. Cf. Bell, 1982: IV: 182.

[27] Hamilton, 1938: 426.

[28] Wheeler-Bennet, 1932: 355.

[29] N.B.K.R. 5/148 K. Zilliacus to H. Dalton, 6th October 1933. Copy sent to P. Noel-Baker.

[30] N.B.K.R. 5/148 P. Noel-Baker to K. Zilliacus, 30th October 1933.

[31] Noel-Baker, 1926: 328.

[32] Zimmern, 1936: 335.

[33] Carlton, 1970: 122.

[34] Madariaga, 1929: 306.

[35] Webster, 1933 (and later via personal contacts); Walters, 1952 and 1969 ed.; Rappard, 1940; Hinsley, 1963. He appears to have found E. H. Carr, a prominent historian, too much concerned deterministically with 'balance of power' and 'regional associations' during the 'Twenty Years Crisis' following the First World War.

[36] Madariaga, 1974: 19.

[37] Madariaga, 1974: 402.

[38] Walters, 1952: 299, 612.

[39] Carlton, 1970: 45, quoting Cecil Papers, Add M.S. 51107, of 16th August 1929. Between Noel-Baker and Mr. and Mrs. Snowden there was little amicability. 'Philip Baker', Mrs. Snowden told a member of the League of Nations Secretariat two years later, 'in particular has played an unworthy part. He is always proposing new compromises.' (Dalton, 1953: 236).

[40] Madariaga, 1974: 237.
[41] Carr, 1968: 38ff.
[42] Cf. Wheeler-Bennett, 1932: 354-355. The literature on this period and on the work of the League of Nations is extensive. Walters, 1969 ed. has a very useful account of events and a clear commentary on ways in which League members responded. See chapters 40, 53, 57-58, 62-63. Carr, 1959, has a brief resume with a distinctive view-point.
[43] G.M.P. 211, P. Noel-Baker to G. Murray, 7th December 1931 and 20th November 1931. In N.B.K.R. there is surprisingly little to be found about the Manchurian crisis.
[44] G.M.P. 286, P. Noel-Baker to G. Murray, 11th October 1931, and G. Murray to P. Noel-Baker, 12th October 1931.
[45] G.M.P. 291, G. Murray to Sir John Simon, 16th March 1932. Simon had followed the Marquis of Reading as Foreign Secretary when Ramsay MacDonald formed his National Government in October 1931.
[46] Cecil Papers, Add MS. 51107, P. Noel-Baker to R. Cecil, 30th April 1932, quoted in Barros, 1979: 368-369.
[47] Cf. the discussion in Bassett, 1968: 564, 575 of the speeches in February 1933 of Chamberlain to the House of Commons and of Churchill at Queens Hall, London and at Waltham Cross, Essex.
[48] G.M.P. 196-197, P. Noel-Baker to G. Murray, 14th October 1932.
[49] N.B.K.R. 9/65 P. Noel-Baker to an unnamed friend, 13th December 1932. Cf. L.N.U., IV, 66. Limitation of Armaments Committee: memo from P. Noel-Baker, 24th November 1933.
[50] *The New Clarion*, 6th January 1934. Founded by Robert Blachford in 1891 this weekly for some years amplified the voice of the Independent Labour Party. (There may be misprints in the original text which explains the confusing double negatives.)
[51] *The New Clarion*, 10th February 1934.
[52] Ceadel, 1980: 3ff.
[53] Shepherd, 1952: 150ff.
[54] N.B.K.R. 9/65 K. Zilliacus to P. Noel-Baker, 22nd November 1933. In respect of the Chinese Kuomintang of the 1930's, Walters, 1969 ed.: 339, declares that neither help nor sympathy was readily evinced by Western powers who feared both the persistance of anti-foreign nationalism and the help and guidance revolutionary China was receiving from the U.S.S.R.
[55] L.N.U. General Council Minutes pt.1, vol. 2. An address by Noel-Baker to London L.N.U. Council, 1942, contained this reference.
[56] Madariaga, 1974: 49.
[57] G.M.P. 223: 34, R. Cecil to G. Murray, 30th July 1936.
[58] Carlton, 1970: 19, quoting the MacDonald Papers. Snowden's antipathy has already been referred to in note 39 above.
[59] The Peace Ballot arrangements and results are discussed in Noel-Baker, 1979: 138-141.
[60] Murray, 1948: 2-3.

61 This is an interesting admission to have from Cecil: delivered at the L.N.U. General Council in London, 1942. L.N.U. General Council Minutes, pt. 1, 10. It is typical of the speaker in its blend of candour and elegance.
62 N.B.K.R. 4/1 P. Noel-Baker to William Gillies, 22nd February 1935. Gillies at that time was Secretary of the Labour Party International Department.
63 Scott, 1973: 335.
64 N.B.K.R. 4/1 John Harvey to P. Noel-Baker, 6th March 1935, after a meeting at the House of Commons of M.P.'s with the Antislavery and Aboriginees Protection Society. Harvey was a fellow-Quaker and well-known in liberal circles.
65 N.B.K.R. 4/1 P. Noel-Baker to R. Cecil, 21st June 1935.
66 N.B.K.R. 4/1 K. Zilliacus to P. Noel-Baker, 16th February 1935.
67 Madariaga, 1973: 352.
68 Walters, 1969: 650; Scott, 1973: 333-334.
69 N.B.K.R. 1X/4 P. Noel-Baker to Walter Layton, 23rd October 1935.
70 N.B.K.R. 4/1 P. Noel-Baker to Léon Blum, 6th July 1935.
71 N.B.K.R. 4/1 P. Noel-Baker to Anthony Eden, 29th July 1935.
72 N.B.K.R. 4/1 P. Noel-Baker report to R. Cecil, 2nd August 1935.
73 N.B.K.R. 4/1 W. Gillies (for Labour Party) to P. Noel-Baker, 30th August 1935.
74 N.B.K.R. 4/1 P. Noel-Baker to Aylmer Vallance, 4th October 1935; P. Noel-Baker to Frank Walters, 3rd and 4th October 1935; Herbert Synett to P. Noel-Baker, 3rd October 1935.
75 N.B.K.R. 4X/23 Transcript of a broadcast of 12th October 1935. Walters, 1969: 657, has a detailed discussion of the negotiations over sanctions at the League of Nations.
76 N.B.K.R. 4/1 P. Noel-Baker to R. Cecil, 15th December 1935. Cf. Scott, 1973: 335ff, for an account of Cabinet discussion in London.
77 Walters, 1969: 671.
78 N.B.K.R. 4/1 K. Zilliacus to P. Noel-Baker, 12th December 1935, copied to Hugh Dalton and Robert Cecil. Cf. the letter to *The Manchester Guardian*, 5th December 1935.
79 N.B.K.R. 4/1 K. Zilliacus to P. Noel-Baker, 16th December 1935.
80 N.B.K.R. 4/1 See e.g. P. Noel-Baker to R. Cecil, 5th May 1936; P. Noel-Baker to F. Walters, 28th May 1936; P. Noel-Baker to H. M. Napier and the 'Friends of Abyssinia', 13th May 1936; P. Noel-Baker letter to *The Times*, 8th May 1936; P. Noel-Baker to F. Walters, 1st May 1936. Cf. Noel-Baker's memo of 23rd June 1936 for the Derby by-election.
81 N.B.K.R. 4/1 Noel-Baker memo of visit to Blum in Paris, 9th May 1936.
82 Neville Chamberlain's speech to the 1900 Club in London, *The Times*, 11th June 1936. It will be clear from indications in the present chapter and in Chapter 2 that Austin and Neville Chamberlain had similar views about 'regional arrangements' and the League of Nations.
83 N.B.K.R. 4/1 K. Zilliacus to P. Noel-Baker, 6th June 1936.
84 N.B.K.R. 4/1 K. Zilliacus to C. Attlee, 6th June 1936. Cf. an open letter to *The Manchester Guardian* from Zilliacus, 4th June 1936. See also P. Noel-Baker to

K. Zilliacus, 9th June 1936; K. Zilliacus to P. Noel-Baker, 27th June 1936; and K. Zilliacus to P. Noel-Baker, 20th June 1936. The phrase alluding to Blum is attributable to Noel-Baker. Cf. N.B.K.R. 4/2, 4X/22, 4X/23 for correspondence with his Derby constituents and others on the Italian situation.

85 *Daily Herald*, 30th June 1936. Cf. the discussion of Labour's *angst* in Martin, 1969 ed.: 93-94.

86 Shepherd, 1951: 385ff. Noel-Baker, watching the political eccentricity of Cripps, saw him by 1939 as a 'queer ally', if not an 'unmitigated disaster'. N.B.K.R. 4X/23 P. Noel-Baker to Walter Layton.

87 Labour Party Annual Conference Report, 1937. Cf. Pimlott, 1977: 150.

88 Taylor, 1957: 192-193 and Chapter VI, *passim*.

89 Woolf, 1937: 337-352.

90 See Chapter 3 above.

91 Beatrice Webb Diary (microfiche), No. 4882 of 20th February 1930. For earlier views see No. 4866 of 21st December 1929, and No. 4816 of 2nd October 1929.

92 Noel-Baker, 1926: 1-2; Farrar, 1952: 82n. Cf. Noel-Baker article in *Labour Magazine*, March 1925, p. 497. Cf. Noel-Baker address to the 11th Session of the League Assembly in 1930 as quoted by Farrar, 1952: 113. See also the discussions in Shepherd, 1951 and Davis, 1950 which are speculative, factual, but not entirely lucid.

93 Marwick, 1964: 293; MacMillan, 1935, *passim*.

94 Dalton, 1936: 481.

95 Pimlott, 1985: 255ff.

96 Gilbert, 1982: 94.

97 Cf. Gilbert, 1976, V, 826n; Churchill, 1950: 170, 181-182; Spier, 1963: *passim*; Angell, 1951: 271. Cf. *G.M.P.*, N. Angell to G. Murray, 2nd February 1938 (looking back to the origin of Focus).

98 Gilbert, 1982, Companion Vol. V, pt. 3: 370. An inference one might draw is that this is Churchill's sense of etiquette; Cecil must have known about the Focus from his confidante, Noel-Baker.

99 Bell, 1982, IV: 34.

100 Gilbert, 1982, Companion Vol. V, pt. 3: 1640. Cf. also correspondence recorded, *idem*, 775, 941.

101 Watt, 1965: 133-135; Gilbert, 1982, Companion Vol. V, pt. 3: 922, 983, 1331.

102 Cf. *G.M.P.* 235: 59. Original correspondence about the Focus and many international problems is with Mrs. Henny Spier in London. See also Spier, 1963. Noel-Baker's zeal is very evident in this correspondence.

Chapter 5

(pages 139-179)

The Years of Defeat 1936-1939

1 Puzzo, 1962: 94-95, commenting on Eden's speech of 14th October 1936. (See also Puzzo, 1962: chapter III.)

[2] Cf. Labour Party Advisory Committee on International Questions, Memo 473a and A.C.I.Q., Memo 480.
[3] 315 H.C. Debs, 27th and 31st July 1936, col. 1892.
[4] 311 H.C. Debs, 17th March 1936, col. 2148.
[5] The exact wording of these Covenant Articles is as follows:
Article XI: 'Any war or threat of war, whether immediately affecting any Members of the League or not is hereby declared a matter of concern to the whole League, and the League shall take any action that may be deemed wise and effectual to safeguard the peace of nations. In case any emergency should arise, the Secretary-General shall, on the request of any member of the League, forthwith summon a meeting of the Council. It is also declared to be the friendly right of each Member of the League to bring to the attention of the Assembly or of the Council any circumstance whatever affecting international relations which threatens to disturb international peace or the good understanding between nations upon which peace depends.'
Article X: 'The Members of the League undertake to respect and preserve as against external aggression the territorial integrity and existing political independence of all Members of the League. In case of any such aggression or in case of any threat or danger of such aggression, the Council shall advise upon the means by which this obligation shall be fulfilled.'
[6] N.B.K.R. 4X/119 Notes, memos from Labour Party Conference, Edinburgh, 5th-9th October 1936.
[7] Dalton, 1957, II: 100, and Naylor, 1969: 62.
[8] N.B.K.R. 4X/119. Several memos by Noel-Baker on the Paris discussions with Léon Blum and Jean Longuet of the French Socialist Party and with Pierre Cot. Undated. Probably late August 1936. See later in this chapter for an account of the International Peace Campaign.
[9] N.B.K.R. 4/656 Memo from Noel-Baker after speaking with Information Bureau, Spanish Peoples Front, London, on 1st December 1936.
[10] N.B.K.R. 4/656 Philip Noel-Baker to Louis Dolivet, 19th October 1936, describing his conversation with Winston Churchill. The comment of Churchill that Italy and Germany and the U.S.S.R. were helping Franco to the extent 'of two per cent' reads rather oddly. A more even picture of Churchill's attitudes in regard to non-intervention and neutrality over Spain may be gained from Gilbert, 1976, V, particularly chapters 39-42.
[11] Pugh, 1975: Appendix.
[12] G.M.P. 267, fol. 17-18, Gilbert Murray to Philip Noel-Baker, 3rd August 1925.
[13] See particularly these Noel-Baker memos: The British Government distinctly pro-Franco; Alleged breaches of non-intervention; The London Supervisory Committee; Labour and non-intervention; Economic sanctions against Spanish democracy, their causes and consequences; The Spanish civil war. Copies of these are in N.B.K.R. Unfortunately, most are neither signed nor dated by their author but they appear to emanate from autumn 1936. Cf. chapter by Noel-Baker in Raymond, 1960.
[14] N.B.K.R. 4/658 K. Zilliacus to Philip Noel-Baker, 25th August 1936.
[15] Quoted in Davis, 1950: 455.

[16] Labour Party Annual Report, 1936: 171.

[17] 318 H.C. Debs, 1st December 1936, col. 1071. Cf. 322 H.C. Debs, 14th April 1937, col. 1142.

[18] N.B.K.R. 4X/119 K. Zilliacus to Philip Noel-Baker, 18th January 1937.

[19] N.B.K.R. 4X/119 K. Zilliacus to Philip Noel-Baker, 21st June 1937.

[20] Labour Party Advisory Committee on International Questions, Memo 473a is referred to.

[21] Quoted in Davis, 1950: 492. A modern re-reading of this speech casts doubt on the strength of the argument advanced and on its articulation.

[22] N.B.K.R. 4X/121 K. Zilliacus to Philip Noel-Baker, 8th November 1937.

[23] N.B.K.R. 4X/121 K. Zilliacus to Philip Noel-Baker, 29th November 1937.

[24] N.B.K.R. 4X/122 P. Noel-Baker to Herbert Morrison, 31st July 1937. Cf. also N.B.K.R. 4X/118 and 4X/121.

[25] N.B.K.R. 4X/122 'Ignotus' (Hampstead) to Philip Noel-Baker, 14th July 1937.

[26] G.M.P. 225, fol. 105, Gilbert Murray to Robert Cecil, 25th June 1936. It is strange that Murray used the surname 'Baker' long after the hyphenated 'Noel-Baker' was customary.

[27] G.M.P. 231, fol. 41, Gilbert Murray to Violet Bonham-Carter, 9th January 1938.

[28] 328 H.C. Debs, 28th October 1937, cols. 287-90. Cf. 315 H.C. Debs, 31st July 1936, col. 1892.

[29] N.B.K.R. 4X/119 Memo by Noel-Baker, 18th September 1936. Regular information by way of letter and cable was coming to Noel-Baker from Wilson Steer, 'your observer in Bilbao' and actually a Special Correspondent for *The Times*. Cf. N.B.K.R. 4X/118. There is a good deal of miscellaneous first-hand information in N.B.K.R. 4/656 about Italian and German involvement in Spain. The informants are located both in Spain and in Britain.

[30] 328 H.C. Debs, 28th October 1937, cols. 286-287.

[31] 342 H.C. Debs, 21st December 1938. The Italian move for British recognition of its imperial possessions is foreshadowed in Noel-Baker's letter to *The Times*, 24th September 1937.

[32] 333 H.C. Debs, 24th March 1938, cols. 1390-1494

[33] 336 H.C. Debs, 20th May 1938, cols. 778-789.

[34] See especially the fuller statements in 333 H.C. Debs, 24th March 1938, cols. 1390-1494 and 338 H.C. Debs, 26th July 1938, cols. 2963-2964.

[35] N.B.K.R. 4X/120 H. N. Brailsford to Philip Noel-Baker, 11th April 1938.

[36] N.B.K.R. 4X/119 P. Noel-Baker to Robert Cecil. Undated, but 1938. Cecil's reply is annotated. (At the time of writing, summer 1986, a veteran Mme. Ibarurri is sometimes to be seen at Socialist rallies in Spain.)

[37] N.B.K.R. 4X/122 C. G. Grey to Philip Noel-Baker, 21st June 1938.

[38] The position is clearly discussed in Starke, 1984: 146ff and 568ff. The point that belligerent recognition did not mean a recognition of legitimacy was stressed by Anthony Eden in 1937 as Starke points out on p. 148. See also the discussion in Edwards, 1979: 119-120 and 184-88.

[39] N.B.K.R. 4X/118 An annotated copy of *The Times*, 12th July 1937. Cf. correspondence with C. R. Attlee, 25th October 1937.

[40] N.B.K.R. 4X/123 P. Noel-Baker to Wogan Phillips, Secretary, Committee of British Shipowners Trading to Spain, 11th September 1938.

[41] N.B.K.R. 4X/123 P. Noel-Baker to Chairman, Committee of British Shipowners Trading to Spain, 9th November 1938. The International Peace Campaign itself is discussed below in this chapter.

[42] N.B.K.R. 4X/118 In Noel-Baker's correspondence with Attlee (see note 39 above) the clear reluctance of Britain to intervene at sea was deplored. The First Sea Lord, indeed, had admitted that Hague Conventions would legitimise picking up 'shipwrecked' men. It was suggested that a deputation to the Prime Minister might bring about an improvement in the situation.

[43] 334 H.C. Debs, 11th April 1938, cols. 734, 736.

[44] 335 H.C. Debs, 12th May 1938, col. 1886. Cf. 334 H.C. Debs, 11th April 1938, col. 900.

[45] 336 H.C. Debs, 2nd June 1938, col. 2269.

[46] See letters to *The Times* of 21st March 1938 and 11th June 1938. N.B.K.R. 4X/119 has a telegram to Philip Noel-Baker from Spain's Foreign Minister, Alvarez del Vayo, dated 20th March 1938, appealing to him to raise in Parliament the urgent matter of 'the extermination of the civilian population of Barcelona!' Aerial warfare was 'a most abominable reality'. See discussion of civilian immunity and aerial warfare in Starke, 1979: 522-523 and Oppenheim, 1955: 417.

[47] N.B.K.R. 4X/119 memo by Noel-Baker, of 19th March 1938. Cf. N.B.K.R. 4X/5 for copies of League of Nations resolutions on Spain. Cf. N.B.K.R. 4X/5/2 for Litvinov's speech at Geneva, 13th May 1938.

[48] N.B.K.R. 4/658 J. L. Brierley to P. Noel-Baker, undated, probably early 1939. Cf. discussion in Starke, 1979: 136ff. Brierley had been Professor of International Law at Oxford since 1922. During the Abyssinian crisis he was legal adviser to the Emperor of Abyssinia.

[49] 328 H.C. Debs, 28th October 1937, col. 293. Cf. Martin, K., 1969 ed.: 110-111.

[50] N.B.K.R. 5/141 P. Noel-Baker to R. Cecil, 20th January 1938.

[51] N.B.K.R. 5/141 R. Cecil and P. Noel-Baker to Raymond Fosdick, Rockefeller Foundation, January 1938; P. Noel-Baker to R. Cecil, 18th February 1938; P. Noel-Baker to Harold Butler, 28th January 1938.

[52] N.B.K.R. 5/134/1 and N.B.K.R. 5/52/2 correspondence and memos, P. Noel-Baker, autumn 1937. N.B.K.R. 5/52/2 P. Noel-Baker to W. Gillies, 28th February 1936.

[53] N.B.K.R. 5/134/1 P. Noel-Baker to Kathleen Courtney, 4th October 1937.

[54] N.B.K.R. 5/45/2 I.P.C. Minutes of 17th March 1936. Louis Dolivet became the I.P.C.'s main organiser.

[55] N.B.K.R. 5/46/1 P. Noel-Baker memo, 5th February 1936; P. Noel-Baker to G. W. Kelling, 8th April 1936; P. Noel-Baker memo, 21st April 1936; R. Cecil to P. Noel-Baker, 26th August 1937, in N.B.K.R. 5/134/1. Cf. I.P.C. Minutes of June 1936.

[56] N.B.K.R. 5/52/4 memo from P. Noel-Baker, undated.

[57] Bisceglia, 1982: xii.

[58] N.B.K.R. 5/55 Nobody legitimately could have accused Noel-Baker of neglecting Party work. Norman Angell was always impressed by his fellow Member's diligence in this respect.

[59] N.B.K.R. 1/65 P. Noel-Baker to Mrs. M. Corbett Ashby, 4th July 1936.

[60] N.B.K.R. 5/142 P. Noel-Baker to Maxwell Garnett, 22nd January 1937.

[61] N.B.K.R. 5/142 R. Cecil to P. Noel-Baker, 29th September 1937. Cf. Minutes of I.P.C. Executive Committee for 1937.

[62] G.M.P. 227-228, P. Noel-Baker to Gilbert Murray, 25th October 1934. Cf. Noel-Baker's attitude to the L.N.U. Youth Group over which he presided some years later. 'We must by some means clear out the Communists who at present simply ruin all constructive work', he wrote to Lord Lytton, 23rd March 1940, N.B.K.R. 4/508.

[63] N.B.K.R. 2/43 and 4/505; G.M.P. 230-231. Cecil's discomfort is revealed in Cecil Papers 51132. The unhappiness occasioned by the sketch and further reflections on officials' attitudes are discussed in some detail.

[64] N.B.K.R. 4/505 G. Murray to R. Cecil, 27th December 1937, and R. Cecil to G. Murray, 30th December 1937.

[65] Cecil Papers 51107, R. Cecil to P. Noel-Baker, 16th November 1932. Cf. Thompson, 1977: 949-959.

[66] For the dissolution of the I.P.C.'s British National Committee see N.B.K.R. 4X/124 and 5/148.

[67] N.B.K.R. 2/36 P. Noel-Baker to Gerald Bailey, 23rd September 1938.

[68] N.B.K.R. 2/36 P. Noel-Baker to Gerald Bailey, 24th October 1938.

[69] Walters, 1952 ed.: 708.

[70] Rock, 1977: 47.

[71] G.M.P. 232-233, 220, particularly G. Murray to R. Cecil, 25th May 1938. Cf. Murray correspondence in Curtis Papers, MMS., fol. 227: 43, e.g. Murray to Curtis, 7th November 1936.

[72] Kennedy, 1983: 16.

[73] Gilbert, 1982, Companion Vol. V, pt. 3: 989.

[74] 333 H.C. Debs, 24th March 1938, col. 1503-1504.

[75] Quoted Wilson, 1978: 126-129, in a discussion of the early days of the Committee. In 1918 Sidney Webb had recommended Woolf to Arthur Henderson as a most useful committee man.

[76] Woolf, 1967: 156.

[77] Cf. Claude Cockburn's dismissal of 'the pacifists and the do-nothing wing of the Labour Party', *The Week*, No. 214, 27th July 1938.

[78] Naylor, 1969: 196.

[79] Donoughue and Jones, 1973: 237, 252, 511. The approval did not outlast the 1940's for Noel-Baker came to deplore the 'defeatism' of Morrison over the United Nations. Domestically, too, Noel-Baker's later opinion of Morrison slumped into disregard. Interview with Baroness Llewelyn-Davies, 27th October 1986.

[80] Cf. Pimlott, 1986: 230, 114, 142.

[81] N.B.K.R. 5/141 Harold Butler to P. Noel-Baker, 8th February 1938.

82 N.B.K.R. 5/141 P. Noel-Baker memo of 28th February 1938.
83 N.B.K.R. 4/35 P. Noel-Baker memos, February-March 1938, referring *inter alia* to British Government reluctance over Mussolini's opposition to appeals to the League of Nations. Cf. Brook-Shepherd, 1961: 199-200.
84 N.B.K.R. 4/35 memo by P. Noel-Baker, 25th January 1934. Cf. Scott, 1973: 291-292.
85 N.B.K.R. 4/35, 4/36 correspondence, particularly in April and May 1938, from Victor Matcjka of Austrian Trade Unions and from Dr. Oscar Pollak of Austrian Socialists. The latter was instrumental in opening a London Bureau on behalf of his party. The student is quoted in Noel-Baker's letter to *The Times*, 27th April 1938.
86 N.B.K.R. 4/35 memo by P. Noel-Baker apropos Drummond, 20th February 1934. Cf. Hildebrand, 1973: 60ff.
87 N.B.K.R. 4/36 P. Noel-Baker to Oscar Pollak, 14th March 1943.
88 N.B.K.R. 5/141 P. Noel-Baker to Edgar P. Young, 8th March 1938.
89 Woolf, 1967: 246-247.
90 Spier, 1963: 12. Lady Bonham-Carter describes this meeting in an introduction to Spiers' book.
91 Labour Party Annual Report, 1939: 242-243 – quotation of P. Noel-Baker.
92 Spier, 1963: 142. Cf. correspondence between Spier and Noel-Baker in July 1938. Cf. note 102 in Chapter 4 above.
93 Unfortunately, the L.N.U. archives housed in the British Library of Economic and Political Sciences at the London School of Economics have scant direct quotation of or allusion to Noel-Baker's part in committee business. His influence has to be inferred in most respects.
94 N.B.K.R. 5/141 P. Noel-Baker memo to I.P.C., undated, but presumably late 1938, unsigned.
95 Walters, 1969: 777.
96 N.B.K.R. 4/47 P. Noel-Baker to Latham, 7th March 1938.
97 N.B.K.R. 4/47 Anthony Eden to P. Noel-Baker, 2nd March 1938; J. M. Keynes to P. Noel-Baker, 23rd March 1938.
98 N.B.K.R. 4/163 Harold Nicolson to P. Noel-Baker, 21st March 1938. Noel-Baker told C. R. Attlee that Nicolson might be persuaded to join the Labour Party. P. Noel-Baker to C. R. Attlee, 16th April 1938, in N.B.K.R. 2/43.
99 Grant Duff, 1938: 669.
100 N.B.K.R. 4/163 P. Noel-Baker to Lord Noel-Buxton, 12th July 1938.
101 333 H.C. Debs, 24th March 1938, col. 1506, and again in 337 H.C. Debs, 20th July 1938, cols. 2176-2177, and 335 H.C. Debs, 26th May 1938.
102 N.B.K.R. 4/135 P. Noel-Baker memo of 21st May 1938. Cf. letter from Szullo to *The Times*, 21st May 1938, and P. Noel-Baker's reply of 24th May 1938.
103 The distinction appears, for instance, in N.B.K.R. 4/167 in a memo from Noel-Baker after a visit to Prague. It was to emerge again in the declaration of Noel-Baker and others after the 1939-45 war broke out. Cf. N.B.K.R. 4/293. See N.B.K.R. 4/135 memo of conversations in Prague with Wenzel Jaksch, 13th/14th September 1938; Wenzel Jaksch to P. Noel-Baker, 22nd September 1938.

104 N.B.K.R. 4/166 P. Noel-Baker to Alexander Cadogan, 28th October 1938, and to Sir Samuel Hoare, 13th December 1938.

105 Walters, 1969: 776.

106 Davis, 1950: 695ff. N.B.K.R. 4/135 has a memo by P. Noel-Baker detailing concerns voiced by the United States League of Nations Association.

107 N.B.K.R. 4/135 has a memo by Seton-Watson, annotated by Noel-Baker and dated 26th September 1938. N.B.K.R. 4/35 has correspondence with Jaksch, 25th February 1939, and in the same month two parliamentary questions from Noel-Baker, dated 20th February 1939, and 6th February 1939. See also memo presumably by Noel-Baker, undated, but about 21st September 1939.

108 N.B.K.R. 4/35 Wenzel Jaksch to P. Noel-Baker, 21st September 1938. Jaksch intended to send the MS. of a book about the Czech crisis to an English publisher.

109 N.B.K.R. 4/163 P. Noel-Baker to Edvard Benes, 21st September 1938.

110 N.B.K.R. 4/163 J. B. Kozak to P. Noel-Baker, undated, but probably October 1938.

111 N.B.K.R. 4/163 P. Noel-Baker to J. B. Kozak, 10th October 1938.

112 N.B.K.R. 4/163 P. Noel-Baker to Wenzel Jaksch and Edvard Benes, 7th October 1938.

113 Cf. N.B.K.R. 4/35 J. B. Kozak to P. Noel-Baker, 23rd September 1938; P. Noel-Baker to J. B. Kozak, 23rd September 1938; N.B.K.R. 4/163 J. B. Kozak to P. Noel-Baker, 2nd October 1938. See discussion in P. Noel-Baker to R. W. Seton-Watson, 29th September 1938. See also Walters, 1969: 775-777. Germany's claim for restoration of her former colonies is dealt with in the Labour Party pamphlet *Common Sense about Colonies,* compiled by Noel-Baker in 1939. These territories should not be handed back to an unacceptable Nazi administration. The mandate system must be extended. Britain could promote 'a new vision of what colonial trusteeship in our generation could mean'. (p. 14) Cf. also 342 H. C. Debs, 7th December 1938, cols. 1199-1209.

114 342 H.C. Debs, 30th November 1938, col. 385; 342 H.C. Debs, 12th December 1938, cols. 1586-1587; 342 H.C. Debs, 21st December 1938, cols. 2852-2853.

115 There is a useful discussion of the distinction in Starke, 1984 ed.: 136-141.

116 N.B.K.R. 4/173 P. Noel-Baker memo 'The proposed recognition by His Majesty's Government of the German annexation of Czechoslovakia'. Rather unevenly argued. Undated, probably March 1939.

117 Citrine, 1967: 20.

118 Cf. Addison, 1975: 70.

119 Interviews with Hon. Francis Noel-Baker, September 1985 and 1987.

120 Gallagher, 1947: 199.

121 Attlee, 1954: 111.

122 Pritt, 1966: 209.

123 Rolph, 1973: 240-241. Virginia Woolf did not hesitate to deplore the defeatism of Martin and his associates. Cf. Bell, 1982, IV: 237-238, and V: 305. There is derision in her opinions.

[124] Cf. Walters, 1969: Pts. IV and V, for a very clear discussion of how the League of Nations handled the crises.
[125] Carr, 1974 ed.: 223.

Chapter 6

(pages 180-213)

Noel-Baker in the Ministries 1942-1951

[1] N.B.K.R. 9/76 C. R. Attlee to P. Noel-Baker, 19th May 1940.
[2] 'Watchman', 1939: 197.
[3] Entry in Hugh Dalton's diary quoted Addison, 1975: 113.
[4] Pimlott, 1986: 156.
[5] N.B.K.R. 9/76 R. Cecil to P. Noel-Baker, 5th August 1941.
[6] Cf. Cecil Papers 51109, fol. 76-79, memo from P. Noel-Baker (but unsigned) to H. Dalton, cc. to R. Cecil, 7th October 1941.
[7] *Labour Party Annual Report*, 1944: 236ff. Cf. Dalton, 1940: 131-132. There is an interesting discussion of Labour's changing view of pacifism in Ceadel, 1980. See also Chapter 4 above.
[8] N.B.K.R. 8/714 Noel-Baker broadcast to the United States, 4th August 1942. (Noel-Baker's involvement in thinking out the lines of a reborn international organisation to take the place of the League is examined in Chapter 7 below.)
[9] Pimlott, 1985: 356.
[10] Pimlott, 1985: 363.
[11] Pimlott, 1986: 360. Strangely, the entry in Dalton's diary recording acceptance is dated Wednesday, 4th February 1941, yet Noel-Baker was not appointed to this Parliamentary Secretaryship until one year later on 4th February 1942. He held the post until 23rd May 1945 (when a Caretaker Government succeeded the Coalition).
[12] Cf. Howard, 1979, IV: 636 et seq.
[13] The aide then was Miss Pat (later Baroness) Llewelyn-Davies. The description is that of Mr. Kenneth East, later Private Secretary to Noel-Baker at the C.R.O.
[14] Behrens, 1955: 441.
[15] Behrens, 1955: 442.
[16] Cf. Court, 1955: 161.
[17] Cf. Hancock & Gowing, 1949; Savage, 1957. N.B.K.R. 8/71/4 has a ministerial broadcast by Noel-Baker which shows his constant concern for all those who worked in the transport industry, the 'unknown soldiers'.
[18] Eventually, losses were assessed at about 11,500,000 tons gross weight. (This compares with 7,750,000 tons in the First World War.) Cf. Churchill, VI, 624n.
[19] 391 H.C. Debs, cols. 258-276, 14th July 1943. Few authorities at this time appear to have foreseen that maritime circumstances would change dramatically and irreversibly within a decade or so. Ernest Shinwell, though, cast doubt on the Minister's 'generalisations'.
[20] Cf. the account of this time in Chapter 7 below.

[21] Noel-Baker was, in fact, already highly informed about military matters. During the war he had got on well with senior members of the Services and he had not hesitated to join them in discussions of strategy. He was particularly keen to promote schemes for strategic bombing of Rumanian oilfields such as those at Ploesti in 1943-44. Interview with Baroness Llewelyn-Davies, 27th October 1986.

[22] Baroness Llewelyn-Davies, personal communication.

[23] K.Y.D. Cf. 435 H.C. Debs, cols. 39-48, 17th March 1947.

[24] 437 H.C. Debs, cols. 1483-1484, 14th May 1947.

[25] K.Y.D. The U.K. Government has had a permanent representative at the U.N. in New York since 1946. In addition, a Minister of State at the Foreign Office has usually been given special responsibility for U.N. affairs, as Noel-Baker was in 1945-46, though never again was he given a post of this nature apart from a brief stand-in when he was Secretary of State for Air in late 1946. From 1964 to 1970 the permanent representative was a Minister of State at the Foreign Office.

[26] K.Y.D. Tito warmed towards Noel-Baker when it was discovered that Tito, as a First World War prisoner of war, had been helped by the Nansen and Noel-Baker relief operation in the Balkans. Interview with Francis Noel-Baker, September 1987.

[27] K.Y.D.

[28] K.Y.D.

[29] Cecil Papers 51109, fol. 192, Noel-Baker notes, 1st June 1947. Cf. N.B.K.R. 4/745 Foreign Office telegrams asking Noel-Baker whether he would stay on as a member of the U.K. Delegation. Ministers of State at the Foreign Office responsible for U.N. affairs were these: P. Noel-Baker from 3rd August 1945, Hector McNeil from 4th October 1946, Kenneth Younger from 28th February 1950 (until 30th October 1951, when the Conservative Government appointed Selwyn Lloyd).

[30] K.Y.D. In fact, McNeil was Parliamentary Under-Secretary of State at the Foreign Office in 1945, working alongside Noel-Baker, and was not subordinate to him.

[31] K.Y.D.

[32] K.Y.D.

[33] K.Y.D.

[34] Cross, 1967: 59, and Cross, 1969: 114. Between 1947 and 1966 the Colonial Office exercised clearly separate functions from the C.R.O., the former being responsible for most of the former colonies mentioned earlier.

[35] Cf. Beloff, 1969: 145ff; Maitland, 1957; Harvey, 1952, for discussion of this issue.

[36] Beloff, 1969: 193. As a Minister Noel-Baker did not himself attend the U.N. but sent delegates and attachés. His participation in the Kashmir debates was an exception.

[37] Garner, 1978: 276.

[38] Gupta, 1975: 99-102.

[39] Morgan, 1984: 231, believes that the broader issues of the 'less-developed world did not have a grass-roots following before the mid-1950's.'

[40] Garner, 1978: 281-282.

[41] Pelling, 1984: 159-160.

[42] Garner, 1978: 292.

[43] Interviews with Baroness Llewelyn-Davies, 27th October 1986, with Mr. Kenneth East, 5th November 1986. Stuart, 1985: 369, 365, records that Lord Reith had been meeting with Liesching, an 'unusual civil servant' and suggests, perhaps in the light of this conversation, that Liesching was not satisfied with Noel-Baker's keeping him informed about 'all-important developments in Commonwealth relations'. Reith was Chairman of the Commonwealth Communications Council and a notoriously demanding person to work with.

[44] Interview with Baroness Llewelyn-Davies, 27th October. The proposal of Mountbatten was for an independence 'D-day' of 15th August 1947. Cf. Ziegler, 1985: 388.

[45] Ziegler, 1985: 441.

[46] Ziegler, 1985: 450. Perhaps if Noel-Baker had been made aware of this rather unspecific allegation he would have retorted that Martin's defeatist attitudes towards the Czechs in 1938, and over a separate peace in 1940 (see Chapter 5 above) did not reveal much strength of purpose in his critic!

[47] Ziegler, 1985: 450. Gordon Walker succeeded to the C.R.O. on 28th February 1950, and Lord Ismay followed on 28th October 1951, with the re-election of the Conservatives.

[48] Garner, 1978: 324. There is a brief reference to the Delegation's work in Ismay, 1960: 447-448. Sir Alexander Cadogan was permanent head of the U.K. Delegation. Noel-Baker was a visiting Minister. Bajpai was responsible for India's Department of External Affairs.

[49] Cf. Attlee Papers, 68, 169-172, P. Noel-Baker to C. R. Attlee, ? March 1948 (undated).

[50] 466 H.C. Debs, col. 184, 7th July 1949. See Mansergh, 1982, II: 145ff, for a useful discussion of the Kashmir dispute.

[51] Gordon Walker, 1970: 150-151.

[52] Pelling, 1984: 161-162. The raiding of Kashmir by Pathans is referred to in Ziegler, 1985: 445-448.

[53] Attlee Papers, 73, 163, C. R. Attlee to P. Noel-Baker, minute of 8th September 1948, and P. Noel-Baker to C. R. Attlee, 14th September 1948.

[54] Noel-Baker, P., 1948. The Olympic Games in retrospect, *World Sports,* for British Olympic Association.

[55] Morrison, 1960: 263.

[56] Enquiries in 1985 of the Air History Branch, Ministry of Defence, and of Mr. John Tusa who has compiled an account of the Airlift reveal no recorded link with Noel-Baker. Cf. Bullock, 1983: 577, who identifies a Service origin elsewhere.

[57] Pound, 1976: 216.

[58] Garner, 1978: 258, writes 'There was the minimum of collusion with the Canadians.'
[59] Herbert, 1950: 447-449. Cf. 462 H.C. Debs, cols. 371-381, 395, 2nd March 1949.
[60] Cf. Pelling, 1984: 255.
[61] Cf. 472 H.C. Debs, 8th March 1950; White Paper of 22nd March 1950; C.R.O. Report 'Bechuanaland Protectorate: Succession to the Chieftainship of the Bamangwato Tribe', Parl. Papers, 1950, xix, 5ff. See also Benson, 1960: passim.
[62] 172 H.C. Debs, col. 407, 27th June 1951. Cf. debate, cols. 380-446. Cf. 483 H.C. Debs, 26th January 1951; 491 H.C. Debs, 31st July 1951. See also Garner, 1978: 334-335.
[63] Cf. Bullock, 1983: 681.
[64] Garner, 178: 332.
[65] Pelling, 1984: 144.
[66] Attlee Papers, 81: 300.
[67] Attlee Papers, 92: 289.
[68] Cf. articles in *Queens Journal*, vol. 77, 1949, no. 12, 1 and *The Queens Review*, vol. 23, November 1949, no. 8, 237-238. (Both publ. Queens University, Ontario.)
[69] Quoted in Pelling, 1984: 232. At this time Prof. Pigou began to write frequent letters, half-humerously airing grievances, to 'My dear Fuel and Power'.
[70] K.Y.D.
[71] Dalton, 1962: 347-348; Pelling, 1984: 235ff; Morgan, 1984: 99ff. In regard to the delay in vesting, the House of Lords insisted that the vesting date had to be after another election, viz. that of February 1950.
[72] Cf. 476 H.C. Debs, col. 1907ff, 26th and 27th June 1950; 476 H.C. Debs, col. 3613, 13th June 1950.
[73] Labour Party Conference Annual Report, 1950.
[74] Labour Party pamphlet 'Coal' (Noel-Baker, P.), September 1950. Cf. 477 H.C. Debs, cols. 1557-1570, 13th July 1950.
[75] 482 H.C. Debs, cols. 205-206, 5th December 1950; 482 H.C. Debs, cols. 1004-1019, 12th December 1950.
[76] 483 H.C. Debs, cols. 1092-1116, 1st February 1951.
[77] The Derby remarks are to be found in Attlee Papers, 94: 164, in a memo from P. Noel-Baker to C. R. Attlee, ? October (undated). The happenings in 1944 and 1947 are referred to respectively in Miliband, 1972: 278, and Morgan, 1984: 68.
[78] P.R.E.M. 8/1275 P. Noel-Baker to C. R. Attlee, 3rd August 1950. Citrine had been something of a bugbear to Communist party members for 20 years. Cf. Macfarlane, 1965: 243-244; Gallacher, 1947: passim.
[79] Morgan, 1984: 465-466, 471. The caution of Noel-Baker is clear in C.A.B. 128/20, of 2nd July 1951.
[80] K.Y.D.
[81] The words are those of Mr. Kenneth East, a former colleague at the C.R.O. They are ingrained in so much of what Noel-Baker said and wrote.

[82] *The Guardian*, obituary of October 1982.

[83] Miss Helen Armstrong, personal communication, 1985. Cf. Wilson, 1971: 11. Cf. Noel-Baker, Francis, 1987: 196-197, and Carlton, David, 1965: 23-24.

Chapter 7

(pages 214-249)

In at the Creation of the U.N.

[1] N.B.K.R. 4/500 P. Noel-Baker memo, 23rd May 1939.

[2] N.B.K.R. 4/507 P. Noel-Baker memo, December 1939. Noel-Baker does not pursue further the distinction between what might be termed 'authoritative publicity' and 'didactic propaganda'. Today's U.N. has departments specially responsible for promulgating the proceedings of conferences and commissions, and for publishing a wide range of information materials to educate the public.

[3] In February 1942 Noel-Baker was appointed Parliamentary Secretary to the Minister of War Transport, Lord Leathers, and he served in that capacity for three years. See Chapter 6 above.

[4] Details are to be found in N.B.K.R. 4/500.

[5] The point about the Foreign Office comes from correspondence with Lord Gladwyn, January 1987.

[6] There are indications in N.B.K.R. 4/500 that Cecil would not have gone as far as his colleague in defining institutional parallels between national and international law.

[7] N.B.K.R. 4/500 P. Noel-Baker to Harold Butler, 24th August 1942. There are also notes which describe the progress of these discussions.

[8] N.B.K.R. 4/500 P. Noel-Baker to William Malkin, February 1944.

[9] 'How to define aggression has defeated the best legal minds since at least 1919!', Lord Gladwyn in correspondence, January 1987.

[10] N.B.K.R. 4X/III A. D. Lindsay to Irene Noel-Baker, March 1941.

[11] N.B.K.R. 4X/III P. Noel-Baker notes for memo 'What Kind of a League', n.d., but clearly the beginning of 1941.

[12] N.B.K.R. 4/512 P. Noel-Baker to Alan Baker, 11th October 1940.

[13] Barros, 1979: 397.

[14] N.B.K.R. 4/719 F. P. Walters to P. Noel-Baker, 31st May 1945; P. Noel-Baker to F. P. Walters, 8th June 1945.

[15] Hazard, 1973, is an example of a marked criticism which has little in the way of constructive suggestion. The work of successive Secretary-Generals receives close attention.

[16] Dalton, 1962, iii: 104.

[17] N.B.K.R. 4X/26 Noel-Baker memo, undated, ? 1919.

[18] Motta, November 1920 and September 1921, quoted in Larus, 1965: 51.

[19] N.B.K.R. 9/89 P. Noel-Baker to R. Cecil, 4th September 1943. Cf. Angell, 1921, xxxiii: 186.

[20] Pratt, 1964: 524-531, 775. N.B.K.R. 8/71/4 has a wartime broadcast of Noel-Baker to Poland where he looks forward from the Atlantic Charter to a new world organisation.
[21] Roosevelt, 1970, II: 1306. Cf. Goodwin, 1957: passim.
[22] N.B.K.R. 4/719 notes of conversation between Smuts, Cecil and Noel-Baker at Hyde Park Hotel, 4th November 1942.
[23] Pratt, 1964: 734-735; Rauch, 1957: 383.
[24] Elmandjra, 1973: 326-327, quotes the statement of Hammarskjöld on this point in 1961.
[25] Clark and Bindoff, 1962: passim. Cf. Webster, 1946 and Morgenthau, 1954.
[26] N.B.K.R. 4/719 P. Noel-Baker memo, 8th March 1943; Lord Gladwyn in correspondence, January 1987.
[27] Cf. Reynolds, 1974: 144; Reynolds and Hughes, 1976: 108.
[28] Barclay, 1975: 78.
[29] N.B.K.R. 9/89 P. Noel-Baker to R. Cecil, 27th July 1945. Bevin was appointed 27th July 1945, and Noel-Baker 3rd August 1945.
[30] Cecil Papers 51109, fol. 163, P. Noel-Baker to R. Cecil, 11th August 1945.
[31] N.B.K.R. 9/58/2 P.Noel-Baker to A. Pigou, 15th August 1945. Attlee's first Cabinet in 1945 had 20 members. The Privy Councillorship came in 1945.
[32] K.Y.D.
[33] K.Y.D.
[34] K.Y.D.
[35] K.Y.D.
[36] K.Y.D.
[37] K.Y.D.
[38] K.Y.D.
[39] See *Commentary on the Report of the Preparatory Commission of the United Nations*, 1946: passim.
[40] Cf. the discussion in Larus, 1965: 205ff; Goodrich, 1947: 3-21.
[41] N.B.K.R. 4/517 Noel-Baker's address to the Preparatory Commission Joint Sub-committee of Committees 2 and 3, 23rd January 1946.
[42] N.B.K.R. 4/517 P. Noel-Baker to Preparatory Commission Committee 8, 15th December 1945; N.B.K.R. 4/719 P. Noel-Baker to same Committee, 18th December 1945.
[43] Campbell and Herring, 1975: 409.
[44] N.B.K.R. 4/719 P. Noel-Baker to Hugh Dalton, 18th December 1945.
[45] Campbell and Herring, 1975: 424.
[46] Campbell and Herring, 1975: 78.
[47] Reynolds and Hughes, 1976: 81.
[48] Campbell and Herring, 1975: 433. Speculation still surrounds the reasons for the Soviet choice.
[49] N.B.K.R. 7/739 U.K. delegation to U.N., telegram to Foreign Office, 6th November 1946.
[50] Campbell and Herring, 1975: 420.
[51] Gladwyn, 1972: 177.

[52] N.B.K.R. 4/727 memo of interview between Attlee, Cecil, and Noel-Baker, 9th March 1948.

[53] N.B.K.R. 4/737 Noel-Baker's speech to U.N. General Assembly, 26th October 1946.

[54] 419 H.C. Debs, col. 1262, 20th February 1946; 416 H.C. Debs, cols. 785-786, 23rd November 1945. Cf. Noel-Baker in 418 H.C. Debs, cols. 630-631, 28th January 1946.

[55] Goodwin, 1957: 426.

[56] N.B.K.R. 4/745 notes by Noel-Baker for speech in U.N. Security Council, 17th November 1946.

[57] N.B.K.R. 4/728 notes by Noel-Baker for speech at Albert Hall, London, 3rd January 1946.

[58] Goodrich, 1960: 76ff.

[59] 413 H.C. Debs, col. 665, 22nd August 1945.

[60] Cf. discussion in Lee, 1947: 33-42; Zimmern, 1936: 271.

[61] Nicolson, 1954: 91. Cf. discussion in Goodwin, 1957: 439, and 1947: 3-21.

[62] Cf. *Commentary on the Report of the Preparatory Commission of the United Nations*, 1946: 39; N.B.K.R. 4/500 P. Noel-Baker to Henri Rolin, 12th March 1943; N.B.K.R. 4/500 P. Noel-Baker to F. P. Walters, 18th May 1942; N.B.K.R. 4/719 P. Noel-Baker to S. King-Hall, 6th March 1946.

[63] Cf. discussion in Goodrich and Hambro, 1949: 73, 120ff.

[64] Quoted in Goodwin, 1957.

[65] N.B.K.R. 4/719 P. Noel-Baker to Air Marshal D. C. Bennett, 17th October 1944; N.B.K.R. 4/728 Liddell Hart to Noel-Baker, 21st November 1945. Cf. N.B.K.R. 4/719 for speech by Noel-Baker to U.N.A. at Albert Hall, London, 10th October 1945. On that occasion the platform included the Prime Minister, Eden, Cecil, Stettinius, the Earl of Lytton, and Megan Lloyd-George.

[66] L.N.U. General Council, Minutes Pt. 1, vol. II, 1943. Held in London.

[67] L.N.U. Papers, memo of interview with Foreign Secretary, 13th January 1944.

[68] Cf. Murray, 1948: 150-151; Goodrich, 1960: 17; Lee, 1947: 33-42; Boyd, 1971: 88ff. Noel-Baker, almost certainly, never accepted the veto as a 'harsh reality'.

[69] Cf. the assertion of Andrei Vishinsky of the U.S.S.R. in the U.N. General Assembly's Political Committee, 10th October 1950: 'Arithmetic is arithmetic. But no arithmetic can solve questions pertaining to matters very far removed from arithmetical problems.' Cf. Emerson and Claude, 1952: 7; N.B.K.R. 4/731 Noel-Baker memo, 15th November 1946.

[70] Smuts, addressing the Canadian press in Ottawa put in these terms: 'The San Fransisco Conference is a framework of peace in a boiling cauldron . . . the world will be alive with danger . . . Do not ask me who is the enemy. I do not know. It may be ourselves.' Quoted in Goodrich, 1960: 160.

[71] Walters, 1969: 814.

[72] Cecil Papers 51109, fol. 192, P. Noel-Baker to R. Cecil, 13th March 1946; L.N.U. Executive Committee Minutes, October 1944, quoting Churchill to Cecil, 14th September 1944. An often-quoted assertion though, strangely, the last sentence is usually left out.

[73] Quoted Scott, 1973: 403-404. Cf. Noel-Baker N.B.K.R. 4/157 for speech notes.

[74] Labour Party Conference Report, 1946: 212. Cf. Bullock, 1983: 198.

[75] N.B.K.R. 4X/126 has press clippings and photographs covering the inauguration of January 1946. The optimism and resolve of Noel-Baker and of his colleagues comes through in his election broadcast of 16th June 1945. See N.B.K.R. 8/71/4 and N.B.K.R. 4/731, *The Spectator*, 4th January 1946.

[76] N.B.K.R. 4/719 Noel-Baker's remarks in Preparatory Commission Committee 1, 5th February 1946. Seven months later the U.K. Delegation sent a telegram to the Foreign Office deploring the number of 'disingenuous organisations' pressing the U.N. for membership. Cf. N.B.K.R. 4/756 telegram of 17th September 1946. See also N.B.K.R. 4/735 Noel-Baker memo, 17th September 1946.

[77] Particularly since 1985 there is much public speculation and controversy about the interventionist role of British forces in Greece at the time of the war's end in Europe.

[78] Vandenberg report to U.S. Senate, 27th February 1946 (in the form of a letter to President Truman), *Keesings Contemporary Archives*, vol. VI, 46-48: 7827.

[79] N.B.K.R. 4/757 Noel-Baker telegram to Foreign Office, 15th October 1946. Cf. N.B.K.R. 4/731 for instructions to U.K. Delegation and the make-up of the advisory team.

[80] Gladwyn, 1972: 194. See also interesting references to the work of the U.K. Delegation in N.B.K.R. 4/745 Noel-Baker memo, re Bevin and the General Assembly, 21st November 1946, and Noel-Baker to Foreign Office, 22nd November 1946; N.B.K.R. 4/738 Noel-Baker telegram to Foreign Office, 30th October 1946; N.B.K.R. 4/736 Noel-Baker telegram to Foreign Office, 23rd October 1946.

[81] Northedge, 1974: 64.

[82] Cf. Bullock, 1983; 83ff: Northedge, 1974: 36; Morgan, 1984: 64, 73. R. A. Butler, in Parliament, voiced his appreciation of a 'diamond lying on a vast heap of coke', a tribute to Bevin quoted in Bullock, 1983: 197-198.

[83] Evans, 1972: 347, 358.

[84] K.Y.D.

[85] 417 H.C. Debs, col. 23, 23rd November 1945.

[86] K.Y.D.

[87] K.Y.D.

[88] N.B.K.R. 4/731 Noel-Baker's footnotes to U.K. Delegation account of General Assembly proceedings of 30th October 1946, dated 6th November 1946.

[89] N.B.K.R. 4/735 Noel-Baker telegram to Secretary of State, 18th September 1946.

[90] K.Y.D.

[91] N.B.K.R. 4/746 clippings with photograph from *World Report*, 19th November 1946, (weekly magazine on international affairs).

[92] Cf. Attlee, 1954: 170.

[93] Bullock, 1983: 74.

[94] K.Y.D. Again, in 1945, Noel-Baker was to be 'distanced' from a leading governmental role at the U.N. See Chapter 6 for reference to this.

[95] Cf. Elmondjra, 1973: 325, 329. Interview with Lord Brockway, November 1984. Cf. *Report of L.N.U. Special Committee on the Future of the U.N.*, IV, 30th November 1944.

[96] N.B.K.R. 4/762 Noel-Baker's notes for speech to Press Association in New York, summer (?) 1946.

[97] N.B.K.R. 4/759 transcript of a Noel-Baker B.B.C. broadcast in 1946.

[98] Nakabayashi (Japan) and P. Noel-Baker interview, 13th June 1982. Transcript in possession D. J. Whittaker.

[99] Luard, 1979: 21.

Chapter 8 *(pages 250-265)*

Magnum Opus: The Arms Race 1958

[1] White, Frieda, review in *International Affairs*, vol. 16, 1937, 981.

[2] Obituary in *The Times*, 9th October 1982; Sims, 1982.

[3] Since 1958 strategies such as M.A.D., the Domino Theory, the Air-Land Model have become increasingly mechanised and ambitious.

[4] Noel-Baker, 1958: 142.

[5] Attlee's appeal took this form: 'Not one of these weapons has any legitimate place in the armaments which are necessary for ordinary purposes of internal security, or for the protection of a government against lawlessness . . . They are weapons of total war designed for mass destruction, and we must banish war from the world if civilisation is to continue.' Cf. 417 H.C. Debs, col. 608, 22nd November 1945.

[6] Ironically, the insistence of the U.S.S.R. that prohibition and destruction of atomic weapons precede the implementation of a control scheme struck most other nations as unacceptable. The issue was one not so much of sovereignty as of timing and procedure.

[7] Noel-Baker, 1958: 201.

[8] Noel-Baker, 1958: 213.

[9] In the earlier days of the League, Noel-Baker and Robert Cecil dismissed the notion of itinerant inspectors. They favoured a permanent commission which would examine all published information and report once or twice a year to the League Council. Cf. R. Cecil in *International Affairs*, vol. 8, 1929: 550. A similar position is taken by Noel-Baker in 1958.

[10] When Noel-Baker mentions the Pacific intentions of Presidents like Wilson, Hoover, Coolidge, Eisenhower, he rarely alludes to the countervailing influence of lobbies on Capitol Hill and their 'mirror images' in the press.

[11] Noel-Baker, 1958: 292.

[12] Noel-Baker, 1958: 250.

[13] Noel-Baker, 1958: 312.

[14] Cf. the case put forward in Noel-Baker, 1979: passim.

[15] Goodwin, 1957: 184.

[16] Noel-Baker, 1958: chapters 38-40.

[17] Noel-Baker, 1958: 498ff.

[18] Noel-Baker, 1958: 543.

[19] Greenwood, Anthony, 1958, 'A warning of the wilderness', *Daily Herald*, 8th June 1958.

[20] Cf. *The Times*, 9th June 1958; the *Manchester Guardian* leader, 9th June 1958.

[21] *The Times Literary Supplement*, 4th July 1958. The reviewer on p. 371 must have had in mind the proposals of Presidents Coolidge and Hoover in the 1920's and 1930's.

[22] Leonard Woolf, *The Political Quarterly*, October-December 1958.

[23] Thomas, Hugh, *New Statesman*, 21st June 1958, 812.

[24] N.B.K.R. 7/44/2 P. Noel-Baker to Moira-, n.d., probably early 1957.

[25] N.B.K.R. 7/44/1 extracts from extra material assembled for a possible further edition of *The Arms Race* in 1977.

[26] Dr. Don Anthony, personal communication.

[27] Nigel Nicolson M.P., in *New World*, September 1953. Cf. other reviews, e.g. *The Sunday Times*, 15th June 1958; the *Manchester Guardian*, 9th June 1958; *Law Library Journal*, vol. 52; *The Nation*, 13th September 1958; *Forward*, 27th June 1958; *The Liberal Forward*, January 1959; *World Affairs* (C. R. Attlee), autumn 1958.

[28] Cf. Sonnenberg pamphlet, 24th August 1961; *Das Politische Buch*, 10/11th May 1962; *Stimme*, 23, 1st December 1961.

[29] Cf. *Fellowship*, (Fellowship of Reconciliation, U.S.A.), 1st May 1959; *Labour's Voice* (Frank Allaun), July 1958.

[30] *Universities and Left Review*, summer 1958; *The New Republic*, (U.S.A.), 1st September 1958.

[31] Goodwin, 1958, 'The Arms Race by Philip Noel-Baker', *International Relations*, vol. 1, 10th October 1958.

[32] Haddow, Alexander, 1958, 'Science and Disarmament', *The New Scientist*, 18th September 1958, 844-846.

[33] N.B.K.R. 9/13 P. Noel-Baker to Gerald Bailey, 11th November 1957. Bailey was Secretary of the American Friends Service Committee in New York.

[34] A reviewer of *The Arms Race* in *The Economist*, 14th June 1958, under the heading 'All or Nothing', puts Noel-Baker in an uncompromising position of 'bold opposition to all the champions of <gradual> disengagement . . .'

[35] The call is expressed by Haddow (cf. note 32 above).

[36] From an obituary in *The Times*, 9th October 1982. In 1959 the Nobel Prize was worth about £15,300. The Nobel gold medal was given to his old school, Bootham in York. Noel-Baker was not entirely pleased at the way his donation to the U.N.A. in London was used. Francis Noel-Baker, interview, 25th September 1987.

[37] *Nobel Peace Prize 1959, Report of Proceedings*, Oslo, 1959. Jahn referred to a visit to Moscow in 1958 by Philip Noel-Baker and his son, Francis. They had had an intensive discussion for 3½ hours with Soviet leaders, Khruschev and Mikoyan, and had come away convinced of their hosts' earnestness about disarmament. Cf. Noel-Baker, Francis, 1987.

[38] Transcript of Noel-Baker's Nobel Lecture given in Oslo, 11th December 1959, in possession D. J. Whittaker. (There is a reference to President Truman's 'Six Principles'.)

Chapter 9 *(pages 266-280)*

Noel-Baker and Greece

[1] N.B.K.R. 8/71/4 transcript of Noel-Baker broadcast, 30th October 1940.
[2] N.B.K.R. 8/71/4 transcript of Noel-Baker broadcast, 6th December 1940.
[3] See Note 1.
[4] Noel-Baker, Francis, 1985: 4.
[5] N.B.K.R. 8/71/4 transcript of Noel-Baker broadcast, 24th August 1945; notes on Noel-Baker's attendance at U.N.R.R.A. Council meetings, London, 1943.
[6] Noel-Baker, Francis, 1985: 4-5.
[7] N.B.K.R. 4/342 Noel-Baker, P., memo to Foreign Office, 29th November 1944.
[8] N.B.K.R. 4/342 Edward Grigg to Philip Noel-Baker, 2nd February 1945; Philip Noel-Baker to Edward Grigg, 19th February 1945; telegram from Athens Embassy to Foreign Office, 29th January 1945.
[9] Pimlott, 1986: 800.
[10] Pimlott, 1986: 826, 842.
[11] N.B.K.R. 4/342 fragments of diary by Irene Noel-Baker, 12th February to 2nd March 1945.
[12] See Note 11.
[13] See Note 11.
[14] N.B.K.R. 4/342 Irene Noel-Baker to Philip Noel-Baker, 2nd March 1945.
[15] N.B.K.R. 4/342 Irene Noel-Baker to Philip Noel-Baker, 7th March 1945.
[16] N.B.K.R. 4/342 Philip Noel-Baker to Francis Noel-Baker, 24th February 1945.
[17] N.B.K.R. 4/342 Philip Noel-Baker to Irene Noel-Baker, 14th March 1945.
[18] Macmillan, 1984: 732.
[19] N.B.K.R. 4/342 Cf. Philip Noel-Baker to Orme Sargent, 17th April 1945 and later letter, Philip Noel-Baker to Irene Noel-Baker, 2nd June 1945.
[20] N.B.K.R. 10/4/2 Philip Noel-Baker to Charles Peake, 22nd April 1954; Charles Peake to Philip Noel-Baker, 3rd June 1954.
[21] N.B.K.R. 10/14/2 fragments of diary by Philip Noel-Baker, April-June 1956, entry for 6th June 1956.
[22] See Note 21.
[23] See Note 21.
[24] Noel-Baker, Francis, 1985: 6-7.
[25] Noel-Baker, Francis, 1987: chapter 17, passim. Cf. *Sunday Times* article, 'Last of the English Milords', 15th June 1984.

Chapter 10 *(pages 281-304)*

Disarmament: The Latter-day Stance

[1] Morgan, 1984: 496ff.
[2] Crossman, 1981: 389-390.

[3] Pimlott, 1986: 605.
[4] N.B.K.R. 2X/6 the quotation is from an address to the Labour Party Conference, Scarborough 1954; the further point is in N.B.K.R. 2/124 P. Noel-Baker to Terence Heelas (Labour Party candidate, Totnes, 1959), 17th October 1960.
[5] N.B.K.R. 2/104 These remarks were made during an address to the Labour Party Conference, Scarborough, 1954.
[6] N.B.K.R. 2/116 clipping from *The Manchester Guardian,* 31st March 1955. Cf. Williams, 1979: 455; McDermott, 1972: 136.
[7] Foot, 1962: 465, 555.
[8] N.B.K.R. 2/119 Noel-Baker firmly told a Labour Party Sub-committee in July 1957, that they must face up to the imbalance and realise that mutual arms reductions would be seen as in the interests of both major power blocs.
[9] Williams, 1979: 455. McDermott, 1972, records that Gaitskell thanked Noel-Baker, Denis Healey, and Kenneth Younger for their help in preparing his Godkin Lectures delivered at Harvard in 1957. Five years later, in March 1960, Noel-Baker launched a disarmament drive at the Annual Council of the U.N.A. which took much the same shape. He saw an effective U.N. system of inspection and control as necessary and possible. The Chairman, Gen. Sir Ronald Adam, added that the drive was possible largely because the speaker had donated his Nobel Prize money to the Association.
[10] N.B.K.R. 2X/6 Report of Labour Party Conference, Scarborough, 1958.
[11] N.B.K.R. 2/116 This is an extract from a House of Commons speech by Noel-Baker reported in *The Manchester Guardian,* 7th March 1955.
[12] N.B.K.R. 2/116 Remarks by Noel-Baker at a Derby Labour Party meeting, 27th March 1955.
[13] N.B.K.R. 2/124 P. Noel-Baker to H. Gaitskell, 21st October 1960; P. Noel-Baker to David Ennals, 17th October 1960.
[14] Brennan, 1961: 456.
[15] N.B.K.R. 2/123 Leaders, articles, correspondence in *Daily Herald, The Manchester Guardian,* both June 1959; P. Noel-Baker to Frank Beswick (Secretary, London Cooperative Society), 4th June 1959. P. Noel-Baker in *The Manchester Guardian,* 16th June 1959, instancing conversation he had with Nikita Khruschev in December 1958. Cf. Noel-Baker, Francis, 1987. Report of Noel-Baker's address at Labour Party Conference, Scarborough, 1960, in *Daily Sketch,* 6th October 1960. N.B.K.R. 2/124 P. Noel-Baker to David Ennals, 14th November 1960.
[16] Goodman, 1979: 300, 264ff.
[17] Goodman, 1979: 308.
[18] Roth, 1977: 260. Cf. 659 H.C. Debs, cols. 229-230, 8th May 1962, and 659 H.C. Debs, cols. 1147-1151, 15th May 1962.
[19] Darby, 1973: 241.
[20] Reported in *The Times,* 3rd October 1960.
[21] Reported in *The Times,* 11th February 1960.
[22] Quoted Sims, 1982.

[23] Haseler, 1969: 182-183, Noel-Baker was President of the Socialist Campaign, a parliamentary organisation aiming to ensure a supply of adequate speakers on defence matters.

[24] N.B.K.R. 2X/7.39 and N.B.K.R. 2/119 Noel-Baker's speech notes in 1955, and notes of Labour Party Parliamentary Committee meetings, 1955-57. N.B.K.R. 2/124 Frank Beswick to P. Noel-Baker, 26th October 1960; to P. Noel-Baker, 2nd January 1961; J. E. Meade to P. Noel-Baker, 2nd January 1961; P. Noel-Baker to J. E. Meade, 7th January 1961. Cf. P. Noel-Baker to David Ennals, 7th January 1961, and P. Noel-Baker to H. Wilson, 23rd April 1963.

[25] Noel-Baker letter to *The Guardian,* 3rd October 1980 (in possession D. J. Whittaker).

[26] Noel-Baker letter to *The Guardian,* 6th October 1980.

[27] Noel-Baker letter to *The Guardian,* 10th October 1981.

[28] Not too much can go into the final paragraph of a letter to a newspaper. The problem of obtaining approval from the U.S.A. and N.A.T.O. to any unilateral decommissioning ought at least to have been pointed out.

[29] Noel-Baker, 1960: 91-93.

[30] Cf. Noel-Baker, 1963, for some reference to the problems. At the Pugwash Conference which he attended regularly (see below in this chapter), Noel-Baker gave likely developments close attention.

[31] Noel-Baker, 1963: 93.

[32] Cf. Cox, 1977: 128.

[33] Noel-Baker, 1980.

[34] Noel-Baker, 1982.

[35] Noel-Baker address to World Assembly of Religious Workers for General and Nuclear Disarmament, 22nd-24th April 1981, Tokyo. Cf. Noel-Baker, 1970: 80-81.

[36] Noel-Baker, 1979. This includes the text of the Commonwealth Prime Minister's Statement of 1961 on Disarmament. The need to accept risks is stressed. Noel-Baker declares that the Statement was written by Earl Mountbatten of Burma.

[37] Galtung, 1984. Cf. Chapter 3 above for pre-war discussion of 'balance' and comparisons.

[38] Although Noel-Baker was not a member of the Just Defence group the beliefs of this non-political association with religious, academic, and military members had much in common with his own standpoint.

[39] Noel-Baker, 1979: 32. Cf. Noel-Baker's remarks quoted Brennan, 1961: 456. See note 14 above.

[40] Noel-Baker, 1979: 94ff.

[41] N.B.K.R. 8/46 Noel-Baker memo about Cheltenham discussion, 19th October 1981; note of meeting in Commons Grand Committee Room shortly afterwards.

[42] The World Disarmament Campaign in Britain produced a regular newsheet *For Human Survival.*

[43] N.B.K.R. 8/46 Speech notes, Hiroshima Day, Hiroshima, 6th August 1981.

[44] Lord Brockway's tribute to Noel-Baker appeared in *Tribune*, 15th October 1982.
[45] Noel-Baker to Sydney Bailey, 25th June 1958 (in possession D. J. Whittaker).
[46] N.B.K.R. 2X/7/4 P. Noel-Baker to Alex Kitson, 9th October 1960. In fact, James Callaghan informed the Shadow Cabinet six days later of his decision to give up the leadership while remaining an M.P.
[47] N.B.K.R. 2X/7/2 P. Noel-Baker to M. Foot, 22nd October 1980.
[48] N.B.K.R. 2X/7/1 P. Noel-Baker to M. Foot, 12th November 1980.
[49] N.B.K.R. 2X/7/2 P. Noel-Baker to M. Foot, 25th March 1981.
[50] N.B.K.R. 2X/7/2 P. Noel-Baker to M. Foot, 11th November 1981. Many of Noel-Baker's proposals for multilateral disarmament went on to be incorporated in Labour Party declarations or those made on behalf of the Socialist International. Michael Foot letter to the author, 9th January 1989.
[51] N.B.K.R. 2X/7/2 P. Noel-Baker to Ron Haywood, 19th March 1981.
[52] N.B.K.R. 2X/7/4 P. Noel-Baker to Austin Mitchell, 11th March 1981.
[53] Cf. the aims of Just Defence mentioned above in note 38.
[54] Noel-Baker quoted *For Human Survival*, World Disarmament Campaign, summer 1981, 4.
[55] N.B.K.R. 8/46 notes for speech in House of Lords, 16th December 1981.
[56] Feld, 1979: 234.
[57] Proc. 13th Pugwash Conference, Karlovy Vary, 13th-19th September 1964, 243-255.
[58] Rottblat, 1972.
[59] N.B.K.R. 8/46 speech notes for 30th Pugwash Conference, Canada, 1981.

Chapter 11

(pages 305-328)

Champion of Collective Security through the U.N. 1949-1982

[1] Taylor, A. J. P., 1965: 299, attributes the coining of the phrase to Edvard Benes in 1932.
[2] The terms are those of Lester Pearson.
[3] Cf. the similar argument of Angell, 1951: 266.
[4] Cf. the criticism of Stromberg, R. M., 1956: 250-263.
[5] Noel-Baker, P., address at the United Nations, New York, on the occasion of a celebration of the Roosevelt centenary, 16th June 1982, transcript in possession of D. J. Whittaker. Cf. Calder, N., 1968, chapter by Noel-Baker; Sims, 1985: passim.
[6] Noel-Baker, 1958.
[7] United Nations Association, 1986, Noel-Baker Memorial Lecture by Brian Urquhart, transcript in possession of D. J. Whittaker.
[8] *United Nations General Assembly, Official Record*, 2nd Part, First Session, 744.
[9] Noel-Baker, 1925: vi.
[10] 419 H.C. Debs, cols. 1262, 1253-1262, of 20th February 1946.

[11] Dalton, 1940: 131-132. The points are elaborated in Zacher, M. W., 1979, and by Haas, E. B., Butterworth, R. L., and Nye, J. S., and by Gasteyger, Curt, 1985.
[12] See Chapter 2 above.
[13] N.B.K.R. 4/428 Noel-Baker's notes for attendance at Labour Party Committee meeting and for further discussion with C. R. Attlee, undated, probably June-July 1950; N.B.K.R. 2/107 Noel-Baker's notes for a public meeting, undefined, 25th July 1950.
[14] N.B.K.R. 2/107 Noel-Baker's notes for an article on Communist propaganda within the Labour Party, undated, probably summer 1951.
[15] N.B.K.R. 4/428 Noel-Baker's notes for attendance at Labour Party Foreign Affairs Committee, 26th June 1952.
[16] N.B.K.R. 4/428 P. Noel-Baker to C. R. Attlee, 25th June 1952.
[17] N.B.K.R. 4/428 P. Noel-Baker to C. R. Attlee, 26th June 1952.
[18] N.B.K.R. 2/104 Noel-Baker's notes for an address to Labour Party Conference, Margate, October 1953.
[19] N.B.K.R. 4/129 Noel-Baker's notes on Congo developments, spring 1962; annotated copy of letter to *The Times,* 30th April 1962, from Brian Urquhart, former U.N. Representative in the Congo.
[20] N.B.K.R. 8/46 Noel-Baker, P., letter to *The Times,* 4th May 1962, and 28th August 1962; P. Noel-Baker to U. Thant, 9th August 1962; P. Noel-Baker to Harold Wilson, 15th August 1962.
[21] N.B.K.R. 7/66/2 correspondence with Japanese press and educational bodies; draft for Tokyo broadcast; annotated North America press clippings.
[22] Howard, A., 1979: 114.
[23] N.B.K.R. 4/863 Noel-Baker, P., letter to *The Times,* 19th July 1965.
[24] N.B.K.R. 4/863 Noel-Baker, P., letter to *The Times,* 24th May 1966.
[25] N.B.K.R. 4/863 memos, speech notes for House of Commons, 7th July 1966.
[26] N.B.K.R. 4/863 P. Noel-Baker to George Brown, 7th September 1966.
[27] N.B.K.R. 4/863 P. Noel-Baker to George Brown, 6th October 1966.
[28] N.B.K.R. 4/863, N.B.K.R. 4/863 Noel-Baker's speech notes for Labour Party Conference, Brighton, October 1966.
[29] N.B.K.R. 4/863 Noel-Baker, P., letter to *The Times,* 13th February 1967.
[30] N.B.K.R. 4/863 speech notes for Commons debate, 21st April 1967.
[31] N.B.K.R. 4/863 Noel-Baker, P., letter to *The Times,* 24th August 1967; sundry correspondence with American Society of International Law.
[32] Noel-Baker, F., 1985: passim.
[33] N.B.K.R. 10/4/2 P. Noel-Baker to Charles Peake, 6th March 1954; Charles Peake to P. Noel-Baker, 26th March 1954 and 2nd April 1954.
[34] N.B.K.R. 10/4/2 Charles Peake to P. Noel-Baker, 11th September 1954.
[35] N.B.K.R. 10/4/2 P. Noel-Baker to Charles Peake, 30th September 1954.
[36] N.B.K.R. 10/4/2 Charles Peake to P. Noel-Baker, 29th December 1954.
[37] N.B.K.R. 10/14/1 Charles Peake to P. Noel-Baker, 6th October 1954; Charles Peake to P. Noel-Baker, ? February 1955.
[38] N.B.K.R. 10/4/2 P. Noel-Baker to Charles Peake, 17th June 1955; Charles Peake to P. Noel-Baker, 29th December 1954, and 1st January 1955.

[39] 547 H.C. Debs, cols. 51, 142, of 5th December 1955; 550 H.C. Debs, col. 39ff, of 14th March 1956. Cf. N.B.K.R. 4/147 Noel-Baker's notes on Selwyn Lloyd's address to United Nations Steering Committee, 23rd September 1955.

[40] 558 H.C. Debs, cols. 355-369, of 14th September 1956.

[41] Noel-Baker, F., 1985: 86.

[42] Noel-Baker, F., 1985: 87. *The House of Commons Select Committee on Cyprus Report* (1976) concludes that Britain's failure to act was both 'illegal' and 'immoral'. Cf. Vanezis, 1977.

[43] N.B.K.R. 4/669 Noel-Baker, P., letter to *The Economist*, 11th August 1956.

[44] 558 H.C. Debs, col. 1451, 1555-1564. Cf. col. 1647.

[45] *The Manchester Guardian*, 1st November 1956.

[46] Nutting, Anthony, 1967: 12.

[47] Nutting, Anthony, 1967: 126.

[48] 558 H.C. Debs, col. 1754, of 2nd November 1956; cols. 1891-1894, of 3rd November 1956; cols. 1640-1652, 1731, of 1st November 1956.

[49] N.B.K.R. 4/673 Noel-Baker's notes for House of Commons debate, undated, but mid-November 1956.

[50] 561 H.C. Debs, cols. 1457-1472, of 6th December 1956. Cf. N.B.K.R. 4/363 P. Noel-Baker to Lord Birdwood, 4th July 1958. N.B.K.R. 4/532 speech notes for House of Commons debates.

[51] 558 H.C. Debs, col. 1477, of 6th December 1956. Cf. sundry speech notes in N.B.K.R. 4/680.

[52] N.B.K.R. 4/706 P. Noel-Baker to Anthony Nutting, Anthony Nutting to P. Noel-Baker, undated, but both May 1967; P. Noel-Baker to Hugh Thomas, 14th October 1966.

[53] N.B.K.R. 9/57/1 A. Benn to P. Noel-Baker, 23rd February 1963.

[54] N.B.K.R. 9/91 Philip Noel-Baker to Francis Noel-Baker, 19th September 1965.

[55] Gordon Evans, personal communication, 1986.

[56] N.B.K.R. 3X/14 P. Noel-Baker to Margaret Thatcher, 5th April 1982; Margaret Thatcher to P. Noel-Baker, 6th April 1982.

[57] Noel-Baker, P., to *Financial Times*, 8th April 1982; Noel-Baker, P., to *Daily Telegraph*, 20th April 1982.

[58] N.B.K.R. 3X/14 P. Noel-Baker to Viscount Watkinson, 20th April 1982. (The latter was then a member of the Falkland Islands Review committee.)

[59] N.B.K.R. 3X/14 Noel-Baker's speech notes for House of Lords, 30th April 1982.

[60] Cf. tributes to Noel-Baker in Huzzard and Meredith, 1985: 10-13.

[61] Lord Brockway's tribute is in *Tribune*, 15th October 1982.

[62] Gordon Evans, personal communication, August 1986.

Chapter 12 *(pages 331-340)*

Epilogue

[1] Cf. *British Year Book of International Law*, 1925: 232, review of Noel-Baker's *The Geneva Protocol*.

[2] Royal Institute of International Affairs, Report of the Council, 1982-83: 24-25.
[3] Harris, 1954: 187.
[4] Quoted Newsweek, January 1946.
[5] Cf. addresses to Labour Party 1980 Annual Conference; Kings College Founders Day, 24th January 1981; meeting of 450 delegates of professional associations, Imperial College, London, 13th February 1982. Lord Thomas of Swynnerton (see Note 2) sees bitterness and disillusion in the last years of his fellow-peer.
[6] Cf. Noel-Baker replying at conferment of Ll.D, University of Nottingham in *University of Nottingham Gazette*, no. 28, 429-431. He was quoting Goldsworthy Lowes Dickenson.
[7] Lorna Lloyd, personal communication, August 1986.
[8] There are signs in Noel-Baker's correspondence that he lamented the complacency of Woolf's *The Journey Not the Arrival Matters*, 1969, and what he regarded as the cynicism of Madariaga.
[9] Cf. Chapter 2 above; Stewart, Marion, 1986: passim.

Acknowledgements

The author is grateful to those mentioned below for permission to quote from texts.

Addison, P., *The Road to 1945* (David Higham Associates).
Attlee Papers (Lord Attlee; University College, Oxford).
Barros, J., *Office Without Power* (Pergamon).
Behrens, C., *Merchant Shipping and the Demands of War* (Controller of H.M.S.O.).
Bell, A. O., *The Diary of Virginia Woolf* (Virginia Woolf estate; A. O. Bell; The Hogarth Press).
Beloff, Max, *Britain's Liberal Empire* (Methuen).
Brockway, Lord, tribute to Lord Noel-Baker, *Tribune*, 15th October 1982 (*Tribune*).
Ceadel, M., *Pacifism in Britain* (Oxford University Press).
Cecil Papers (British Library Board).
Dalton, Hugh, *Memoirs* (Century Hutchinson).
Evans, T. P., *Bevin* (Unwin Hyman).
Feld, B. T., *A Voice Crying in the Wilderness* (Pergamon).
Garner, Lord, *The Commonwealth Office* (William Heinemann).
Gilbert, M., *Winston S. Churchill* (William Heinemann).
Hamilton, M., *Arthur Henderson* (William Heinemann).
Hankey, Lord, *The Supreme Control* (Unwin Hyman).
Headlam, Morley, J., *Sir James Headlam-Morley* (Methuen).
Herbert, A. P., *Independent Member* (A. P. Watt).
Jameson, Storm, *Challenge to Death* (Constable).
Kennedy, P., *Strategy and Diplomacy* (Collins).
Madariaga, S. de, *Disarmament* (The heirs of S. de Madariaga).
Medlicott, W., *Documents on British Foreign Policy* (Controller of H.M.S.O.).
Morgan, K. O., *Labour in Power* (Oxford University Press).
Murray, Gilbert, *From the League to the U.N.* (Oxford University Press).
Gilbert Murray Papers (Mr. Alexander Murray).
Nicolson, H., *The Evolution of Diplomatic Method* (Constable).
Noel-Baker Papers (The Master, Fellows and Scholars of Churchill College, University of Cambridge).
Noel-Baker, P. J., *The First World Disarmament Conference* (Pergamon).
Noel-Baker, P. J., *Disarmament* (The Hogarth Press); *The Arms Race* (Stevens); speech at 13th Pugwash Conference (Prof. J. Rotblat).
Northedge, F. S., *Descent from Power* (Unwin Hyman).

Pimlott, B., *Hugh Dalton; The Second World War Diary of Hugh Dalton* (Jonathan Cape).
Raymond, J., *The Baldwin Age* (Eyre and Spottiswode).
Reynolds, P. A., and Hughes, E. J., *The Historian as Diplomat* (Blackwell).
Robbins, K. G., article 1983, on Labour foreign policy and international Socialism (Prof. K. G. Robbins).
Rock, W. R., *British Appeasement in the 1930's* (Edward Arnold).
Roskill, S., *Hankey: Man of Secrets* (Collins).
Royal Institute of International Affairs, *Annual Report of Council* (Royal Institute of International Affairs).
Scott, G., *The Rise and Fall of the League of Nations* (Century Hutchinson).
Smuts, J. C., *Jan Christian Smuts* (Macmillan).
Swartz, M., *The Union of Democratic Control* (Oxford University Press).
Thomas, Lord, review of *The Arms Race* in *New Statesman,* 21st June 1958 *(New Statesman* and *New Society).*
Walters, F. M. A., *History of the League of Nations* (Oxford University Press).
Beatrice Webb Diary (London School of Economics).
Woolf, Leonard, *Beginning Again; Downhill all the Way* (Leonard Woolf estate; The Hogarth Press).
Ziegler, P., *Mountbatten* (Collins).

References

The list below contains only those primary sources (books and journal articles) mentioned in the text and in the notes following it. The numerous secondary sources consulted by the author are not included.

A. Collections of personal papers

Attlee Papers, Bodleian Library, Oxford.
Cecil Papers, British Library.
Curtis Papers, Bodleian Library, Oxford.
Gilbert Murray Papers, Bodleian Library, Oxford (cited in notes as G.M.P.).
Noel-Baker Papers, Archive Centre, Churchill College, Cambridge (cited in notes as N.B.K.R.).
Younger Papers (by courtesy of Lady Younger who possesses them; cited in notes as K.Y.D.).

B. Other institutional collections

Cabinet Minutes, Public Record Office (cited in notes as C.A.B.).
Dictionary of National Biography.
Documents on British Foreign Policy, Second Series.
Foreign Office Minutes, Public Record Office (cited in notes as P.R.O. F.O. Mins.).
House of Commons Debates, Parliamentary Papers (cited in notes as H.C. Debs).
House of Lords Debates, Parliamentary Papers.
Labour Party Advisory Committee on International Questions Minutes.
Labour Party Annual Conference Reports.
Labour Party Annual Party Reports.
League of Nations Union archives, B.L.E.P.S., London School of Economics (cited in notes as L.N.U.).
Nobel Peace Prize Report of Proceedings, 1959.
Proceedings of Pugwash Conferences.
Royal Commission on Armaments 1935 Report, H.M.S.O.

C. Books

ADDISON, PAUL, (1975) *The Road to 1945: British Politics and the Second World War*. Jonathan Cape.

ALEXANDER, HORACE, (1982) A Long Memory of Philip Noel-Baker. *The Friend*. 19th November, 1982, 1467-1468.

ANGELL, NORMAN, (1910) *The Great Illusion*. Heinemann; (1921) *The Fruits of Victory*. Garland; (1951) *After All*. Hamish Hamilton.

ATTLEE, C. R., (1954) *As it Happened*. Odhams.

BALFOUR, MICHAEL, (1960) *The Kaiser and His Times*. Cresset.

BARCLAY, RODERICK, (1975) *Ernest Bevin and the Foreign Office 1932-1969*. Latimer.

BARROS, JAMES, (1979) *Office Without Power*. Clarendon.

BARTLETT, R. J., (1944) *The League to Enforce Peace*. Univ. North Carolina.

BASSETT, R., (1968) *Democracy and Foreign Policy – A Case History: The Sino-Japanese Dispute 1931-33*. Cass.

BEHRENS, C. B. A., (1955) *History of the Second World War: General Series. Merchant Shipping and the Demands of War*. H.M.S.O.

BELL, A. O., (1982) *Diaries of Virginia Woolf*, vols. IV, V. Hogarth.

BELOFF, MAX, (1969) *Britain's Liberal Empire 1897-1921*. Methuen.

BENSON, MARY, (1960) *Tshekedi Khama*. Faber.

BERRIDGE, G. R. & JENNINGS, A. eds., (1985) *Diplomacy at the U.N.* Macmillan.

BINKLEY, R. C., (1929) Ten years of peace conference history. *Jour. Mod. Hist.*, Sept. 1929; (1931) Some references on disarmament & history. *Int. Affairs*, Sept. 1931.

BIRN, D. S., (1981) *The League of Nations Union*. O.U.P.

BISCEGLIA, LOUIS, (1972) The Politics of a Peace Prize. *Jour. Contemp. Hist.*, vii, July-Oct. 1972; (1982) *Norman Angell & Liberal Internationalism* in Britain 1931-35. Garland.

BOYD, ANDREW, (1964) *United Nations: Piety, Myth & Truth*. Penguin; (1971) *Fifteen Men on a Powder Keg: A History of the U.N. Security Council*. Methuen.

BRENNAN, D. G., (1967) *Arms Control & Disarmament*. Jonathan Cape.

BRETTON, H. L., (1953) *Stresemann and the Revision of Versailles*. Stanford Univ. Press.

British Year Book of International Law, (1925). Review of Noel-Baker's *The Geneva Protocol*.

BROOK-SHEPHERD, NORMAN, (1961) *Dollfuss*. Macmillan.

BULLOCK, ALAN, (1960) *The Life and Times of Ernest Bevin*, vol. 1. Heinemann; (1983) *Ernest Bevin, Foreign Secretary*. Heinemann.

CALDER, NIGEL, (ed) (1968) *Unless Peace Comes*. Spokesman.

CAMPBELL, T. M. & HERRING, C. C., (1975) *The Diaries of Edward R. Stettinius Jr. 1943-1945*. New Viewpoints, New York.

CARLTON, DAVID, (1970) *MacDonald Versus Henderson: The Foreign Policy of the Second Labour Government*. Macmillan.

CARR, E. H., (1959) *International Relations between the Two World Wars*. Macmillan; (1968) *Nationalism and After*. Macmillan; (1974 ed.) *The Twenty Years Crisis*. 1919-1939.

CEADEL, MARTIN, (1980) *Pacifism in Britain 1914-1945*. O.U.P.

CECIL, LORD ROBERT (Viscount Cecil), (1929) The Tenth Assembly. *Int. Affairs*, 8 (1929), 550; (1941) *A Great Experiment*. Hodder & Stoughton; (1949) *All The Way*. Hodder & Stoughton.

CHURCHILL, W. S., (1950) *The Second World War: The Gathering Storm*. Cassell.

CITRINE, SIR WALTER (LORD), (1967) *Two Careers*. Hutchinson.

CLARKE, G. N. and BINDOFF, S. T., (1962) Charles Kingsley Webster 1886-1961. *Proc. British Acad.*, vol. XLVIII, 445.

CONNELL, J., (1958) *The Office, A Study in British Foreign Policy and its Maker, 1919-51*. Wingate.

COURT, W. H. B., (1955) *Coal*. H.M.S.O.

COX, JOHN, (1977) *Overkill: The Story of Modern Weapons*. Pelican.

CROSS, J. A., (1967) *Whitehall and the Commonwealth: British Departmental Organisation for Commonwealth Relations*. Routledge & Kegan Paul; (1969) The Beginning and End of the Commonwealth Office. *Publ. Admin.*, 47, (1969), 113-119.

CROSSMAN, RICHARD, (1981) *The Backbench Diaries of Richard Crossman*. Hamish Hamilton.

DALTON, HUGH, (1931) British foreign policy 1929-31. *Political Quarterly*, 11, (1931), 485-505; (1936) The popular front *Political Quarterly*, Oct.-Dec. 1935, vii, 4; (1940) *Hitler's War Before and After*. Penguin; (1953) *Call Back Yesterday: Memoirs 1887-1931*. Muller; (1957) *The Fateful Years: Memoirs 1931-1945*. Muller; (1962) *High Tide and After: Memoirs 1945-60*. Muller.

DARBY, PHILIP, (1973) *British Defence Policy East of Suez 1947-68*. O.U.P.

DAVIS, SAMUEL, (1950) The British Labour Party and British Foreign Policy 1933-39. Unpubl. Ph.D thesis, Univ. London.

DILKS, DAVID, ed. (1971) *The Diaries of Sir Alexander Cadogan 1938-45*. Putnam.

DONOGHUE, BERNARD & JONES, G. W., (1973) *Herbert Morrison, Portrait of a Politician*. Weidenfeld & Nicholson.

DUBLIN, M. D., (1983) Transgovernmentalism in the League of Nations. *Int. Organ.*, 37, 3, Summer 1983, 469-493.

EDWARDS, JILL, (1979) *The British Government and the Spanish Civil War 1936-39*. Macmillan.

EGERTON, G. W., (1978) *Great Britain and the Creation of the League of Nations, 1914-1919*. Univ. N. Carolina.

ELMANDJRA, M., (1973) *The United Nations System*. Faber.

EVANS, T. E., (1972) *The Killearn Diaries, 1934-1946*. Sidgwick & Jackson.

EVANS, T. M., (1946) *Bevin*. Allen & Union.

FARRAR, ELEANOR, (1952) The British Labour Party and international organisations; a study of the Party's policy towards the League of Nations, the United Nations, and Western Union. Unpubl. Ph.D thesis, Univ. London.

FELD, B. T., (1979) *A Voice Crying in the Wilderness: Essays on the Problem of Science & World Affairs*. Pergamon.

FOOT, MICHAEL, (1962) *Aneurin Bevan*, vol. 1, 1897-1945. Macgibbon & Kee.

GALLAGHER, WILLIAM, (1947) *Revolt on the Clyde*. Lawrence & Wishart.

GALTUNG, JOHAN, (1984) P.N.B. Memorial Lecture (Transcript). *United Nations Association.*

GARNER, LORD, (1978) *The Commonwealth Office 1925-68.* Heinemann.

GASTEYGER, CURT, (1985) *Searching for World Security.* Pinter.

GILBERT, MARTIN, (1976-1982) *Winston S. Churchill,* vol. V, V Companion. Heinemann.

GLADWYN, LORD, (Jebb, Gladwyn), (1972) *Memoirs of Lord Gladwyn.* Weidenfeld & Nicholson.

GOODMAN, GEOFFREY, (1979) *The Awkward Warrior, Frank Cousins: His Life and Times.* Davis-Poynter.

GOODRICH, L. M., (1947) From League of Nations to United Nations. *Int. Organ.,* 1, 3-21; (1960) *The United Nations.* Stevens.

GOODRICH, L. M. & HAMBRO, EDWARD, (1949) *Charter of the United Nations: Commentary & Documents.* Stevens.

GOODWIN, G. L., (1957) *Britain and the United Nations.* New York: Manhattan; (1958) Review of *The Arms Race. Int. Rels.,* 1, 10, Oct. 1958, 482-493.

GORDON-WALKER, PATRICK, (1970) *The Cabinet.* Jonathan Cape.

GRANT, DUFF S., (1938) The Czechs and the crisis, *Contemporary Review,* Dec. 1938.

GREENWOOD, ARTHUR, (1958) A warning of the wilderness, *Daily Herald,* 8th June 1958.

GREENWOOD, J. O., (1975) *Quaker Encounters,* vol. 1, *Friends and Relief.* Ebor Press.

GUPTA, P. S., (1975) *Imperialism and the British Labour Movement 1914-64.* Macmillan.

HAAS, E. B., BUTTERWORTH, R. L. & NYE, J. S., (1972) *Conflict Management by International Organisations.*

HADDOW, ALEXANDER, (1958) Science and Disarmament. *The New Scientist,* 18th September 1958, pp. 844-846.

HAMILTON, M. A., (1938) *Arthur Henderson: A Biography.* Heinemann.

HANCOCK, W. K. & GOWING, M. M., (1949) *History of the Second World War: Civil Series: British War Economy.* H.M.S.O.

HANKEY, LORD, (1963) The Supreme Control: *At the Paris Peace Conference 1919.* Allen & Unwin.

HARVEY, HEATHER J., (1952) *Consultation and Cooperation in the Commonwealth.* O.U.P.

HASELER, STEPHEN, (1969) *The Gaitskellites.* Macmillan.

HAZZARD, SHIRLEY, (1973) *Defeat of an Ideal.* Macmillan.

HEADLAM-MORLEY, AGNES, (ed.) (1972) *Sir James Headlam-Morley: A Memoir of the Paris Peace Conference 1919.* Methuen.

HENIG, R. B., (1973) *The League of Nations.* Oliver & Boyd.

HERBERT, A. P., (1950) *Independent Member.* Methuen.

HILDEBRAND, KLAUS, (1973) *The Foreign Policy of the Third Reich.* Batsford.

HINSLEY, F. H., (1963) *Power and the Pursuit of Peace.* C.U.P., (1973) *Nationalism and the International System.* Hodder & Stoughton.

HOETZCH, OTTO, (1932) A German view of disarmament. *Int. Affairs*, 11, (1932), 51.
HOWARD, MICHAEL, (1979) *Restraints on War: Studies in the Limitations of Armed Conflict.*
HUZZARD, R. & MEREDITH, C., (1985) *World Disarmament: An Idea Whose Time Has Come.* Spokesman Press.
ISMAY, H. L., (1960) *The Memories of General The Lord Ismay.* Heinemann.
KENNEDY, P. M., (1983) *Strategy and Diplomacy 1870-1945.* Fontana.
LARUS, JOEL, (1965) *From Collective Security to Preventive Diplomacy; Readings in International Organisation and the Maintenance of Power.* John Wiley.
LEE, D. E., (1947) The genesis of the veto. *Int. Organ.*, 1, (1947), 33-42.
LLOYD-GEORGE, DAVID, (1939) *War Memoirs*, vol. 1, 2. Odhams; *The Truth about the Peace Treaties*, vol. 1, 2. Gollancz.
LUARD, EVAN, (1979) *The United Nations: How it Works and What it Does.* Macmillan.
MCDERMOTT, GEOFFREY, (1972) *Leader Lost, a Biography of Hugh Gaitskell.* Frewin.
MACFARLANE, L. J., (1965) *The British Communist Party.* Macgibbon & Kee.
MACMILLAN, HAROLD, (1935) *The Next Five Years: An Essay in Political Agreement.* Macmillan; (1984) *War Diaries: The Mediterranean 1943-45.* Macmillan.
MADARIAGA, S. DE, (1929) *Disarmament.* Milford; (1935) *Price of Peace.* Cobden Sanderson; (1974) *Morning Without Noon.* Saxon House.
MAITLAND, PATRICK, (1957) *Task for Giants: An Expanding Commonwealth.* Longmans, Green.
MALCOLM, NEIL, (1926) Review of *Disarmament. Int. Affairs*, vol. 5, 1926, 160-161.
MANSERGH, NICHOLAS, (1982 ed.) *The Commonwealth Experience from British to Multiracial Commonwealth.* Weidenfeld & Nicholson.
MARTIN, KINGSLEY, (1969) *Harold Laski 1893-1950.* Jonathan Cape.
MARWICK, A., (1964) Middle opinion in the 30's: planning, progress and political agreement. *Eng. Hist. Rev.*, 1964, 28-98.
MAURICE, FREDERICH, (1926) A British view of the possibilities of disarmament. *Int. Affairs*, vol. 5, (1926), 117-132.
MEDLICOTT, W. N., et al, (1966) *Documents on British Foreign Policy 1919-39.* Series 1A, vols. 1-16. H.M.S.O.
MILIBAND, R., (1972) *Parliamentary Socialism.* New York: Monthly Review Press.
MILLER, D. H., (1928) *The Drafting of the Covenant.* (Reprinted by Johnson Reprint Corp.; New York 1969 – 2 vols.)
MORGAN, K. O., (1984) *Labour in Power 1945-51.* O.U.P.
MORGENTHAU, H. J., (1954) The new United Nations and the revision of the Charter. *Review of Politics*, XVI, (1954), 3-21.
MORRISON, HERBERT, (1960) *Herbert Morrison.* Odhams.
MOSLEY, SIR OSWALD, (1968) *My Life.* Nelson.
MUIR, AUGUSTUS, (1968) *The History of Baker Perkins.* Heffer.
MUNCH, PAUL, (ed.) (1923-24) *Les Origins et l'oeuvre de la societé des nations.* Copenhagen. (Chapter by Noel-Baker on the Covenant.)
MURRAY, GILBERT, (1948) *From the League to the United Nations.* O.U.P.

NAYLOR, J. F., (1969) *Labour's International Policy*. Weidenfeld & Nicholson.
NICHOLSON, NIGEL, (1958) *Review of the Arms Race* in *New World*, Sept. 1958.
NICOLSON, HAROLD, (1954) *The Evolution of Diplomatic Method*. Constable.
NOEL-BAKER, FRANCIS, (1985) *My Cyprus File*. Ross Features International; (1987) *A Taste of Hardship*. Ross Features International.
NORTHEDGE, F. S., (1962) *British Foreign Policy: the Process of Readjustment*. Allen & Unwin; (1969) *The Troubled Giant*. G. Bell; (1974) *Descent from Power*. Allen & Unwin.
NUTTING, ANTHONY, (1967) *No End of a Lesson:* Story of Suez. Constable.
OPPENHEIM, (1955 ed.) *International Law*.
PARMOOR, LORD, (1936) A Retrospect: *Looking Back Over a Life of More than Eighty Years*. Heinemann.
PELLING, HENRY, (1984) *The Labour Governments 1945-51*. Macmillan.
PIMLOTT, BEN, (1977) *Labour and the Left in the 1930's*. C.U.P.; (1985) *Hugh Dalton*. Jonathan Cape; (1986) *The Second World War Diary of Hugh Dalton 1940-45*. Jonathan Cape.
POOLE, R., (1978) *The Unknown Virginia Woolf*. C.U.P.
POUND, REGINALD, (1976) *Alan Patrick Herbert: A Biography*. Michael Joseph.
PRATT, J. W., (1964) *Cordell Hull 1933-44*, vols. 1, 2. New York: Cooper Square.
PRITT, D. N., (1966) *The Autobiography of D. N. Pritt. Pt. 2. Brasshats & Bureaucrats*. Lawrence & Wishart.
PUGH, M. C., (1975) British public opinion and collective security, 1926-1936. Unpubl. Ph.D thesis, Univ. East Anglia.
PUZZO, D. H., (1962) *Spain and the Great Powers 1936-41*. Books for Libraries Press.
RAFFO, P. S., (1967) Viscount Cecil and the League of Nations. Unpubl. Ph.D thesis, Univ. Liverpool; (1974) The Anglo-American preliminary negotiations for a League of Nations. *Jour. Contemp. Hist.*, 9, (1974), 153-176; (1974) The League of Nations philosophy of Lord Robert Cecil. *Austr. Jour. Pol. Hist.*, XX, (1974), 186-196.
RAPPARD, W. E., (1925) *International Relations as Viewed from Geneva*. Yale Univ. Press; (1940) *The Quest for Peace*. Harvard Univ. Press.
RAUNCH, BASIL, (ed.) (1957) *The Roosevelt Reader*. Holt, Rinehart & Winston.
RAYMOND, JOHN, (ed.) (1960) *The Baldwin Age*. Eyre & Spoltiswoode.
REYNOLDS, P. A., (1974) *British Foreign Policy in the Inter-War Years*.
REYNOLDS, P. A. & HUGHES, E. J., (1976) *The Historian as Diplomat: Charles Kingsley Webster and the United Nations 1939-1940*. Martin Robertson.
RICHARDSON, R. C., (1969) The problem of disarmament in British diplomacy, 1932-34. Unpubl. M.A. thesis, Univ. British Columbia; (1986) *Rattling an Olive Branch: the Conservative Government of 1924-29 and the Disarmament Problem*. (now in press); (1987) In quest of arms control or rattling an olive branch? Some lessons of history. *European Consortium for Political Research*, Amsterdam, April 10th-15th 1987.
ROBBINS, K. G., (1983) Labour Foreign Policy and international socialism: MacDonald and the League of Nations. *Annali della Fondazione Giangiacomo Feltrinelli 1984/1985*.

Rock, W. R., (1977) *British Appeasement in the 1930's*. Arnold.
Rolph, C. H., (1973) *Kingsley*. Gollancz.
Roosevelt, Elliott, (ed.) (1970) *F.D.R.: His Personal Letters*. Duell, Sloan, & Pearce.
Roskill, Stephen, (1972) *Hankey: Man of Secrets 1919-31*, vol. 2. Collins.
Rotblat, J., (1972) Scientists in the Quest for Peace. *A History of the Pugwash Conference*. Mass. Inst. Tech. Press.
Roth, Andrew, (1977) *Lord Reith*.
Rothwell, V. H., (1971) *British War Aims & Peace Diplomacy 1914-18*. Clarendon.
Royal Commission on the Private Manufacture and Trading in Arms, (1935). Ldn: H.M.S.O.
Royal Institute of International Affairs, (1983). Report of the Council 1982-83. (Obituary of Noel-Baker by Hugh Thomas.)
Savage, C. I., (1957) *History of the Second World War: General Series: Inland Transport*. H.M.S.O.
Scott, George, (1973) *The Rise and Fall of the League of Nations*. Hutchinson.
Shepherd, George W., (1952) The Theory and practice of internationalism in the British Labour Party with specific reference to the inter-war period. Unpubl. Ph.D thesis, Univ. London.
Sims, Nicholas, (1982) Philip Noel-Baker, *The Friend*, 22nd Oct. 1982.
Skidelsky, Robert, (1983) *John Maynard Keynes*, vol. 1, 1883-1920. Macmillan.
Slocombe, George, (1938) *A Mirror to Geneva, Its Growth, Grandeur and Decay*. Henry Holt.
Smuts, J. C., (1918) *The League of Nations: A Practical Suggestion*. Hodder & Stoughton; (1952) *Jan Christian Smuts*. Cassell.
Sorensen, Jan, (1932) *The Saga of Fridtjof Nansen*. W. W. Norton, New York.
Spier, Eugen, (1963) *Focus*. Oswald Wolff.
Starke, J. G., (1984 ed.) *Introduction to International Law*. Butterworths.
Stewart, Marian, (1986) *Philip Noel-Baker: From the Archives*. Noel-Baker Memorial Lecture, Achmetaga, Greece.
Stromberg, R. M., (1956) The idea of collective security. *Jour. Hist. Ideas*, vol. 17, 250-263.
Stuart, Charles, (ed.) (1975) *The Reith Diaries*. Collins.
Swartz, Marrin, (1971) *The Union of Democratic Control in British Politics during the First World War*. O.U.P.
Taylor, A. J. P., (1957) *The Trouble Makers*. Hamish Hamilton; (1965) *English History 1914-45*. O.U.P.
Temperley, H. N. V., (ed.) (1920) *History of the Peace Conference* vols. 1-6. Hodder & Stoughton.
Tennyson, Charles, (ed.) (1974) *Basileon – A. Magazine of Kings College, Cambridge 1900-1914*. Scholar Press.
Thomas, Hugh, (1958) Book review of *The Arms Race*. *New Statesman*, 21st June 1958, 812.
Thomson, J. H., (1977) Lord Cecil and the pacifists in the League of Nations Union. *The History Journal*, 20, 4, (1977), 949-959.

THORNE, CHRISTOPHER, (1972) *The Limits of Foreign Policy: The West, the League and the Far Eastern Crisis of 1931-33*. Hamish Hamilton.

UNITED NATIONS (1946) *Commentary on the Report of the Preparatory Commission of the United Nations*, Parliamentary Papers, Cmd. 6934. H.M.S.O.; (1946) *General Assembly Official Record*, 2nd Part, First Session.

WALTERS, F. P., (1969 ed.) *A History of the League of Nations*, vols. 1, 2. O.U.P. for RIIA.

WATCHMAN, (1939) *Right Honourable Gentlemen*. Hamish Hamilton.

WATT, D. C., (1965) *Personalities and Politics; Studies in the Formulation of British Foreign Policy in the Twentieth Century*. Westport, Conn.: Greenwood.

WEBB, BEATRICE, (1978) *The Diary of Beatrice Webb 1873-1943*, microfiche, L.S.E. and Cambridge: Chadwyck-Healey.

WEBSTER, C. K., (1933) *The League of Nations in Theory & Practice*. Allen & Unwin; (1946) The Making of the Charter of the United Nations. Creighton Lecture, Univ. London, Nov. 1946. London: RIIA.

WHEELER-BENNETT, J. W., (1932) *Disarmament and Security since Locarno 1925-1931; being the political and technical background of the general disarmament conference 1932*. Reprinted 1973, New York: Fertis.

WHITE, FRIEDA, (1937) Review of the private manufacture of arms. *Int. Affairs*, 16, (1937).

WHITTAKER, DAVID J., (1989) Philip Noel-Baker 1889-1982. *Der Nobel Friedenspreize vom 1900 bis Heute*, vol. vii, Munich: Edition Pacis.

WILLIAMS, P. M., (1979) *Hugh Gaitskell*. Jonathan Cape.

WILSON, DUNCAN, (1978) *Leonard Woolf: a Political Biography*. Hogarth; (1987) *Gilbert Murray O. M.*, 1866-1957. Clarendon.

WILSON, HAROLD, (1971) *The Labour Government 1964-1970. A Personal Record*. Weidenfeld & Nicholson.

WINKLER, H. R., (1948) The development of the League of Nations idea in Great Britain 1914-19. *Jour. Mod. Hist.*, xx, June 1948, 2, 95-112; (1955) *The League of Nations Movement in Great Britain*. Rutgers Univ. Press; (1956) The emergence of a Labour Foreign Policy in Great Britain. *Jour. Mod. Hist.*, xxviii, (1956), 247-258.

WOOLF, LEONARD, (1937) The resurection of the League. *Political Quarterly*, viii, (1937), pt. 3, 337-352; (1958) Review of *The Arms Race. Political Quarterly*, Oct.-Dec. 1958, 399; (1964) *Beginning Again: An Autobiography of the Years 1911-1918*. Hogarth; (1967) *Downhill all the Way*. Hogarth.

YOUNG, HILTON, (1926) The work of the Eighth Assembly of the League of Nations. *Int. Affairs*, vol. 5, 1925, 368-383.

ZIMMERN, ALFRED, (1924) The League and the old diplomacy. *Contemp. Review*, Feb. 1924; (1936) *The League of Nations and the Rule of Law 1918-1935*. Macmillan.

ZACHER, M. W., (1979) *International Conflicts and Collective Security 1946-77*. Praeger.

ZIEGLER, PHILIP, (1985) *Mountbatten*. Collins.

D. Newspapers and magazines consulted

The Aeroplane, Bootham School Magazine, British Friend, Daily Herald, Daily Sketch, Das Politische Buch, The Economist, F.A.U. Monthly Magazine, Fellowship, For Human Survival, Forward, Granta, The Guardian, International Affairs, Labour Magazine, Labour's Voice, Law Literary Journal, The Liberal Forward, The Listener, Manchester Guardian, Nation, The New Clarion, The New Republic, The New Scientist, New World, Newsweek, The Political Quarterly, Queens Journal, The Queens Review, Socialist Commentary, Socialist Review, The Spectator, Stimme, Sunday Times, The Times, The Times Literary Supplement, Tribune, Universities and Left Review, University of Nottingham Gazette, The Week, The World, World Affairs, World Sports.

E. Select list of Philip Noel-Baker's writings

Not everything written by Noel-Baker through his long life is listed below. The works cited are those consulted during the compilation of this biography. The list is chronological. Readers turning to Lloyd, Lorna and Sims, N. H., (1979) *British Writing on Disarmament from 1914 to 1978 : A Bibliography*, London : Francis Pinter, will find that Noel-Baker has more entries there than any other writer.

'P. J. B.', (1912) Olympiads and the noble English press, *Granta*, 23rd Nov. 1912.

BAKER, P. J., (1920) Olympic reflections, *Sports and Sportsmen*, no. 1, vol. 1, Nov. 1920.

NOEL-BAKER, P. J., (1924) Real plan to outlaw war, *Our World*, vol. 5, 19-25; (1924a) M. Herriot's offer, *Nation*, vol. 35, 431-432; (1924b) Menace of armaments, *Nation*, vol. 35, 613-614; (1924c) The Olympic Games, *Empire Review*, May 1924; (1925) *The Geneva Protocol for the Pacific Settlement of International Disputes*, London: P. S. King; (1926) *Disarmament*, London: Hogarth Press (Reprint 1970, New York: Kennicat Press); (1926a) Locarno or the League: Sir Austen's collapse and its lessons, *Socialist Review*, May 1926; (1927) *Disarmament and the Coolidge Conference*, London: Hogarth Press.

BAKER, P. J., and BAKER, E. B., (1927a) *J. Allen Baker: A Memoir*, London: Swarthmore Press.

NOEL-BAKER, P. J., (1927b) *The League of Nations at Work*, London: Nisbet; (1929) *The Present Juridical Status of the British Dominions in International Law*, London: Longmans; (1933) *The End of a Myth*, N. Friends Peace Board, (4 pp. pamphlet reprinted from Headway).

NOEL-BAKER, P. J., et al, (1934) *Challenge to Death*, London: Constable.

NOEL-BAKER, P. J., (1934a) Disarmament, *International Affairs*, vol. 13, 3-25; (1934b) *War in the Air? The Attitude of the Government*, London: National Peace Council, (4 pp. pamphlet); (1934c) *Hawkers of Death: The Private Manufacture and Trade in Arms*, London, (28 pp. pamphlet); (1934d) *Suppressing the Private Manufacture of Armaments: the Objections Answered*,

London: National Peace Council, (8 pp. pamphlet); (1936) *The Private Manufacture of Armaments*, London: Gollancz, (Reprint 1972, New York: Dover Publics); (1936a) the future of the collective system, *Problems of Peace*, 10th series, 178-198, Geneva Institute of International Relations; (1939) *Common Sense and the Colonies*, London: Labour Party pamphlet; (1948) The Olympic Games in retrospect, *World Sports*, (for British Olympic Association); (1958) *The Arms Race: A Programme for World Disarmament*, London: Stevens, (Reprints 1960 – London: John Calder, New York: Oceana); (1960) Prospects for world disarmament, *Jour. Roy. Commonwealth Soc.*, vol. 3, 1960, 91-93; (1960a) *Weltabrüsting Heute Möglich*, Geneva: Swiss Peace Council, (German translation of Nobel Peace Prize acceptance speech in Oslo, 11th Dec. 1959); (1961) 'Foreign comment' in Brennan, D. G. (ed.), *Arms Control and Disarmament: American Views and Studies*, New York: Cape, 451-456; (1962) *Nansen's Place in History*, Oslo: Universitetsförlaget, (26 pp. pamphlet); (1963) *The Way to World Disarmament*, London: Union of Democratic Control, (48 pp. pamphlet); (1965) *A Policy for Disarmament*, London: U.N.A., (22 pp. pamphlet); (1965a) The supreme objective, *Socialist Commentary*, Mar. 1965, 16-17, (see also Socialist Commentary, Jan. 1965, 23-24); (1965b) Science and disarmament, *Impact of Science in Society*, Paris: Unesco, vol. 15, no. 4, 211-246; (1968) 'We have been here before', in Calder, Nigel (ed.), *Unless Peace Comes: A Scientific Forecast of New Weapons*, New York: Viking, London: Penguin (1970), 193-205, (in 1968 ed.); (1970) Putting a stop to C.B.W., *Science Journal*, Jan. 1970, 80-81.

NOEL-BAKER, P. J., (1970a) The arms race: escalation of total madness, *U.N.E.S.C.O. Courier*, Paris: Unesco, vol. 23, Nov. 1970, 4-12; (1972) *Hunger will Rage until the Arms Race is Stopped*, London: Soc. Friends Peace and Int. Rels. Committee, (4 pp. pamphlet); (1978) *Disarm or Die: A Disarmament Reader for the Leaders and Peoples of the World*, London: Taylor and Francis; (1978a) Disarmament and development in Jolly, Richard (ed.), *Disarmament and World Development*, Oxford: Pergamon, 3-6; (1979) *The First World Disarmament Conference 1932-33 and Why it Failed*, Oxford: Pergamon; (1980) What nuclear war would mean, (Conference speech reprinted), London: Quaker Peace and Service, March 1980; (1982) Why 1932 failure must not be repeated in 1982, *For Human Survival*, London: World Disarmament Campaign, Spring 1982.

Index